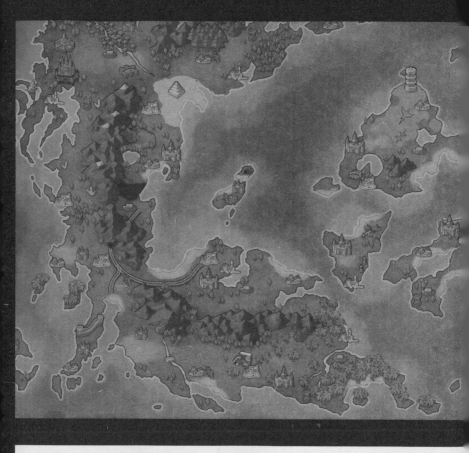

THE STORY SO FAR

The continent of Consume is plagued by a war for domination between the blue-eyed Kingdom of Segua and the red-eyed Ninteldo Empire. In the rural village of Marcthree, young Gear is motivated by the death of a friend to join the Segua Army. Recognized as a talented "killer", Gear is given a spot among the army's elite and sent to Tatrand's Fortress Hope. His mission: to infiltrate the fortress and rescue an imprisoned General. However, Gear discovers the trapped General is none other than his missing father, Alex! Alex, on the verge of death, asks Gear to absorb him so that he can bequeath all of his power to his son. Gear makes the difficult decision, accepting his father's life and power. This gives him the strength to single-handedly subdue the entire Fortress. This grand victory for Segua catapults Gear into continent-wide fame.

But Gear isn't the only well-known killer. Killers from other nations each begin to take to the stage as a new war begins to brew throughout Consume...

WORLD WAR BLUE

VOLUME 3

art by **Crimson**
story by **Anastasia Shestakova**

STAFF CREDITS

translation	**Adrienne Beck**
adaptation	**Patrick King**
lettering	**Laura Scoville**
logo design	**Courtney Williams**
cover design	**Nicky Lim**
proofreader	**Janet Houck, Conner Crooks**
editor	**Adam Arnold**
publisher	**Jason DeAngelis**
	Seven Seas Entertainment

AOI SEKAI NO CHUSINDE KANZENBAN VOL. 3
© 2010 ANASTASIA SHESTAKOVA / © 2010 CRIMSON
This edition originally published in Japan in 2010 by
MICROMAGAZINE PUBLISHING CO., Tokyo. English translation
rights arranged with MICROMAGAZINE PUBLISHING CO., Tokyo
through TOHAN CORPORATION, Tokyo.

ISBN: 978-1-937867-98-0
Printed in Canada
First Printing: November 2013
10 9 8 7 6 5 4 3 2 1

FOLLOW US ONLINE: www.gomanga.com

READING DIRECTIONS

This book reads from *right to left*, Japanese style.
If this is your first time reading manga, you start
reading from the top right panel on each page and
take it from there. If you get lost, just follow the
numbered diagram here. It may seem backwards
at first, but you'll get the hang of it! Have fun!!

NO ONE CAN STAND IN OUR WAY

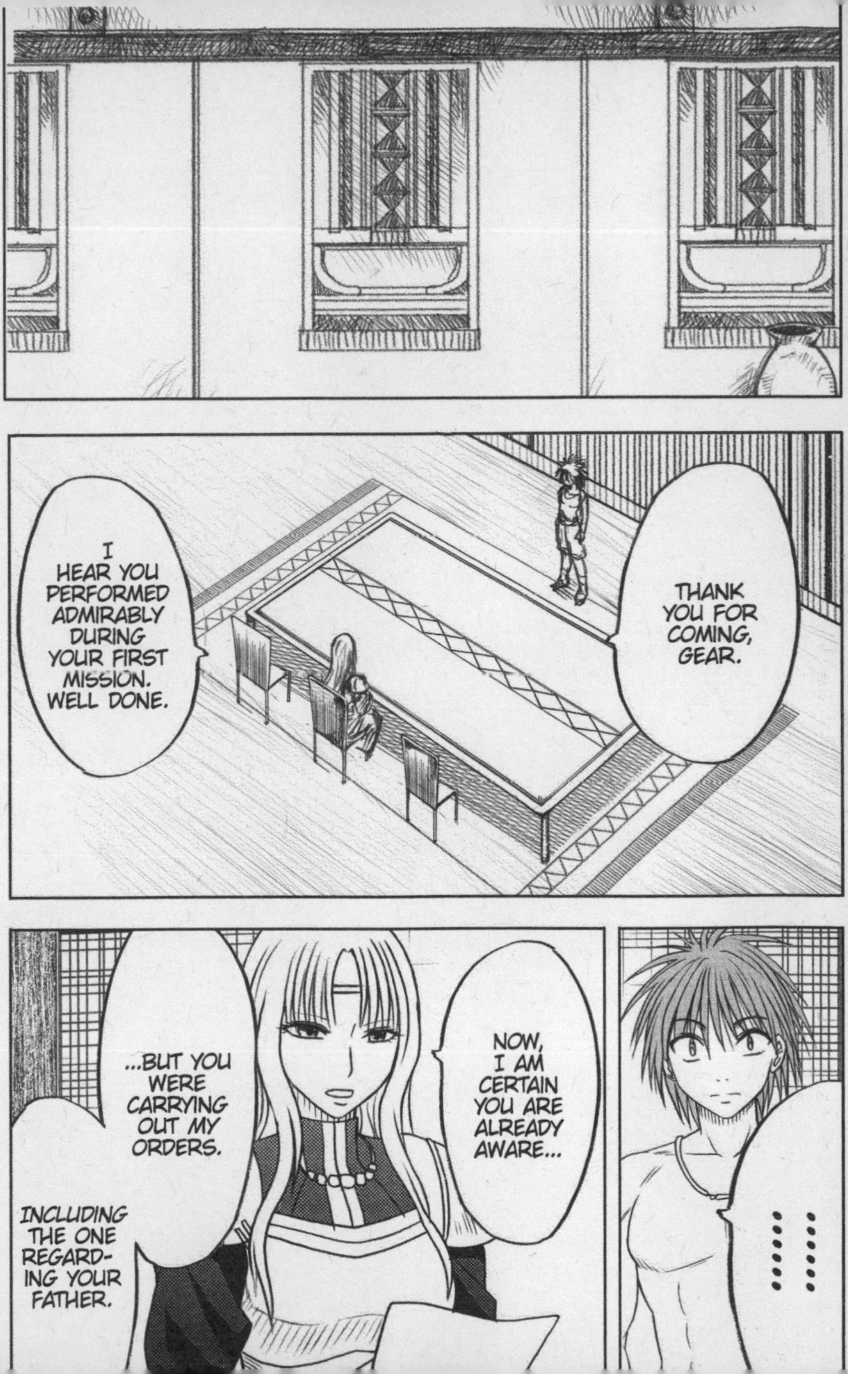
THANK YOU FOR COMING, GEAR.
I HEAR YOU PERFORMED ADMIRABLY DURING YOUR FIRST MISSION. WELL DONE.
......
NOW, I AM CERTAIN YOU ARE ALREADY AWARE...
...BUT YOU WERE CARRYING OUT MY ORDERS.
INCLUDING THE ONE REGARDING YOUR FATHER.

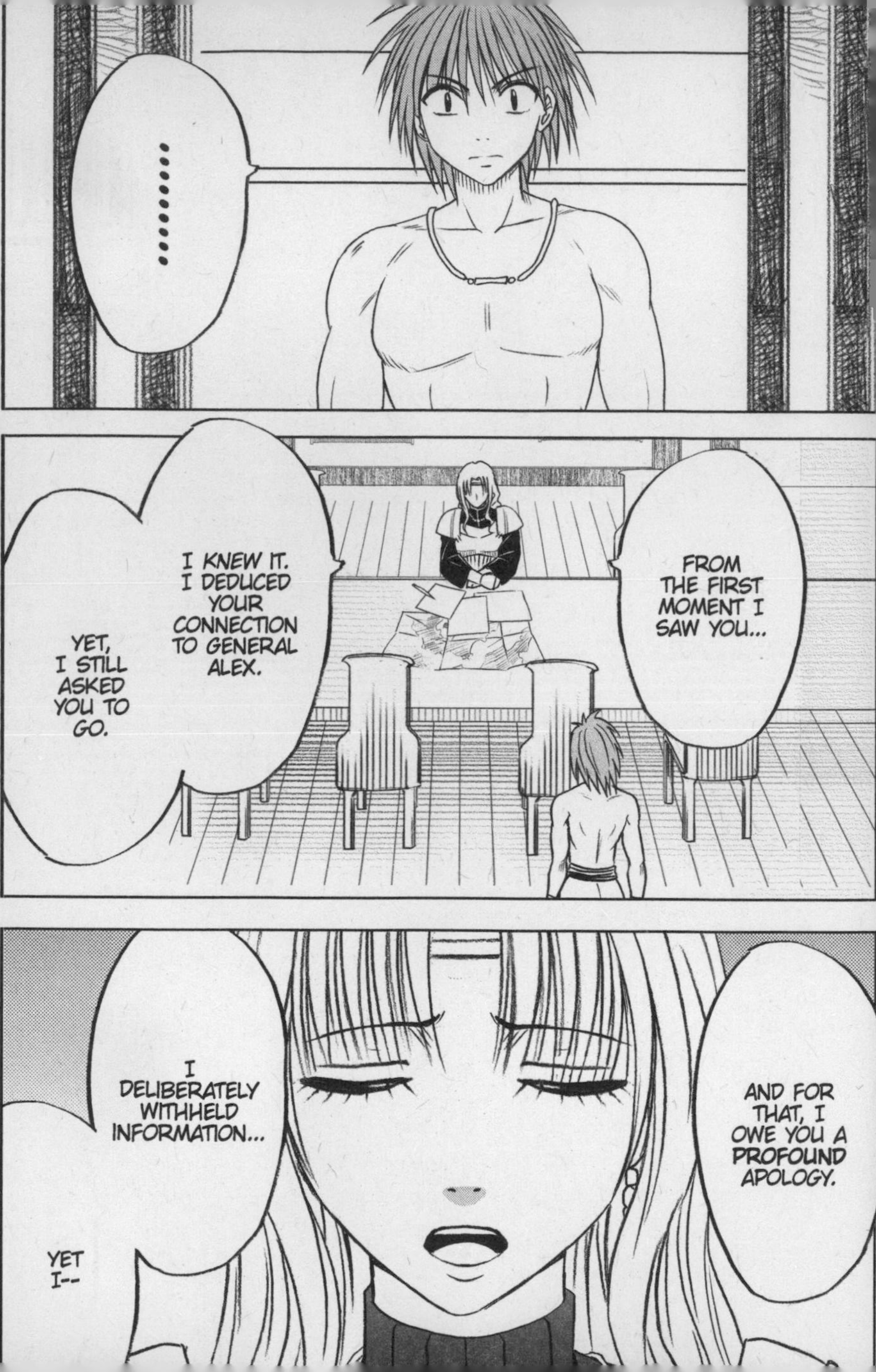
....
FROM THE FIRST MOMENT I SAW YOU...
I KNEW IT. I DEDUCED YOUR CONNECTION TO GENERAL ALEX.
YET, I STILL ASKED YOU TO GO.
AND FOR THAT, I OWE YOU A PROFOUND APOLOGY.
I DELIBERATELY WITHHELD INFORMATION...
YET I--

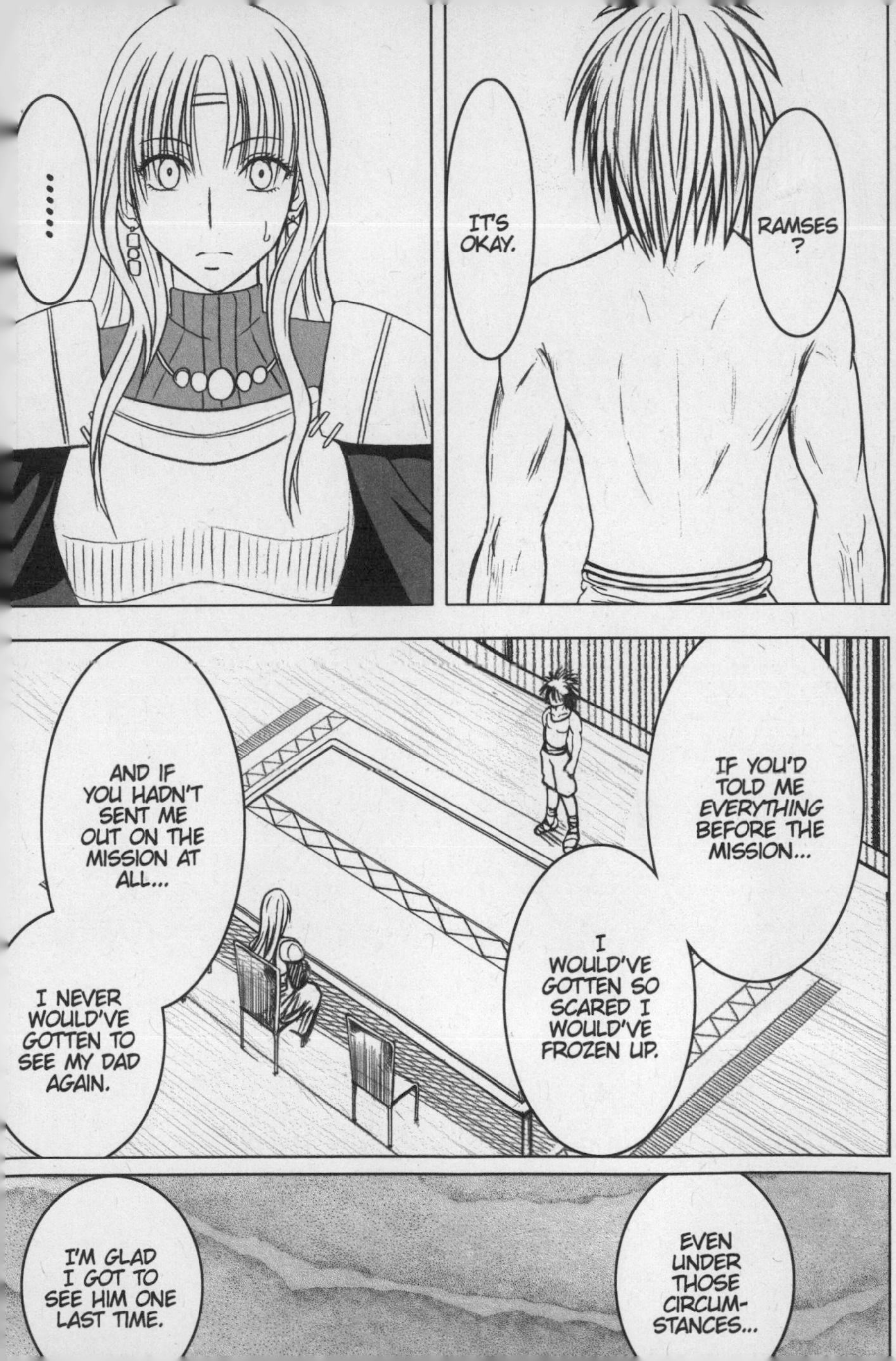
RAMSES ?
IT'S OKAY.
......
IF YOU'D TOLD ME EVERYTHING BEFORE THE MISSION...
I WOULD'VE GOTTEN SO SCARED I WOULD'VE FROZEN UP.
AND IF YOU HADN'T SENT ME OUT ON THE MISSION AT ALL...
I NEVER WOULD'VE GOTTEN TO SEE MY DAD AGAIN.
EVEN UNDER THOSE CIRCUM-STANCES...
I'M GLAD I GOT TO SEE HIM ONE LAST TIME.

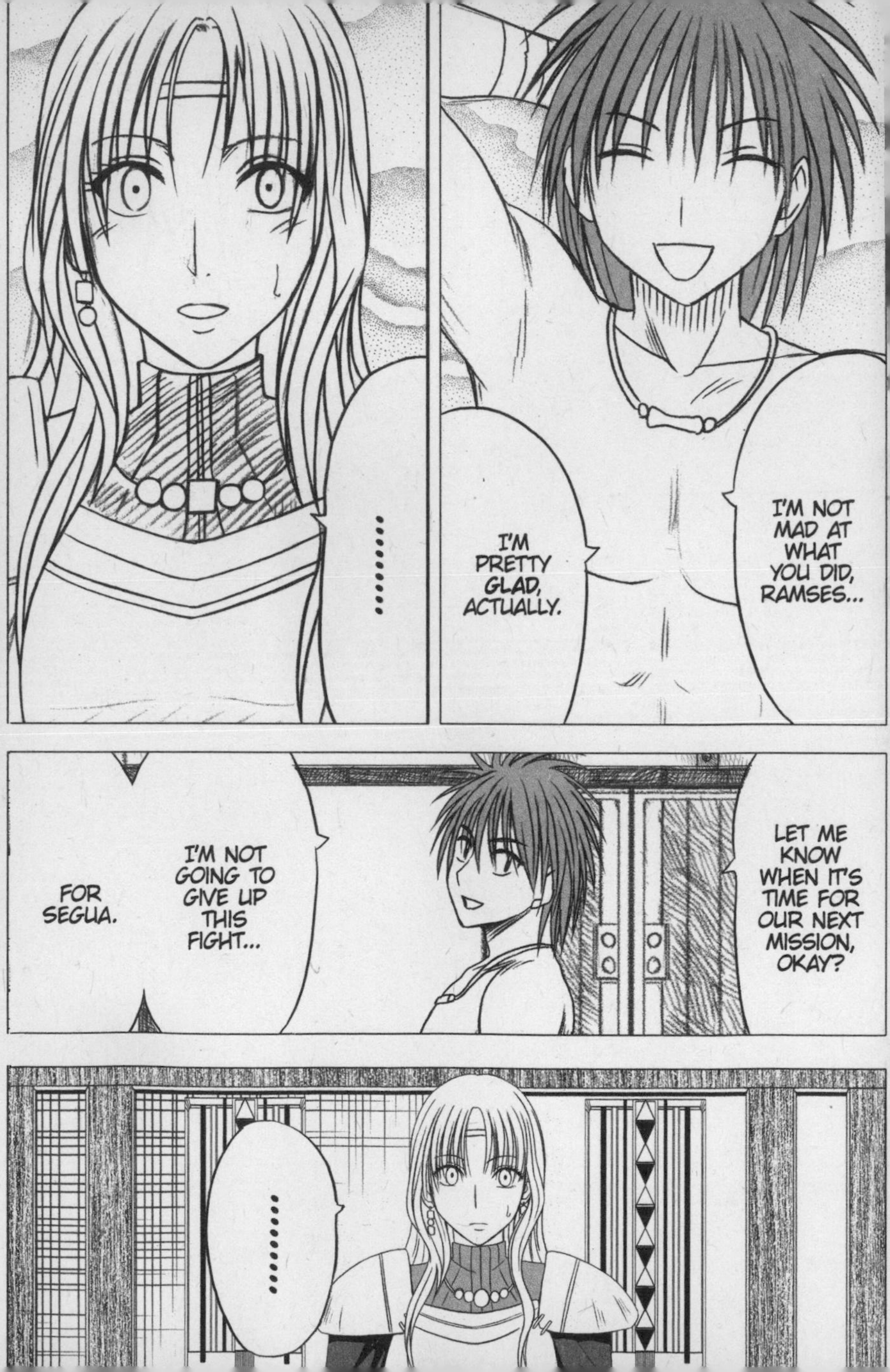
I'M NOT MAD AT WHAT YOU DID, RAMSES...
I'M PRETTY GLAD, ACTUALLY.
....
LET ME KNOW WHEN IT'S TIME FOR OUR NEXT MISSION, OKAY?
I'M NOT GOING TO GIVE UP THIS FIGHT...
FOR SEGUA.
....

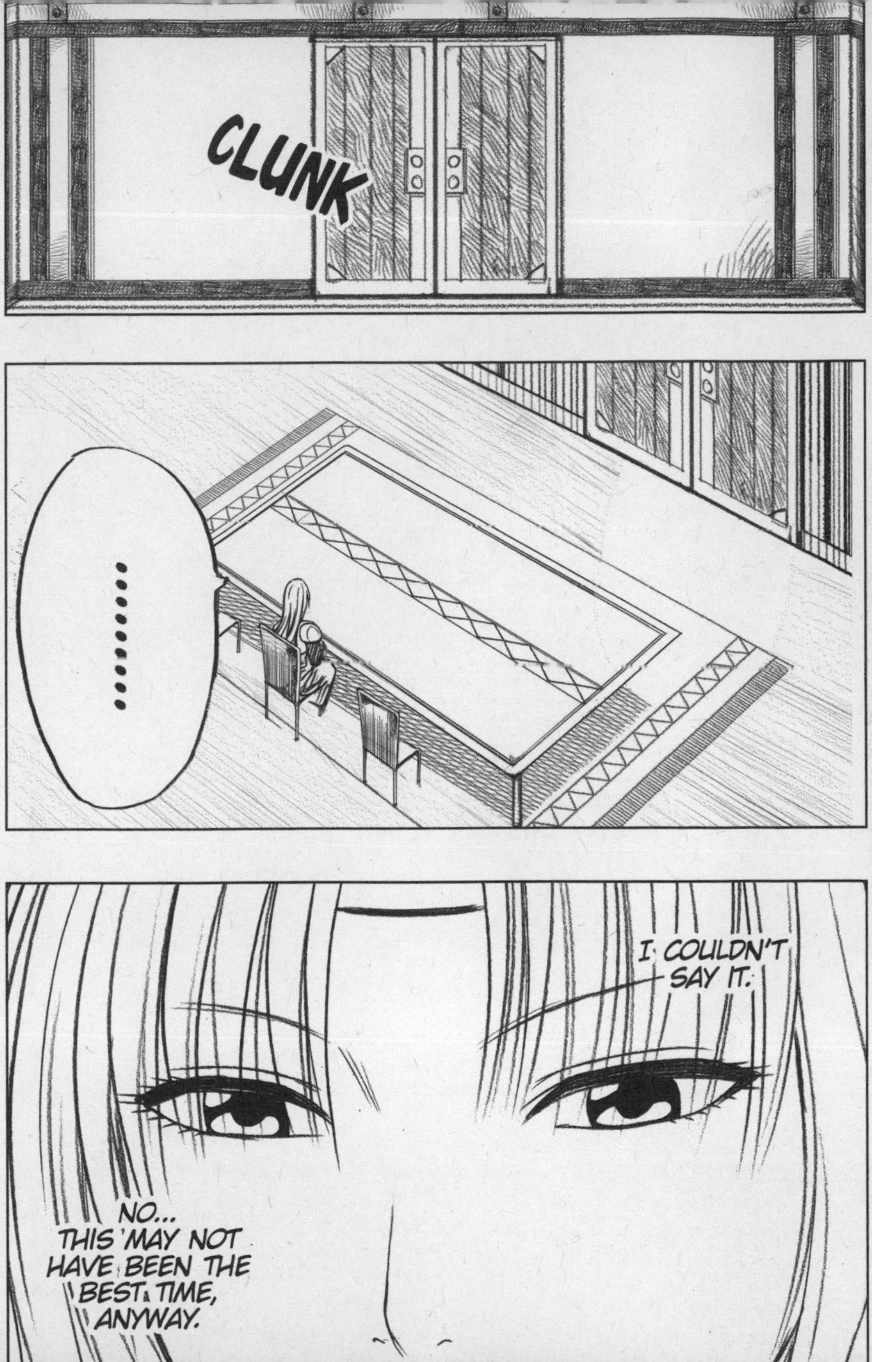
CLUNK
....
I COULDN'T SAY IT.
NO... THIS MAY NOT HAVE BEEN THE BEST TIME, ANYWAY.

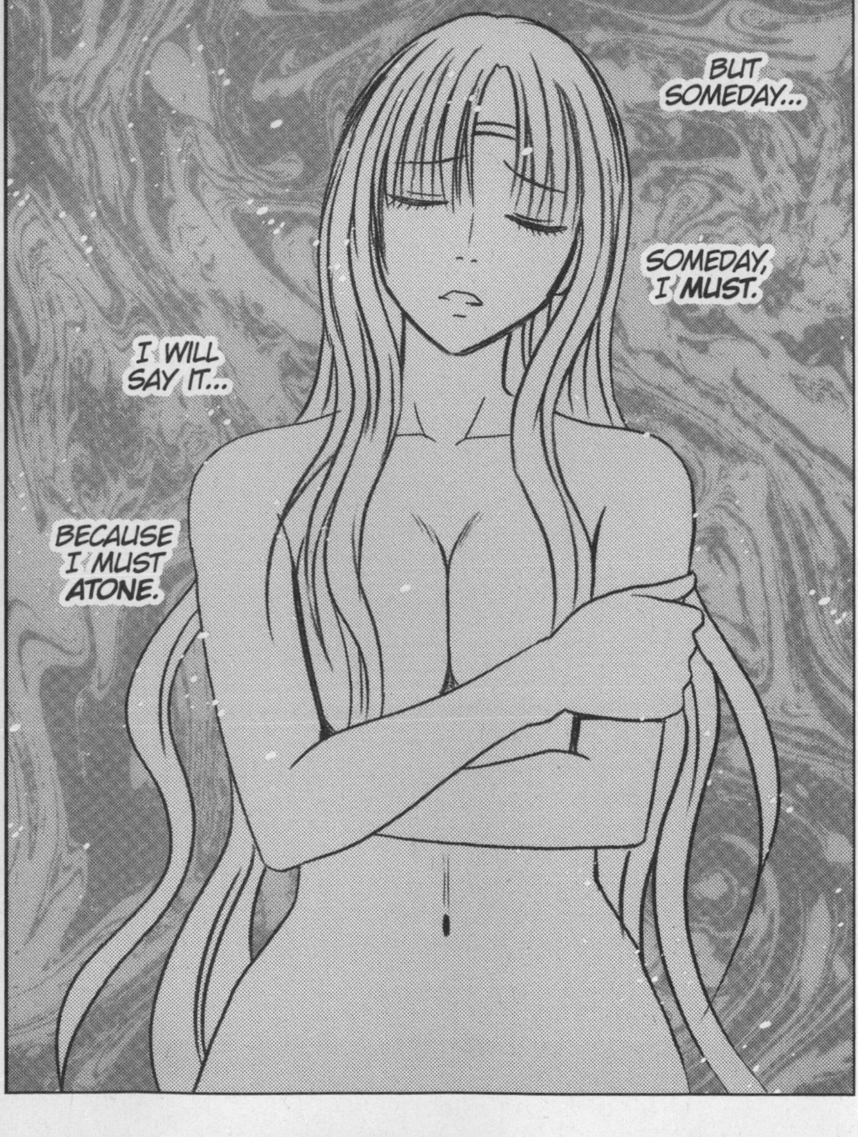
BUT SOMEDAY...
SOMEDAY, I MUST.
I WILL SAY IT...
BECAUSE I MUST ATONE.

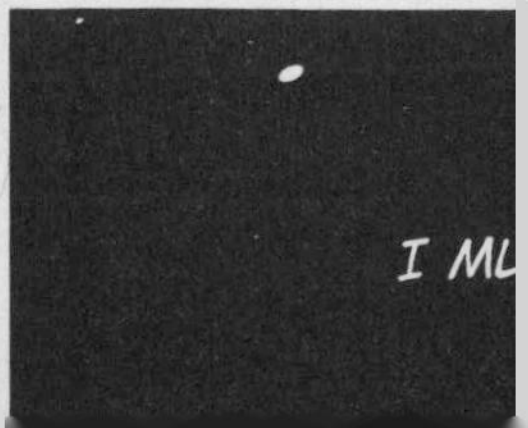
I MU

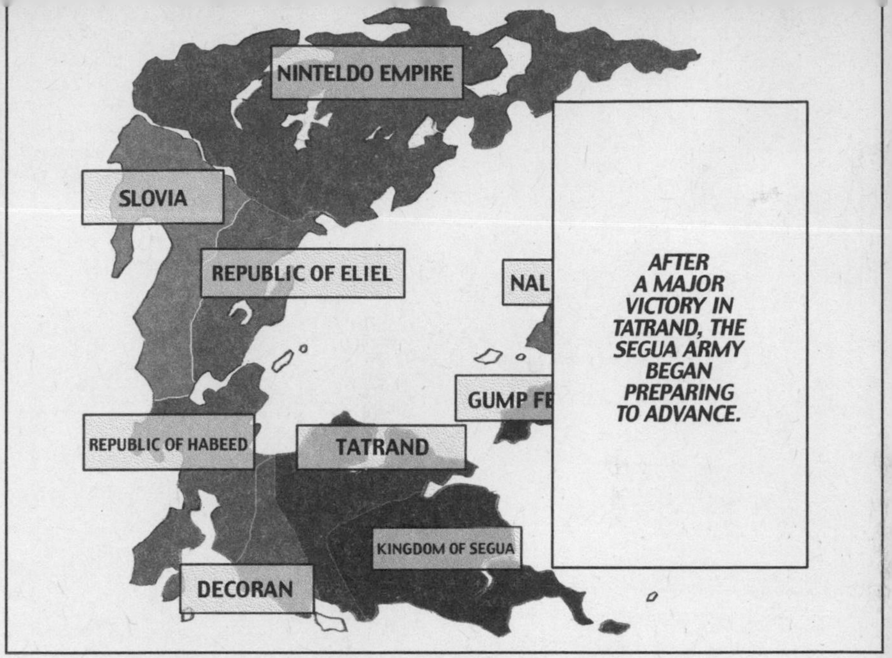
AFTER A MAJOR VICTORY IN TATRAND, THE SEGUA ARMY BEGAN PREPARING TO ADVANCE.
NINTELDO EMPIRE
SLOVIA
REPUBLIC OF ELIEL
NAL
GUMP FE
REPUBLIC OF HABEED
TATRAND
KINGDOM OF SEGUA
DECORAN

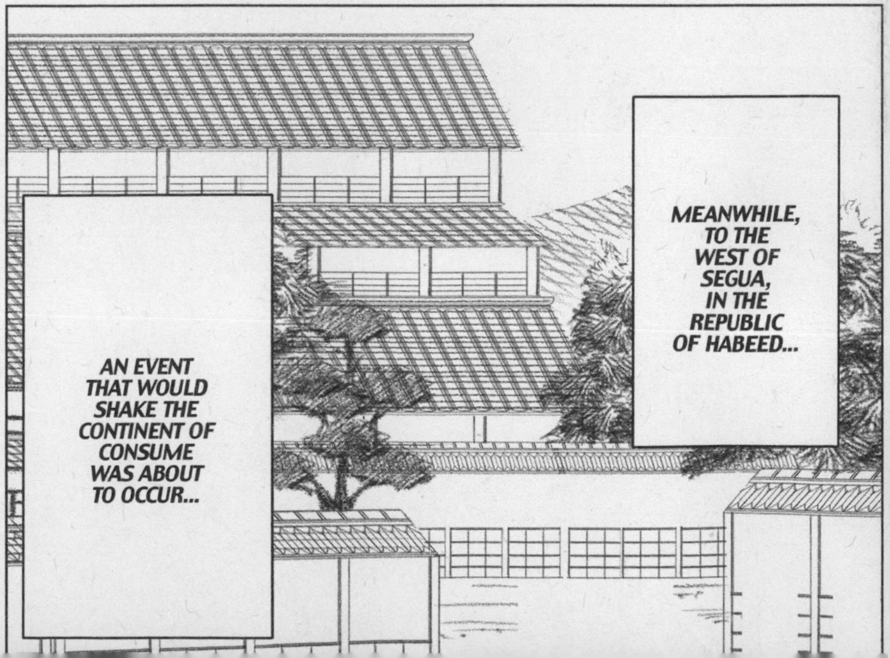
MEANWHILE, TO THE WEST OF SEGUA, IN THE REPUBLIC OF HABEED...
AN EVENT THAT WOULD SHAKE THE CONTINENT OF CONSUME WAS ABOUT TO OCCUR...

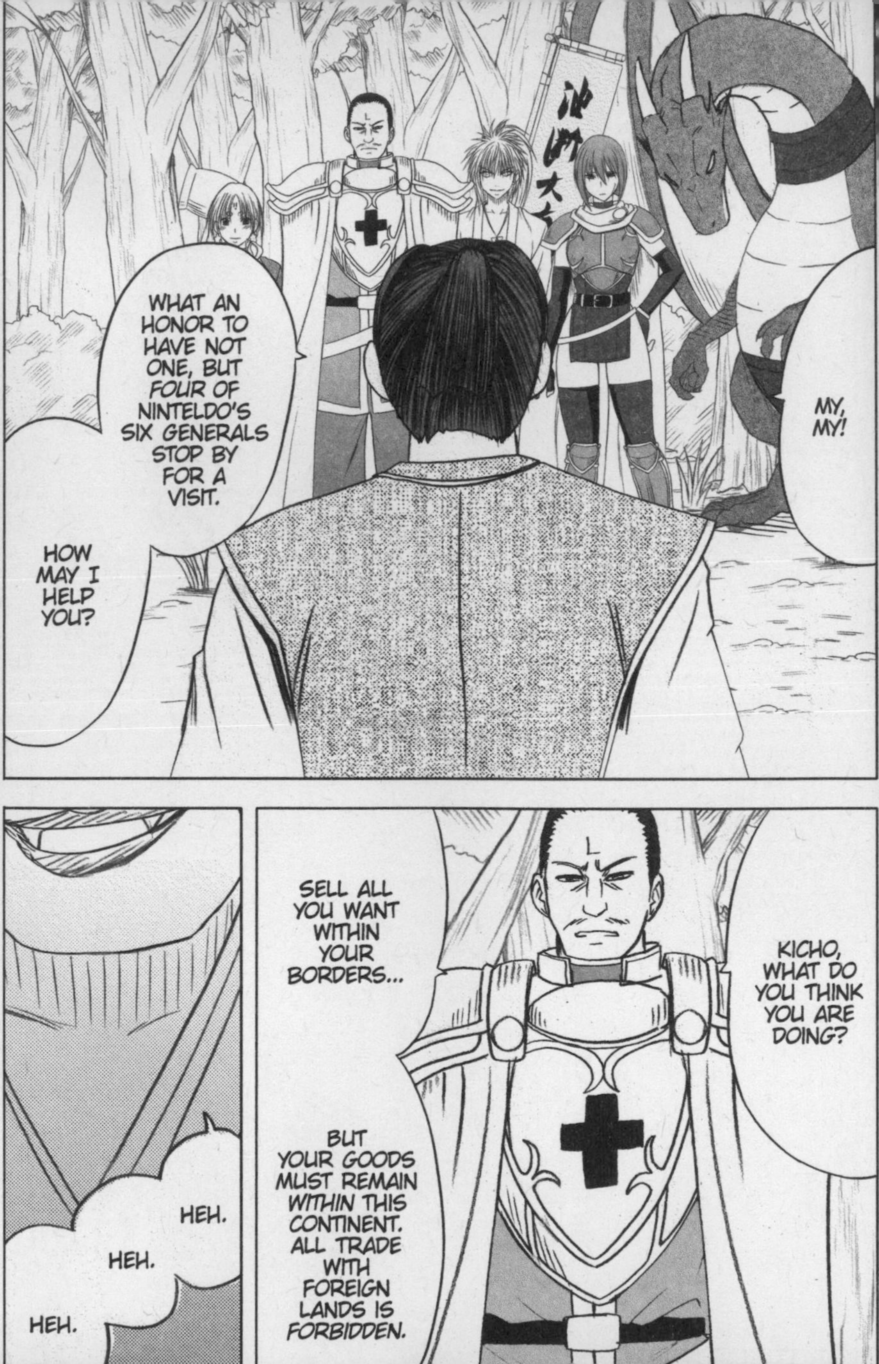
MY, MY!
WHAT AN HONOR TO HAVE NOT ONE, BUT FOUR OF NINTELDO'S SIX GENERALS STOP BY FOR A VISIT.
HOW MAY I HELP YOU?
KICHO, WHAT DO YOU THINK YOU ARE DOING?
SELL ALL YOU WANT WITHIN YOUR BORDERS...
BUT YOUR GOODS MUST REMAIN WITHIN THIS CONTINENT. ALL TRADE WITH FOREIGN LANDS IS FORBIDDEN.
HEH.
HEH.
HEH.

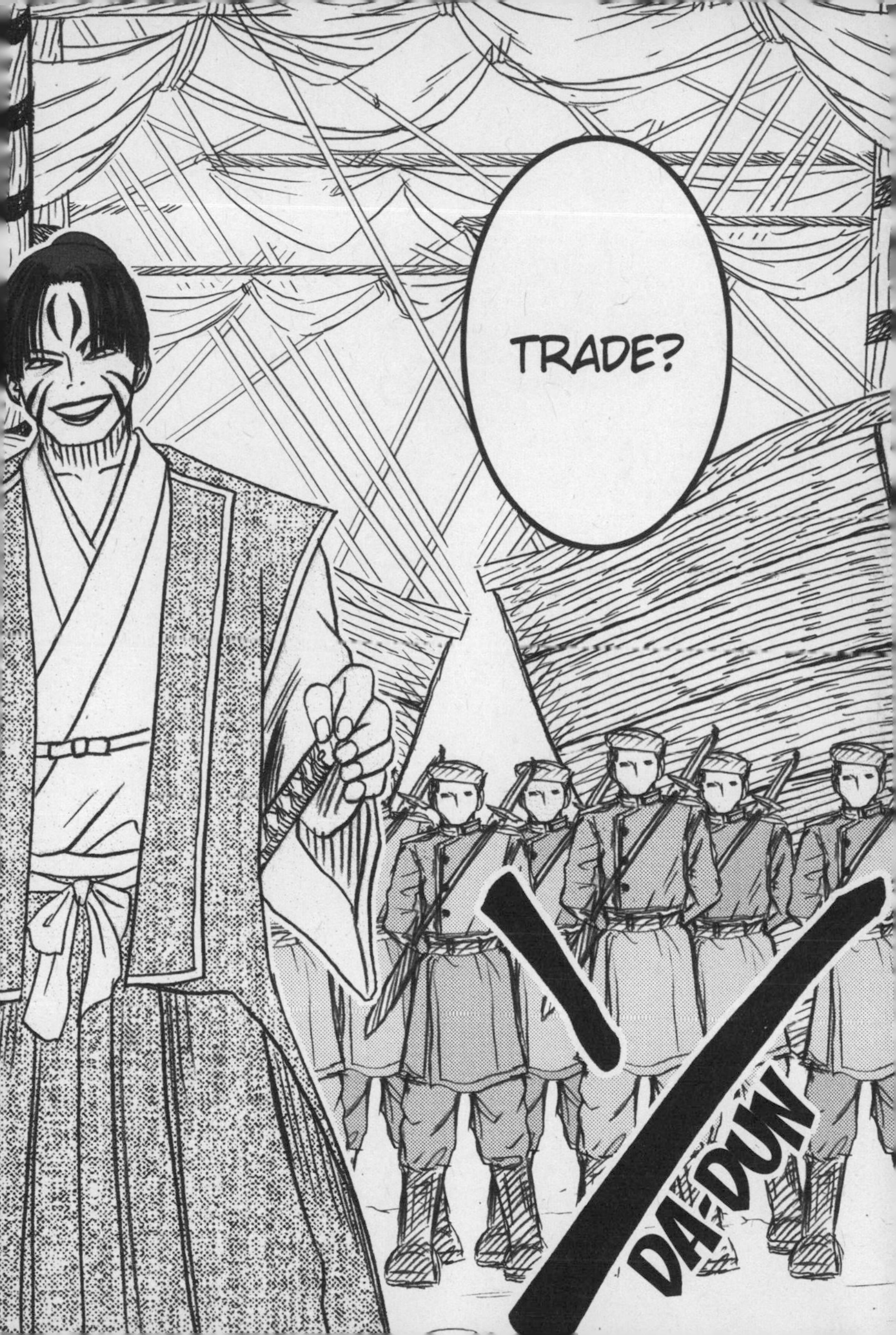
TRADE?
DA-DUN

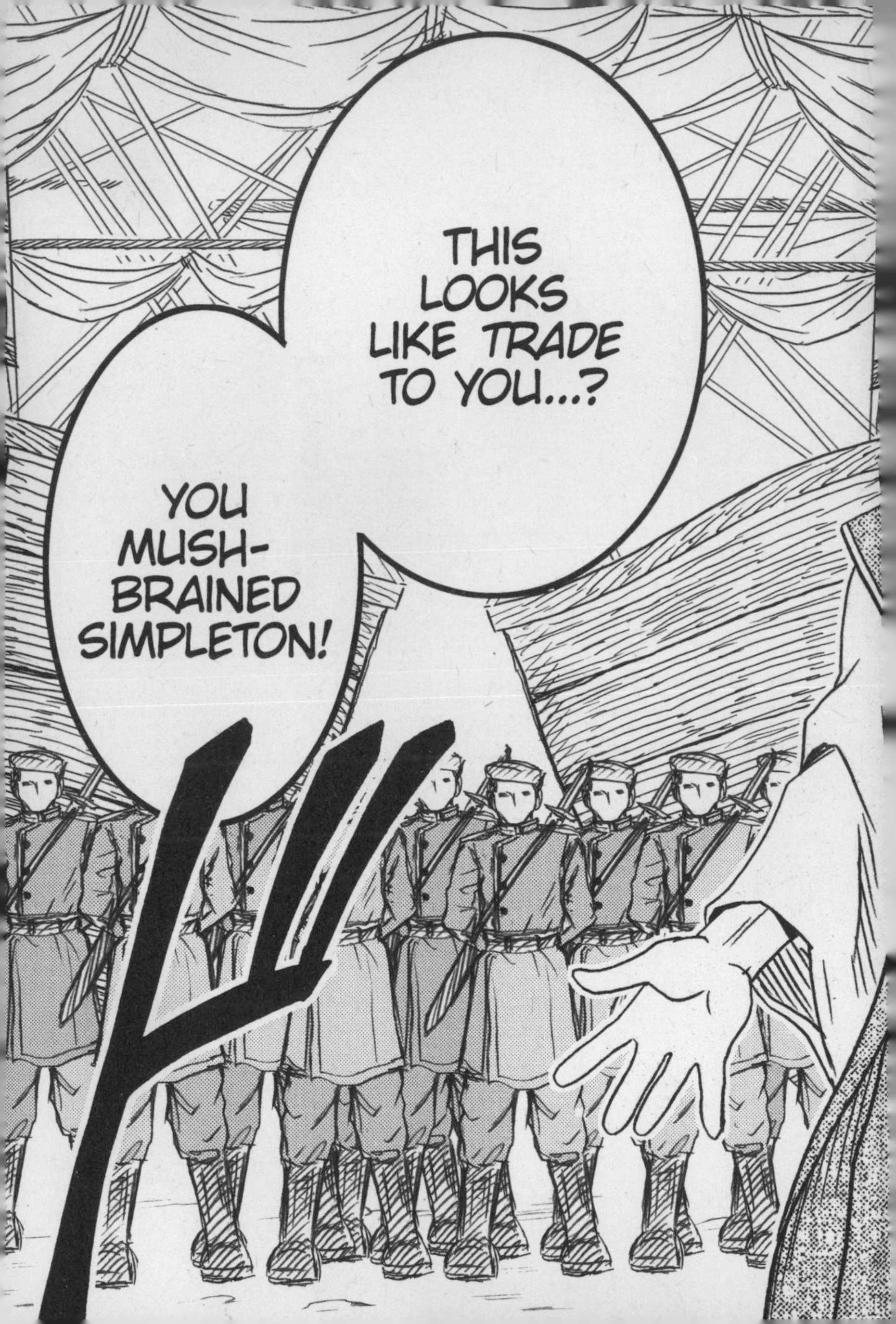
THIS LOOKS LIKE *TRADE* TO YOU...?
YOU MUSH-BRAINED SIMPLETON!

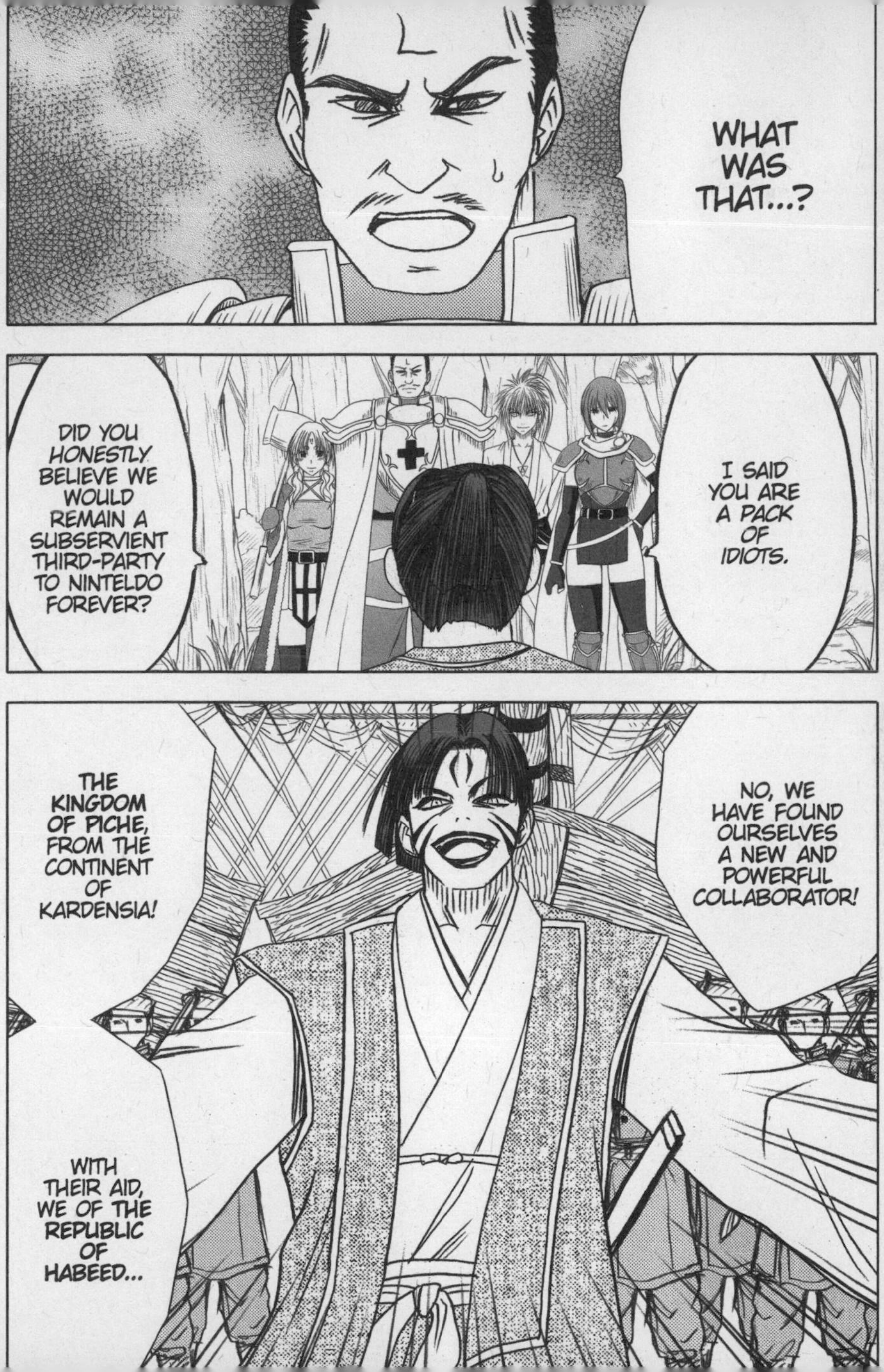
WHAT WAS THAT...?
I SAID YOU ARE A PACK OF IDIOTS.
DID YOU HONESTLY BELIEVE WE WOULD REMAIN A SUBSERVIENT THIRD-PARTY TO NINTELDO FOREVER?
NO, WE HAVE FOUND OURSELVES A NEW AND POWERFUL COLLABORATOR!
THE KINGDOM OF PICHE, FROM THE CONTINENT OF KARDENSIA!
WITH THEIR AID, WE OF THE REPUBLIC OF HABEED...

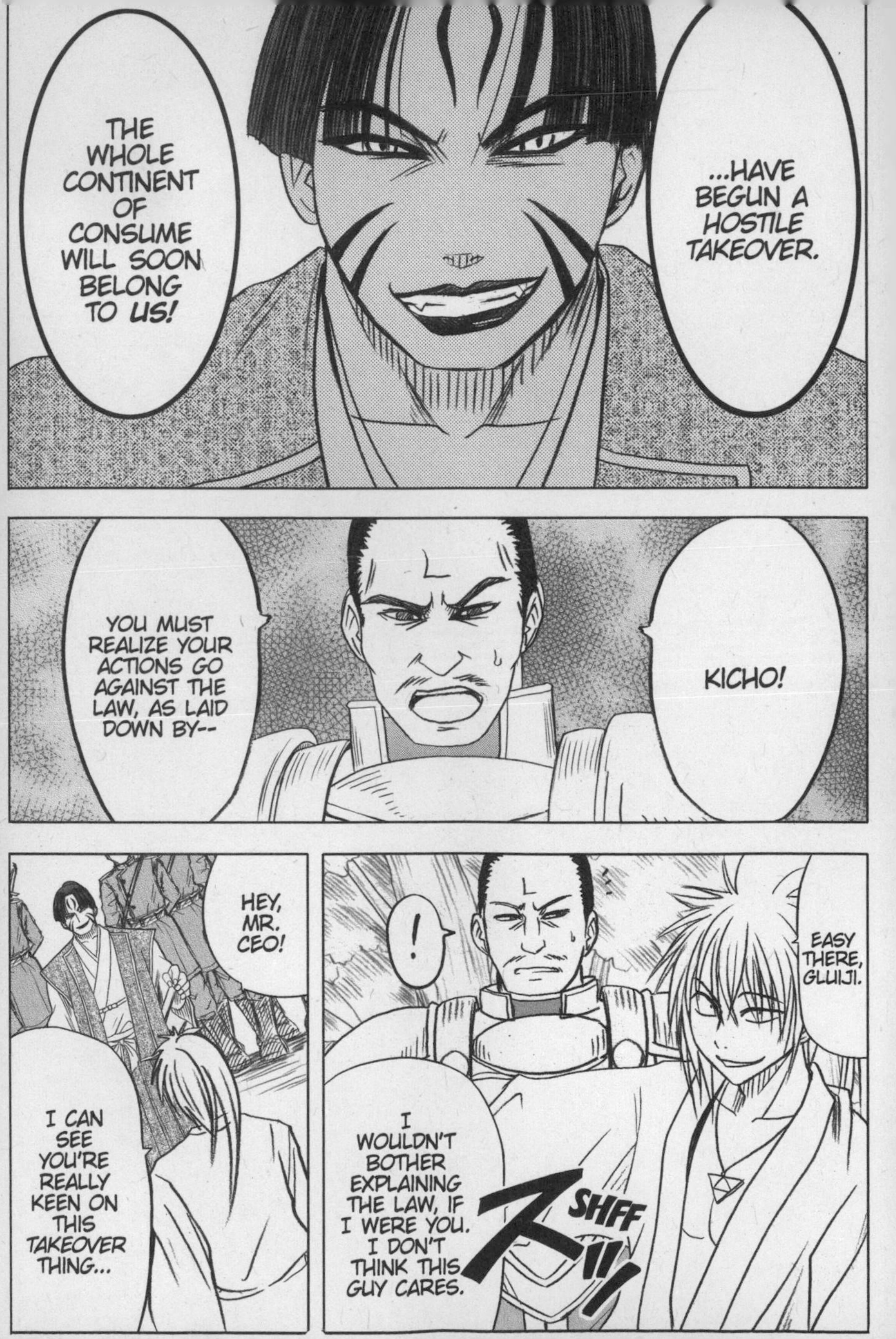
...HAVE BEGUN A HOSTILE TAKEOVER.
THE WHOLE CONTINENT OF CONSUME WILL SOON BELONG TO US!
KICHO!
YOU MUST REALIZE YOUR ACTIONS GO AGAINST THE LAW, AS LAID DOWN BY--
EASY THERE, GLUIJI.
!
I WOULDN'T BOTHER EXPLAINING THE LAW, IF I WERE YOU. I DON'T THINK THIS GUY CARES.
SHFF
HEY, MR. CEO!
I CAN SEE YOU'RE REALLY KEEN ON THIS TAKEOVER THING...

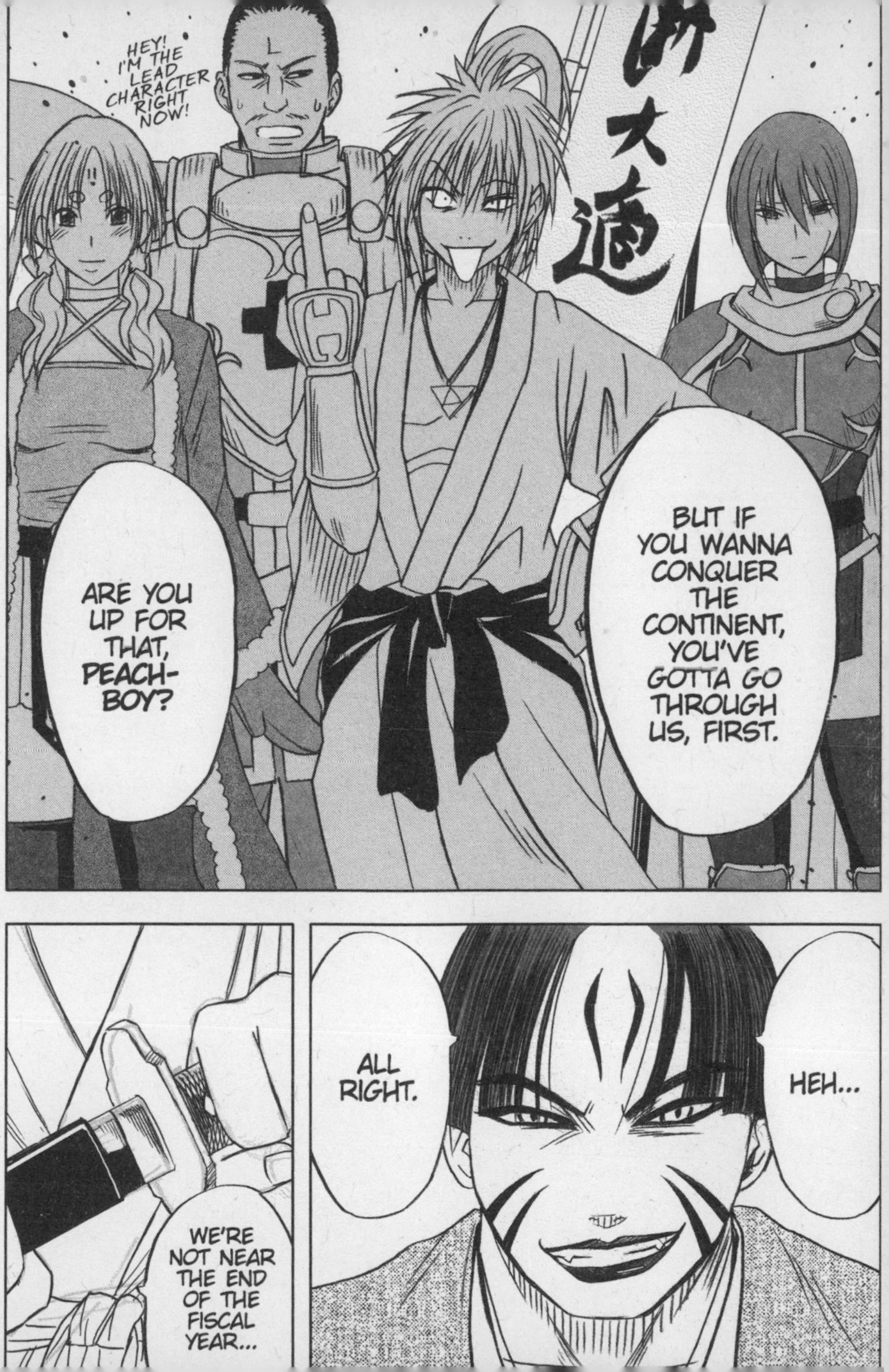
BUT IF YOU WANNA CONQUER THE CONTINENT, YOU'VE GOTTA GO THROUGH US, FIRST.
ARE YOU UP FOR THAT, PEACH-BOY?
HEY! I'M THE LEAD CHARACTER RIGHT NOW!
HEH...
ALL RIGHT.
WE'RE NOT NEAR THE END OF THE FISCAL YEAR...

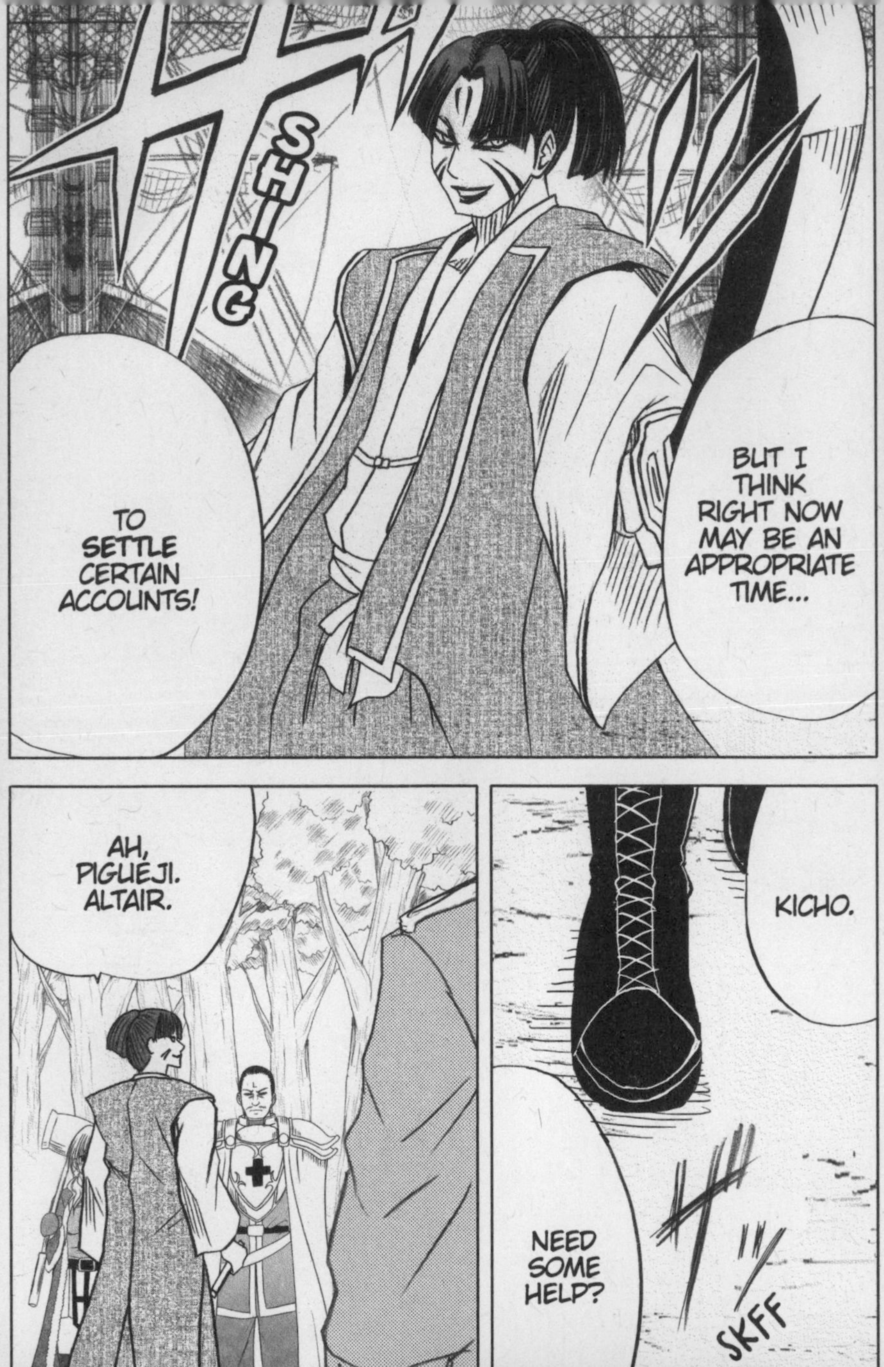
SHING
BUT I THINK RIGHT NOW MAY BE AN APPROPRIATE TIME...
TO SETTLE CERTAIN ACCOUNTS!
KICHO.
NEED SOME HELP?
SKFF
AH, PIGUEJI. ALTAIR.

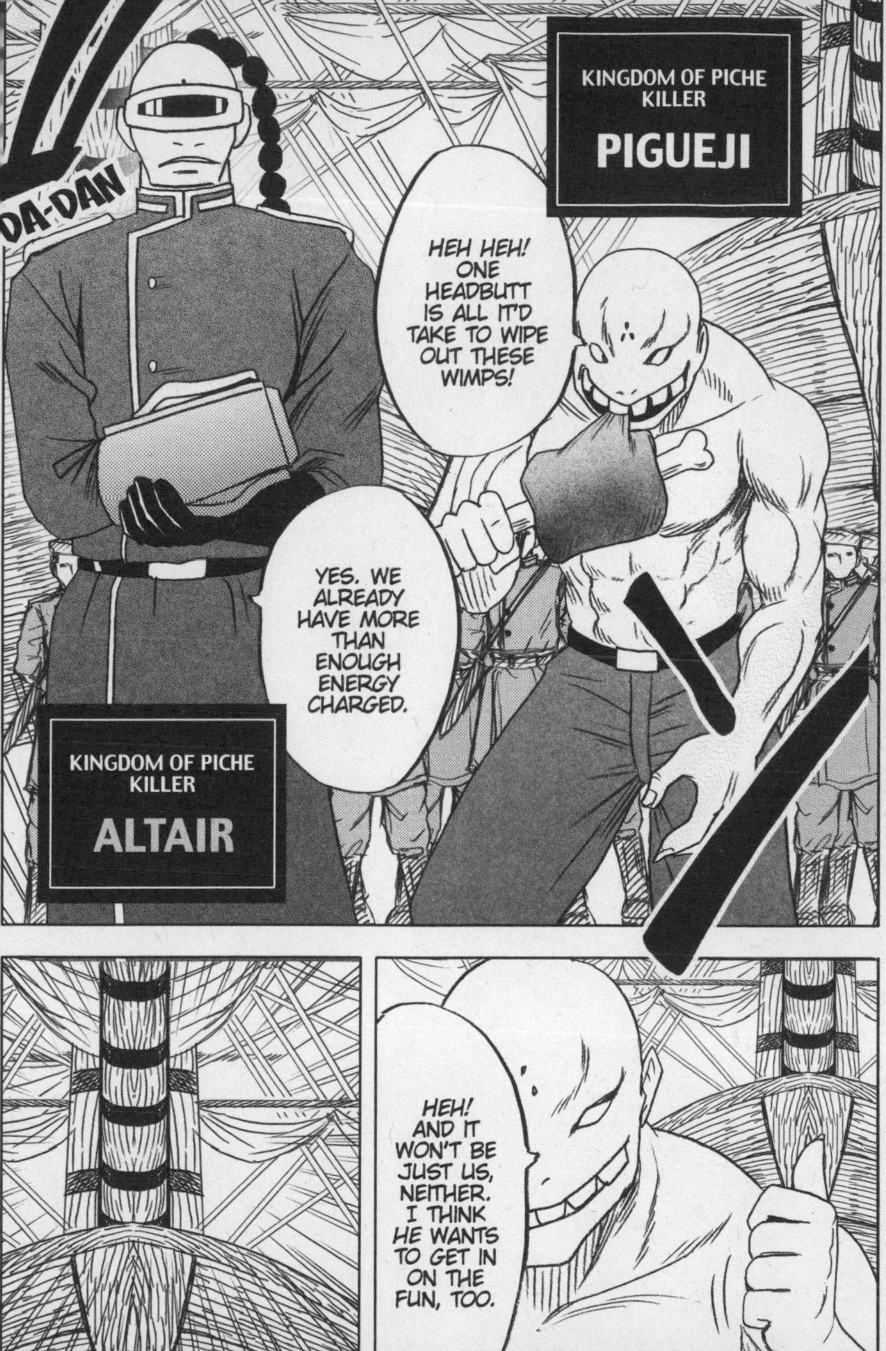
KINGDOM OF PICHE KILLER
PIGUEJI
HEH HEH! ONE HEADBUTT IS ALL IT'D TAKE TO WIPE OUT THESE WIMPS!
DA-DAN
YES. WE ALREADY HAVE MORE THAN ENOUGH ENERGY CHARGED.
KINGDOM OF PICHE KILLER
ALTAIR
HEH! AND IT WON'T BE JUST US, NEITHER. I THINK HE WANTS TO GET IN ON THE FUN, TOO.

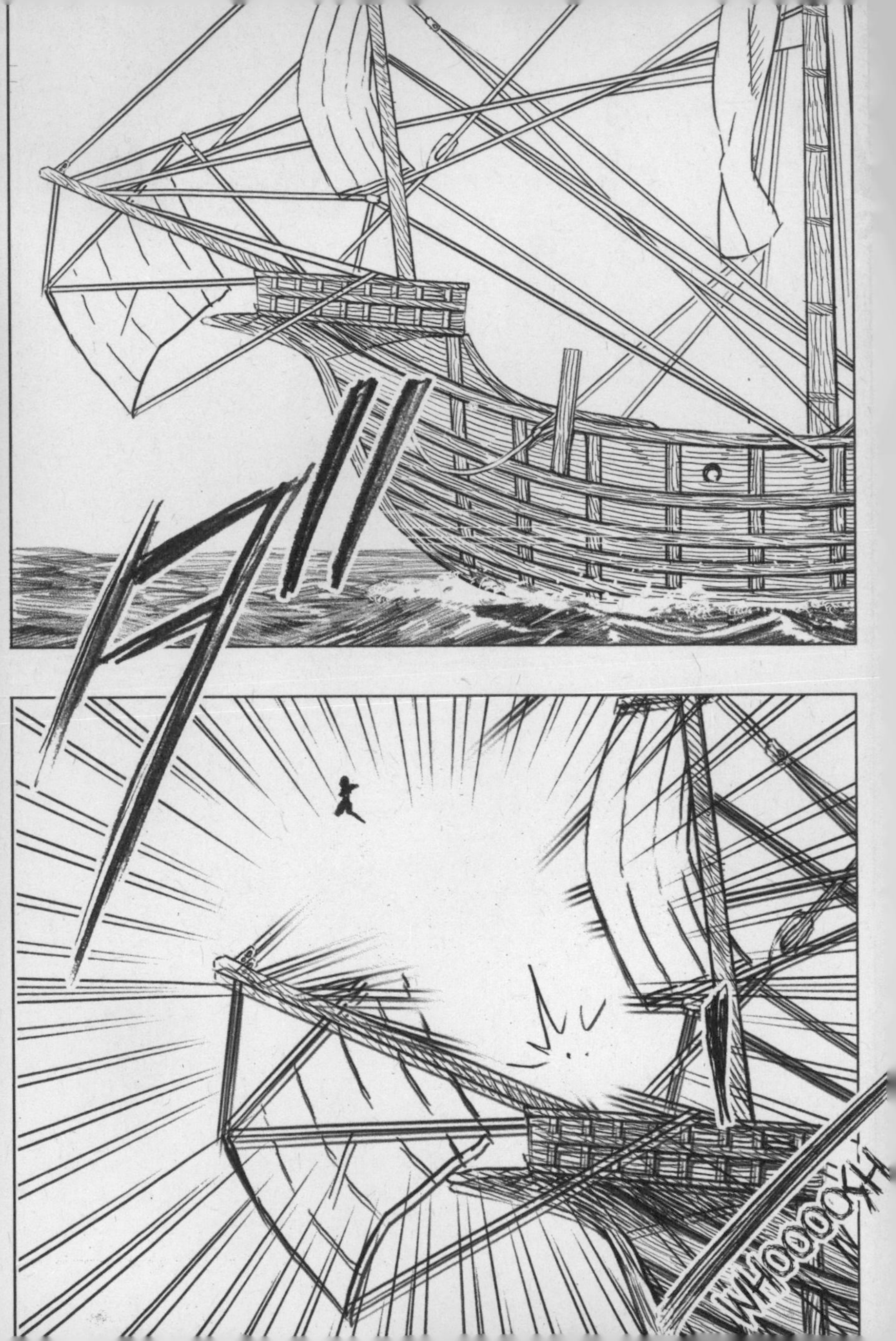
WHOOOCKH

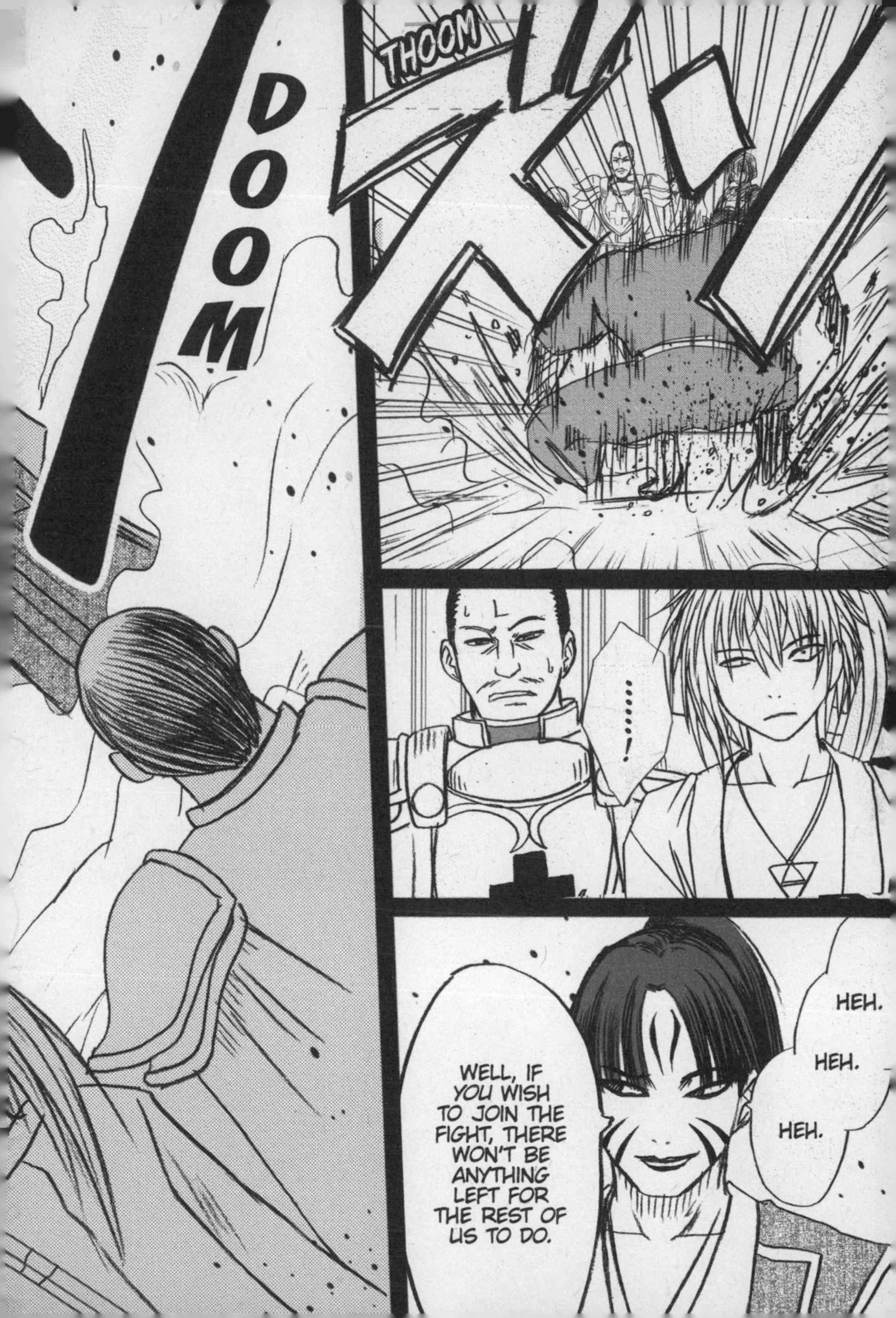
THOOM
......!
HEH.
HEH.
HEH.
WELL, IF YOU WISH TO JOIN THE FIGHT, THERE WON'T BE ANYTHING LEFT FOR THE REST OF US TO DO.
DOOM

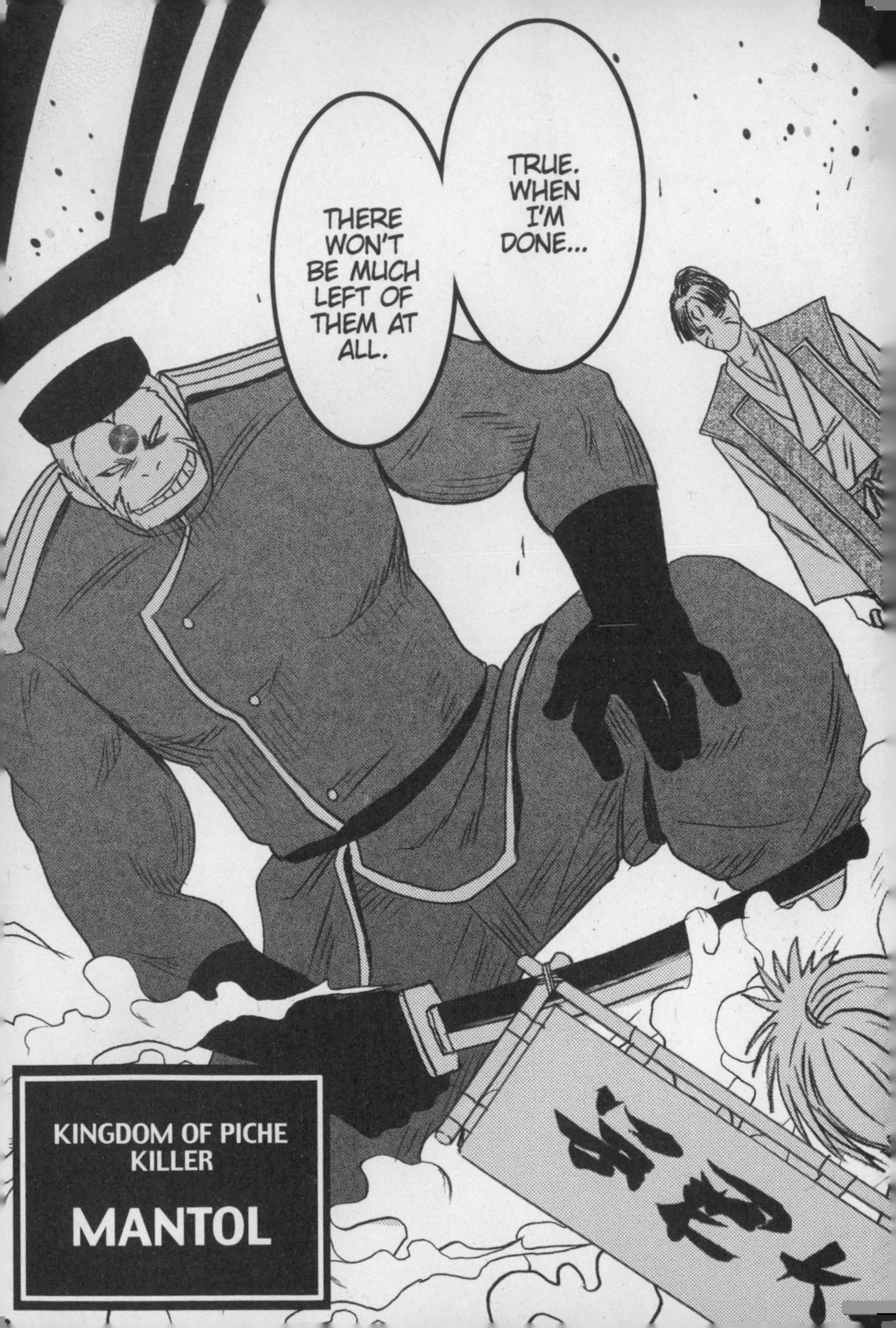
TRUE. WHEN I'M DONE...
THERE WON'T BE MUCH LEFT OF THEM AT ALL.
KINGDOM OF PICHE KILLER
MANTOL

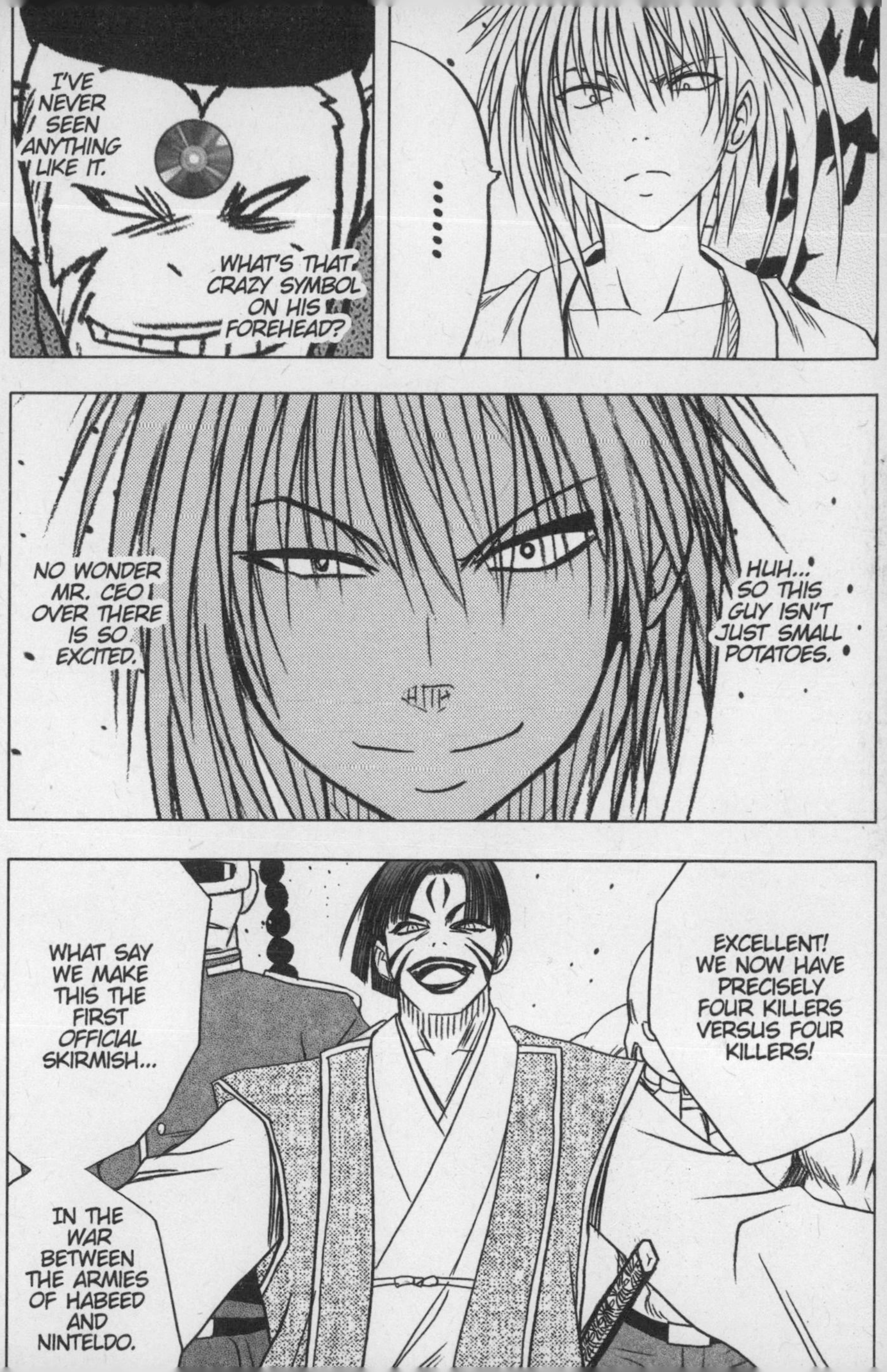
......
I'VE NEVER SEEN ANYTHING LIKE IT.
WHAT'S THAT CRAZY SYMBOL ON HIS FOREHEAD?
HUH... SO THIS GUY ISN'T JUST SMALL POTATOES.
NO WONDER MR. CEO OVER THERE IS SO EXCITED.
EXCELLENT! WE NOW HAVE PRECISELY FOUR KILLERS VERSUS FOUR KILLERS!
WHAT SAY WE MAKE THIS THE FIRST OFFICIAL SKIRMISH...
IN THE WAR BETWEEN THE ARMIES OF HABEED AND NINTELDO.

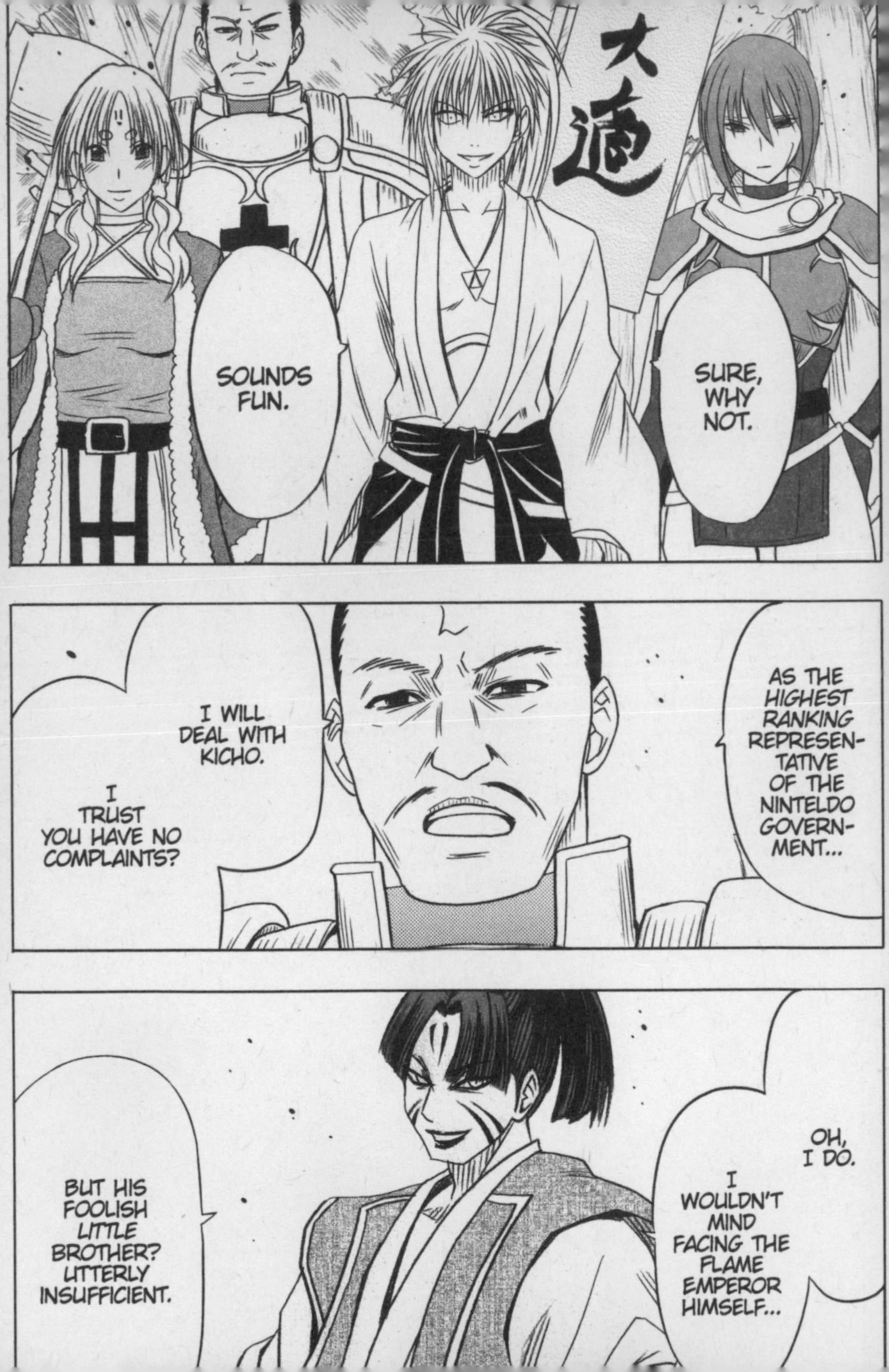
SURE, WHY NOT.
SOUNDS FUN.
AS THE HIGHEST RANKING REPRESENTATIVE OF THE NINTELDO GOVERNMENT...
I WILL DEAL WITH KICHO.
I TRUST YOU HAVE NO COMPLAINTS?
OH, I DO.
I WOULDN'T MIND FACING THE FLAME EMPEROR HIMSELF...
BUT HIS FOOLISH LITTLE BROTHER? UTTERLY INSUFFICIENT.

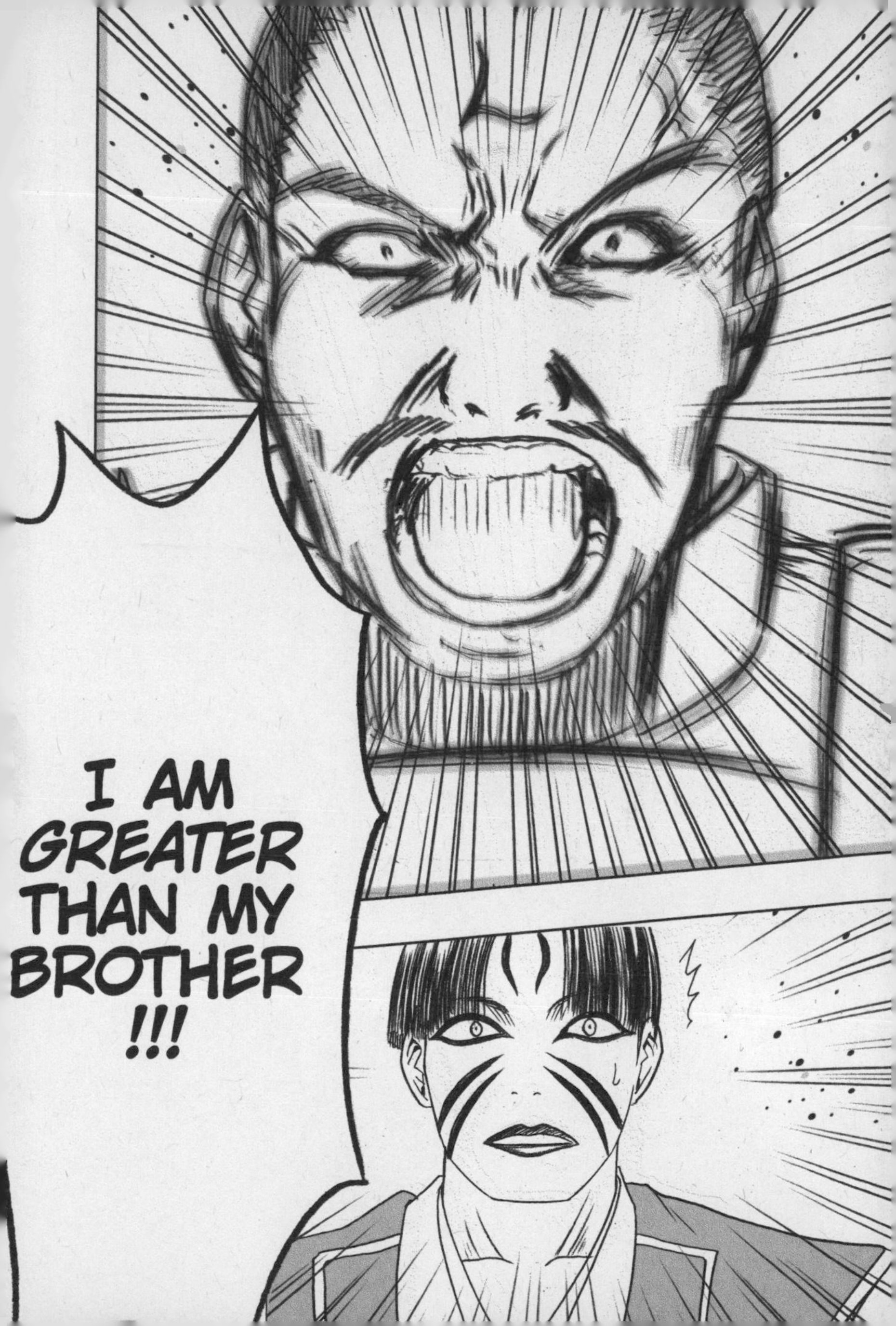
I AM GREATER THAN MY BROTHER !!!

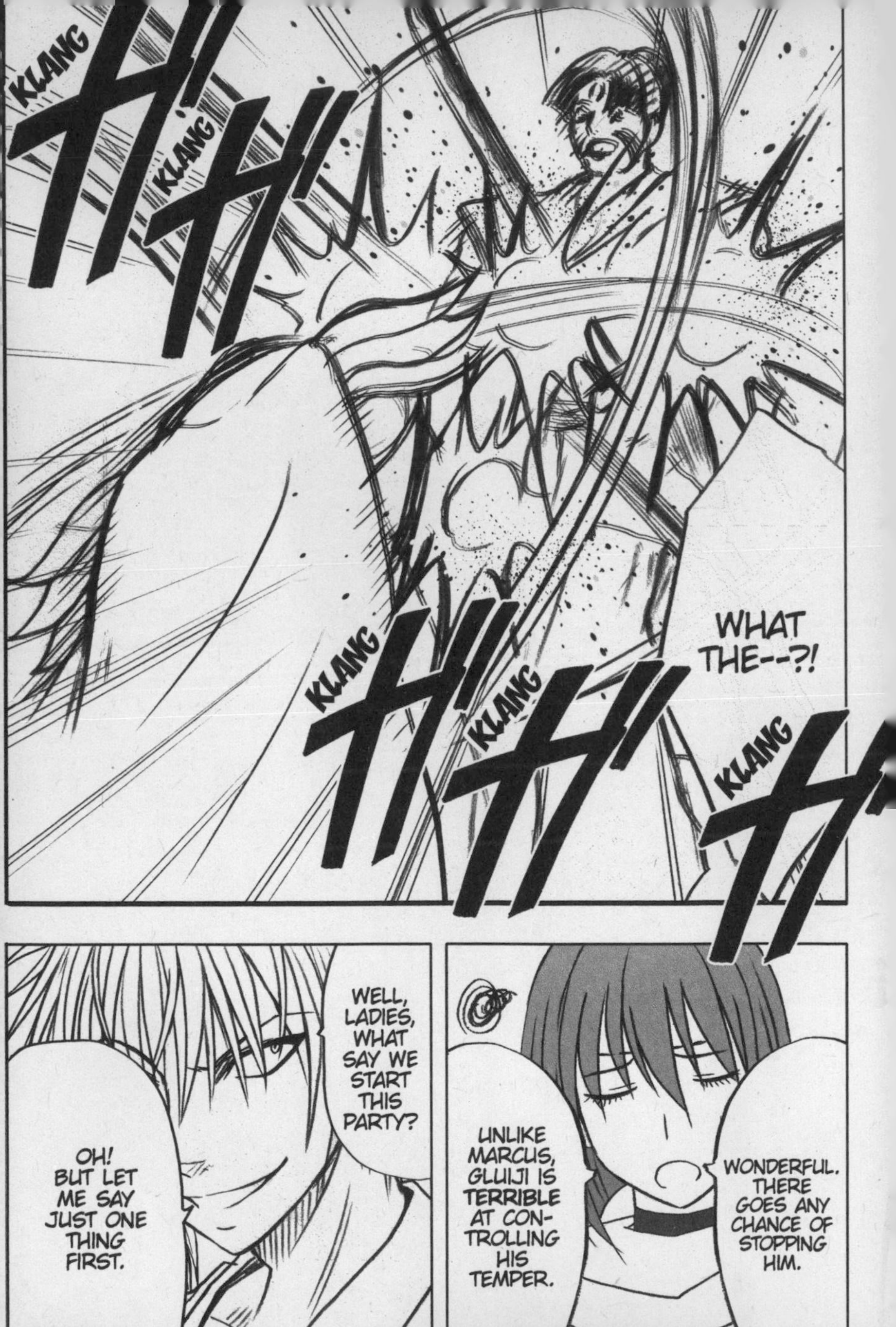
KLANG
KLANG
WHAT THE--?!
KLANG
KLANG
KLANG
WONDERFUL. THERE GOES ANY CHANCE OF STOPPING HIM.
UNLIKE MARCUS, GLUIJI IS TERRIBLE AT CON-TROLLING HIS TEMPER.
WELL, LADIES, WHAT SAY WE START THIS PARTY?
OH! BUT LET ME SAY JUST ONE THING FIRST.

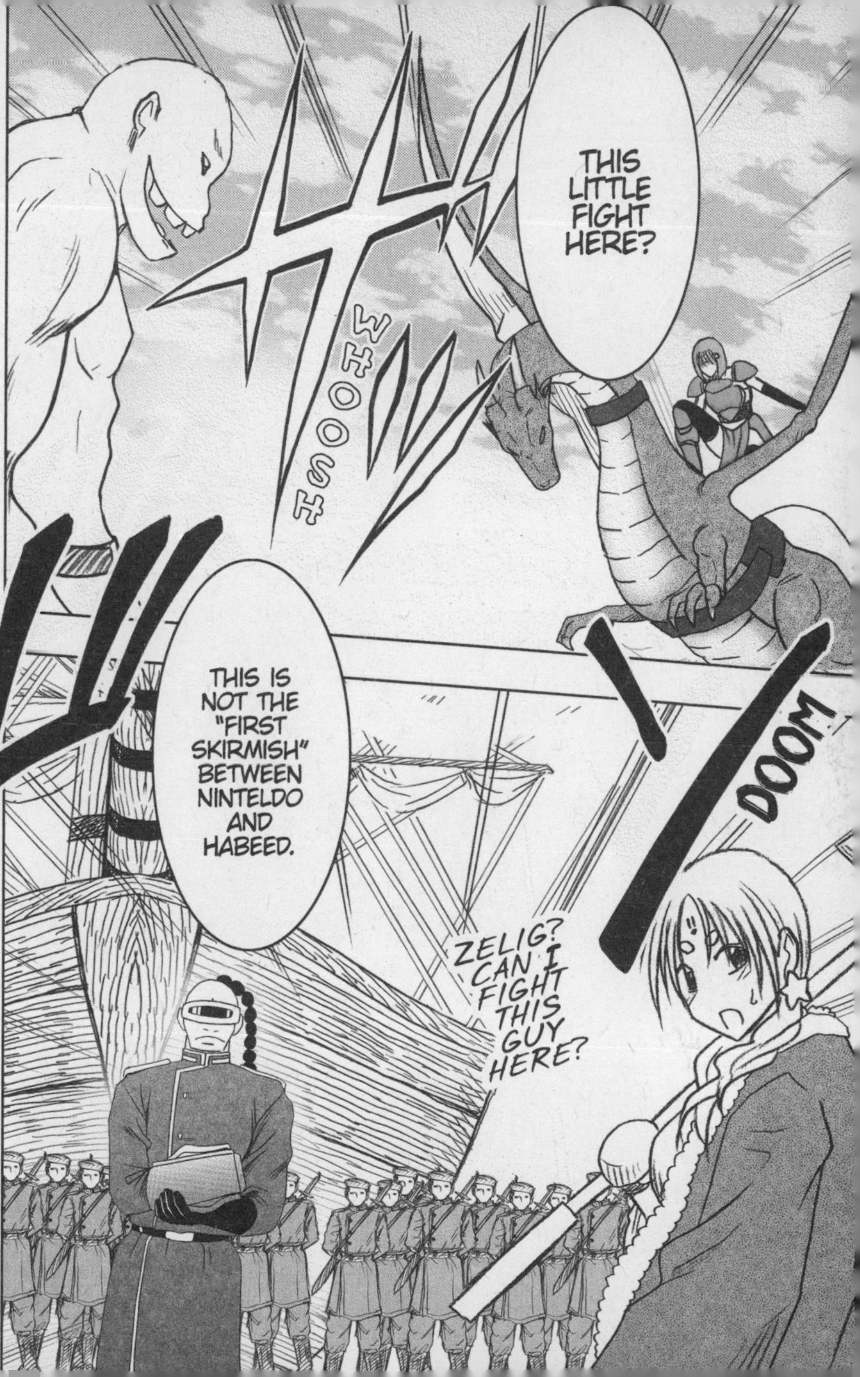
THIS LITTLE FIGHT HERE?
WHOOSH
DOOM
THIS IS NOT THE "FIRST SKIRMISH" BETWEEN NINTELDO AND HABEED.
ZELIG? CAN I FIGHT THIS GUY HERE?

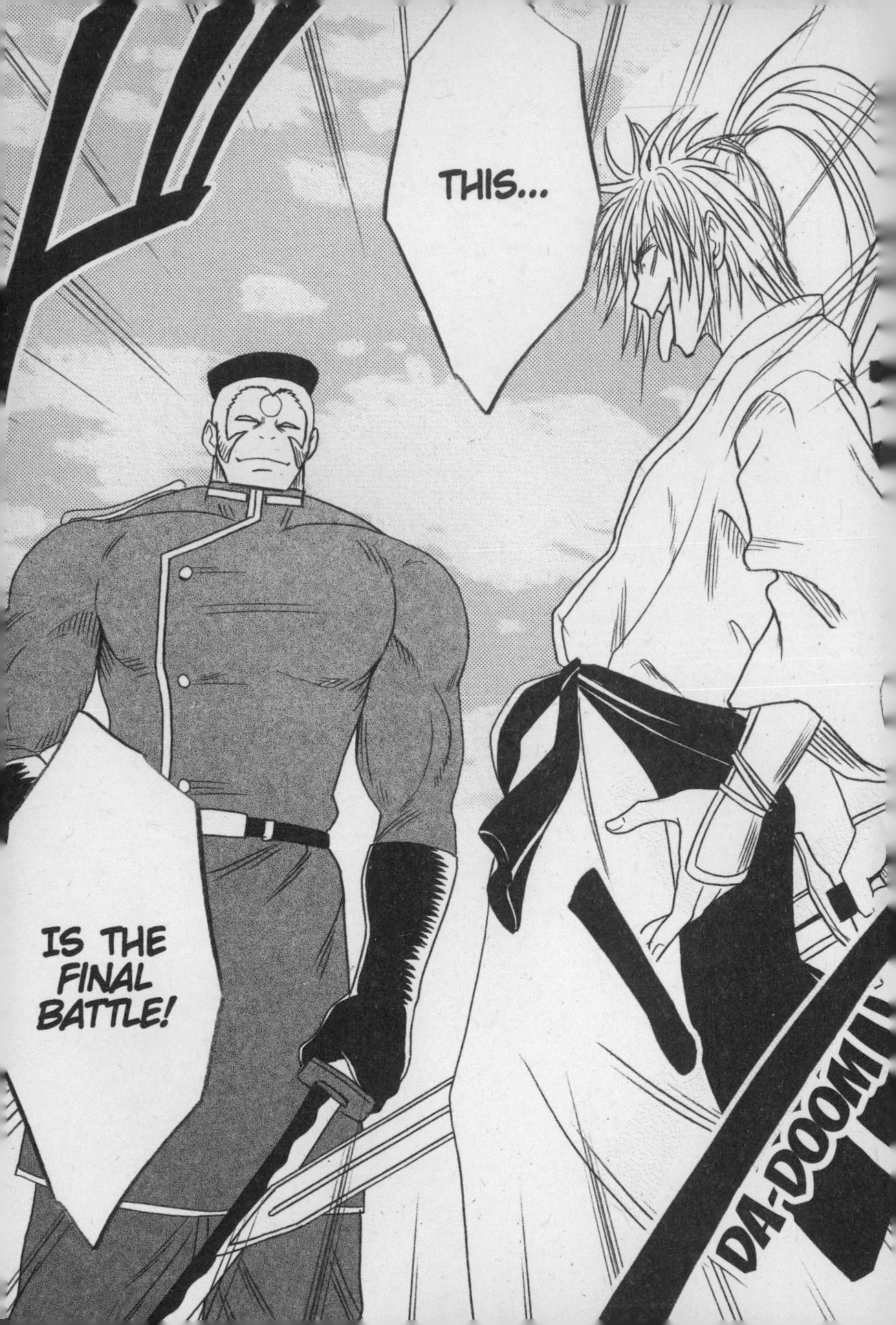
THIS...
IS THE FINAL BATTLE!
DA-DOOM

Perusing Video Game History

ON THE EDGE OF THE BLUE WORLD

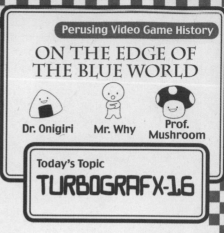

Dr. Onigiri

Mr. Why

Prof. Mushroom

Today's Topic

TURBOGRAFX-16

Mr. Why: Hello, everyone! As with the previous volumes, in this chat corner, the Doctor, the Professor, and I are going to talk a little about video games and their history. Just as a warning, it's not going to have much to do with what's going on in the story.

Dr. Onigiri: Hi! I'm Dr. Onigiri, and I don't puff up, even when you put me in water!

Prof. Mushroom: Yo. I'm Professor Mushroom, and I'd really appreciate it if you'd, y'know, not drop me in a lava lake. That'd be swell.

Mr. Why: By the way, I've been wondering about this for a while now. Why are we doing this corner, again?

Prof. Mushroom: Well, if you'll recall all the way back to the first one we did in Volume 1, we said it's because there were so many dang console makers out there, it was confusing.

Mr. Why: Really? So it wasn't just Nintendo and Sega who made consoles?

Prof. Mushroom: Yep! We're even going to talk about one of them today: NEC Home Electronics, Ltd.

Mr. Why: Oh! I've heard of NEC! They made computers, right?

Dr. Onigiri: Right! NEC Home Electronics (NEC-HE, for short) was a subsidiary of the well-known computer maker NEC. They made electronic appliances, like AC units and refrigerators.

Mr. Why: Wow. I don't know why, but when I think of a refrigerator made by NEC, I imagine it as being super high-tech, with loads of buttons and features.

KINGDOM OF PICHE KILLER
PIGUEJI
HEH HEH! ONE HEADBUTT IS ALL IT'D TAKE TO WIPE OUT THESE WIMPS!
DA-DAN
YES. WE ALREADY HAVE MORE THAN ENOUGH ENERGY CHARGED.
KINGDOM OF PICHE KILLER
ALTAIR

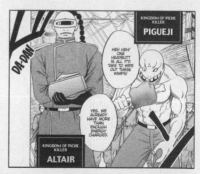

Altair and Pigueji are two assassins sent from the kingdom of Piche, on the foreign continent called Kardensia. Both are powerful killers.

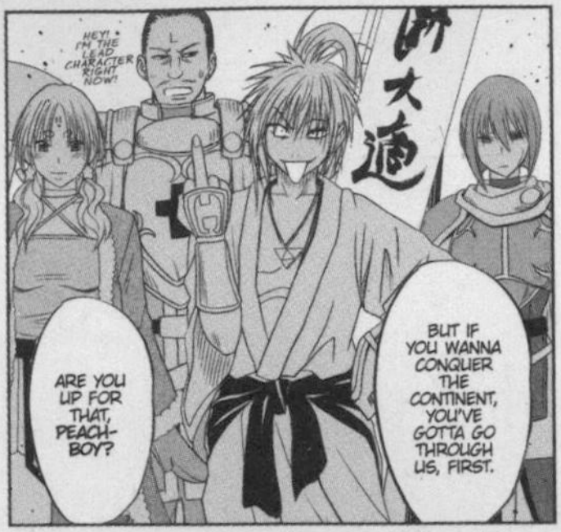
BUT IF YOU WANNA CONQUER THE CONTINENT, YOU'VE GOTTA GO THROUGH US, FIRST.
ARE YOU UP FOR THAT, PEACH-BOY?
HEY! I'M THE LEAD CHARACTER RIGHT NOW!

Kicho's name comes from splitting the character for "peach" into its component parts, "ki" and "cho."

Prof. Mushroom: Nah, they were just plain old, regular refrigerators! Now, four years after Nintendo released the Famicom (the Japanese version of the NES), on October 30th, 1987, NEC-HE released their own game console, called the PC Engine in Japan, and the TurboGrafx-16 Entertainment SuperSystem in the rest of the world.

Mr. Why: "TurboGrafx-16"?

Dr. Onigiri: Yes. But NEC-HE was an appliance maker. They didn't have any experience building a game console. So they collaborated with a third-party game maker to develop it.

Prof. Mushroom: And that third party game maker was Hudson Soft, the creators of *Momotaro Dentetsu*--an RPG series featuring characters from Japanese folklore.

Dr. Onigiri: Exactly! The TurboGrafx-16 was a system co-owned by both NEC-HE and Hudson Soft.

Prof. Mushroom: The NES couldn't even touch TurboGrafx-16 in terms of sound and graphics quality. NEC-HE really shocked the gaming world when it released a nearly flawless port of the uber-popular arcade shooter *R-Type.*

Dr. Onigiri: The system had several exclusive killer games as well. One of the more popular ones was *Bonk's Adventure*, a side-scroller about a prehistoric cave-boy who defeats enemies by headbutting them and eats meat to power himself up.

Mr. Why: Huh. What other popular games did it have?

Prof. Mushroom: Lessee... There's *Super Momotaro Dentetsu*, their big remake of the NES title. They added a whole lot of new features, like colored squares that did different things if you landed on them, seasonal differences to profits and a card system, all of which became staples in later games.

Dr. Onigiri: Well... I, uh, hate to say it, but the TurboGrafx-16 had a lot more momentum behind it than Sega did at the time. Having computer-giant NEC's name attached to it gave it some powerful brand recognition. In Japan, anyway. I hear it was different in the U.S. and Europe.

Prof. Mushroom: And with NEC's computer know-how, they powered up the TurboGrafx-16 in a big way. We'll talk about that next time.

To Be Continued...

WORLD WAR BLUE
CHARACTER INTRODUCTION

The Samurai CEO
KICHO

Kicho originally made his fame as a swordsman. However, on a lark, he founded a rail business that became a huge commercial success, making him even more famous as a CEO.

His favorite season is summer, and he despises winter. He loves the color blue, and is fond of yellow, but he hates red.

Smart and a shrewd businessman, he has an unexpected fondness for toilet humor.

Author Comment

The different facets of Kicho's personality make him an interesting character to me. He'll get some time in the limelight again later in the series.

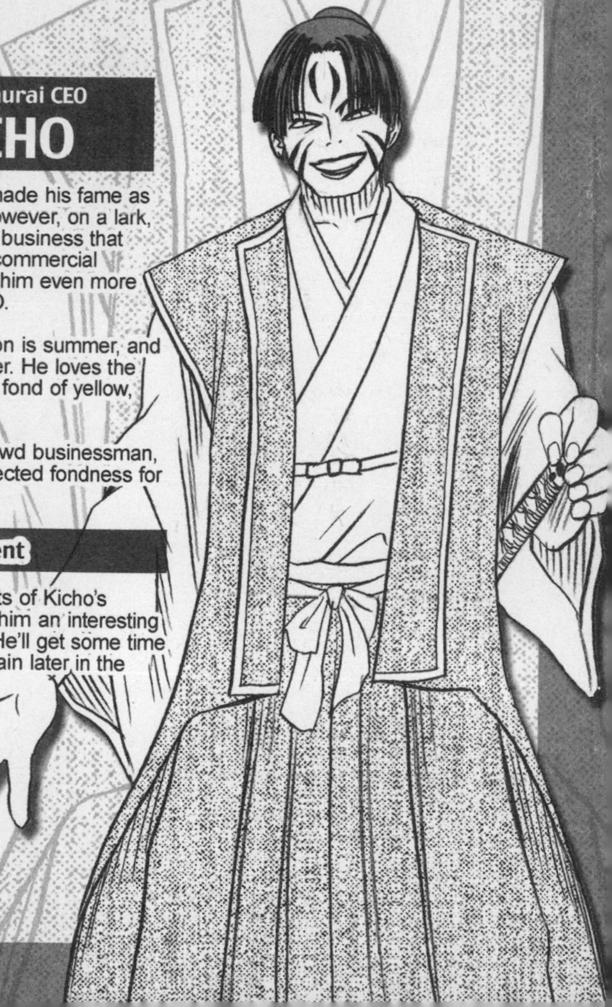

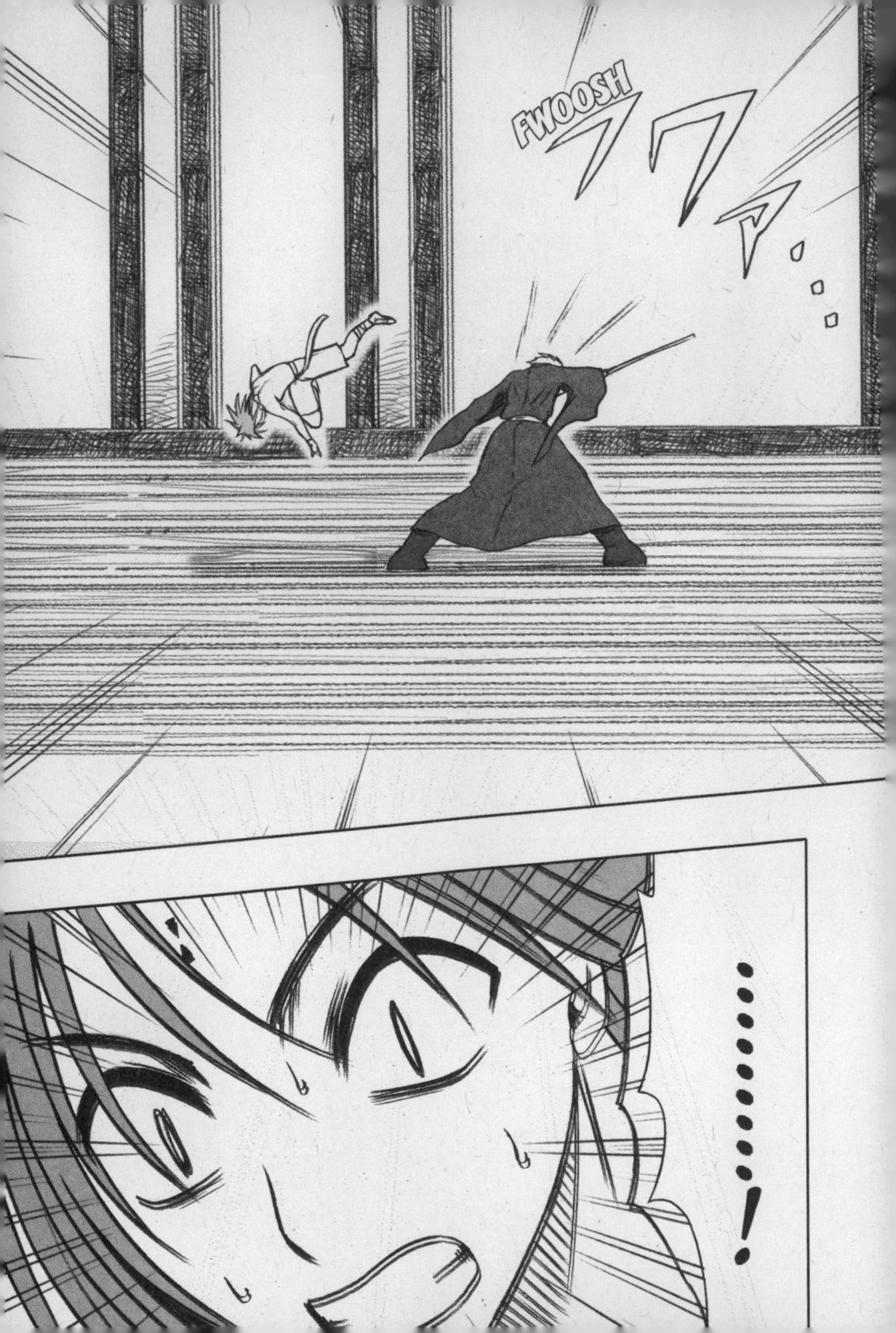
FWOOSH
.........!

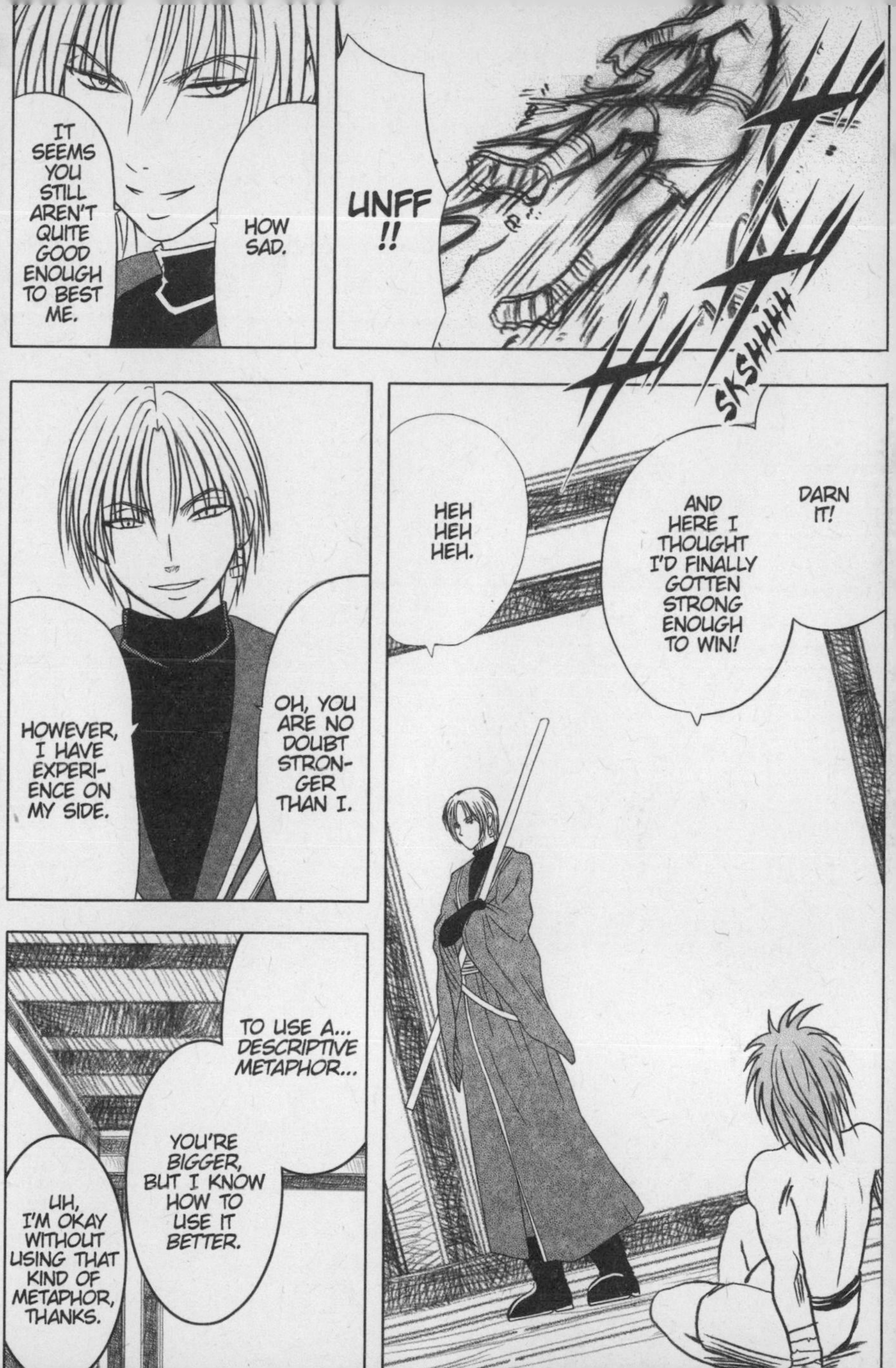
UNFF!!
SKSHHHH
HOW SAD.
IT SEEMS YOU STILL AREN'T QUITE GOOD ENOUGH TO BEST ME.
DARN IT!
AND HERE I THOUGHT I'D FINALLY GOTTEN STRONG ENOUGH TO WIN!
HEH HEH HEH.
OH, YOU ARE NO DOUBT STRONGER THAN I.
HOWEVER, I HAVE EXPERIENCE ON MY SIDE.
TO USE A... DESCRIPTIVE METAPHOR...
YOU'RE BIGGER, BUT I KNOW HOW TO USE IT BETTER.
UH, I'M OKAY WITHOUT USING THAT KIND OF METAPHOR, THANKS.

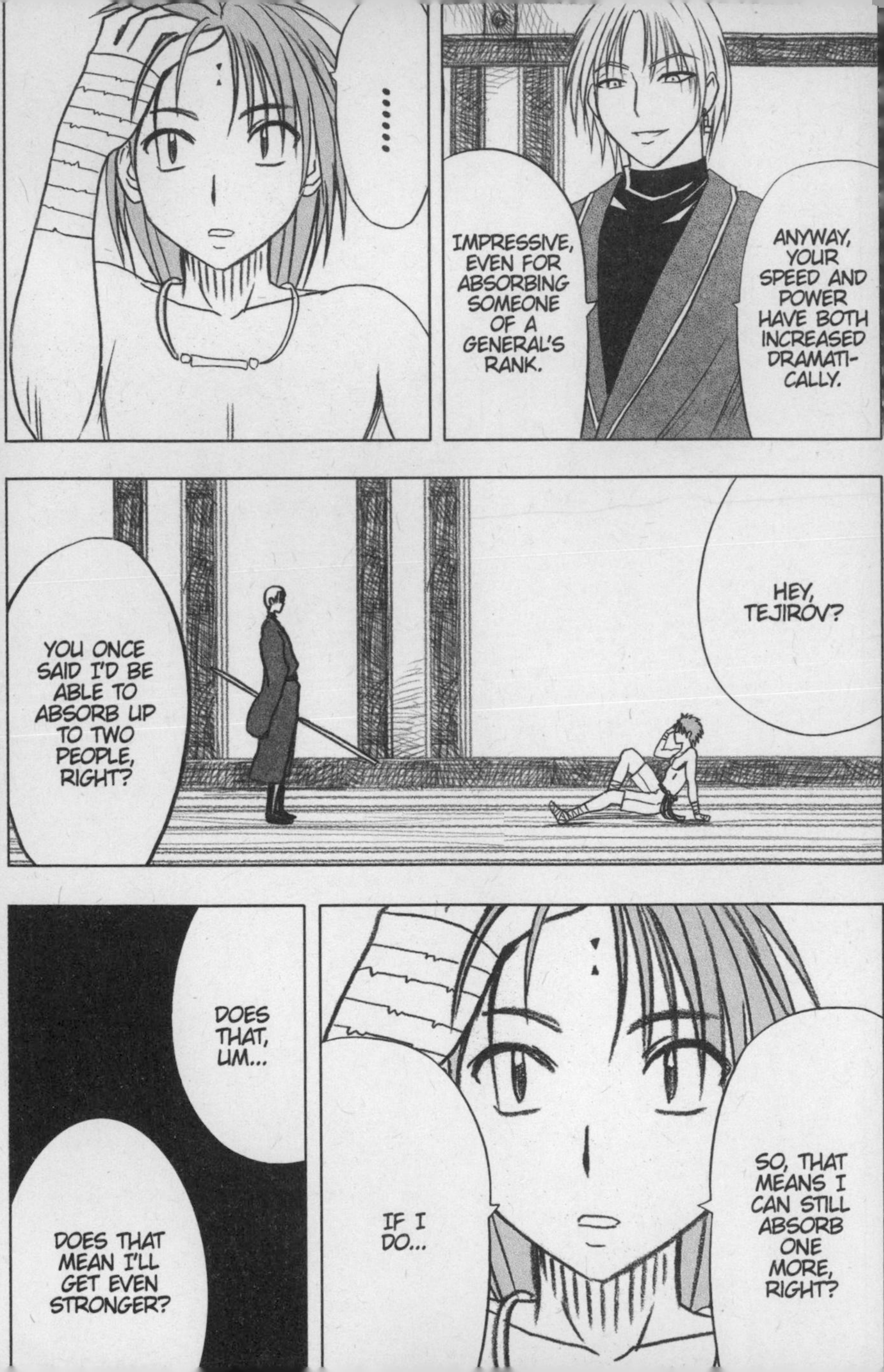
ANYWAY, YOUR SPEED AND POWER HAVE BOTH INCREASED DRAMATI- CALLY.
IMPRESSIVE, EVEN FOR ABSORBING SOMEONE OF A GENERAL'S RANK.
......
HEY, TEJIROV?
YOU ONCE SAID I'D BE ABLE TO ABSORB UP TO TWO PEOPLE, RIGHT?
SO, THAT MEANS I CAN STILL ABSORB ONE MORE, RIGHT?
IF I DO...
DOES THAT, UM...
DOES THAT MEAN I'LL GET EVEN STRONGER?

Part 2

CHAPTER 3

CD

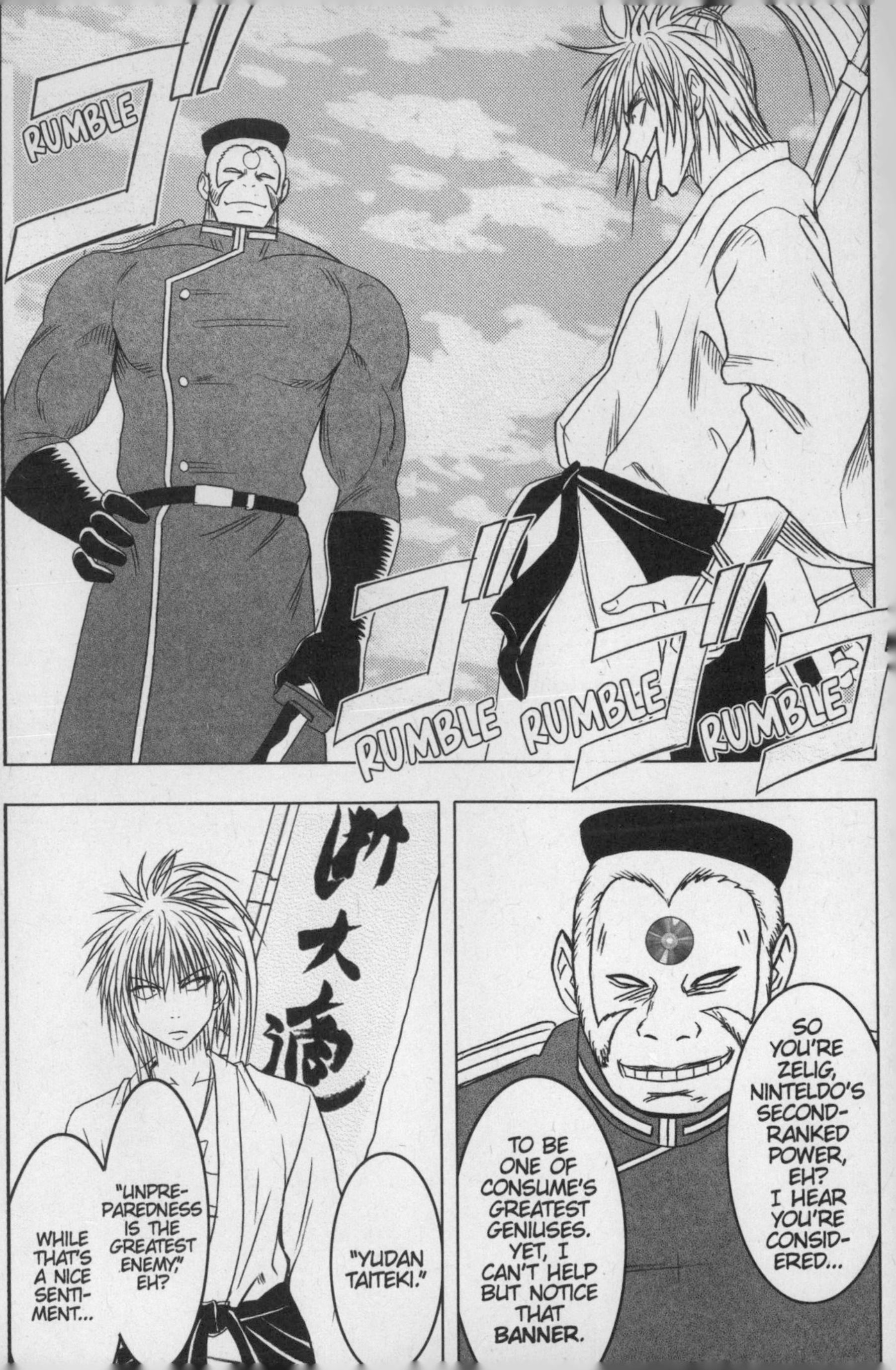
RUMBLE
RUMBLE
RUMBLE
RUMBLE
SO YOU'RE ZELIG, NINTELDO'S SECOND-RANKED POWER, EH? I HEAR YOU'RE CONSIDERED...
TO BE ONE OF CONSUME'S GREATEST GENIUSES. YET, I CAN'T HELP BUT NOTICE THAT BANNER.
"YUDAN TAITEKI."
"UNPREPAREDNESS IS THE GREATEST ENEMY," EH?
WHILE THAT'S A NICE SENTIMENT...

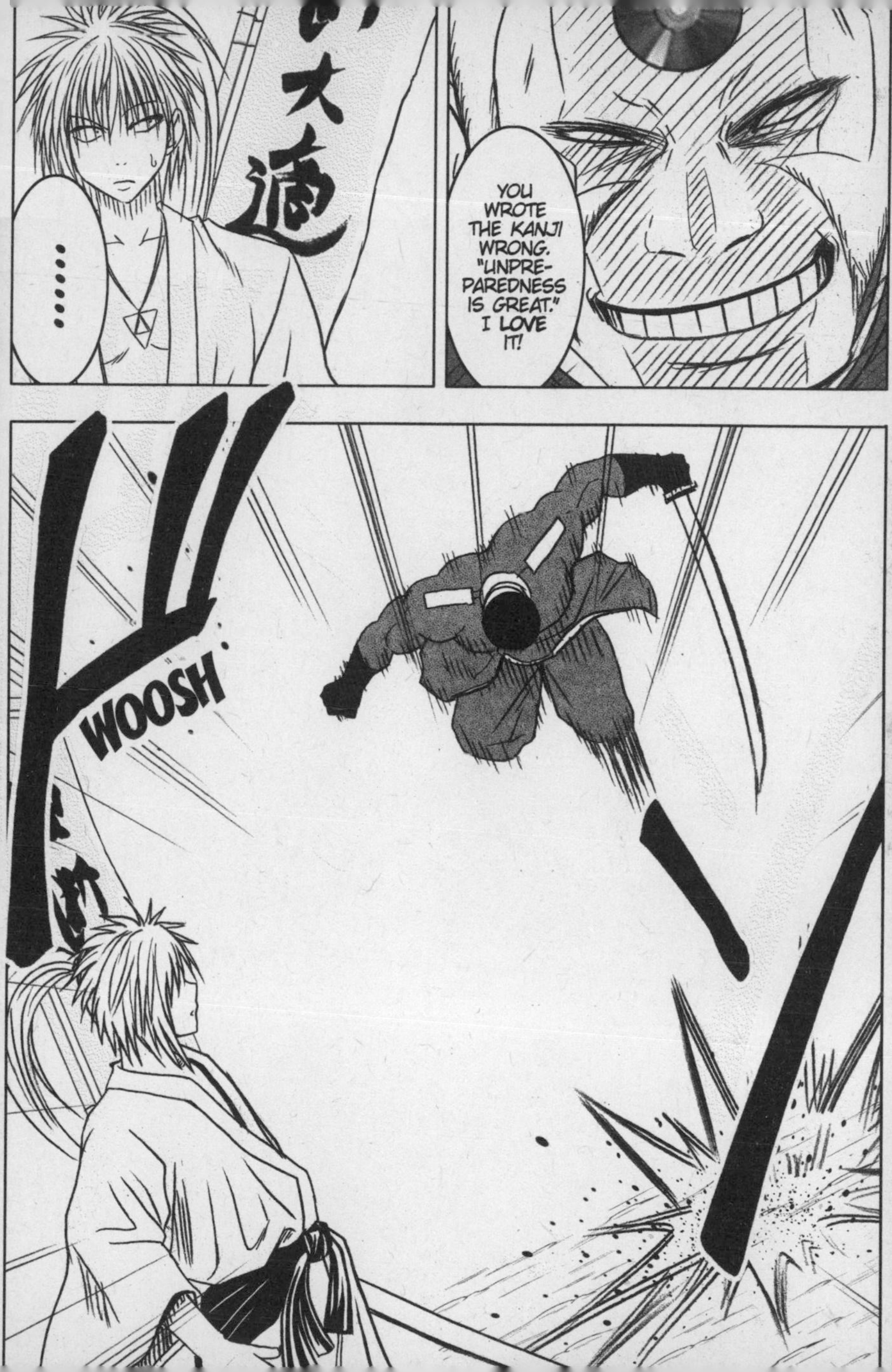
YOU WROTE THE KANJI WRONG. "UNPREPAREDNESS IS GREAT." I LOVE IT!
......
WOOSH

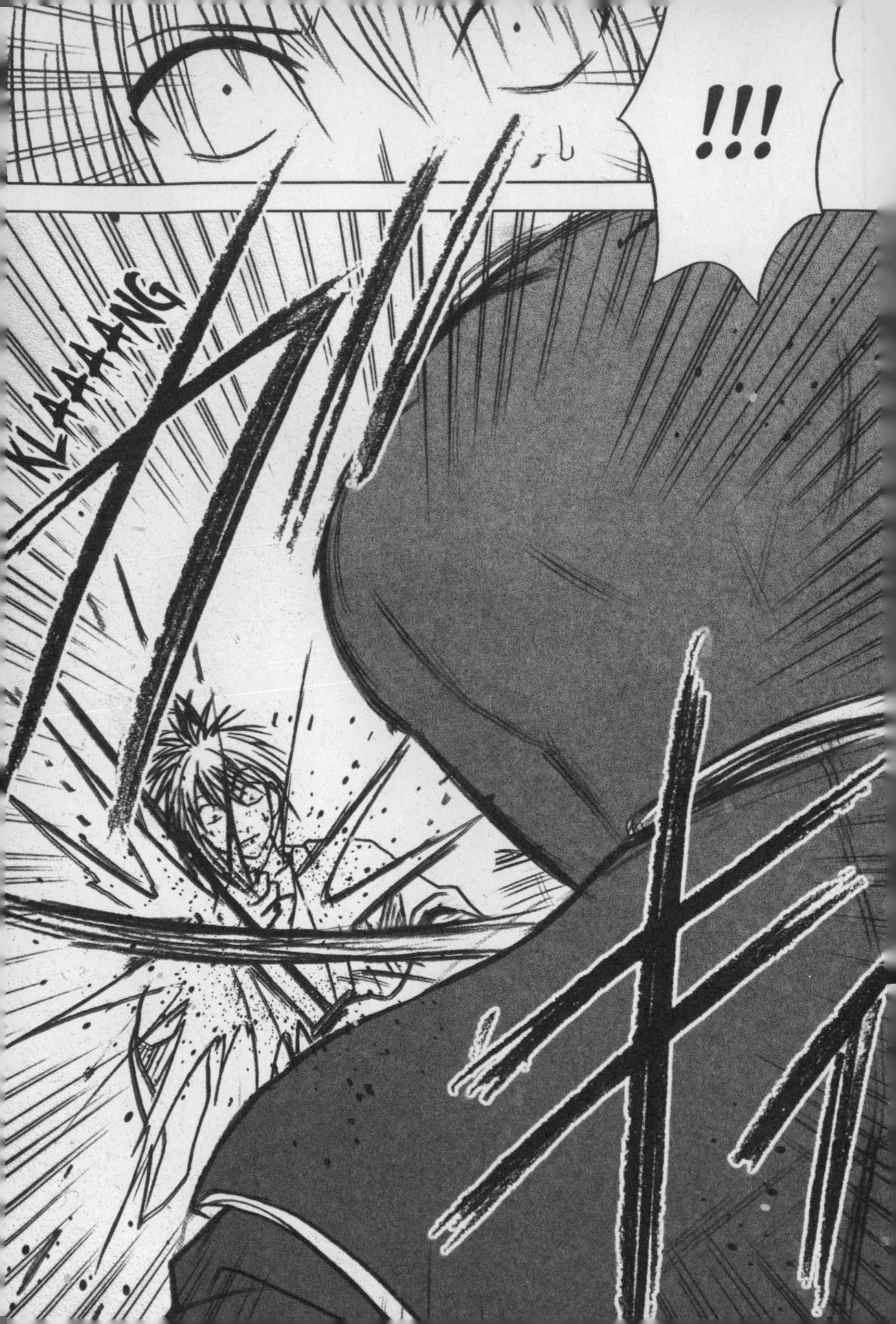
!!!
KLAAAANG

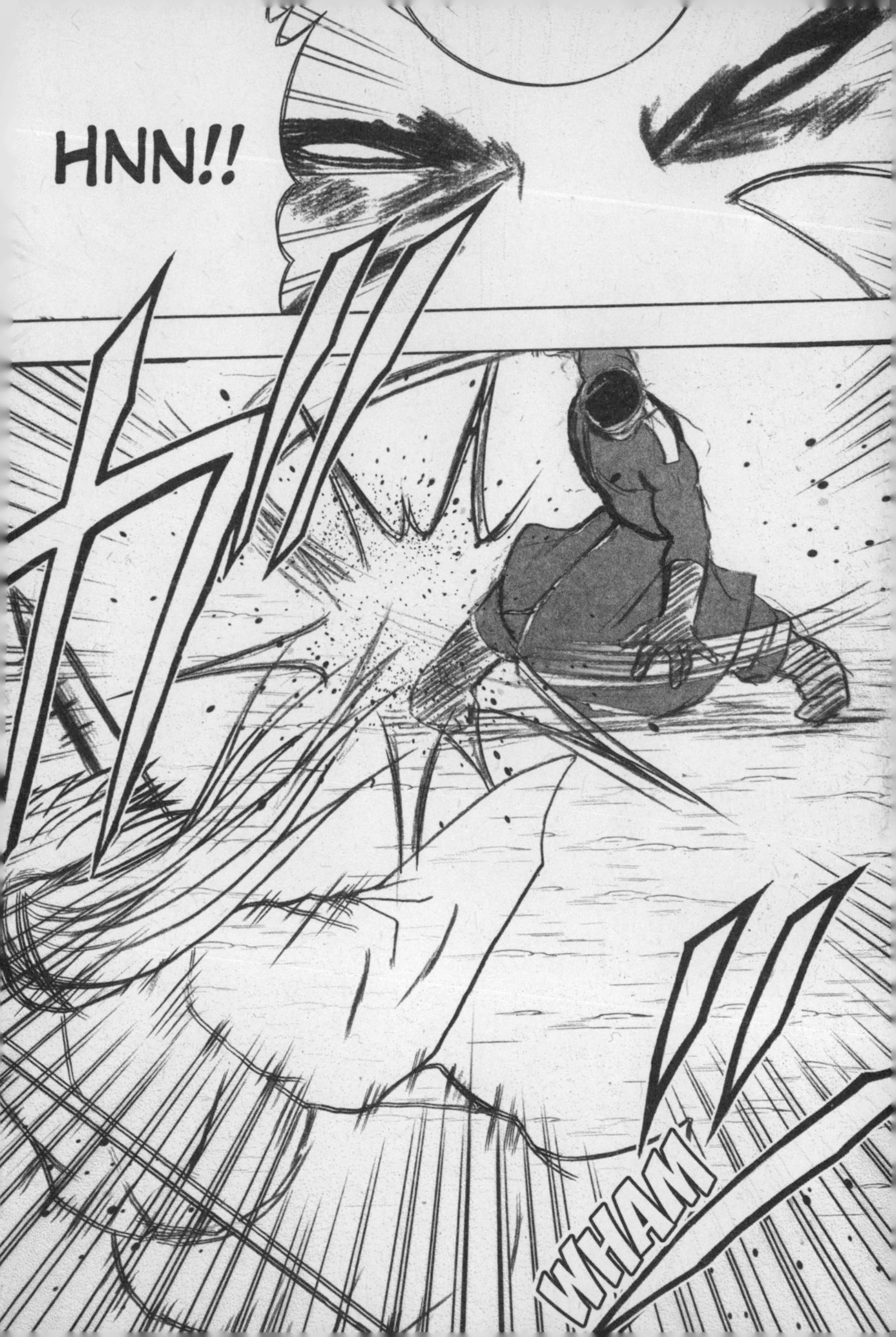
HNN!!
WHAM

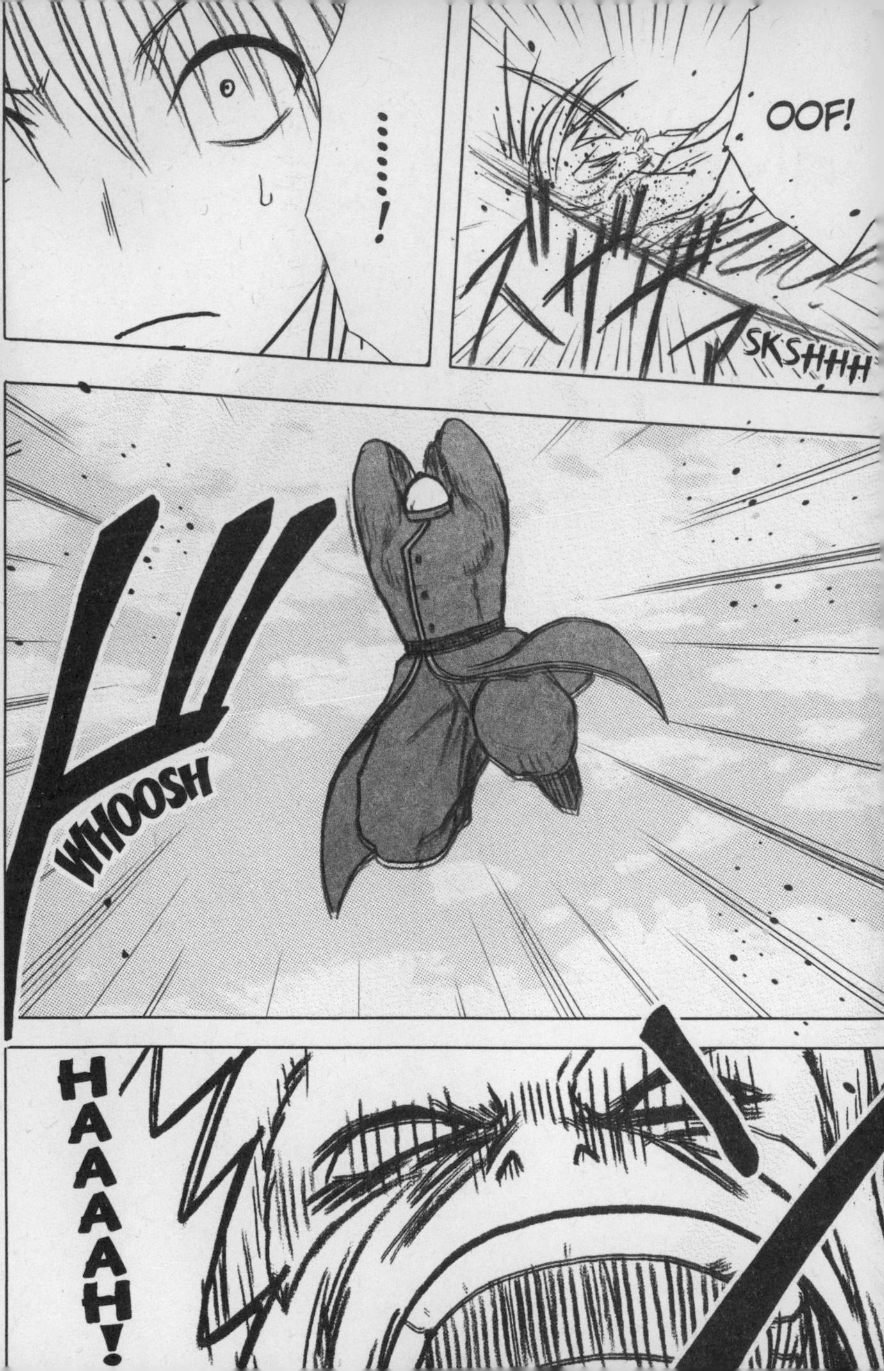
OOF!
SKSHHH
.....!
WHOOSH
HAAAAAH!

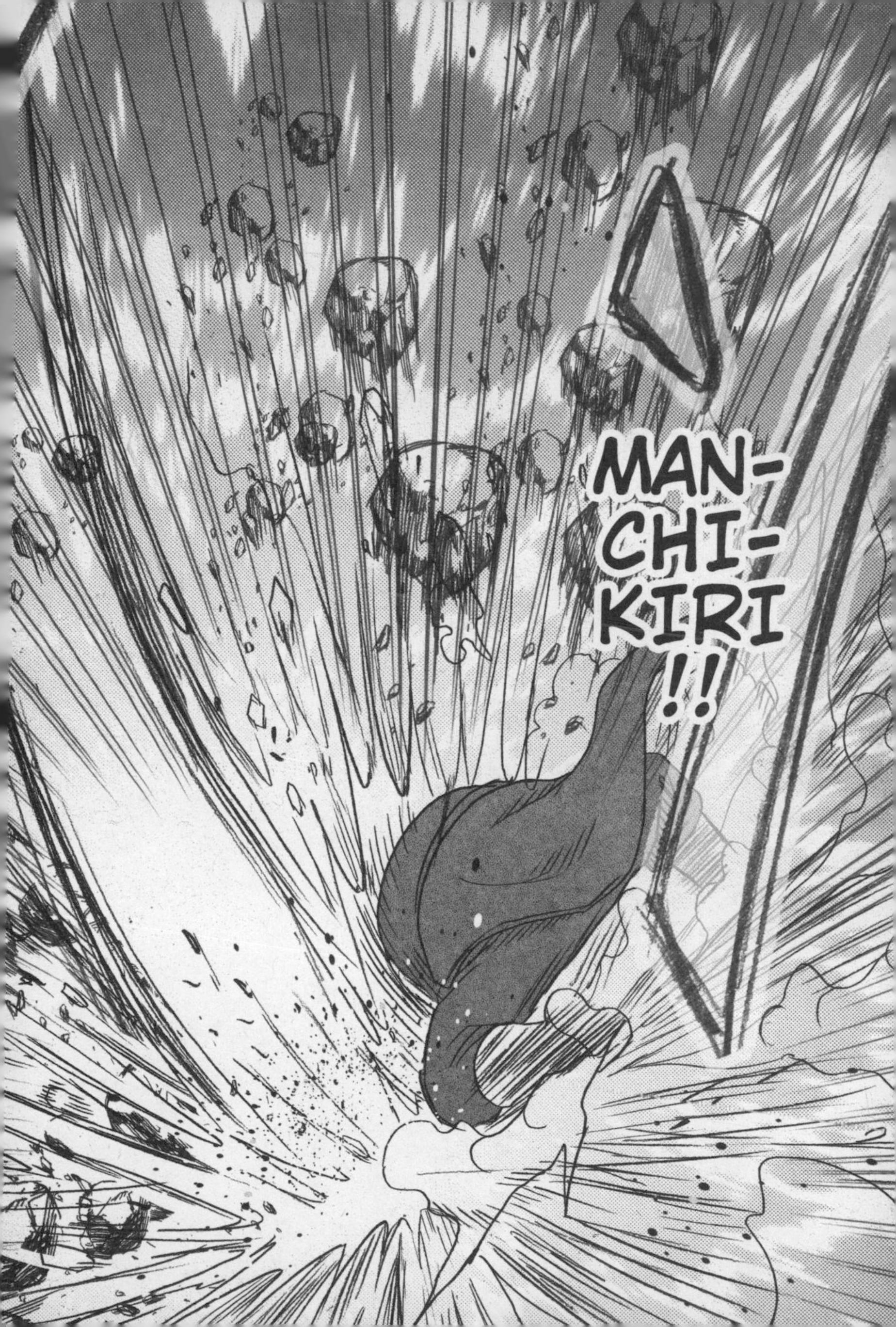
MAN-
CHI-
KIRI
!!

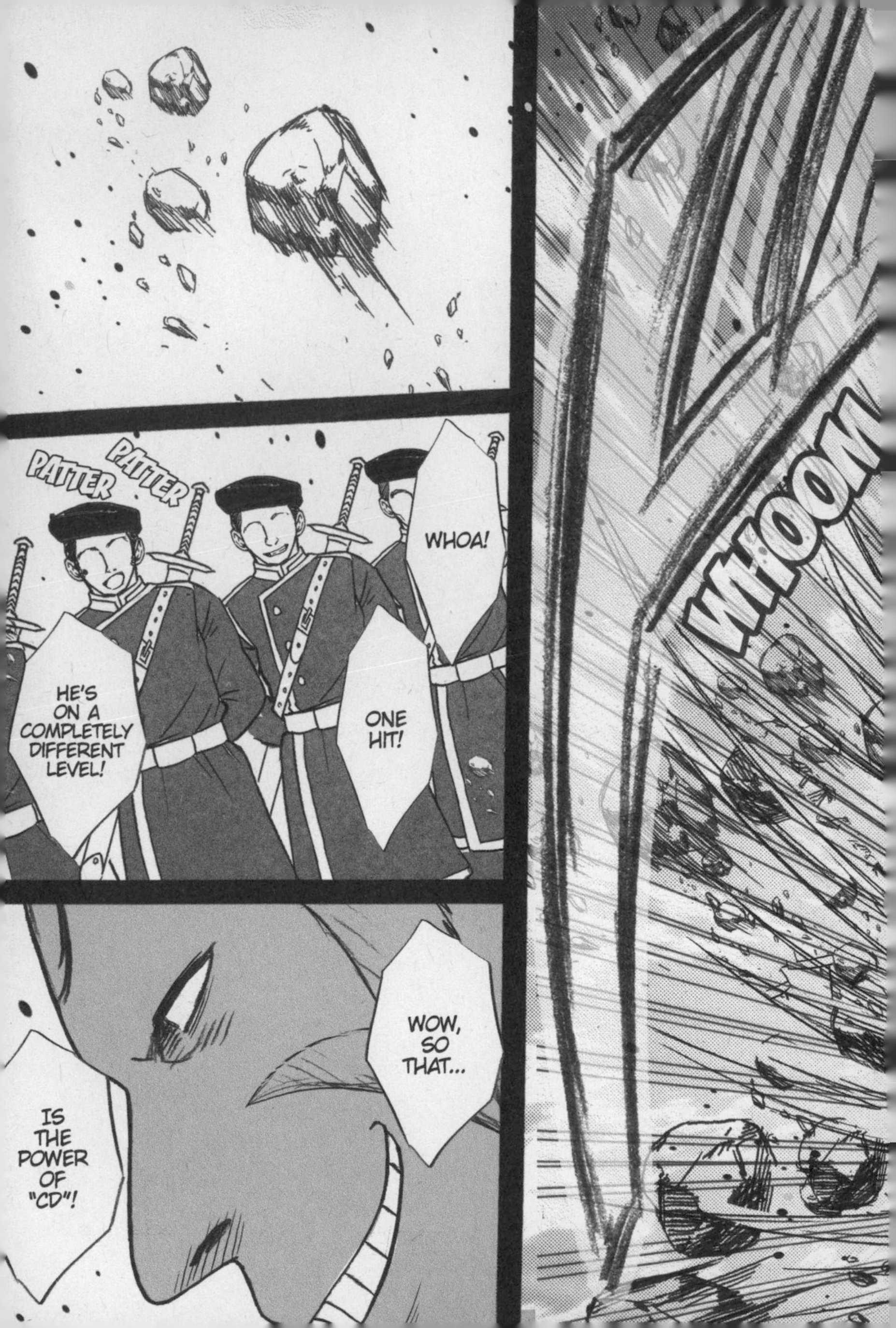
WHOOM
WHOA!
PATTER
PATTER
ONE HIT!
HE'S ON A COMPLETELY DIFFERENT LEVEL!
WOW, SO THAT...
IS THE POWER OF "CD"!

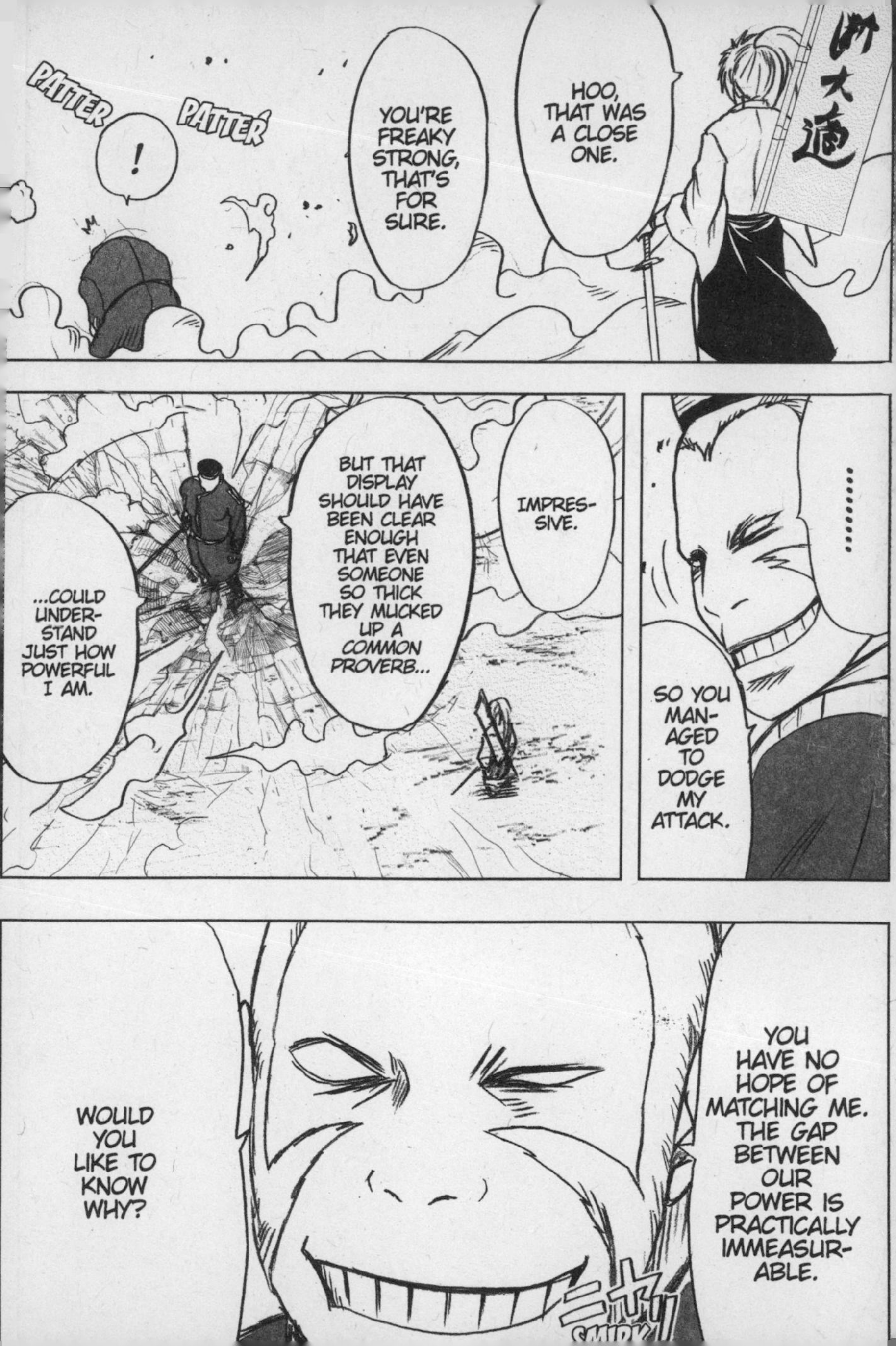
HOO, THAT WAS A CLOSE ONE.
YOU'RE FREAKY STRONG, THAT'S FOR SURE.
PATTER
PATTER
!
......
SO YOU MANAGED TO DODGE MY ATTACK.
IMPRESSIVE.
BUT THAT DISPLAY SHOULD HAVE BEEN CLEAR ENOUGH THAT EVEN SOMEONE SO THICK THEY MUCKED UP A COMMON PROVERB...
...COULD UNDERSTAND JUST HOW POWERFUL I AM.
YOU HAVE NO HOPE OF MATCHING ME. THE GAP BETWEEN OUR POWER IS PRACTICALLY IMMEASURABLE.
WOULD YOU LIKE TO KNOW WHY?

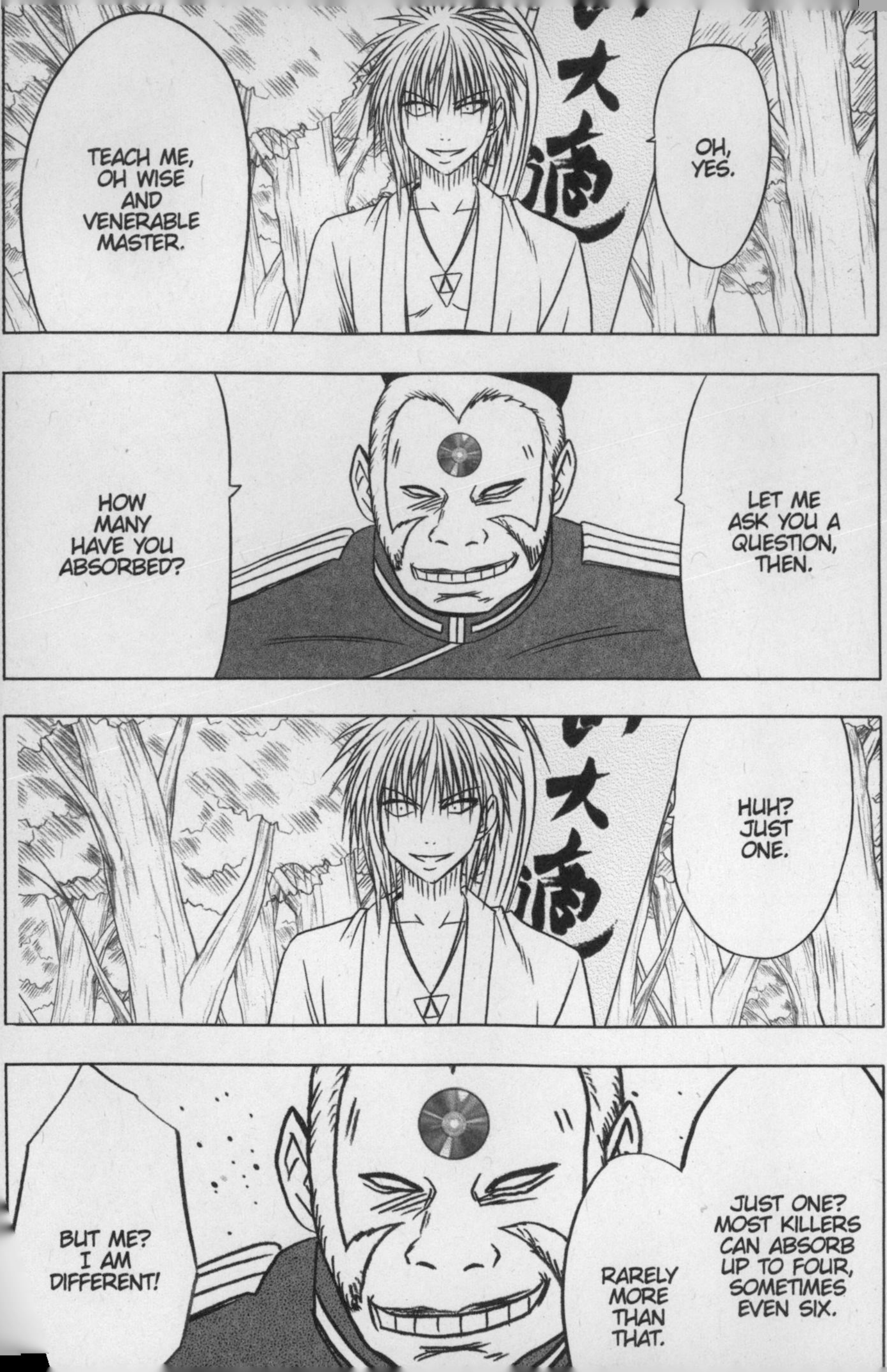
OH, YES.
TEACH ME, OH WISE AND VENERABLE MASTER.
LET ME ASK YOU A QUESTION, THEN.
HOW MANY HAVE YOU ABSORBED?
HUH? JUST ONE.
JUST ONE? MOST KILLERS CAN ABSORB UP TO FOUR, SOMETIMES EVEN SIX.
RARELY MORE THAN THAT.
BUT ME? I AM DIFFERENT!

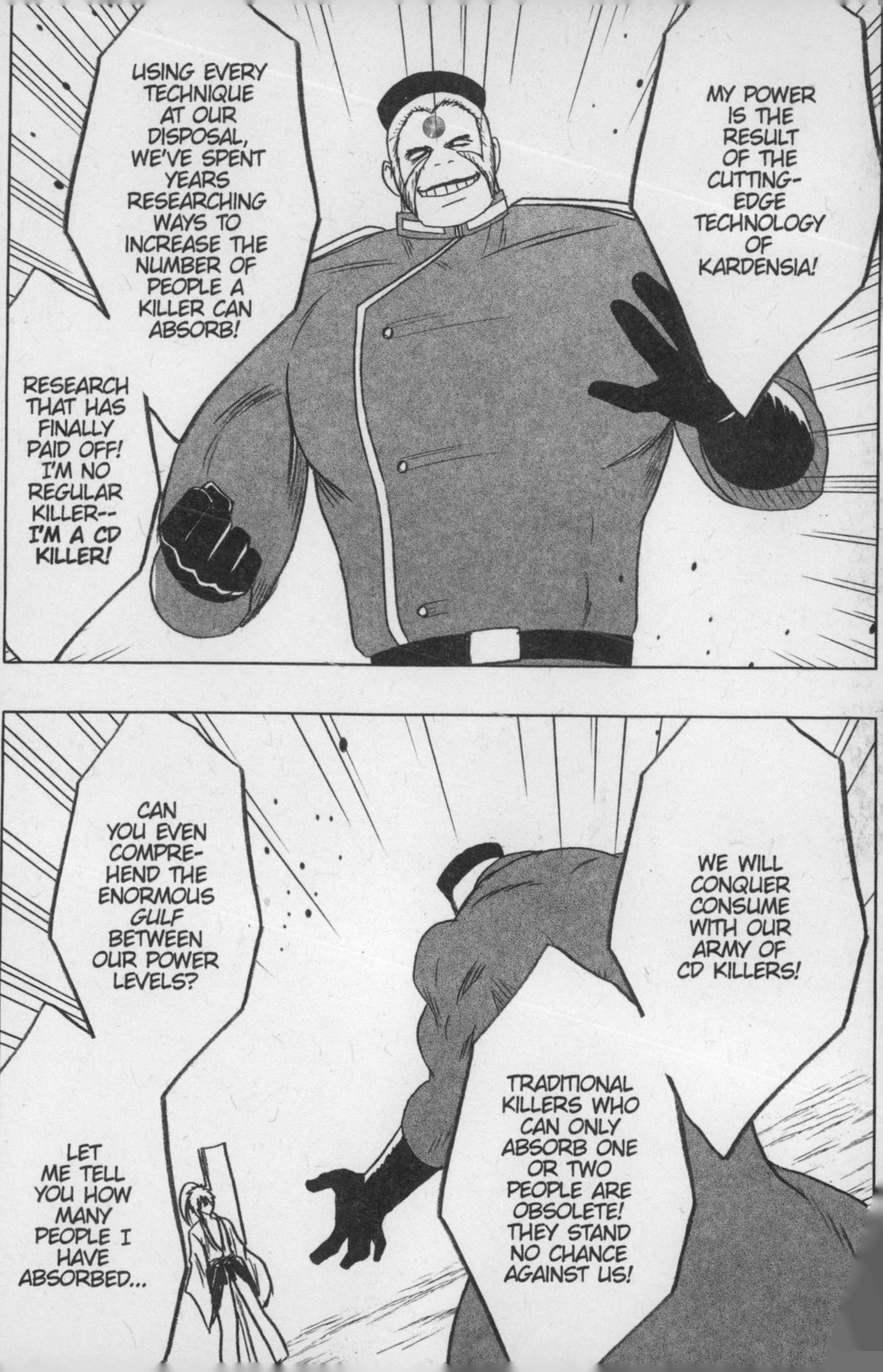
MY POWER IS THE RESULT OF THE CUTTING-EDGE TECHNOLOGY OF KARDENSIA!
USING EVERY TECHNIQUE AT OUR DISPOSAL, WE'VE SPENT YEARS RESEARCHING WAYS TO INCREASE THE NUMBER OF PEOPLE A KILLER CAN ABSORB!
RESEARCH THAT HAS FINALLY PAID OFF! I'M NO REGULAR KILLER-- I'M A CD KILLER!
WE WILL CONQUER CONSUME WITH OUR ARMY OF CD KILLERS!
CAN YOU EVEN COMPRE-HEND THE ENORMOUS GULF BETWEEN OUR POWER LEVELS?
TRADITIONAL KILLERS WHO CAN ONLY ABSORB ONE OR TWO PEOPLE ARE OBSOLETE! THEY STAND NO CHANCE AGAINST US!
LET ME TELL YOU HOW MANY PEOPLE I HAVE ABSORBED...

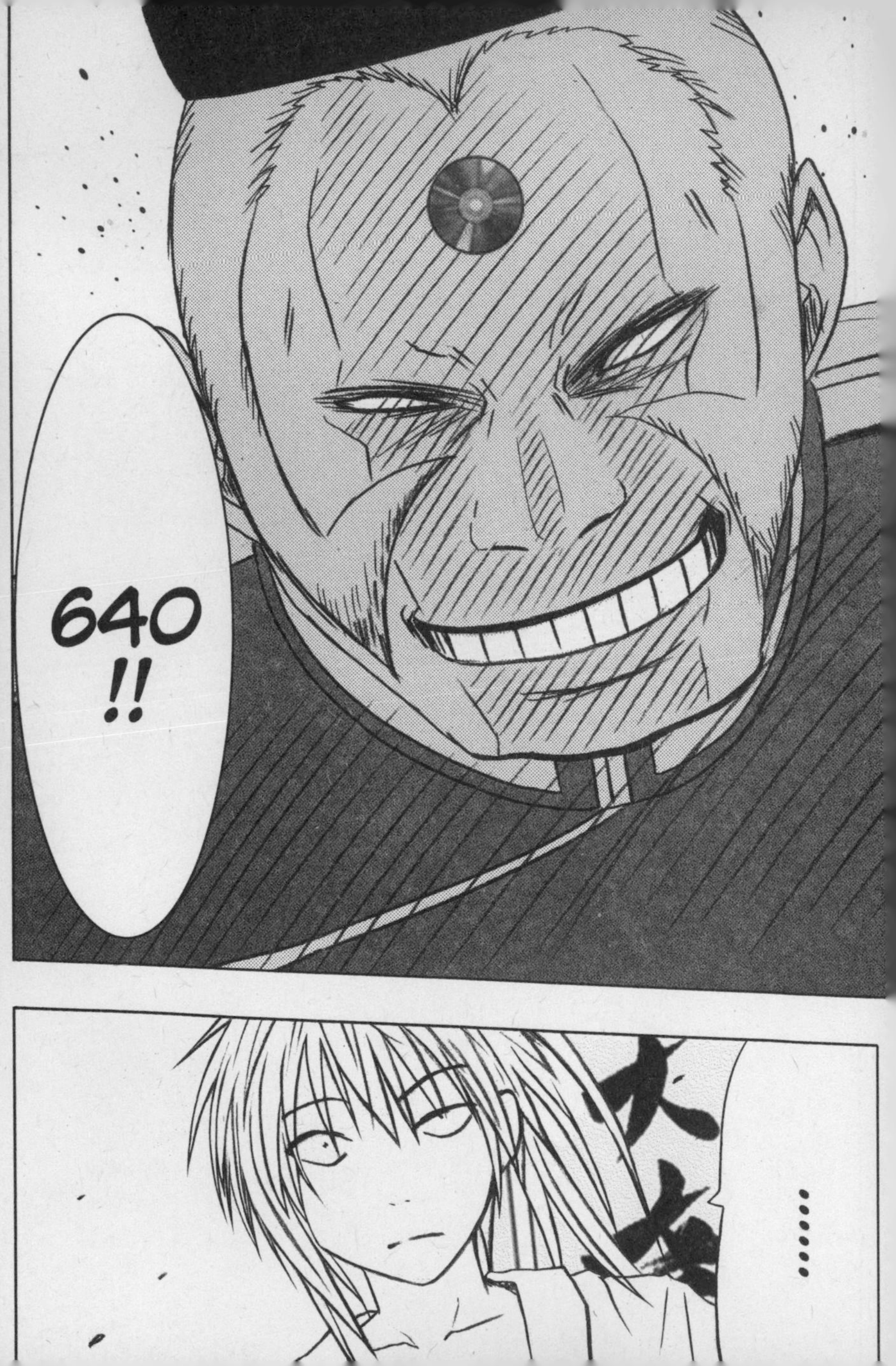
640 !!
......

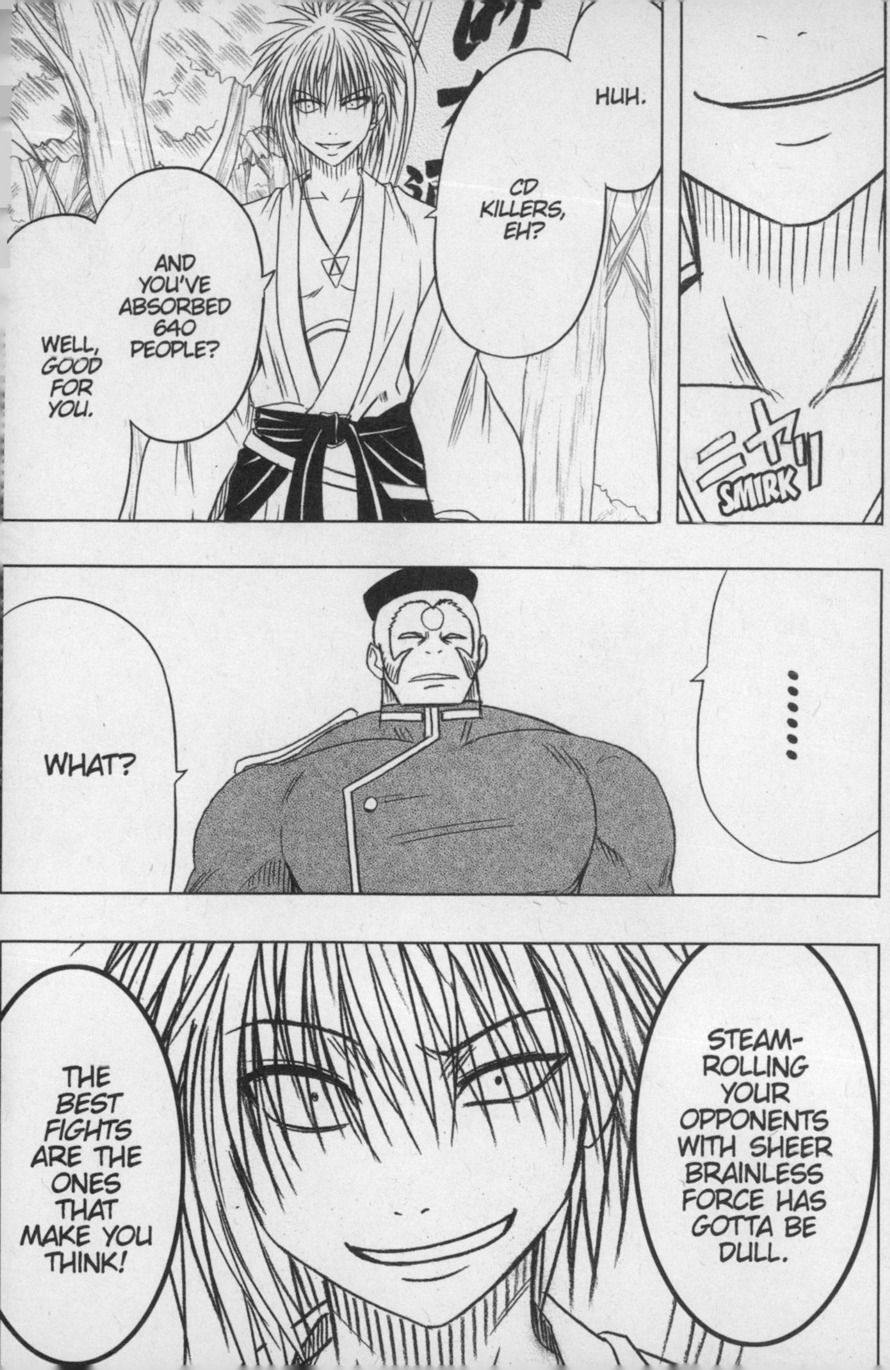
SMIRK
HUH.
CD KILLERS, EH?
AND YOU'VE ABSORBED 640 PEOPLE?
WELL, GOOD FOR YOU.
......
WHAT?
STEAM-ROLLING YOUR OPPONENTS WITH SHEER BRAINLESS FORCE HAS GOTTA BE DULL.
THE BEST FIGHTS ARE THE ONES THAT MAKE YOU THINK!

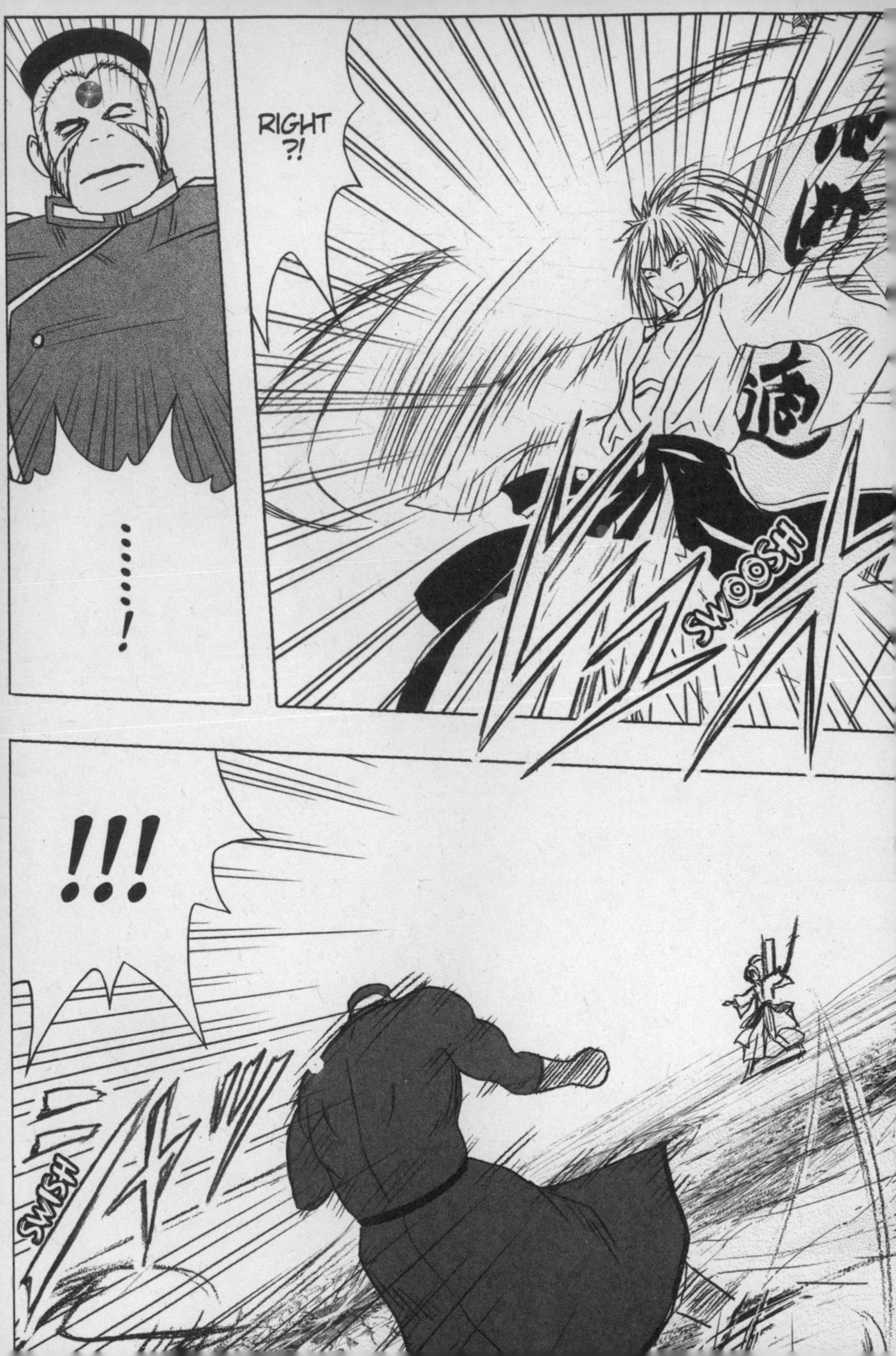
RIGHT ?!
SWOOSH
......!
!!!
SWISH

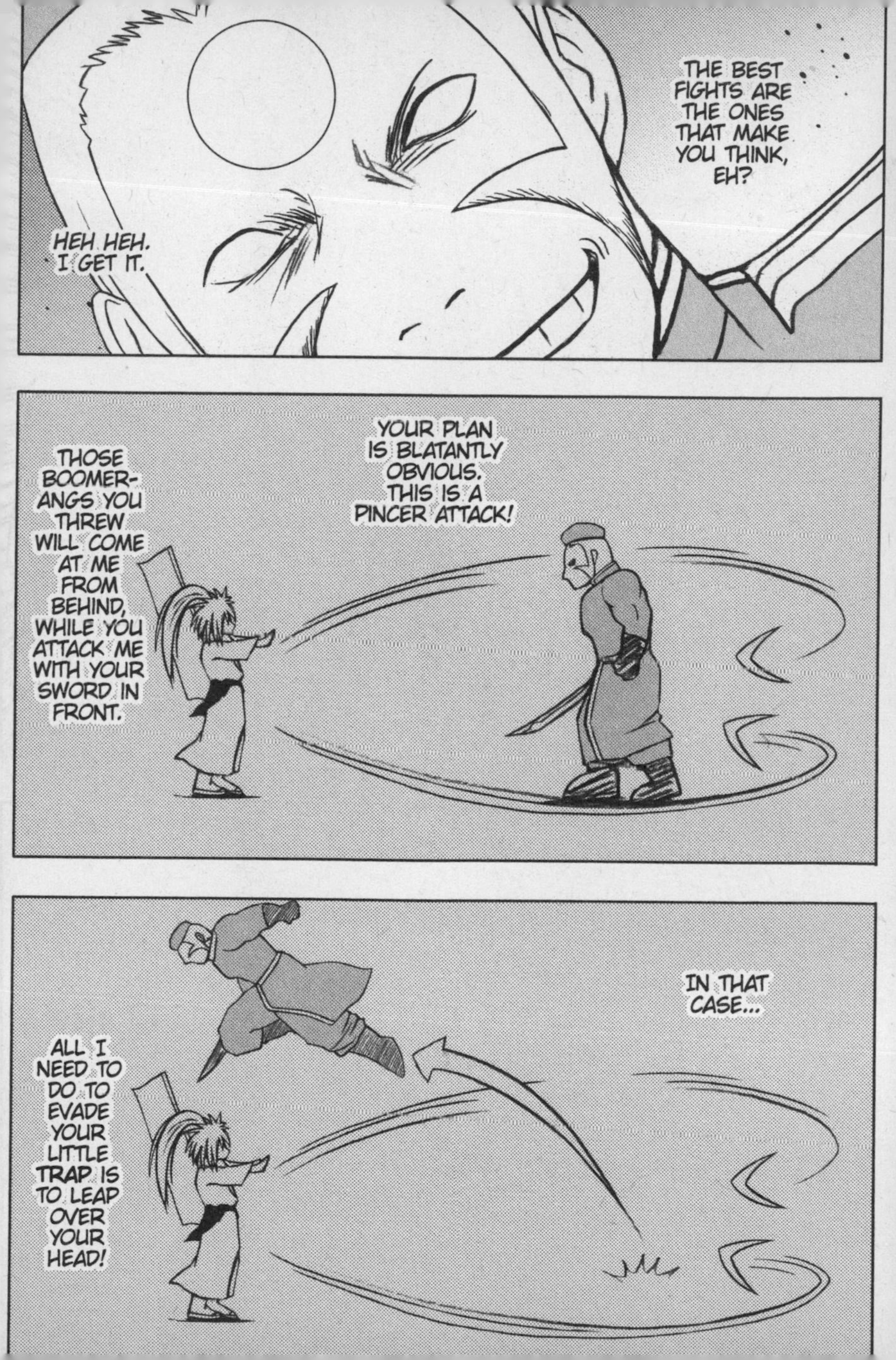
THE BEST FIGHTS ARE THE ONES THAT MAKE YOU THINK, EH?
HEH HEH. I GET IT.
YOUR PLAN IS BLATANTLY OBVIOUS. THIS IS A PINCER ATTACK!
THOSE BOOMER-ANGS YOU THREW WILL COME AT ME FROM BEHIND, WHILE YOU ATTACK ME WITH YOUR SWORD IN FRONT.
IN THAT CASE...
ALL I NEED TO DO TO EVADE YOUR LITTLE TRAP IS TO LEAP OVER YOUR HEAD!

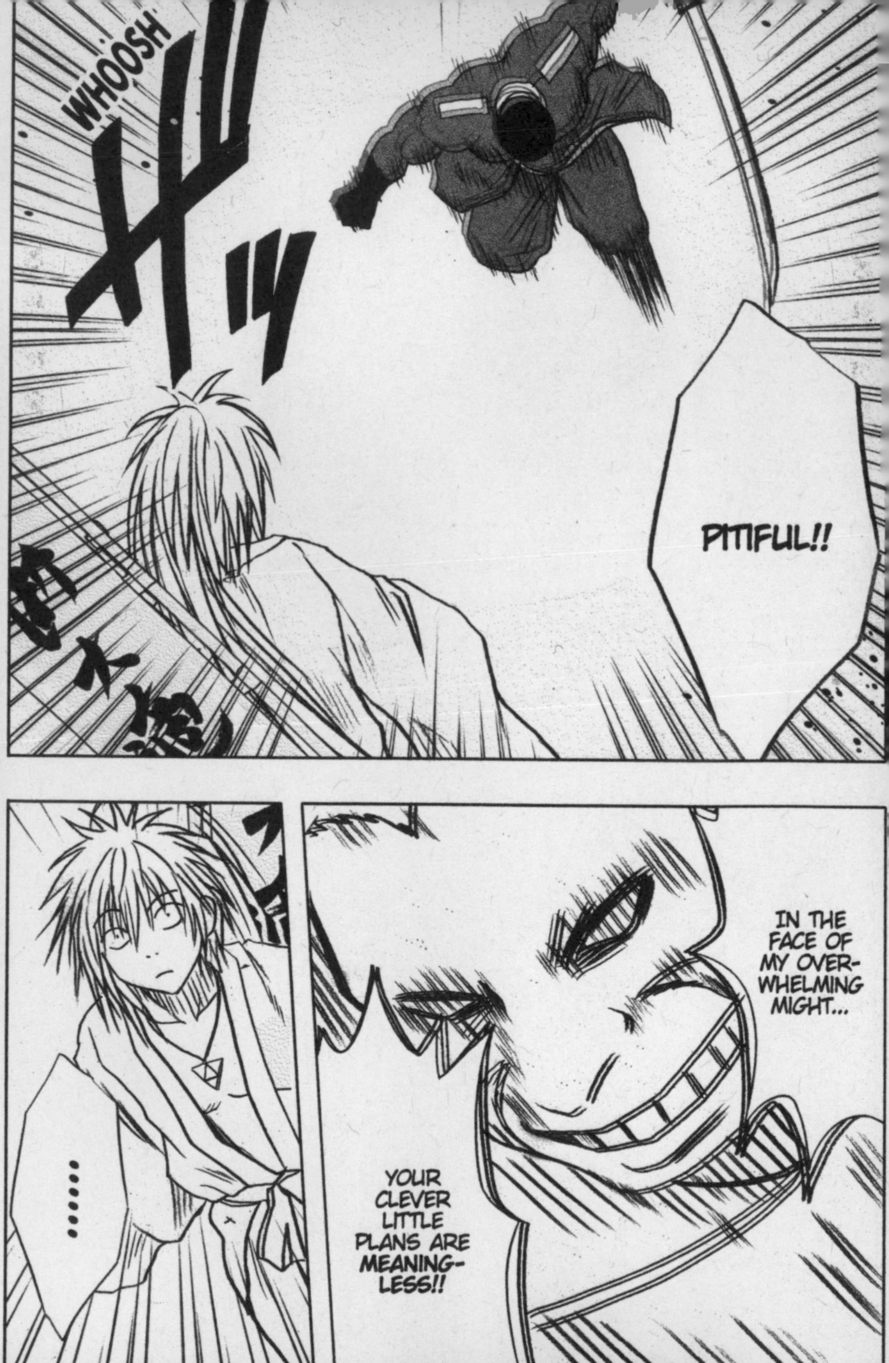
WHOOSH
PITIFUL!!
IN THE FACE OF MY OVER-WHELMING MIGHT...
YOUR CLEVER LITTLE PLANS ARE MEANING-LESS!!
......

HA-HAH!!

UH...
YOU DO
KNOW I
PLANTED
BOMBS
OVER
THERE,
RIGHT?

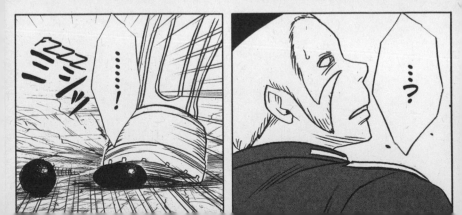

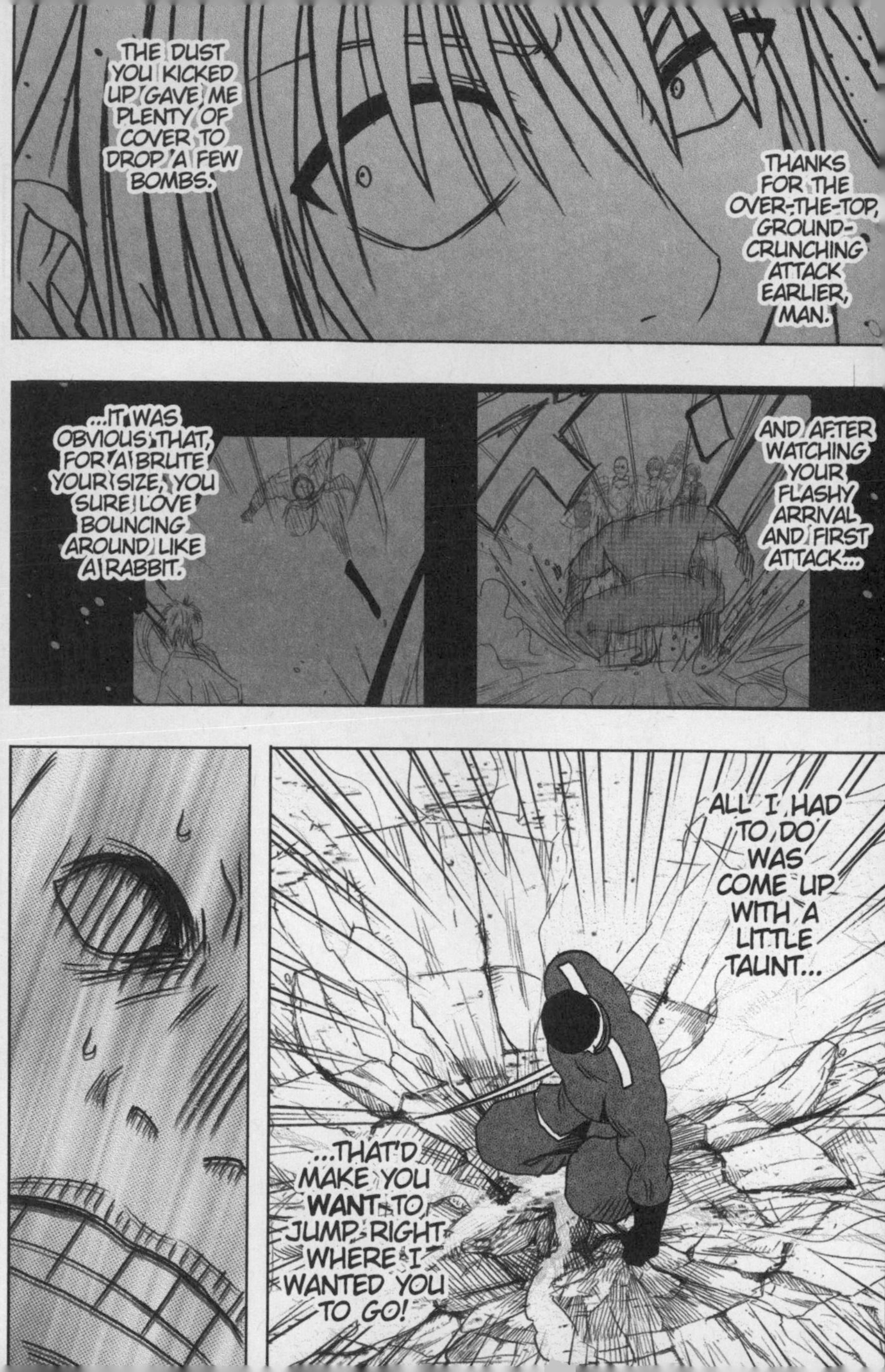
THANKS FOR THE OVER-THE-TOP, GROUND-CRUNCHING ATTACK EARLIER, MAN.
THE DUST YOU KICKED UP GAVE ME PLENTY OF COVER TO DROP A FEW BOMBS.
AND AFTER WATCHING YOUR FLASHY ARRIVAL AND FIRST ATTACK...
...IT WAS OBVIOUS THAT, FOR A BRUTE YOUR SIZE, YOU SURE LOVE BOUNCING AROUND LIKE A RABBIT.
ALL I HAD TO DO WAS COME UP WITH A LITTLE TAUNT...
...THAT'D MAKE YOU WANT TO JUMP RIGHT WHERE I WANTED YOU TO GO!

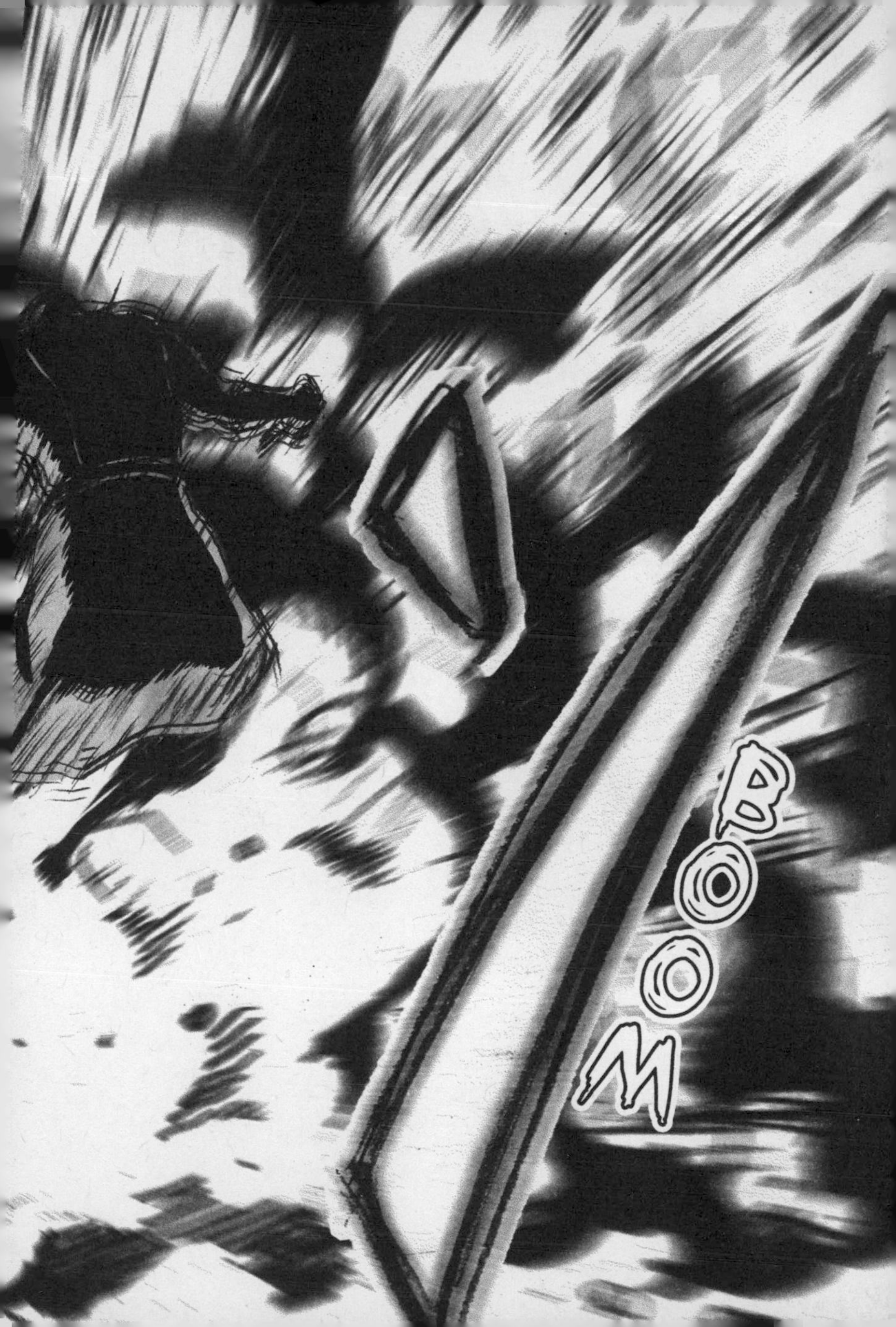
BOOOM

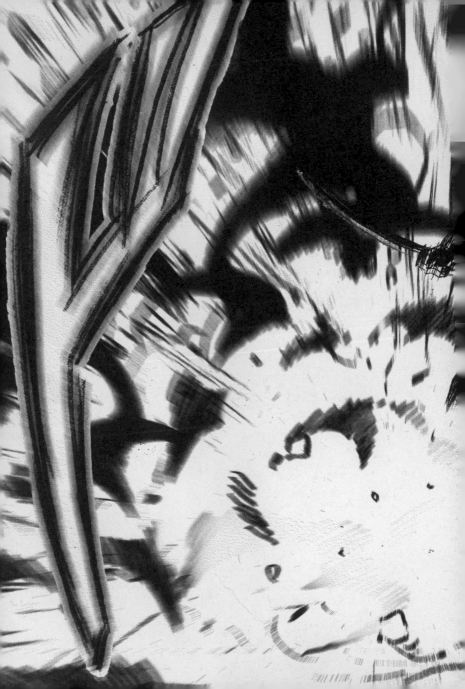

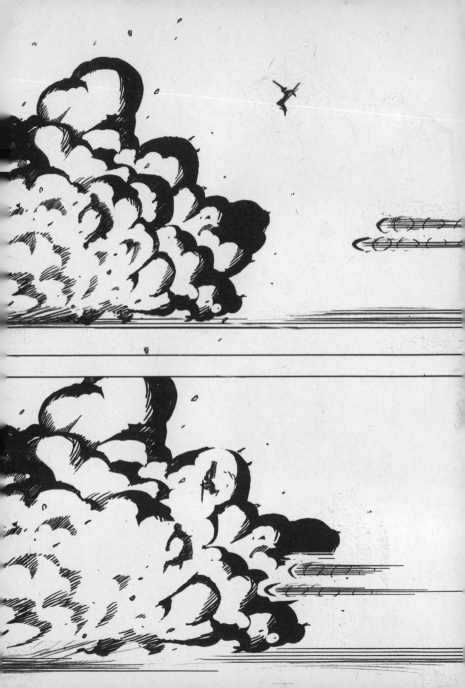

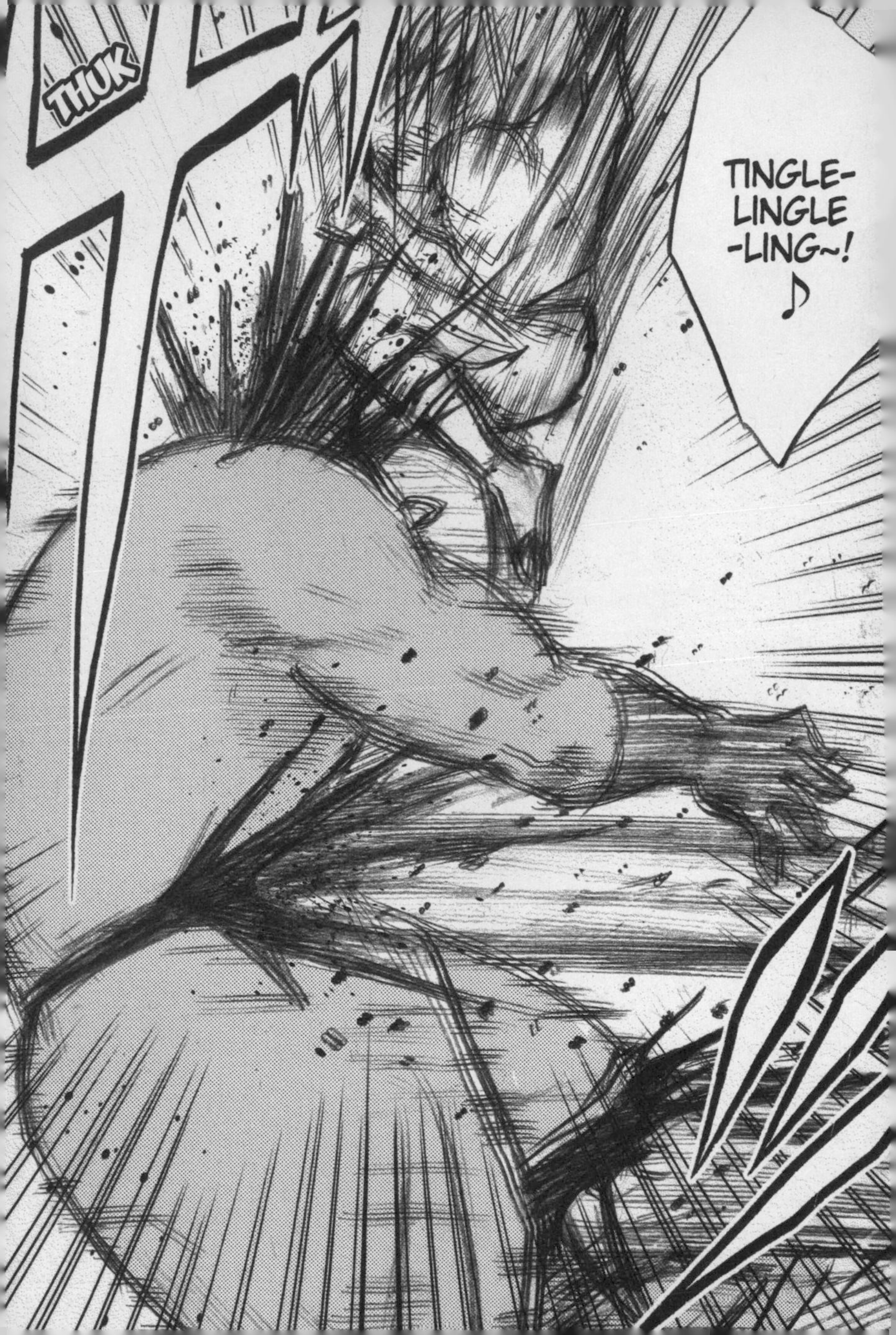
TINGLE-
LINGLE
-LING~! ♪
THUK

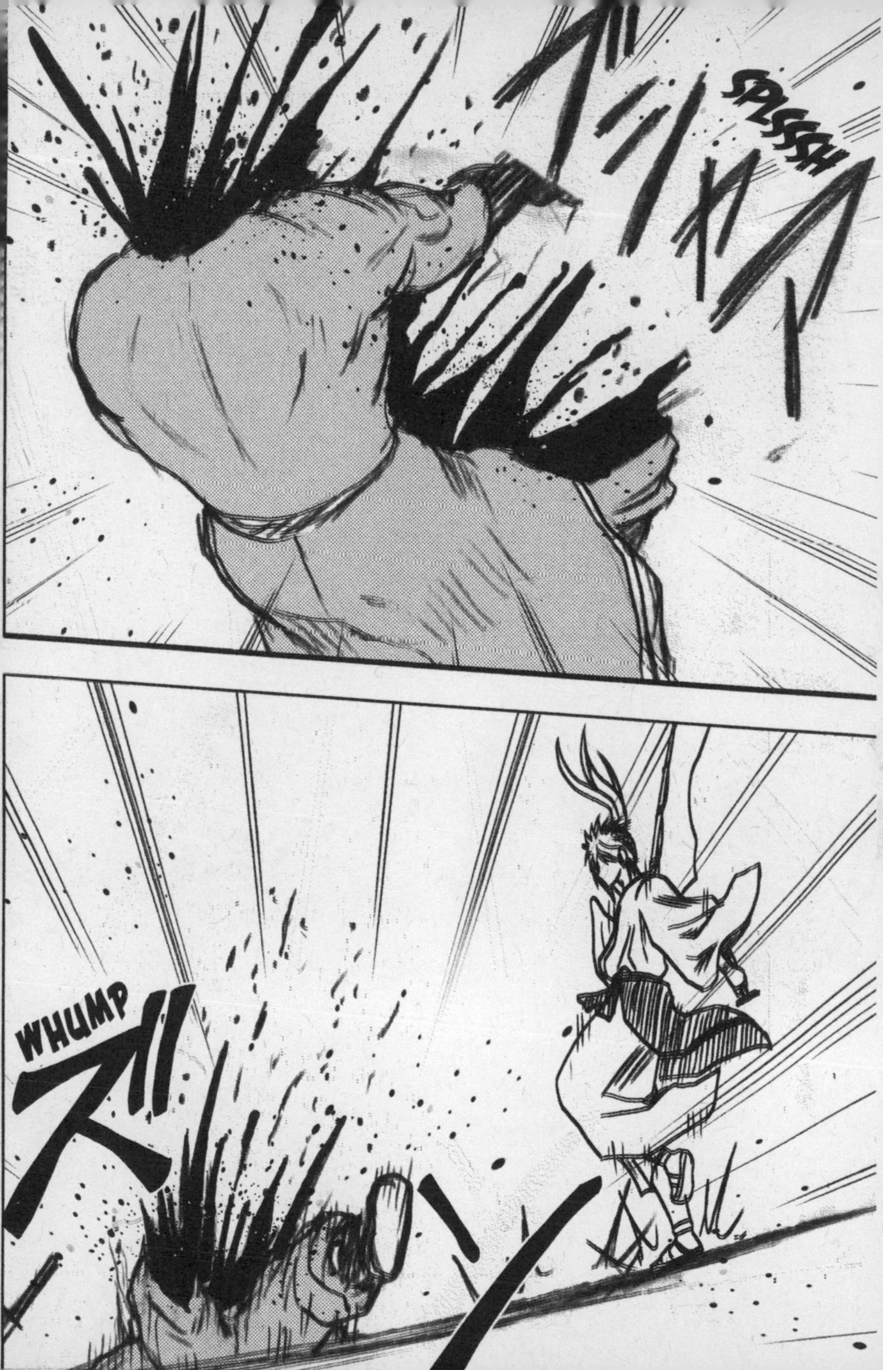
SPLSSSH
WHUMP

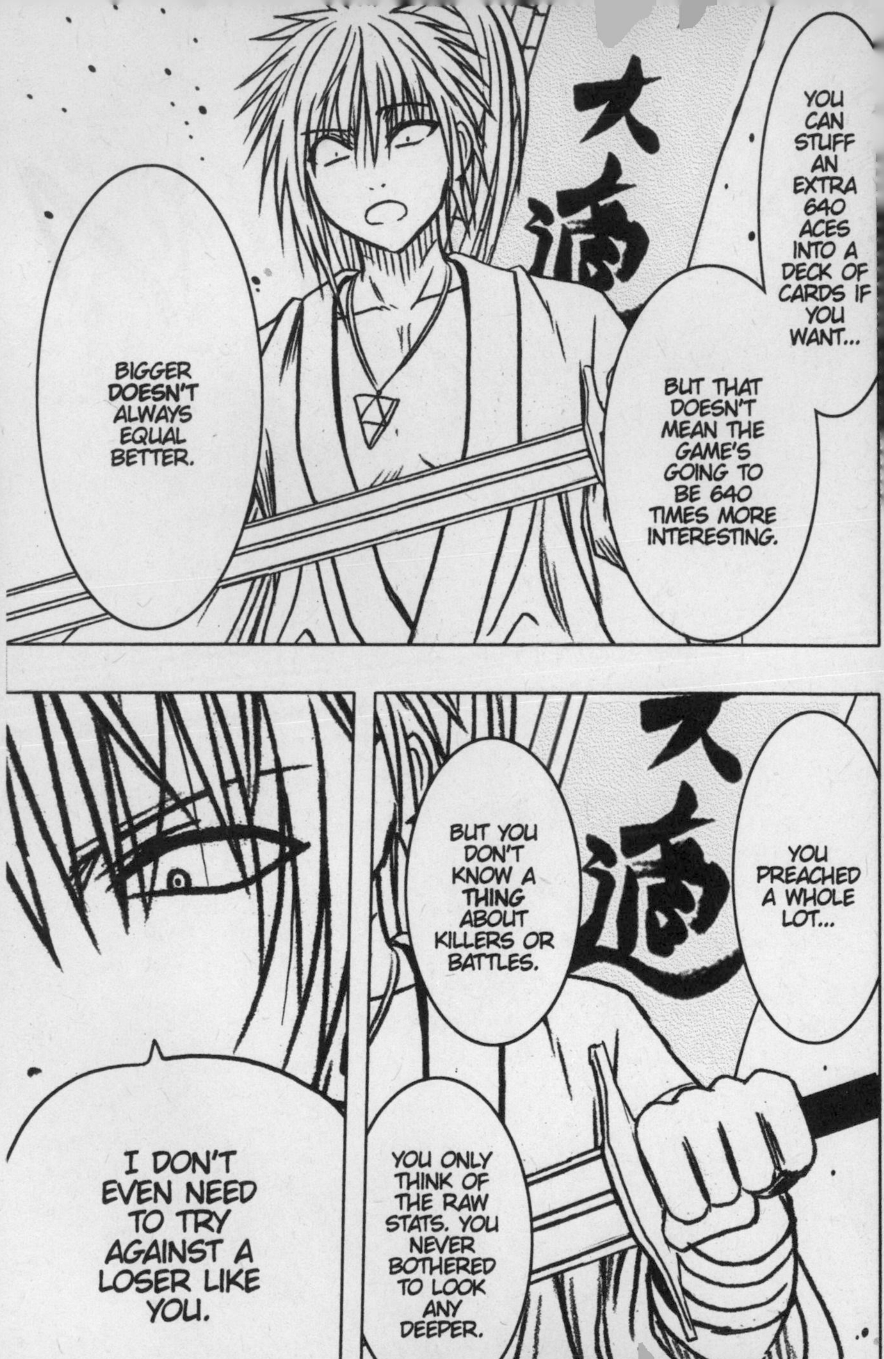
YOU CAN STUFF AN EXTRA 640 ACES INTO A DECK OF CARDS IF YOU WANT...
BUT THAT DOESN'T MEAN THE GAME'S GOING TO BE 640 TIMES MORE INTERESTING.
BIGGER DOESN'T ALWAYS EQUAL BETTER.
YOU PREACHED A WHOLE LOT...
BUT YOU DON'T KNOW A THING ABOUT KILLERS OR BATTLES.
YOU ONLY THINK OF THE RAW STATS. YOU NEVER BOTHERED TO LOOK ANY DEEPER.
I DON'T EVEN NEED TO TRY AGAINST A LOSER LIKE YOU.

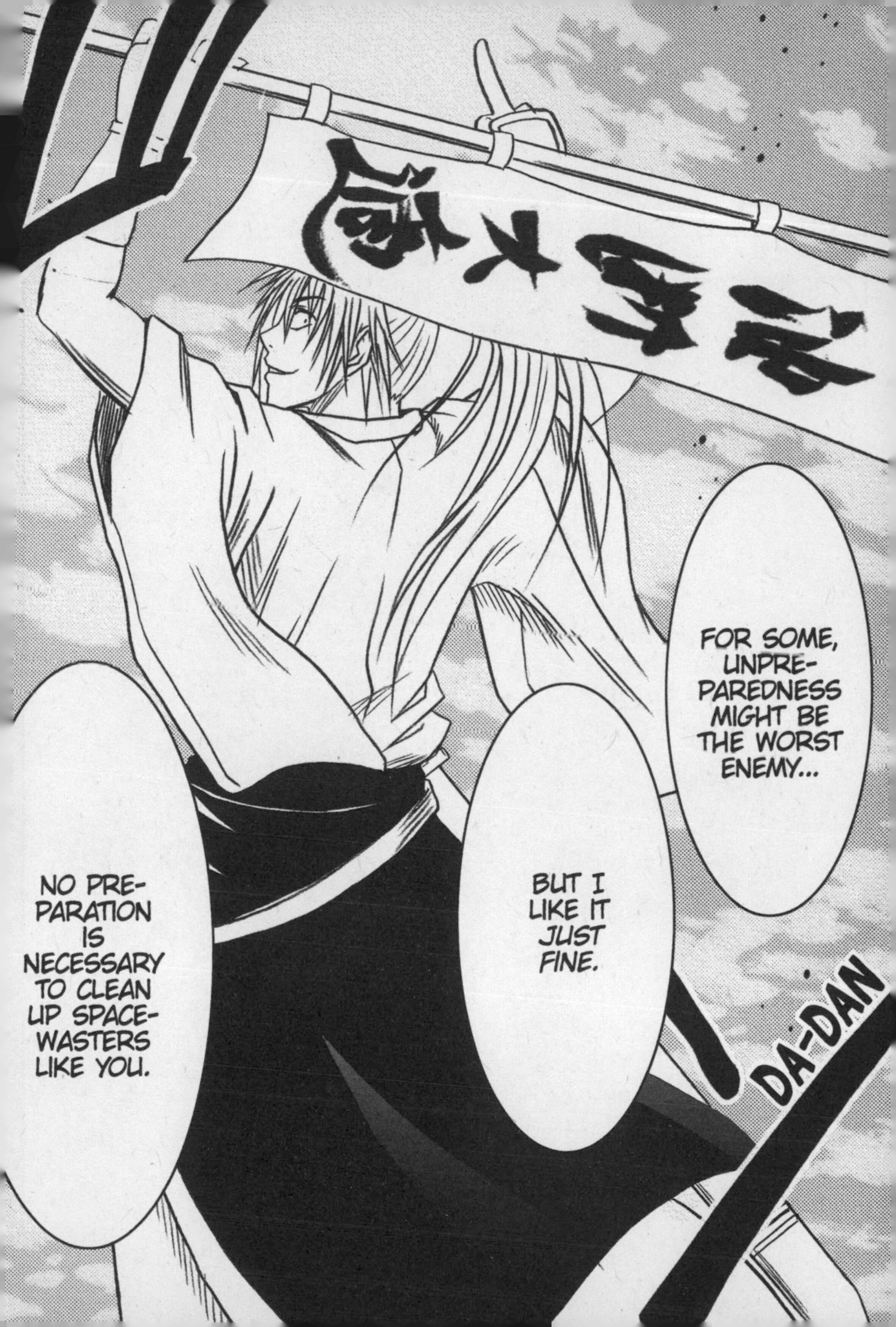
FOR SOME, UNPRE-PAREDNESS MIGHT BE THE WORST ENEMY...
BUT I LIKE IT JUST FINE.
NO PRE-PARATION IS NECESSARY TO CLEAN UP SPACE-WASTERS LIKE YOU.
DA-DAN

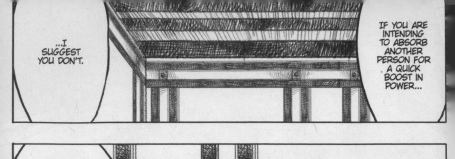

IF YOU ARE INTENDING TO ABSORB ANOTHER PERSON FOR A QUICK BOOST IN POWER...
...I SUGGEST YOU DON'T.
ABSORBING WHOEVER HAPPENS TO BE CONVENIENT IS HARDLY EFFICIENT.
IN FACT, MOST EXPERTS AGREE THERE ARE UNWRITTEN REQUIREMENTS THAT MUST BE FULFILLED FOR IT TO BE EFFECTIVE.
REQUIRE-MENTS?
WHAT ELSE IS THERE BESIDES PICKING SOMEBODY WHO'S POWERFUL?
WHO KNOWS?
I MYSELF AM NOT A KILLER, SO I CANNOT SAY WITH CERTAINTY.
STILL...
I ENCOURAGED YOU TO ABSORB YOUR FATHER BECAUSE THAT WAS THE MISSION PLAN.
PERSONALLY, I DID NOT SUPPORT THE IDEA.

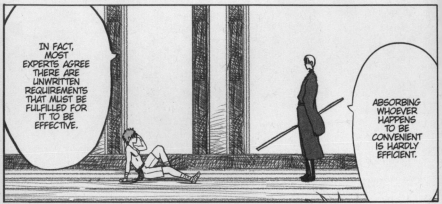

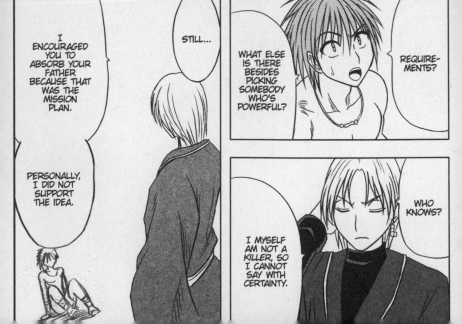

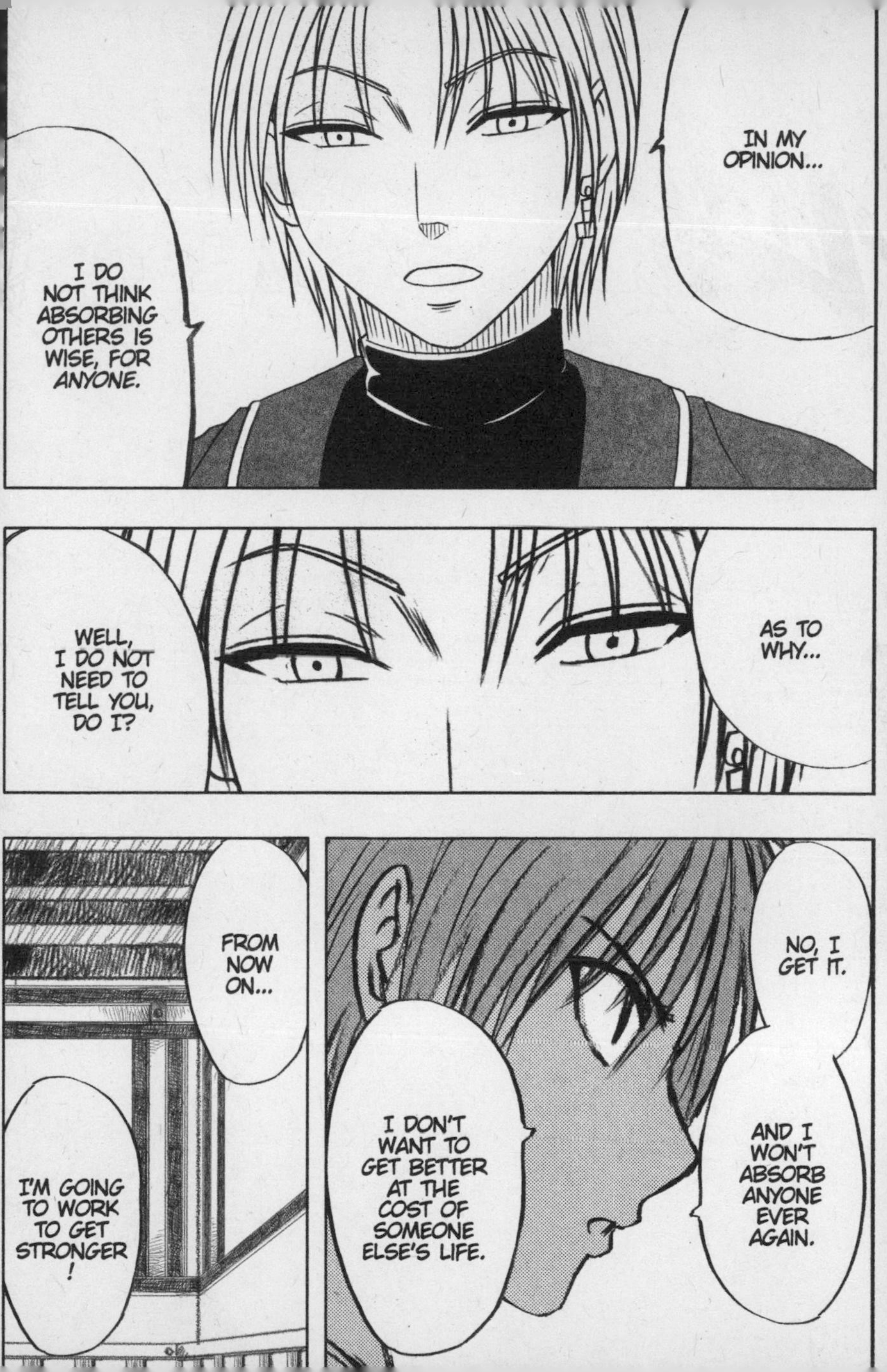
IN MY OPINION...
I DO NOT THINK ABSORBING OTHERS IS WISE, FOR ANYONE.
AS TO WHY...
WELL, I DO NOT NEED TO TELL YOU, DO I?
NO, I GET IT.
AND I WON'T ABSORB ANYONE EVER AGAIN.
I DON'T WANT TO GET BETTER AT THE COST OF SOMEONE ELSE'S LIFE.
FROM NOW ON...
I'M GOING TO WORK TO GET STRONGER!

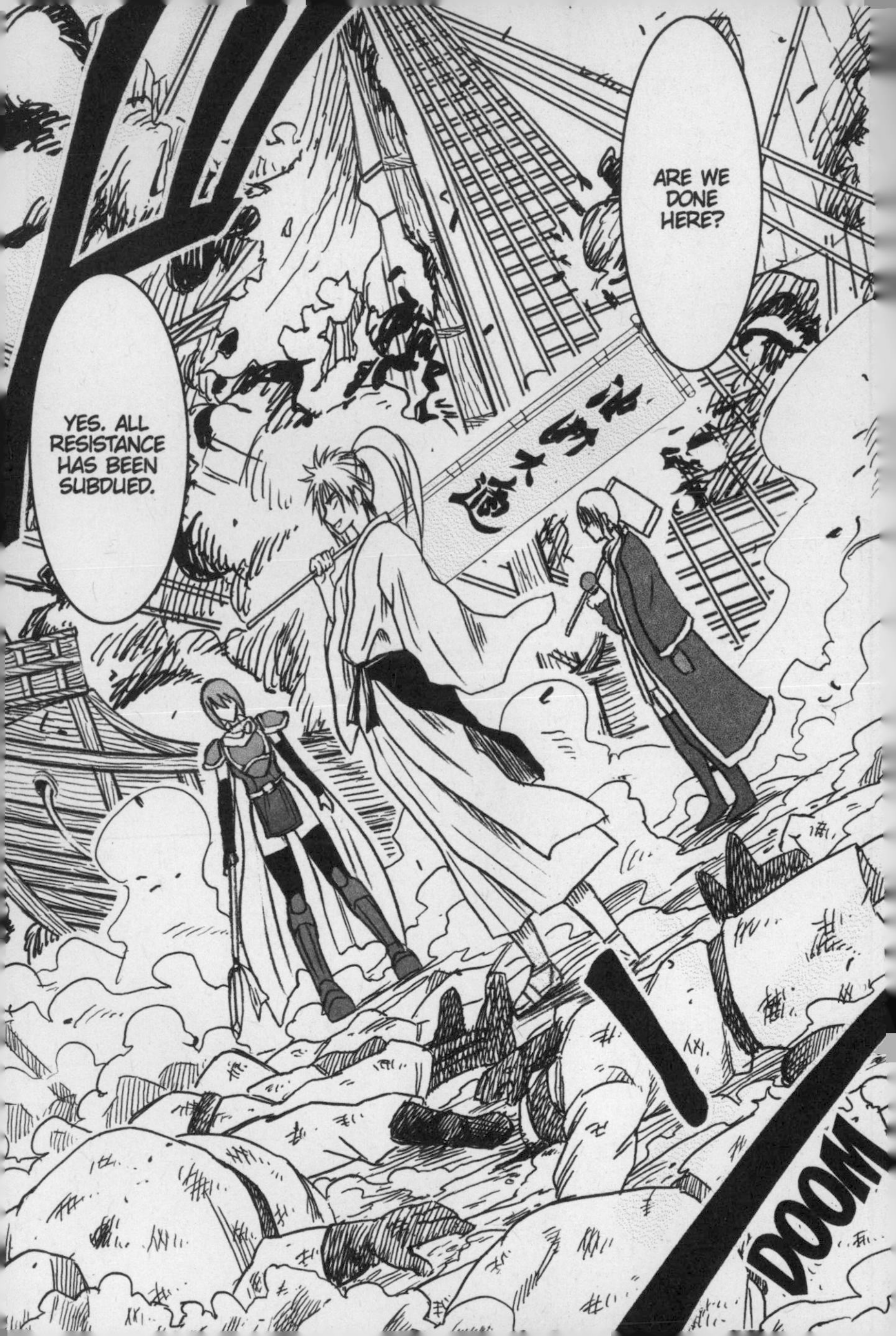
ARE WE DONE HERE?
YES. ALL RESISTANCE HAS BEEN SUBDUED.
DOOM

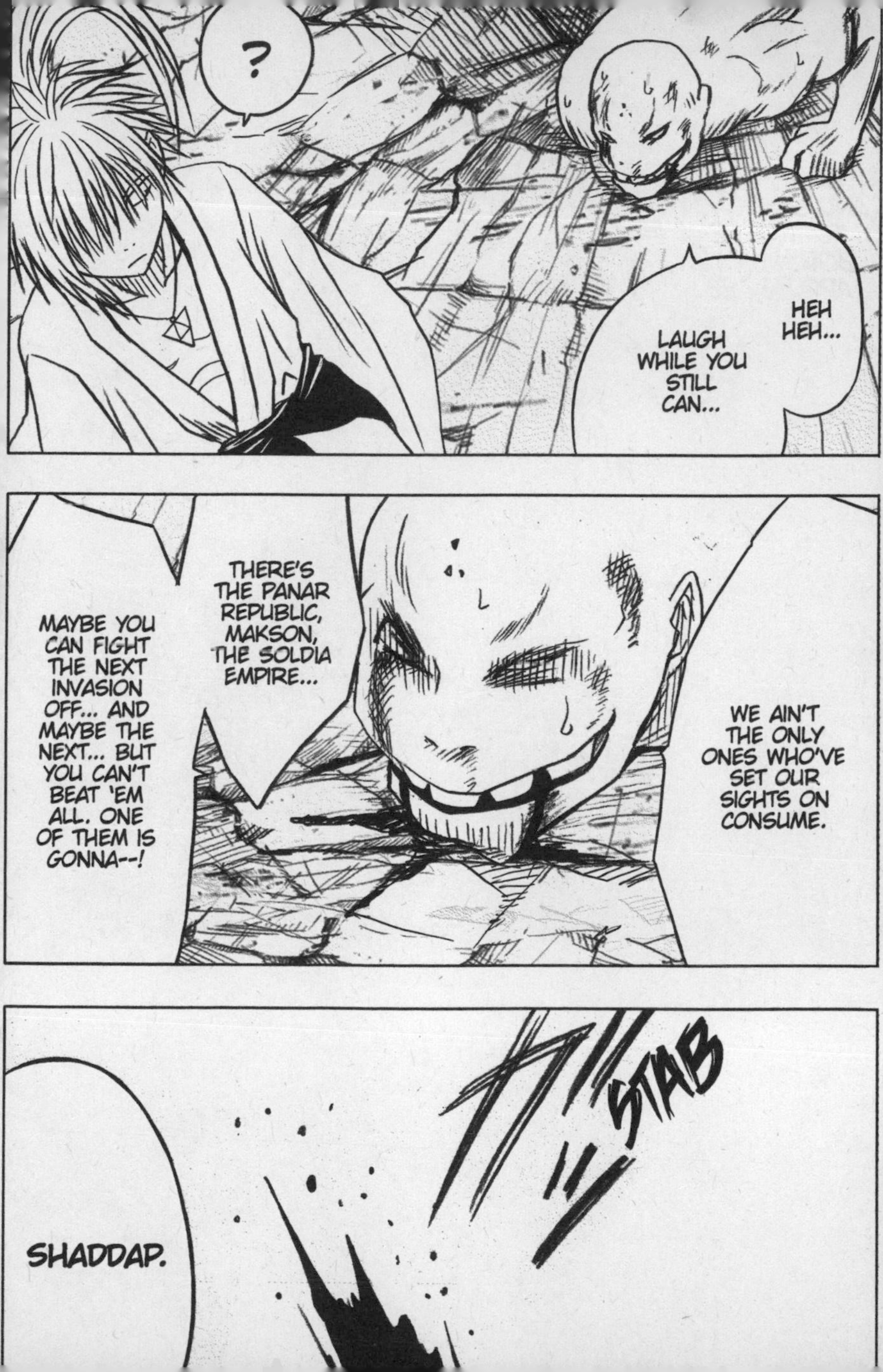
?
HEH HEH... LAUGH WHILE YOU STILL CAN...
WE AIN'T THE ONLY ONES WHO'VE SET OUR SIGHTS ON CONSUME.
THERE'S THE PANAR REPUBLIC, MAKSON, THE SOLDIA EMPIRE...
MAYBE YOU CAN FIGHT THE NEXT INVASION OFF... AND MAYBE THE NEXT... BUT YOU CAN'T BEAT 'EM ALL. ONE OF THEM IS GONNA--!
STAB
SHADDAP.

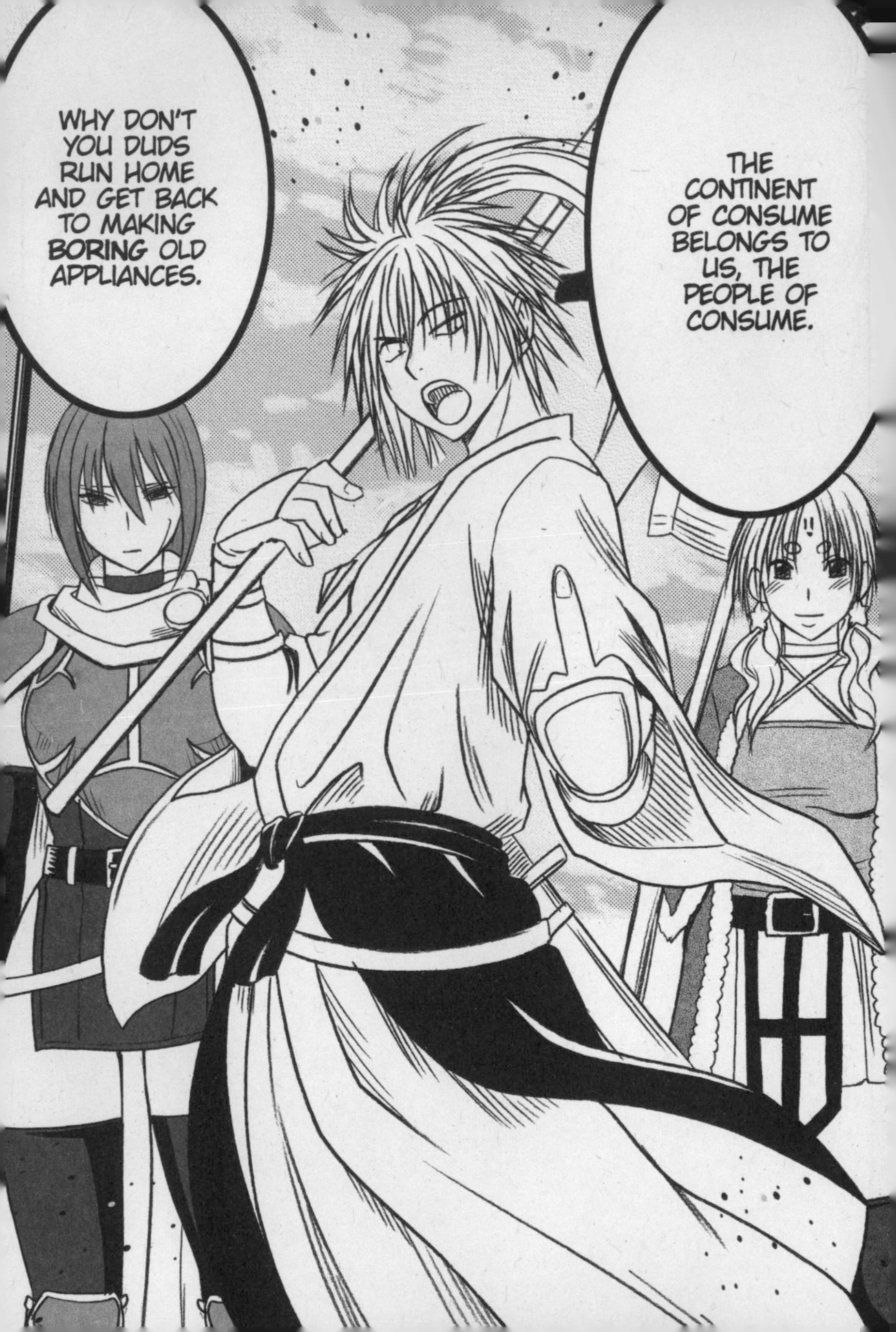
THE CONTINENT OF CONSUME BELONGS TO US, THE PEOPLE OF CONSUME.
WHY DON'T YOU DUDS RUN HOME AND GET BACK TO MAKING BORING OLD APPLIANCES.

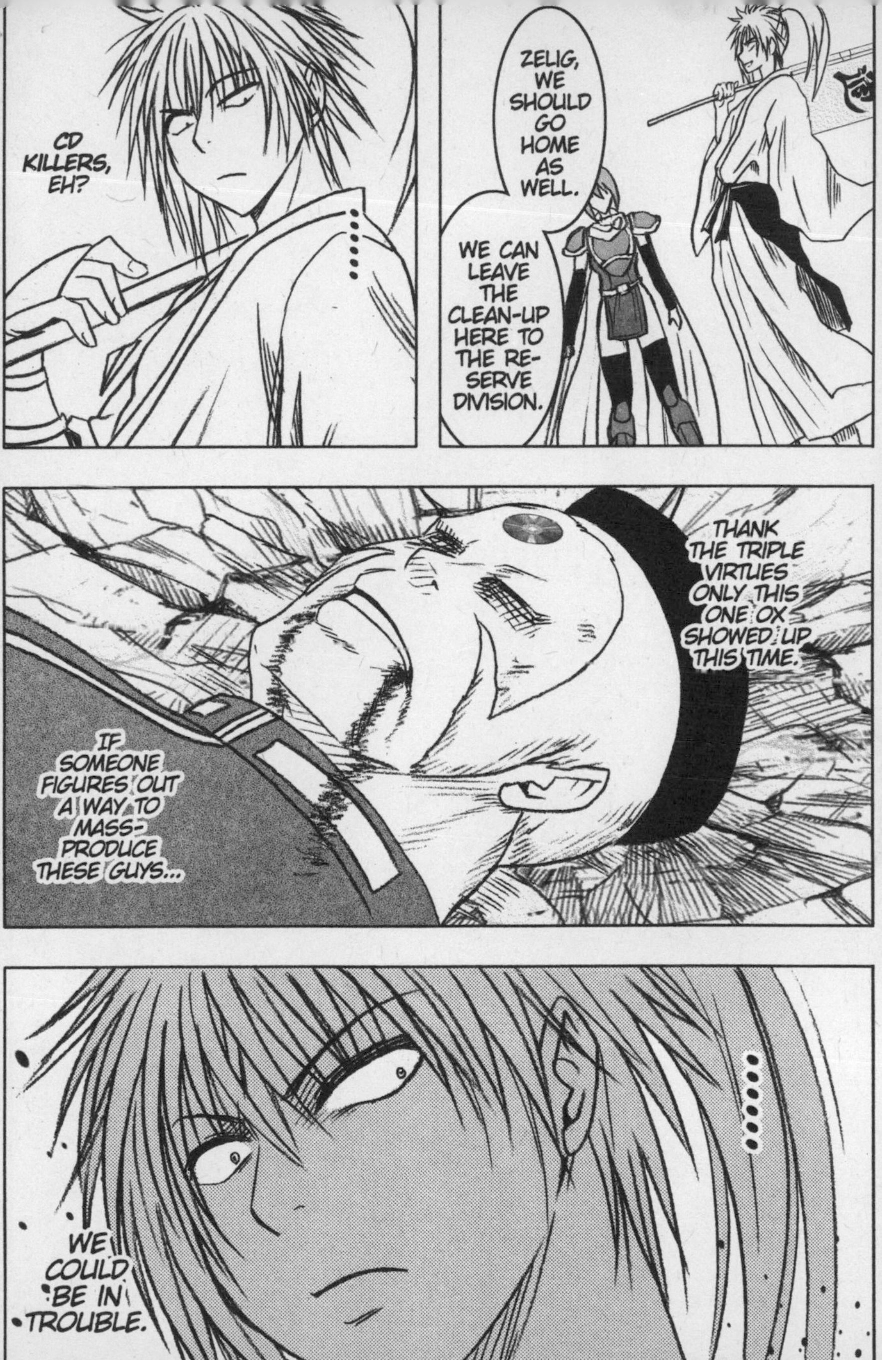
ZELIG, WE SHOULD GO HOME AS WELL.
WE CAN LEAVE THE CLEAN-UP HERE TO THE RE-SERVE DIVISION.
CD KILLERS, EH?
......
THANK THE TRIPLE VIRTUES ONLY THIS ONE OX SHOWED UP THIS TIME.
IF SOMEONE FIGURES OUT A WAY TO MASS-PRODUCE THESE GUYS...
......
WE COULD BE IN TROUBLE.

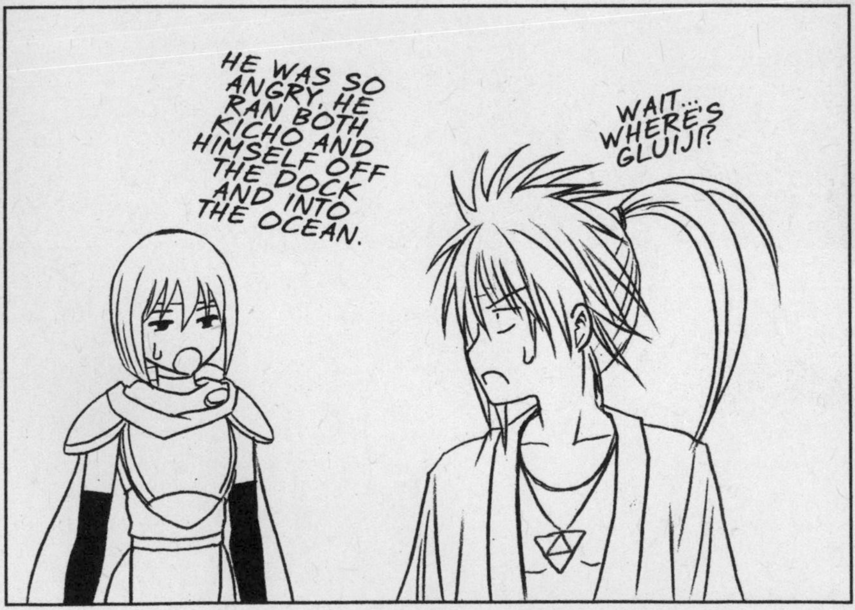
WAIT... WHERE'S GLUIJI?
HE WAS SO ANGRY, HE RAN BOTH KICHO AND HIMSELF OFF THE DOCK AND INTO THE OCEAN.

Perusing Video Game History

ON THE EDGE OF THE BLUE WORLD

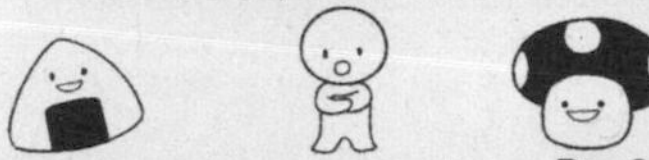

Dr. Onigiri   Mr. Why   Prof. Mushroom

Today's Topic

TURBOGRAFX-CD

Mr. Why: Okay, I hear the TurboGrafx-16 had an upgrade. Tell me about it.

Dr. Onigiri: Sure thing! The TurboGrafx-16 started out as a console that was capable of adding a lot of peripherals.

Prof. Mushroom: You know how in Japan right now, you can add a Torne adapter to your PlayStation 3 to turn it into a TV Tuner and DVR (digital video recorder), right? The TurboGrafx-16 had stuff like that.

Dr. Onigiri: The first of the peripherals to come out for it was the TurboGrafx-CD, in 1988. It played games that were on CDs instead of cartridges. Nowadays, most games are published on discs, but back then, this was the first time any home console had done it.

Mr. Why: Okay. What made that so amazing?

Prof. Mushroom: Well, the one big advantage CDs had over cartridges was storage space.

Dr. Onigiri: Exactly. Games for the Famicom or Sega Mark III were no more than 1 to 2 megabytes in size. But CDs could store up to *640 megabytes* of data! With hundreds of times as much available storage, games could branch out and do things they'd never done on a cartridge, like add full-motion video or recorded dialogue. Graphics could be greatly upgraded as well.

Prof. Mushroom: That kind of difference was *revolutionary*.

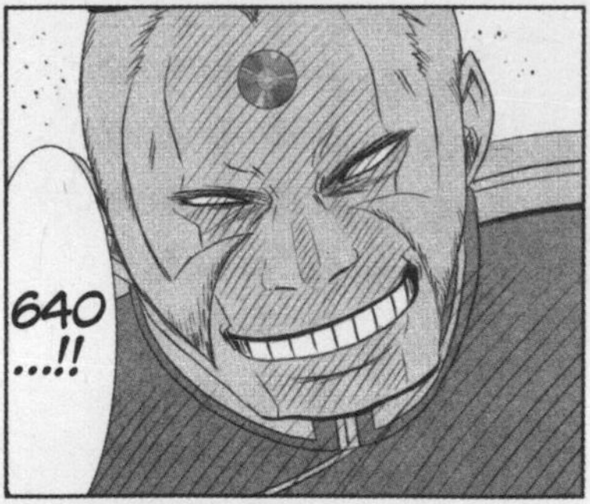
640
....!!

CD killers can absorb hundreds of times the number of people a normal killer can; up to an astounding 640.

Dr. Onigiri: One of the biggest titles on the TurboGrafx-CD was the *Far East of Eden* RPG series.

Prof. Mushroom: Yeah. That series had quirky characters, over-the-top attacks, and an enemy boss that was a powerful but dumb giant ape. The whole game played out like an anime series.

Dr. Onigiri: CDs seemed like nothing but a great idea, but they did create one massive problem.

Mr. Why: Oooh, what was it?

Dr. Onigiri: The graphics-above-all mindset. People began to focus entirely on the game's appearance, letting the actual substance of the game fall by the wayside.

Mr. Why: Oh?

Prof. Mushroom: Now, I'm not one to knock graphics. A game's beauty does contribute to how fun it is overall, but that's not all there is to it. Take *Super Mario Bros.*, for example. It's a small game with really simple graphics, but even today, it still has the feel of a complete game. *Super Mario Bros. 2* (a.k.a. *Super Mario Bros.: The Lost Levels*), its sequel, didn't upgrade the graphics much, but it let you choose between Mario and Luigi (who played a bit differently), which massively increased how fun that game was in light of its difficulty. Then there's *The Legend of Zelda*. Again, it had simple graphics, but the main character Link had to use his weapons in interesting ways to solve innovative puzzles, keeping it engrossing. Focusing only on the graphics kinda clouded what the real substance of a game should be.

Dr. Onigiri: And that may have played a part in the TurboGrafx-16's gradual, but inexorable loss to Nintendo. It eventually faded from the market completely, but Nintendo's victory wasn't a resounding one. Other companies looked at what NEC-HE had done, and started to think about doing it themselves. Electronics makers Panasonic and Sony, as well as software developer Microsoft started eying the home game console market. It would be a little while before they dove in to compete with Nintendo and Sega, but this was definitely the beginning of the age of fierce console wars.

To Be Continued...

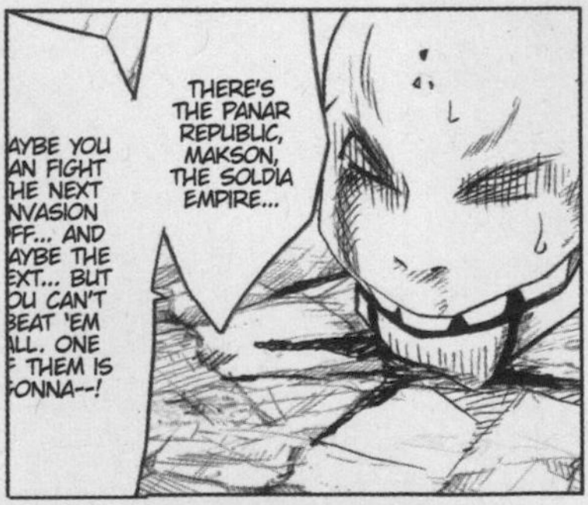
THERE'S THE PANAR REPUBLIC, MAKSON, THE SOLDIA EMPIRE...
AYBE YOU AN FIGHT HE NEXT NVASION FF... AND AYBE THE EXT... BUT OU CAN'T BEAT 'EM ALL. ONE F THEM IS ONNA--!

Foreign continent Kardansia has set its sights on conquering Consume. New forces may soon arrive to wage war against Ninteldo and Segua.

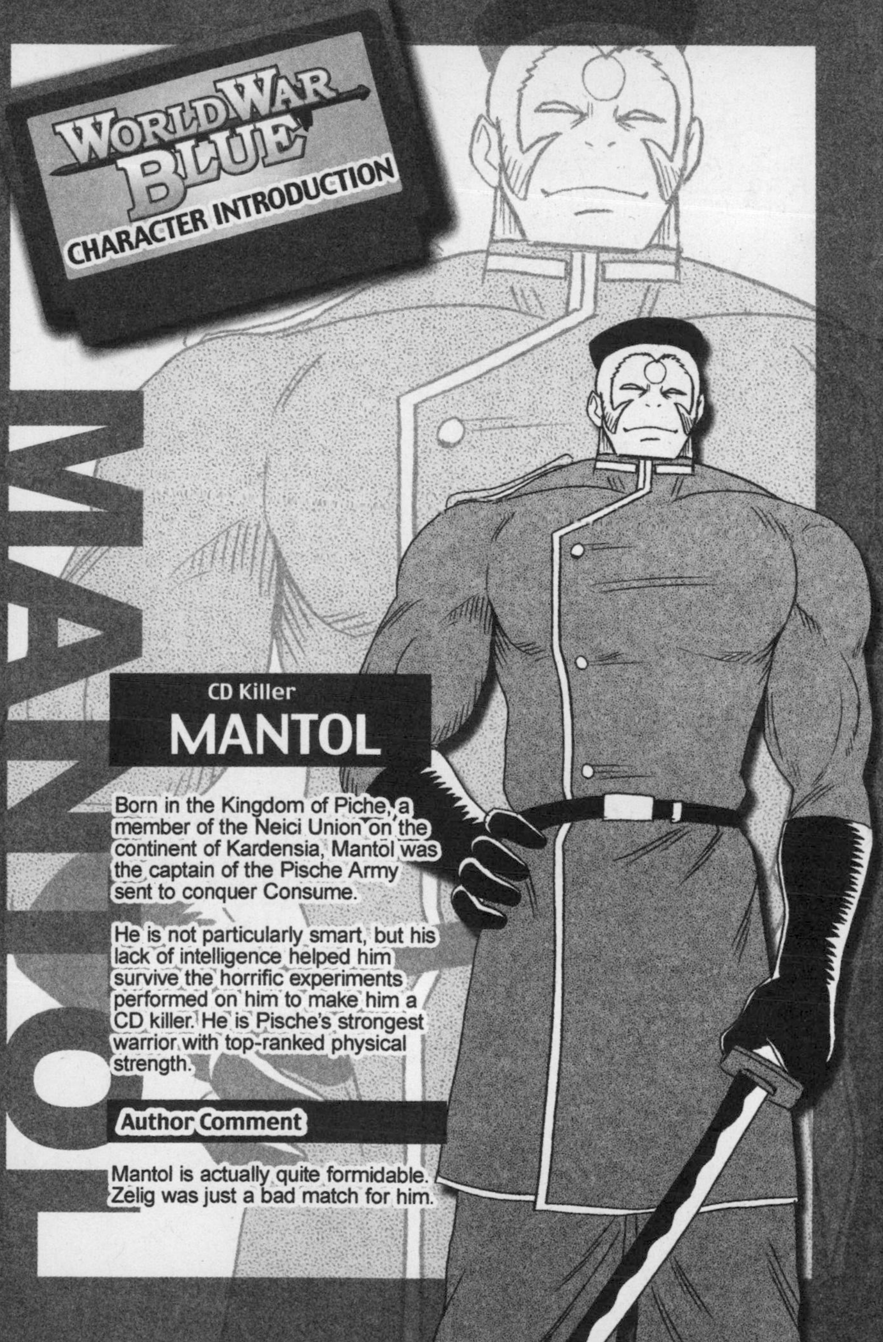

WORLD WAR BLUE

CHARACTER INTRODUCTION

CD Killer

MANTOL

Born in the Kingdom of Piche, a member of the Neici Union on the continent of Kardensia, Mantol was the captain of the Pische Army sent to conquer Consume.

He is not particularly smart, but his lack of intelligence helped him survive the horrific experiments performed on him to make him a CD killer. He is Pische's strongest warrior with top-ranked physical strength.

Author Comment

Mantol is actually quite formidable. Zelig was just a bad match for him.

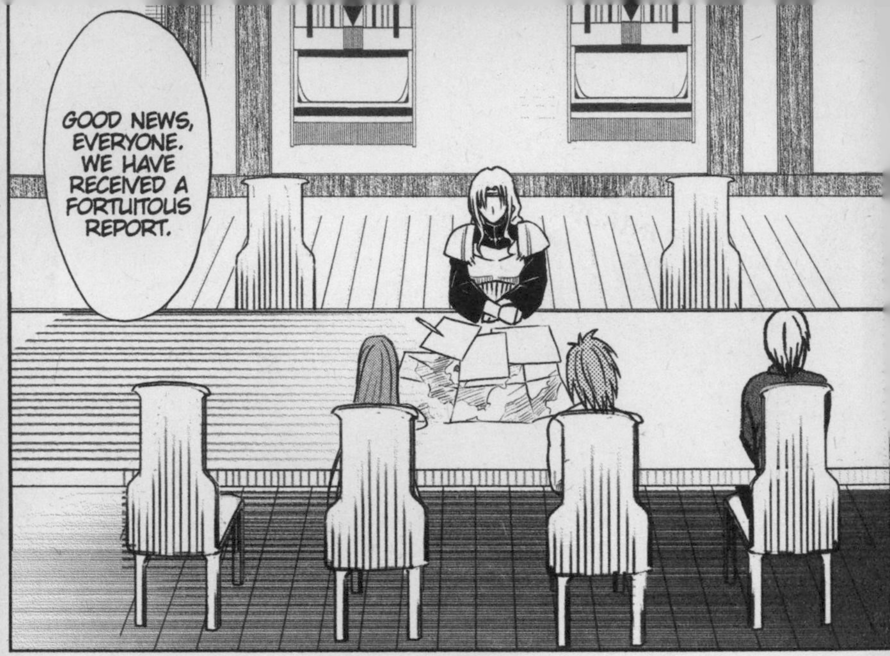
GOOD NEWS, EVERYONE. WE HAVE RECEIVED A FORTUITOUS REPORT.

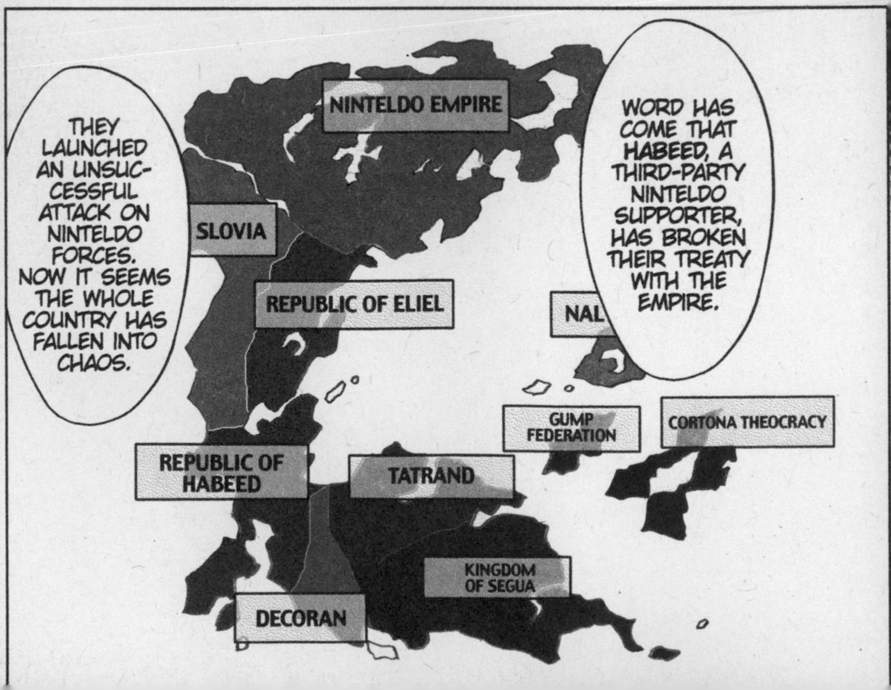
WORD HAS COME THAT HABEED, A THIRD-PARTY NINTELDO SUPPORTER, HAS BROKEN THEIR TREATY WITH THE EMPIRE.
THEY LAUNCHED AN UNSUC-CESSFUL ATTACK ON NINTELDO FORCES. NOW IT SEEMS THE WHOLE COUNTRY HAS FALLEN INTO CHAOS.
NINTELDO EMPIRE
SLOVIA
REPUBLIC OF ELIEL
GUMP FEDERATION
CORTONA THEOCRACY
REPUBLIC OF HABEED
TATRAND
KINGDOM OF SEGUA
DECORAN

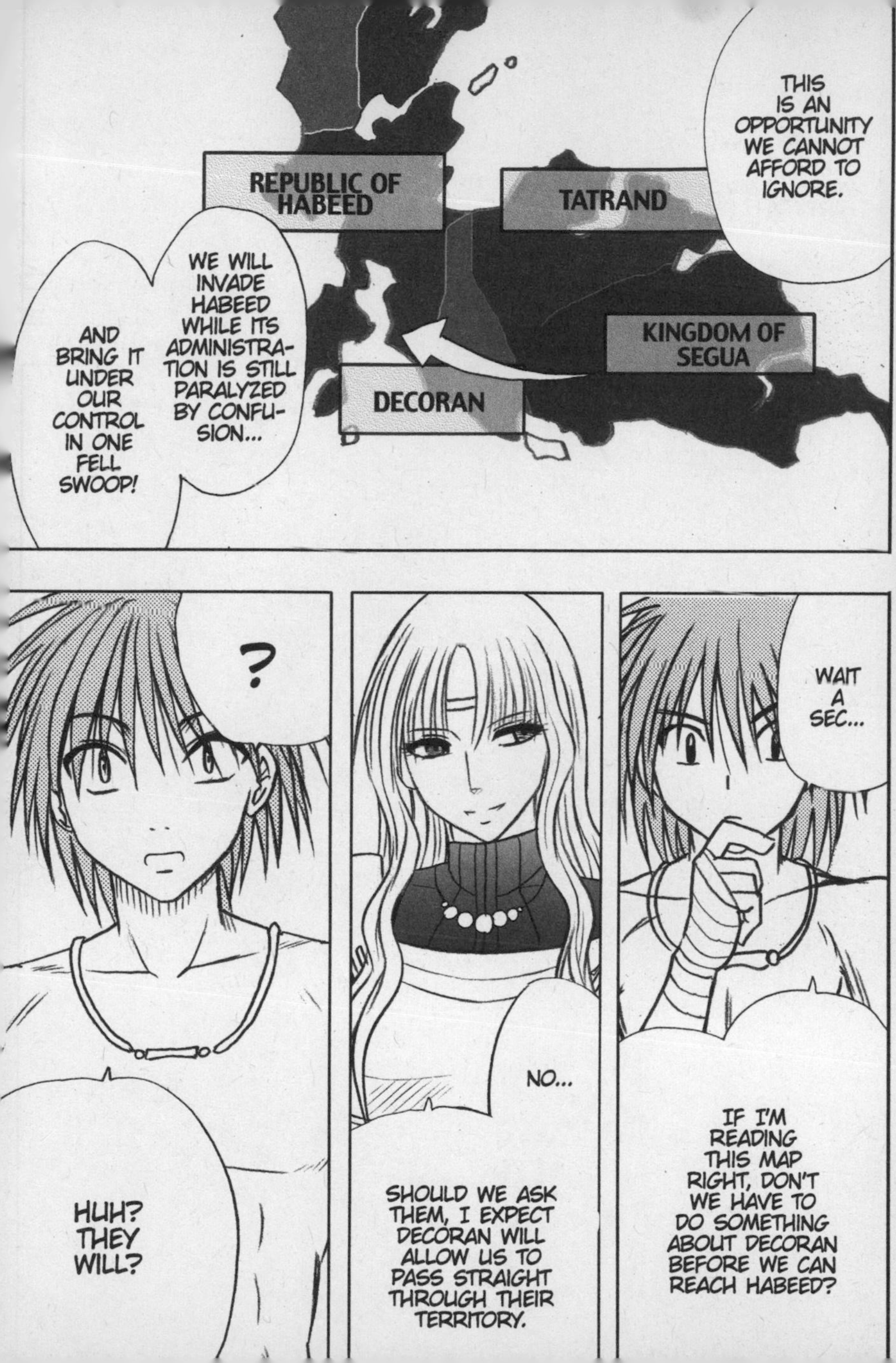
THIS IS AN OPPORTUNITY WE CANNOT AFFORD TO IGNORE.
TATRAND
REPUBLIC OF HABEED
KINGDOM OF SEGUA
DECORAN
WE WILL INVADE HABEED WHILE ITS ADMINISTRATION IS STILL PARALYZED BY CONFUSION...
AND BRING IT UNDER OUR CONTROL IN ONE FELL SWOOP!
WAIT A SEC...
IF I'M READING THIS MAP RIGHT, DON'T WE HAVE TO DO SOMETHING ABOUT DECORAN BEFORE WE CAN REACH HABEED?
NO...
SHOULD WE ASK THEM, I EXPECT DECORAN WILL ALLOW US TO PASS STRAIGHT THROUGH THEIR TERRITORY.
?
HUH? THEY WILL?

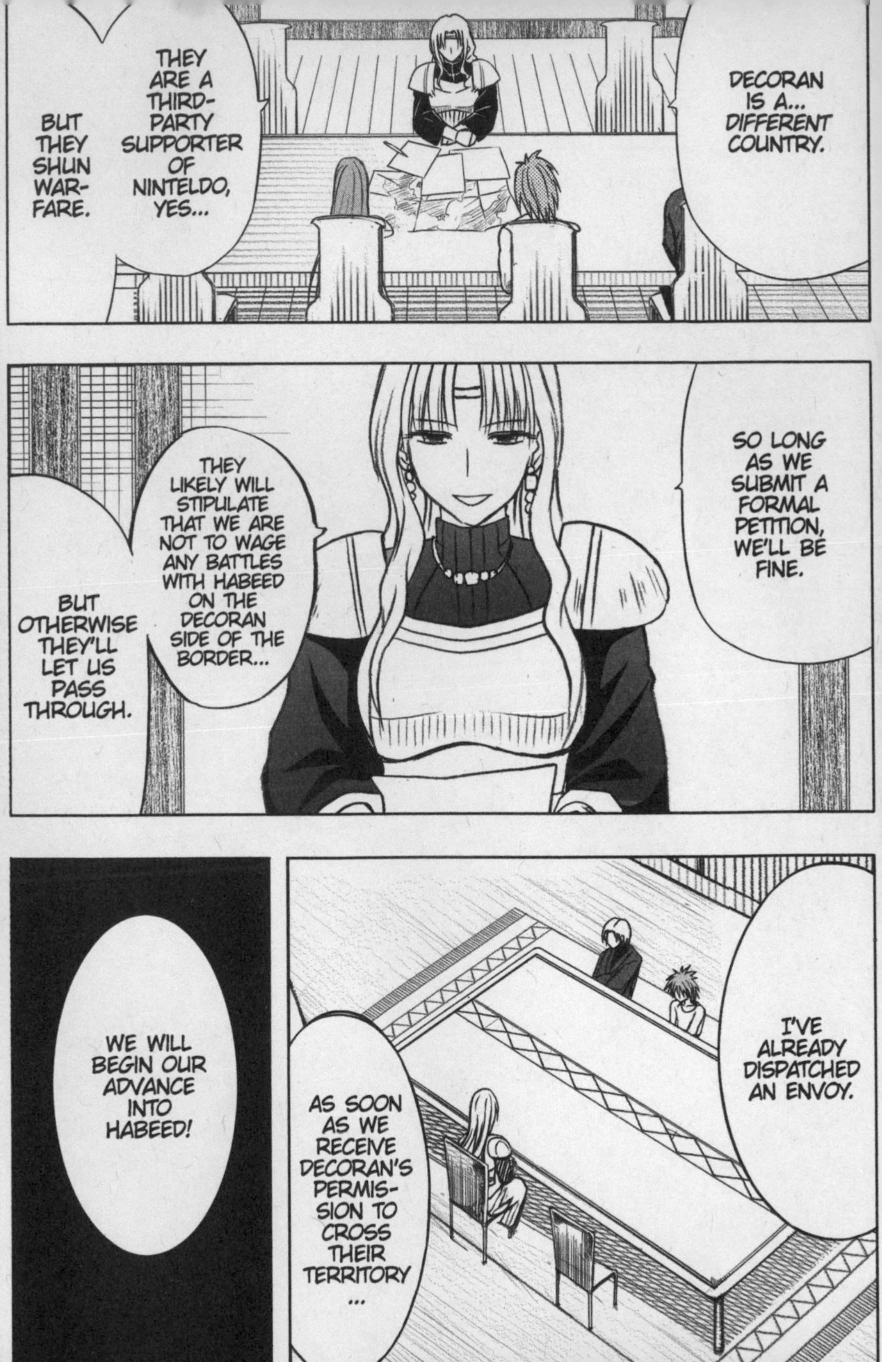
DECORAN IS A... DIFFERENT COUNTRY.
THEY ARE A THIRD-PARTY SUPPORTER OF NINTELDO, YES...
BUT THEY SHUN WARFARE.
SO LONG AS WE SUBMIT A FORMAL PETITION, WE'LL BE FINE.
THEY LIKELY WILL STIPULATE THAT WE ARE NOT TO WAGE ANY BATTLES WITH HABEED ON THE DECORAN SIDE OF THE BORDER...
BUT OTHERWISE THEY'LL LET US PASS THROUGH.
I'VE ALREADY DISPATCHED AN ENVOY.
AS SOON AS WE RECEIVE DECORAN'S PERMISSION TO CROSS THEIR TERRITORY...
WE WILL BEGIN OUR ADVANCE INTO HABEED!

Part 2

CHAPTER 4

RUNNING

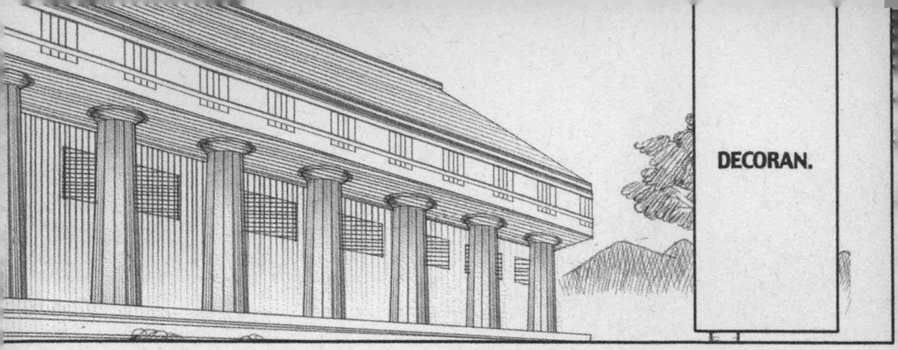
DECORAN.

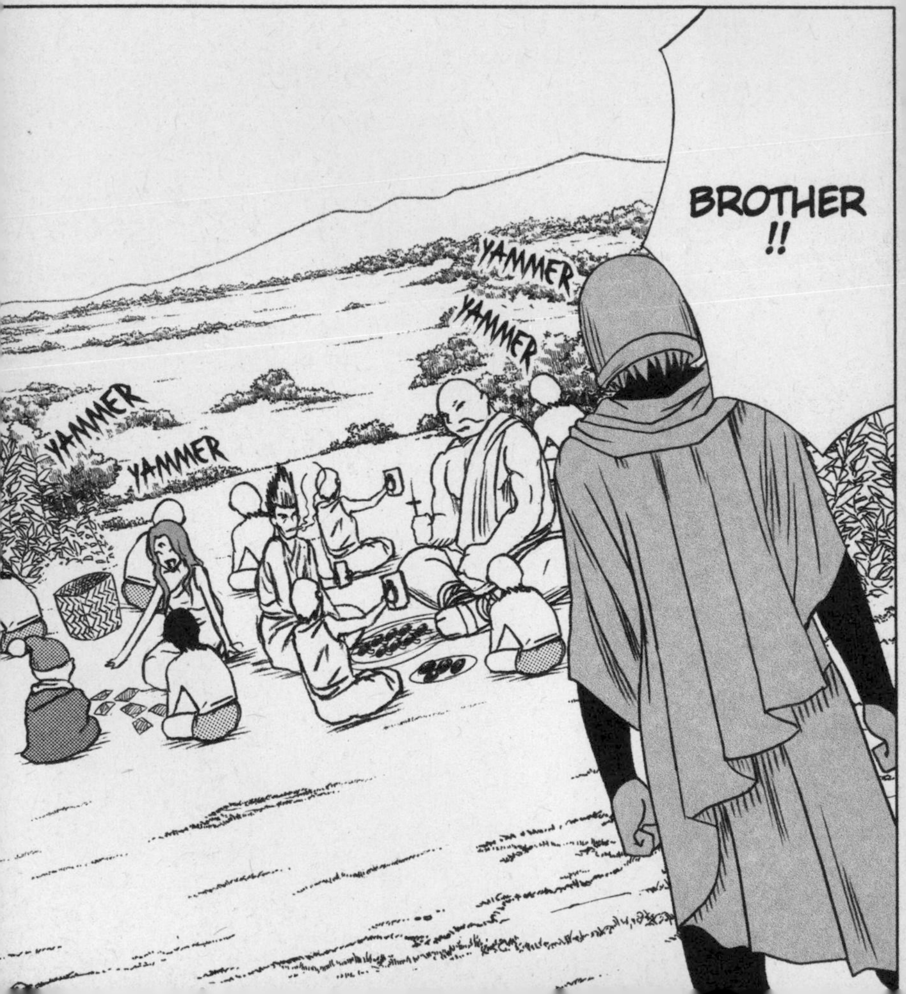
BROTHER !!
YAMMER
YAMMER
YAMMER
YAMMER

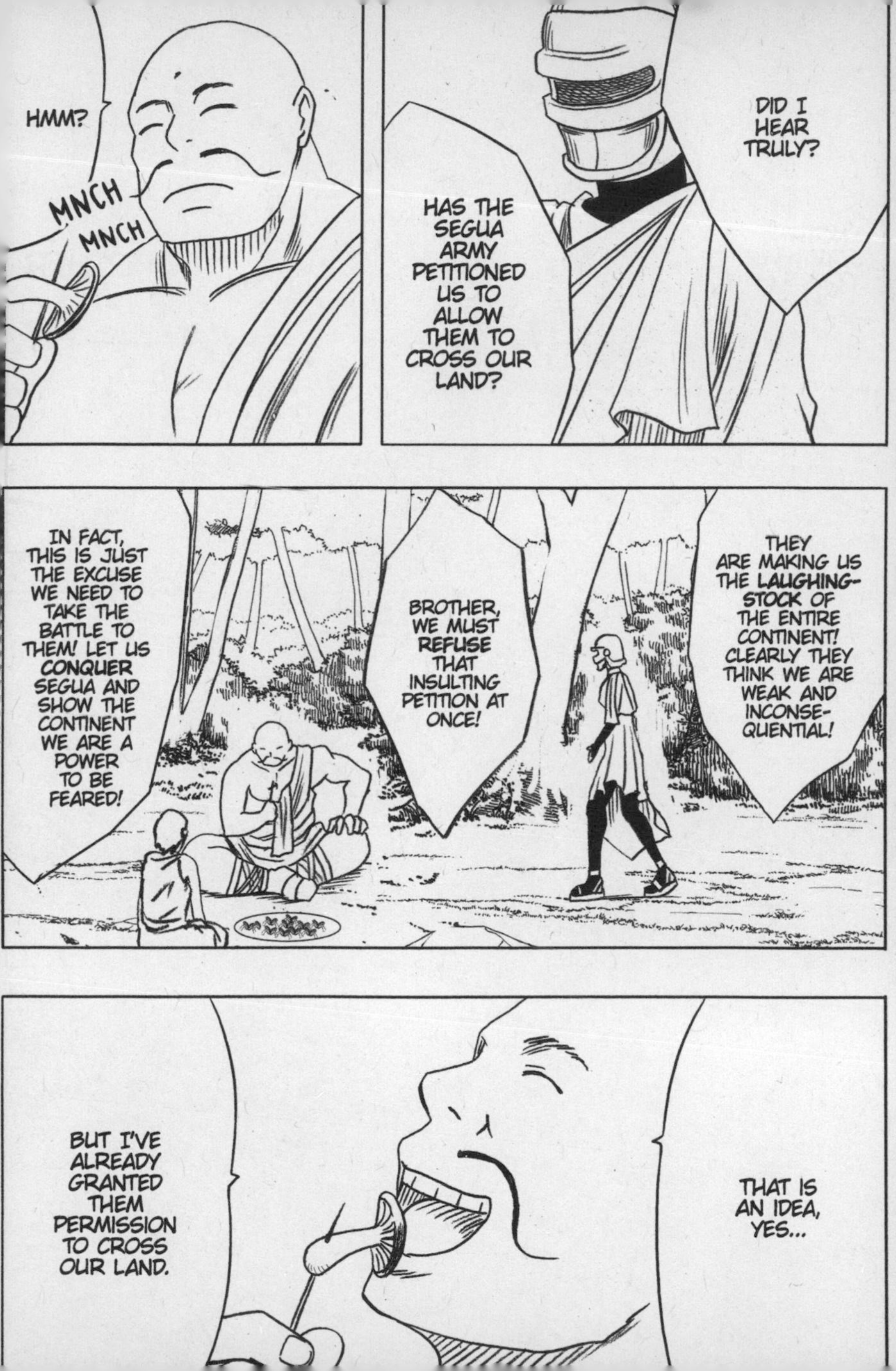
DID I HEAR TRULY?
HAS THE SEGUA ARMY PETITIONED US TO ALLOW THEM TO CROSS OUR LAND?
HMM?
MNCH MNCH
THEY ARE MAKING US THE LAUGHING-STOCK OF THE ENTIRE CONTINENT! CLEARLY THEY THINK WE ARE WEAK AND INCONSE-QUENTIAL!
BROTHER, WE MUST REFUSE THAT INSULTING PETITION AT ONCE!
IN FACT, THIS IS JUST THE EXCUSE WE NEED TO TAKE THE BATTLE TO THEM! LET US CONQUER SEGUA AND SHOW THE CONTINENT WE ARE A POWER TO BE FEARED!
THAT IS AN IDEA, YES...
BUT I'VE ALREADY GRANTED THEM PERMISSION TO CROSS OUR LAND.

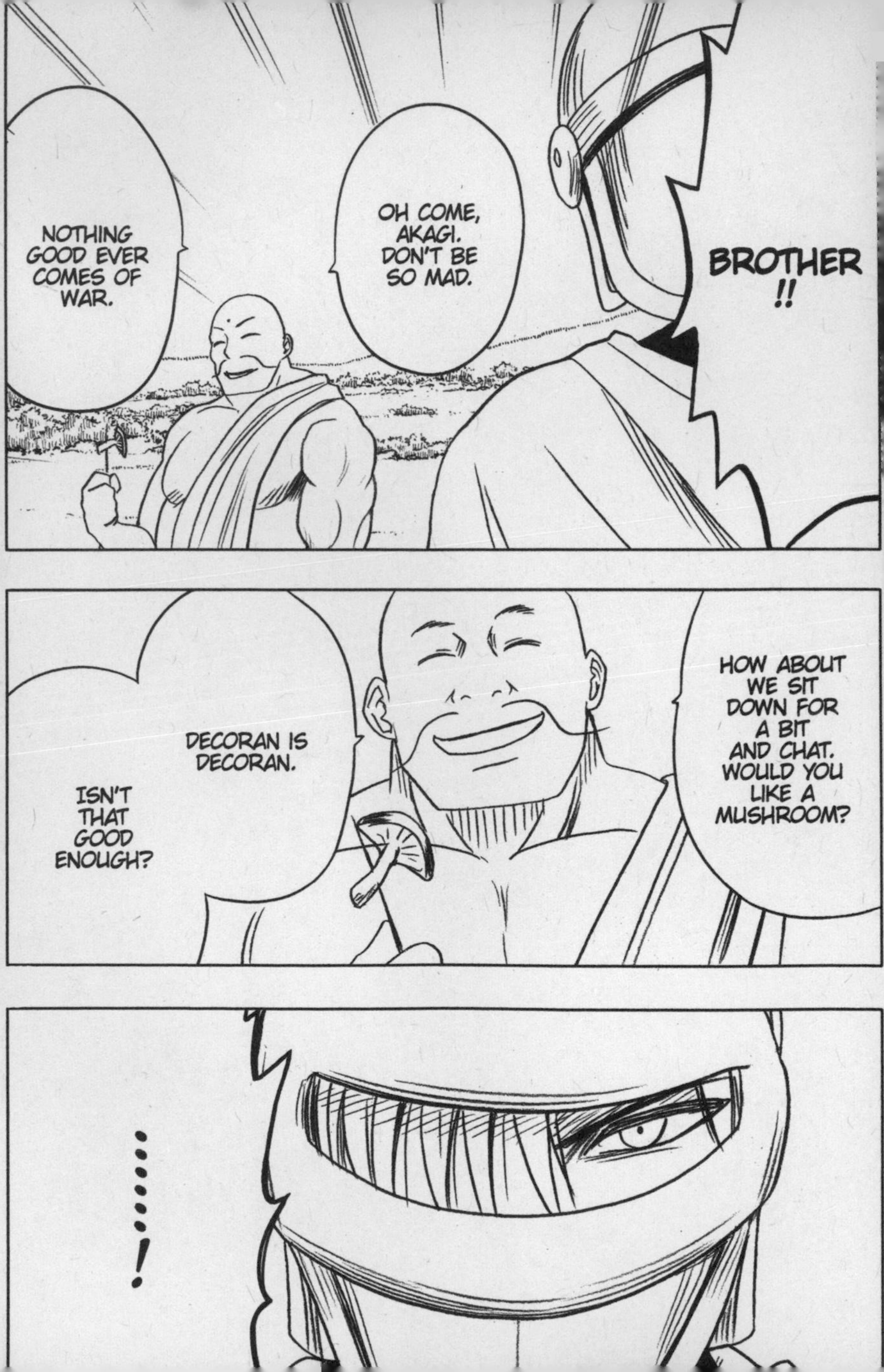
BROTHER !!
OH COME, AKAGI. DON'T BE SO MAD.
NOTHING GOOD EVER COMES OF WAR.
HOW ABOUT WE SIT DOWN FOR A BIT AND CHAT. WOULD YOU LIKE A MUSHROOM?
DECORAN IS DECORAN.
ISN'T THAT GOOD ENOUGH?
......!

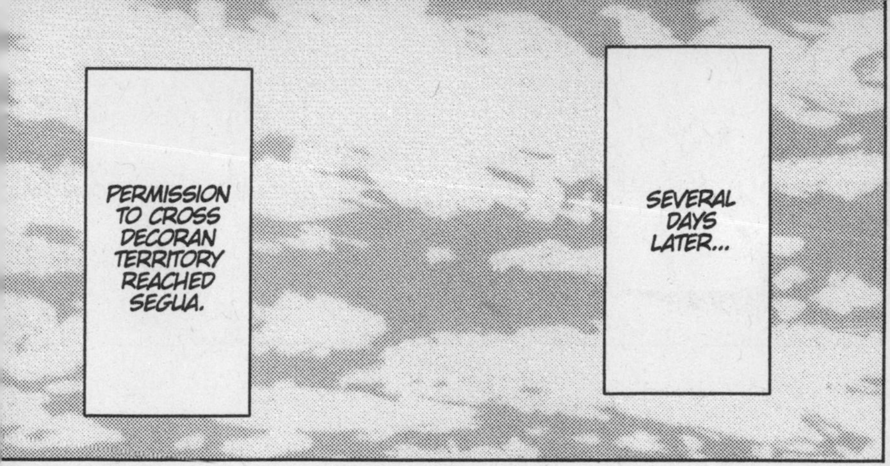
SEVERAL DAYS LATER...
PERMISSION TO CROSS DECORAN TERRITORY REACHED SEGUA.
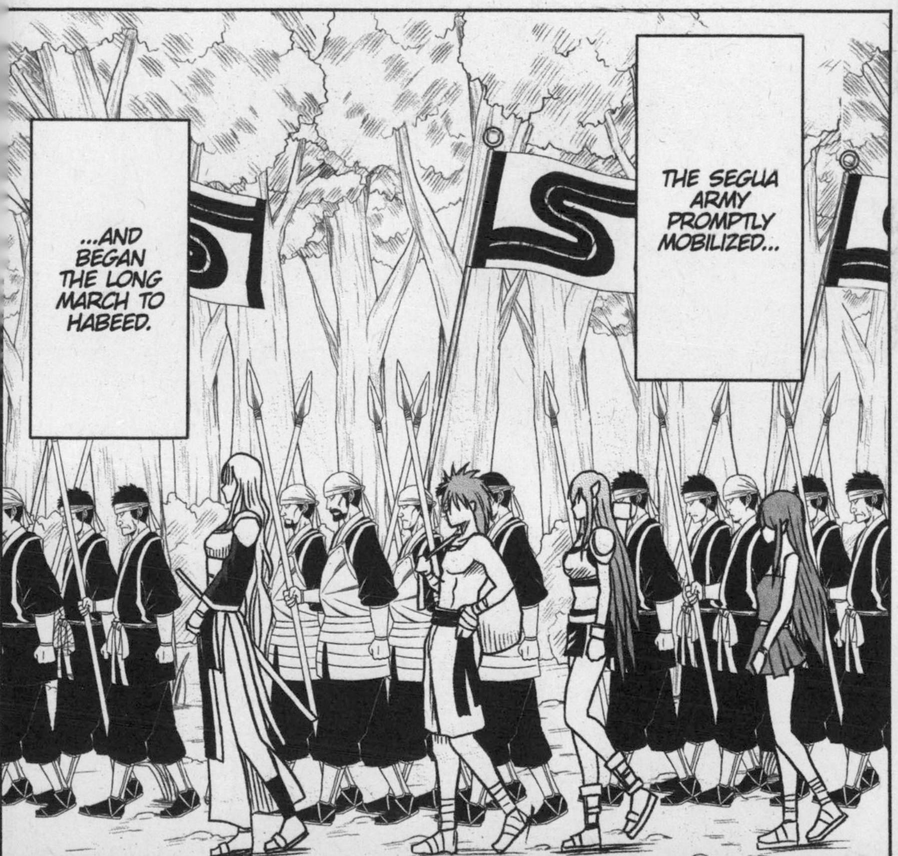
THE SEGUA ARMY PROMPTLY MOBILIZED...
...AND BEGAN THE LONG MARCH TO HABEED.

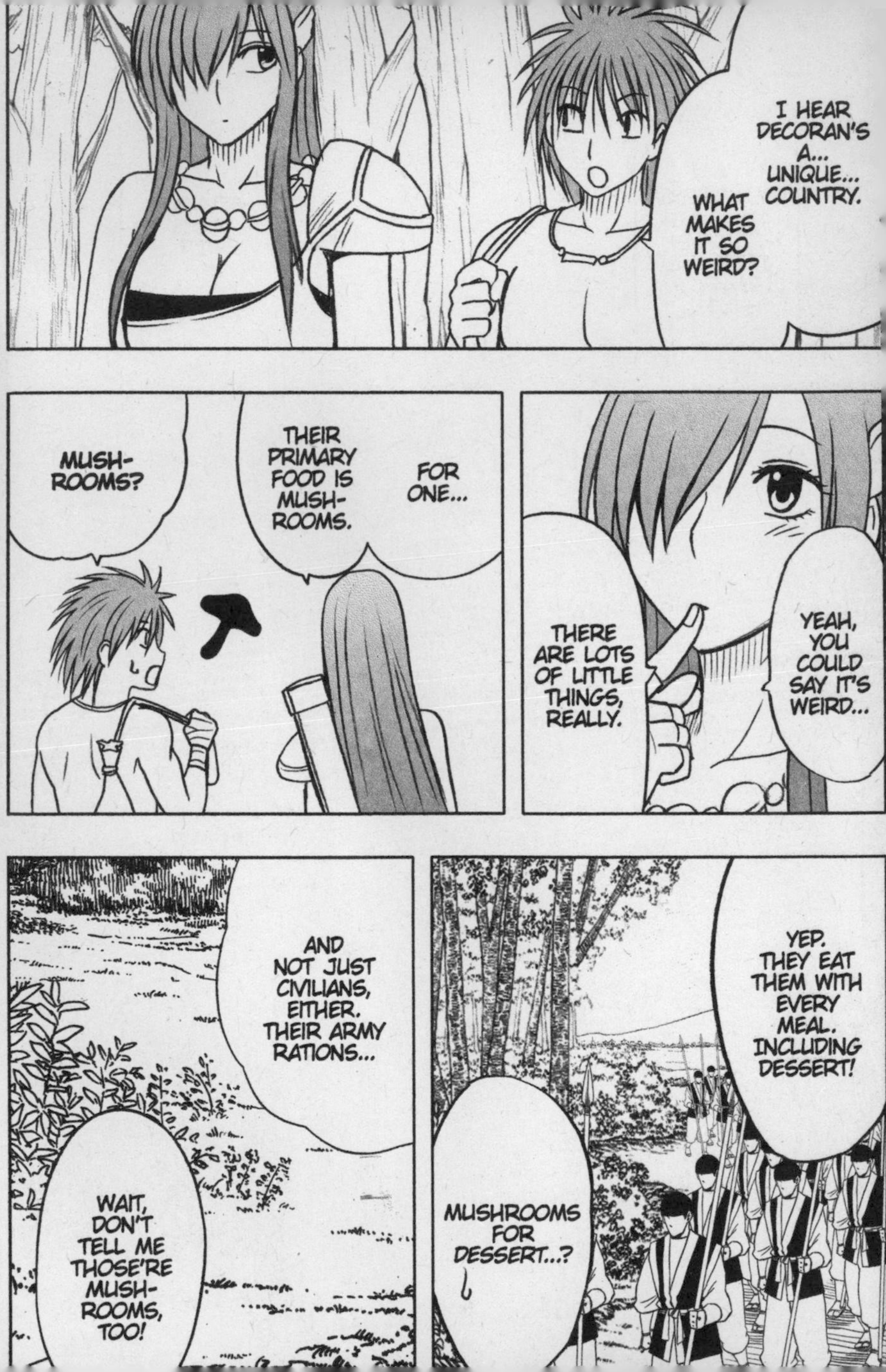
I HEAR DECORAN'S A... UNIQUE... COUNTRY.
WHAT MAKES IT SO WEIRD?
YEAH, YOU COULD SAY IT'S WEIRD...
THERE ARE LOTS OF LITTLE THINGS, REALLY.
FOR ONE...
THEIR PRIMARY FOOD IS MUSH-ROOMS.
MUSH-ROOMS?
YEP. THEY EAT THEM WITH EVERY MEAL. INCLUDING DESSERT!
MUSHROOMS FOR DESSERT...?
AND NOT JUST CIVILIANS, EITHER. THEIR ARMY RATIONS...
WAIT, DON'T TELL ME THOSE'RE MUSH-ROOMS, TOO!

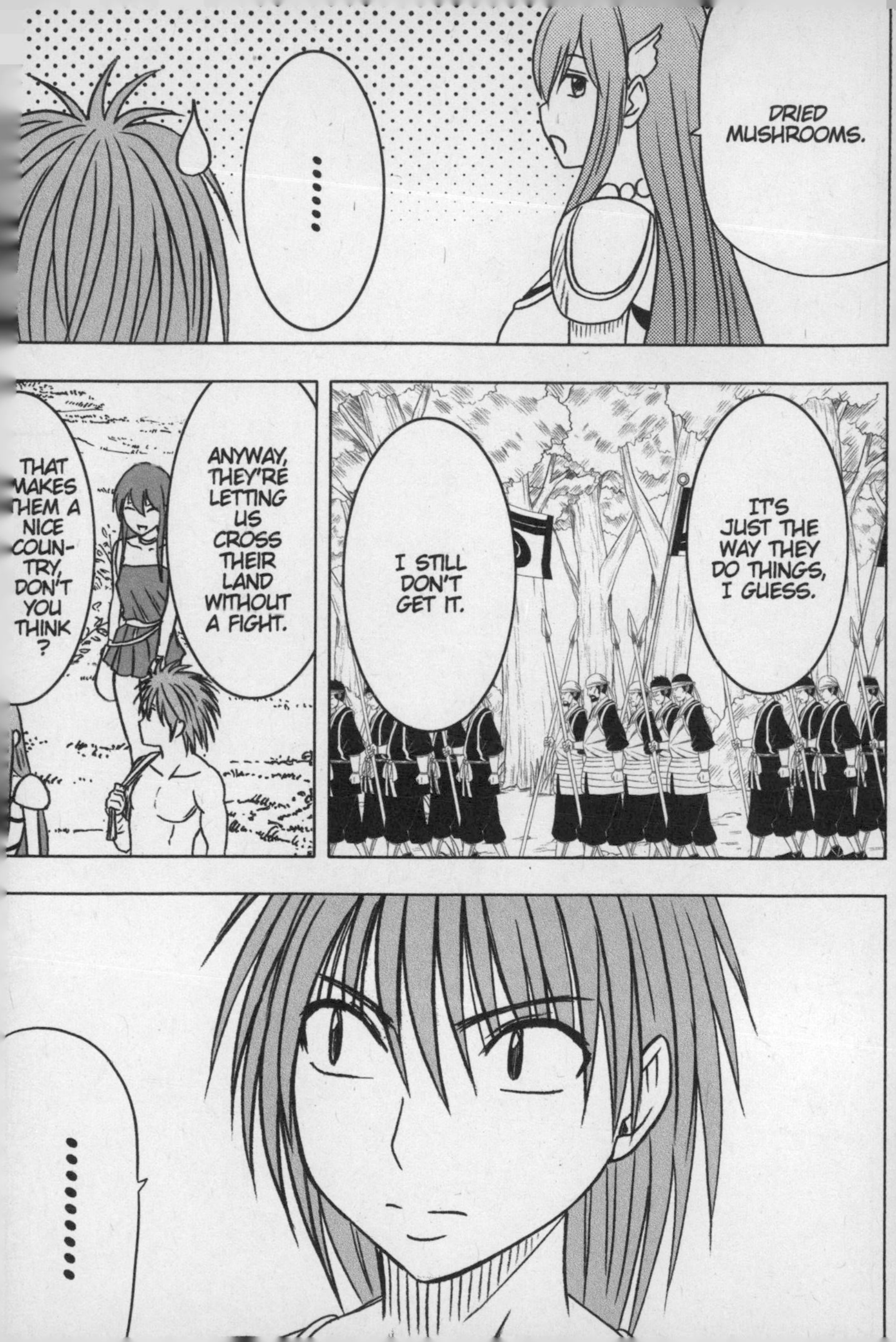
DRIED MUSHROOMS.
......
IT'S JUST THE WAY THEY DO THINGS, I GUESS.
I STILL DON'T GET IT.
ANYWAY, THEY'RE LETTING US CROSS THEIR LAND WITHOUT A FIGHT.
THAT MAKES THEM A NICE COUNTRY, DON'T YOU THINK?
....

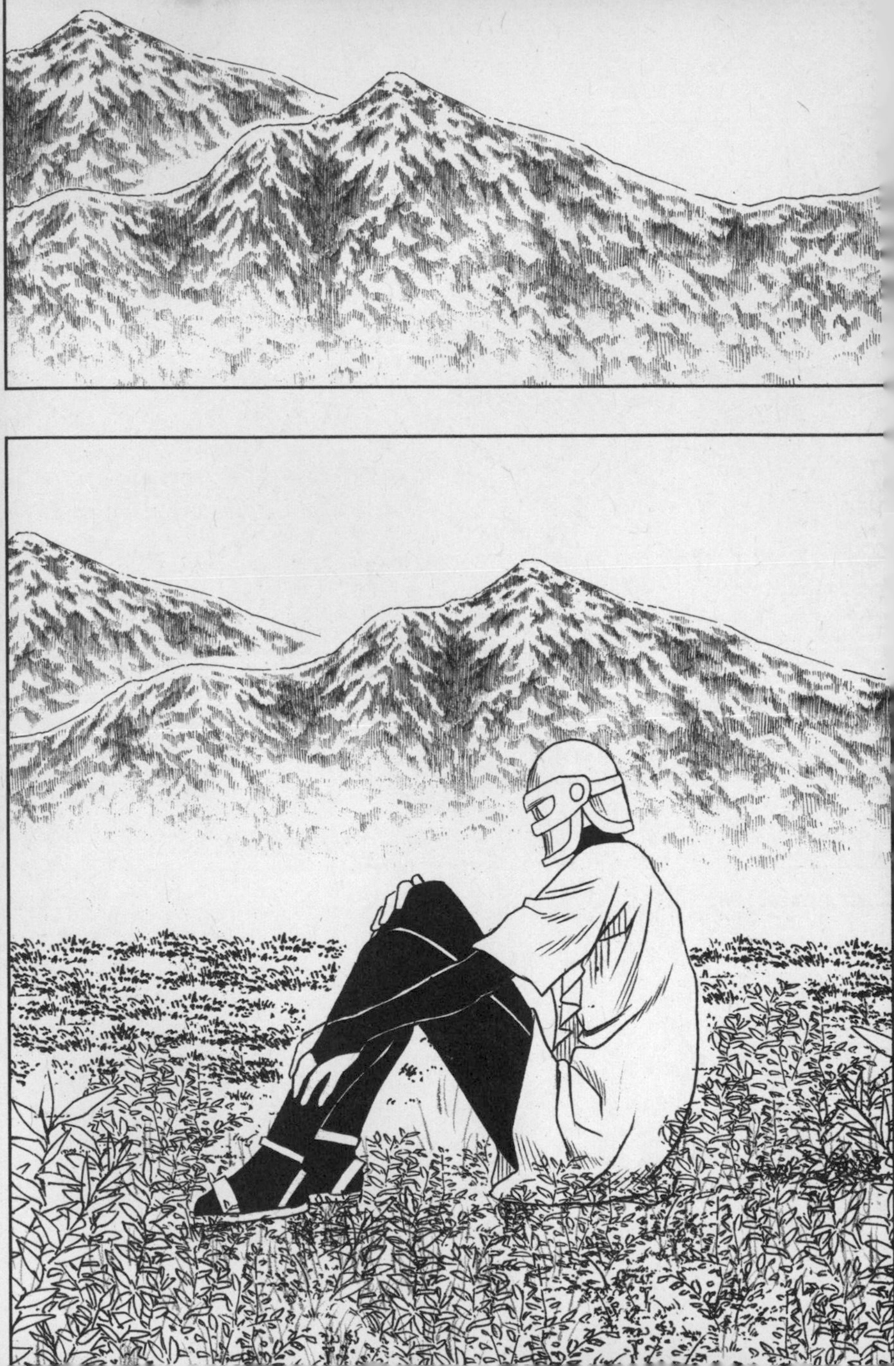

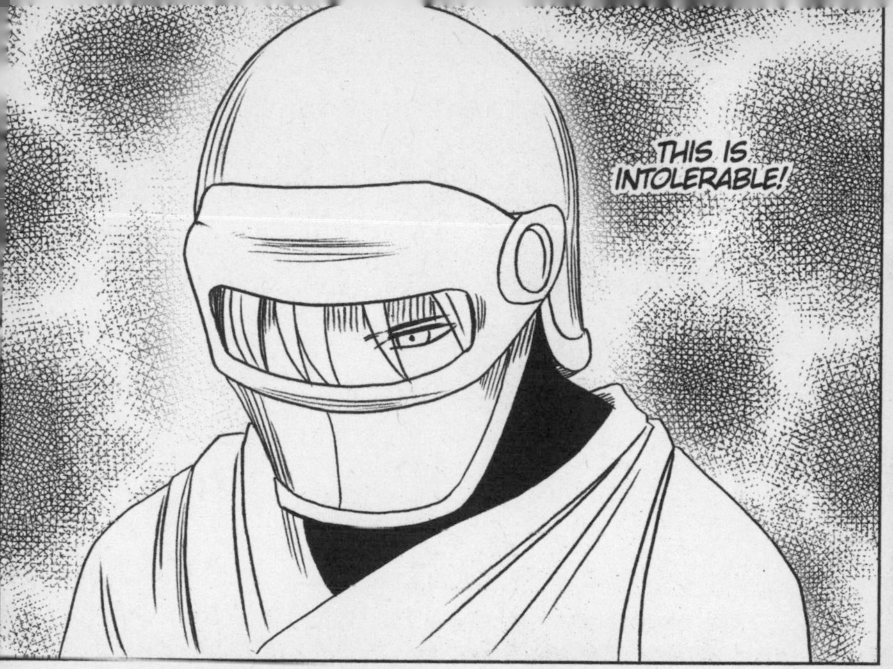
THIS IS INTOLERABLE!

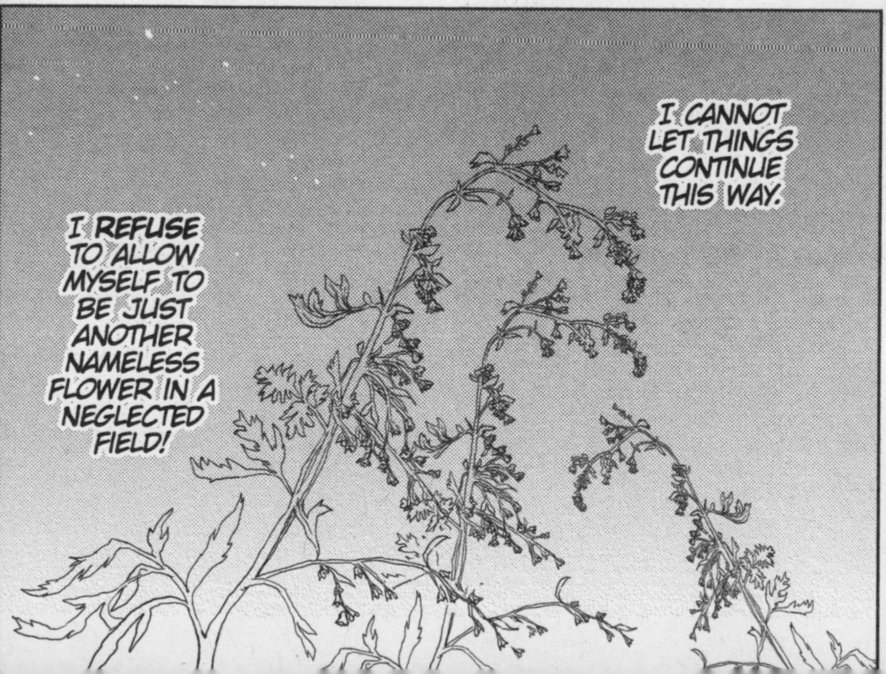
I CANNOT LET THINGS CONTINUE THIS WAY.
I REFUSE TO ALLOW MYSELF TO BE JUST ANOTHER NAMELESS FLOWER IN A NEGLECTED FIELD!

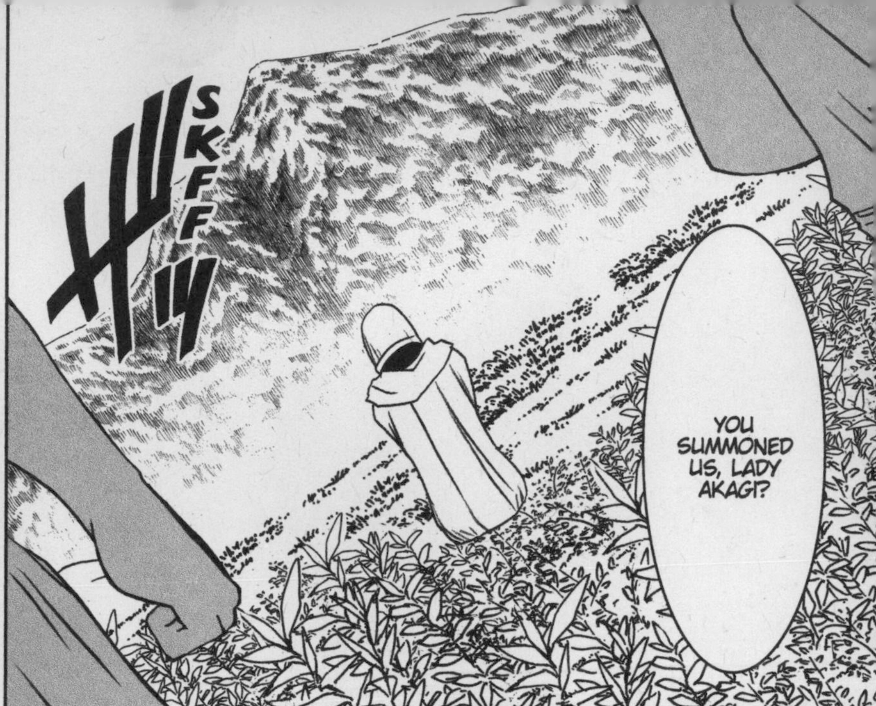
SKFFFF
YOU SUMMONED US, LADY AKAGI?
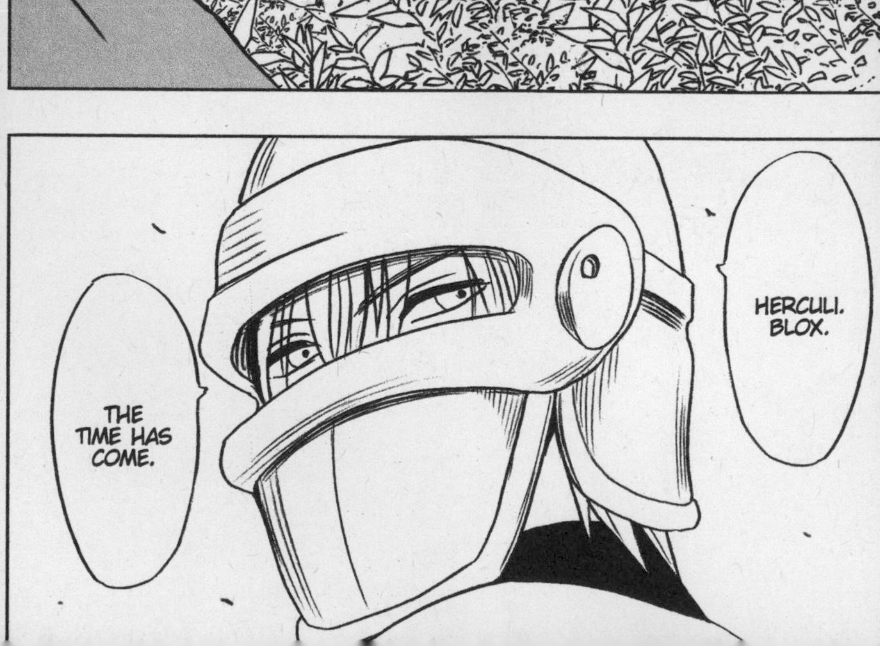
HERCULI. BLOX.
THE TIME HAS COME.

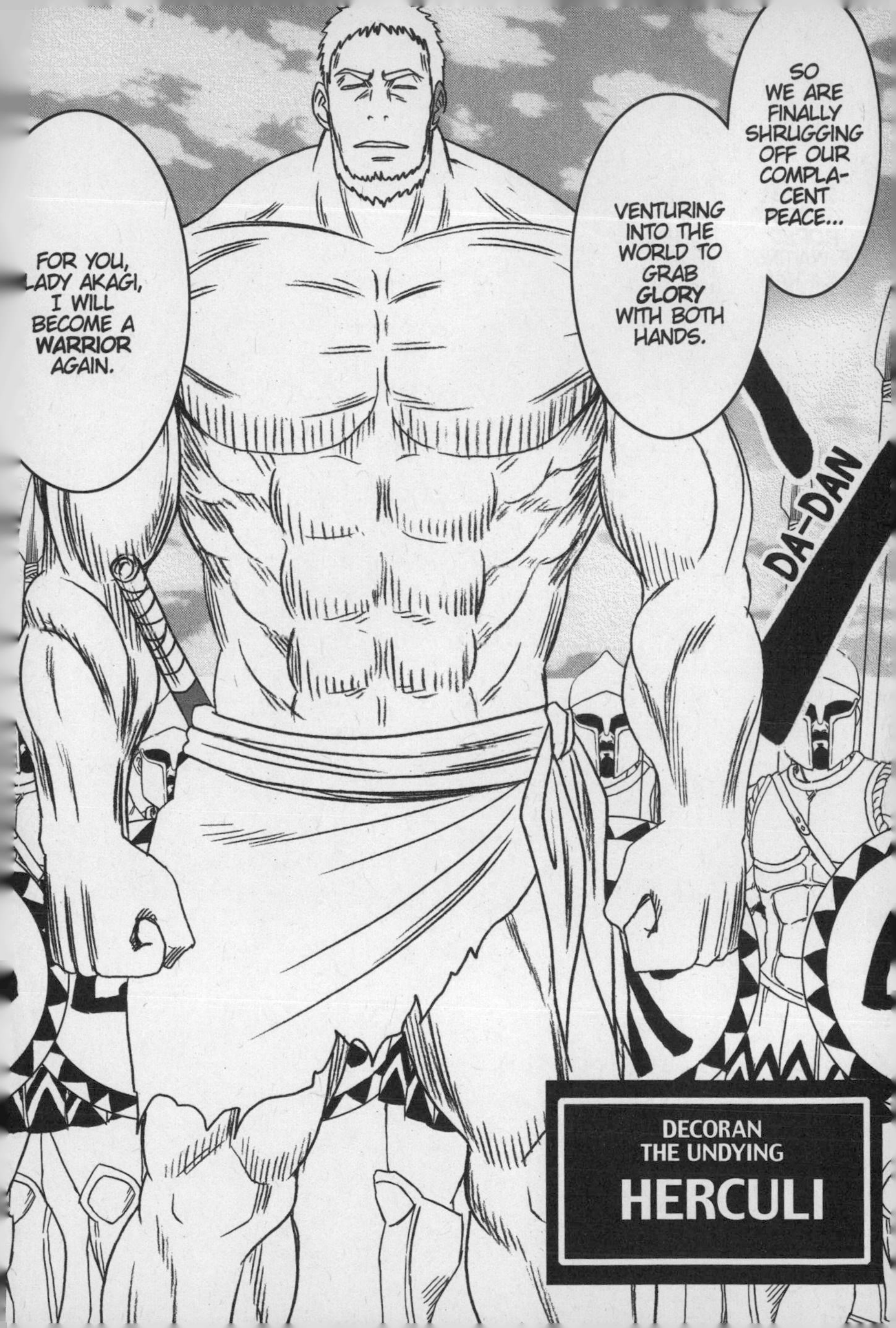
SO WE ARE FINALLY SHRUGGING OFF OUR COMPLA-CENT PEACE...
VENTURING INTO THE WORLD TO GRAB GLORY WITH BOTH HANDS.
DA-DAN
FOR YOU, LADY AKAGI, I WILL BECOME A WARRIOR AGAIN.
DECORAN THE UNDYING
HERCULI

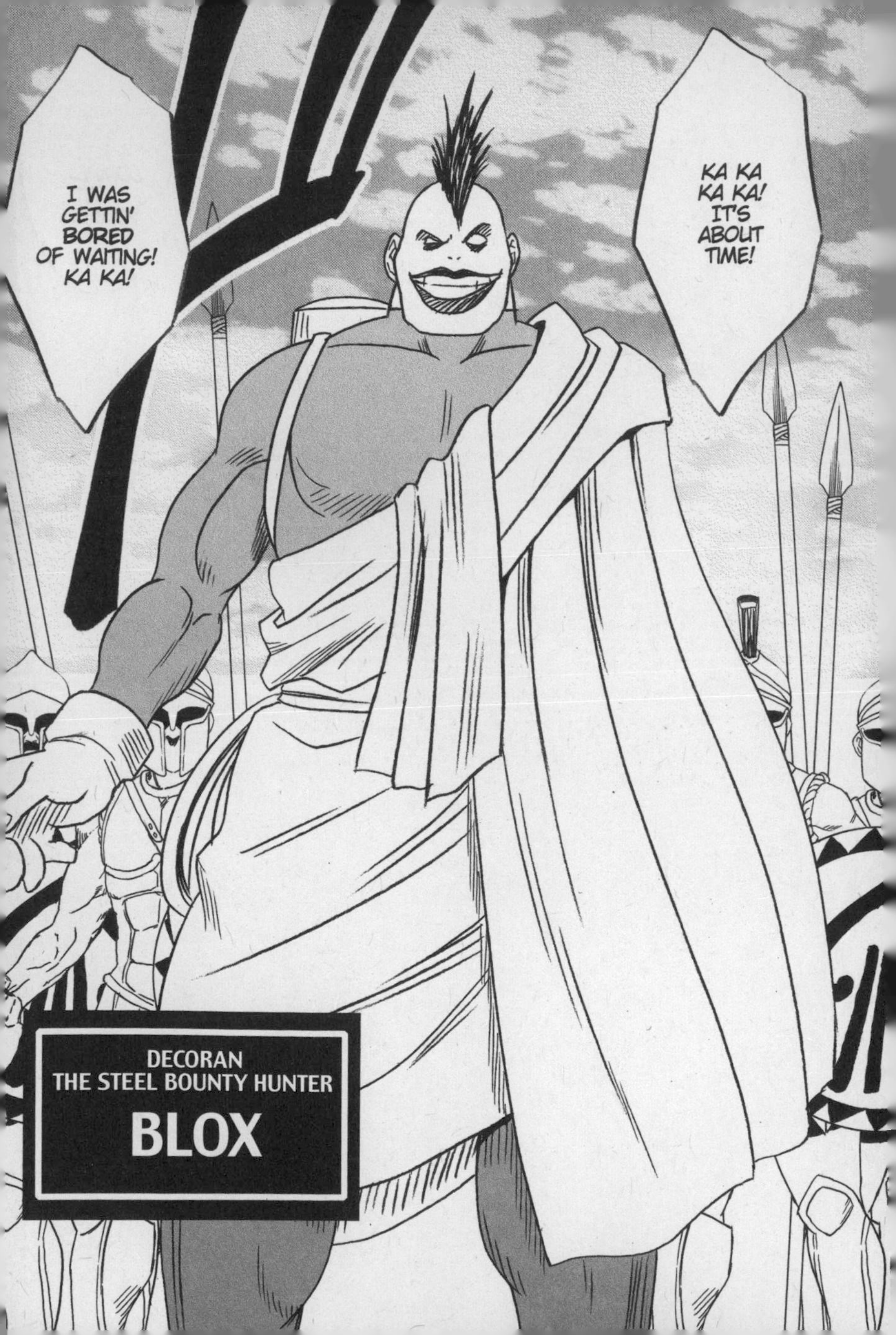
KA KA KA KA! IT'S ABOUT TIME!
I WAS GETTIN' BORED OF WAITING! KA KA!
DECORAN THE STEEL BOUNTY HUNTER
BLOX

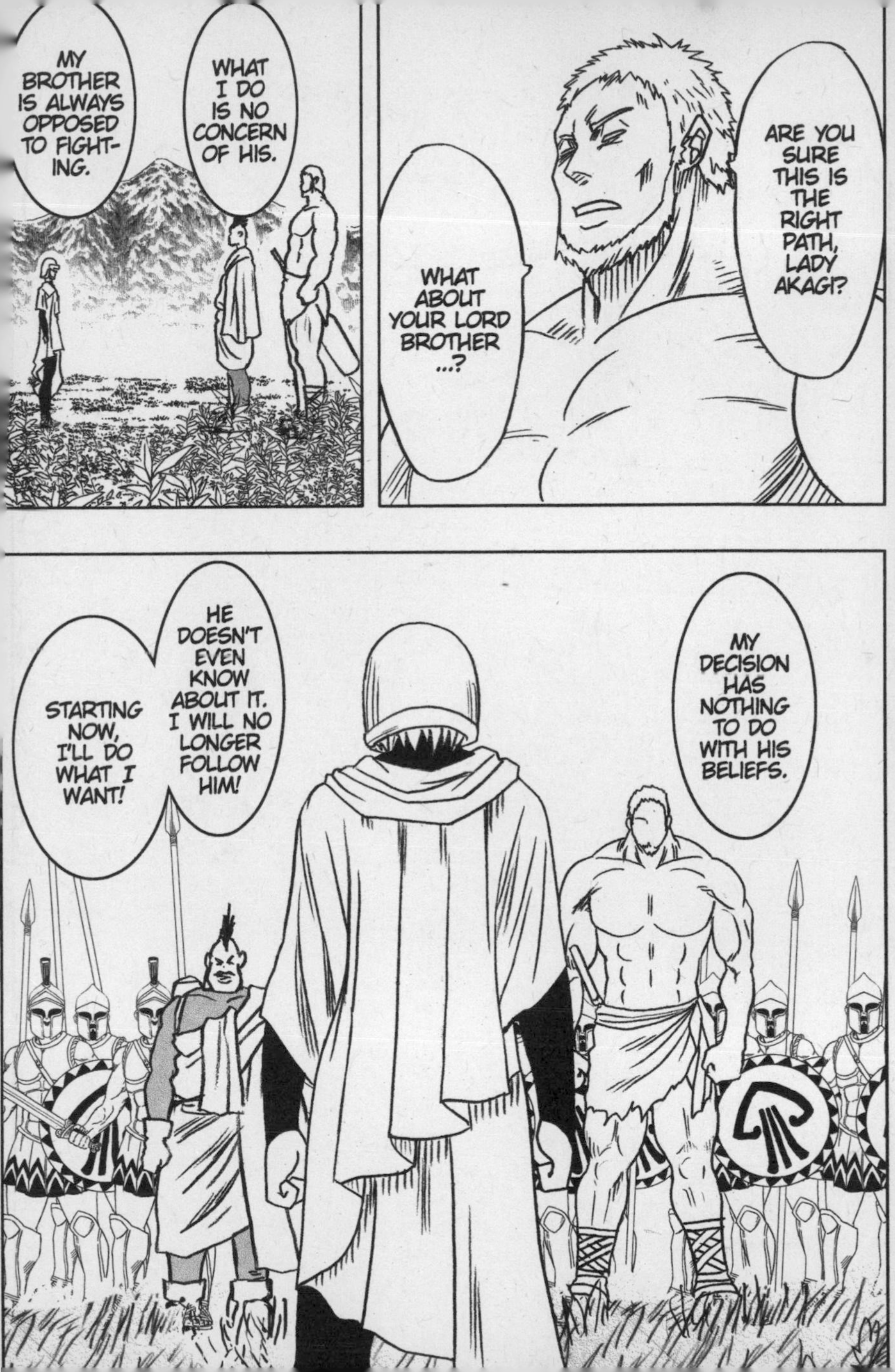
ARE YOU SURE THIS IS THE RIGHT PATH, LADY AKAGI?
WHAT ABOUT YOUR LORD BROTHER ...?
WHAT I DO IS NO CONCERN OF HIS.
MY BROTHER IS ALWAYS OPPOSED TO FIGHT-ING.
MY DECISION HAS NOTHING TO DO WITH HIS BELIEFS.
HE DOESN'T EVEN KNOW ABOUT IT. I WILL NO LONGER FOLLOW HIM!
STARTING NOW, I'LL DO WHAT I WANT!

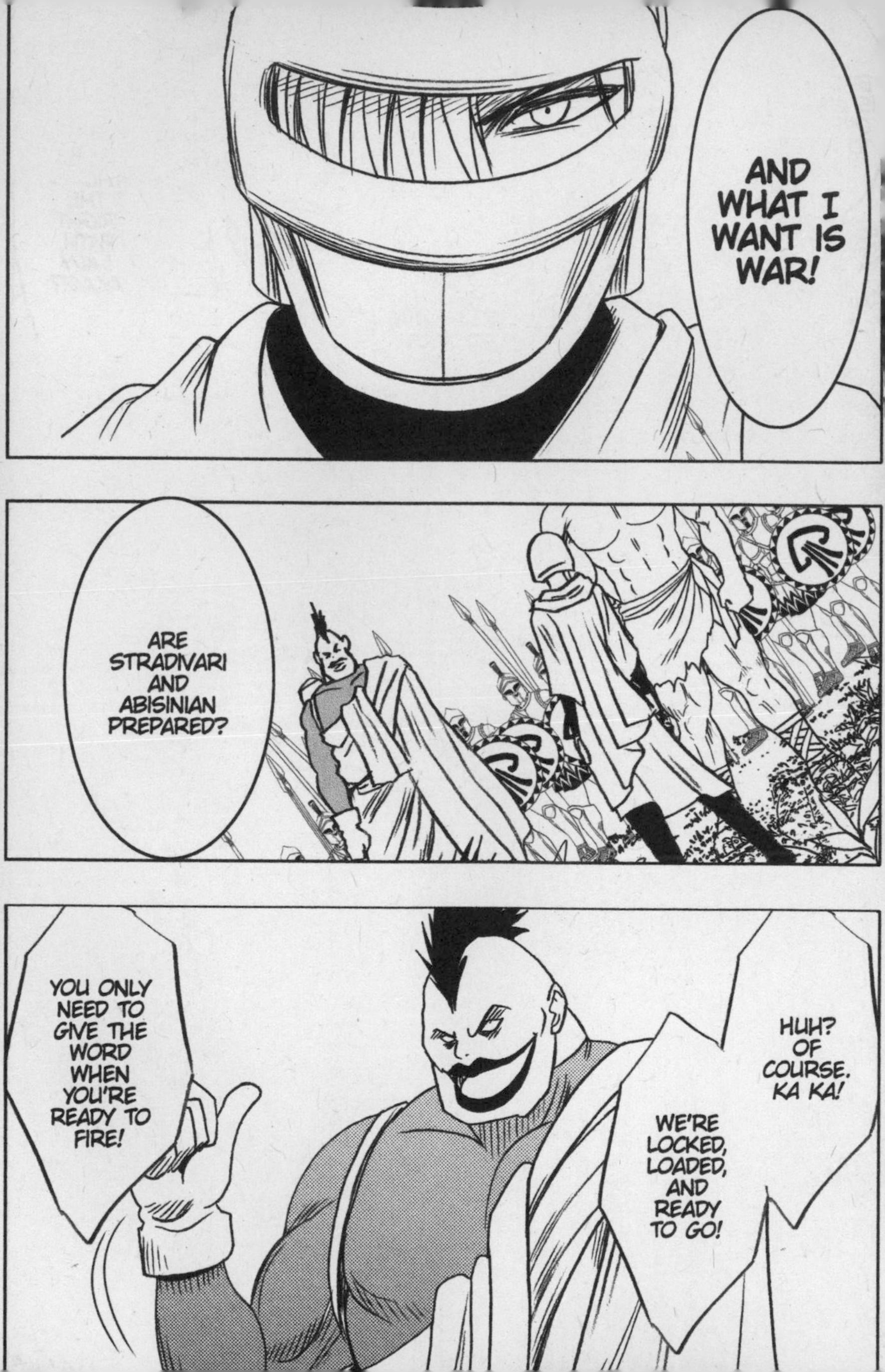
AND WHAT I WANT IS WAR!
ARE STRADIVARI AND ABISINIAN PREPARED?
HUH? OF COURSE. KA KA!
WE'RE LOCKED, LOADED, AND READY TO GO!
YOU ONLY NEED TO GIVE THE WORD WHEN YOU'RE READY TO FIRE!

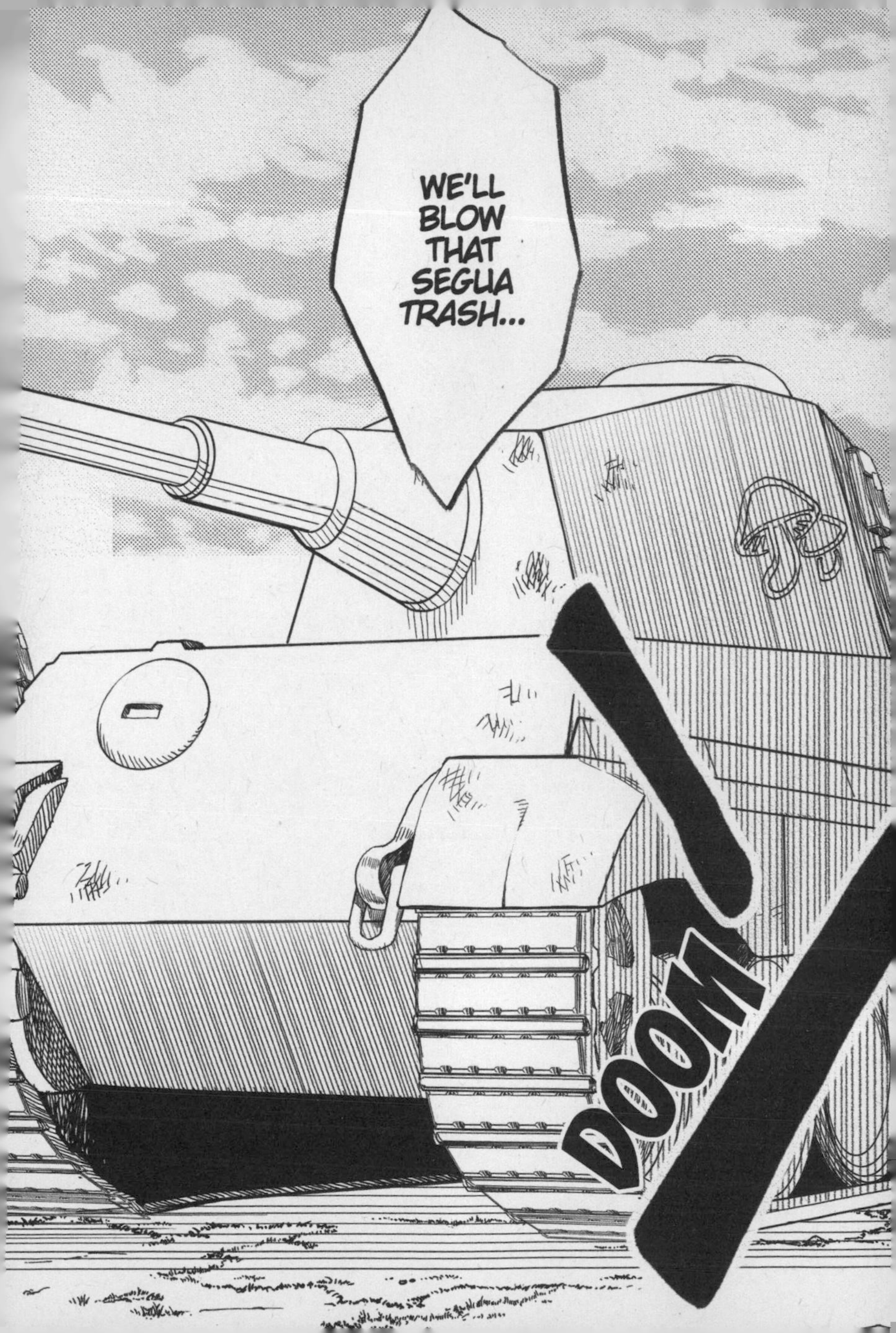
WE'LL BLOW THAT SEGUA TRASH...
DOOM

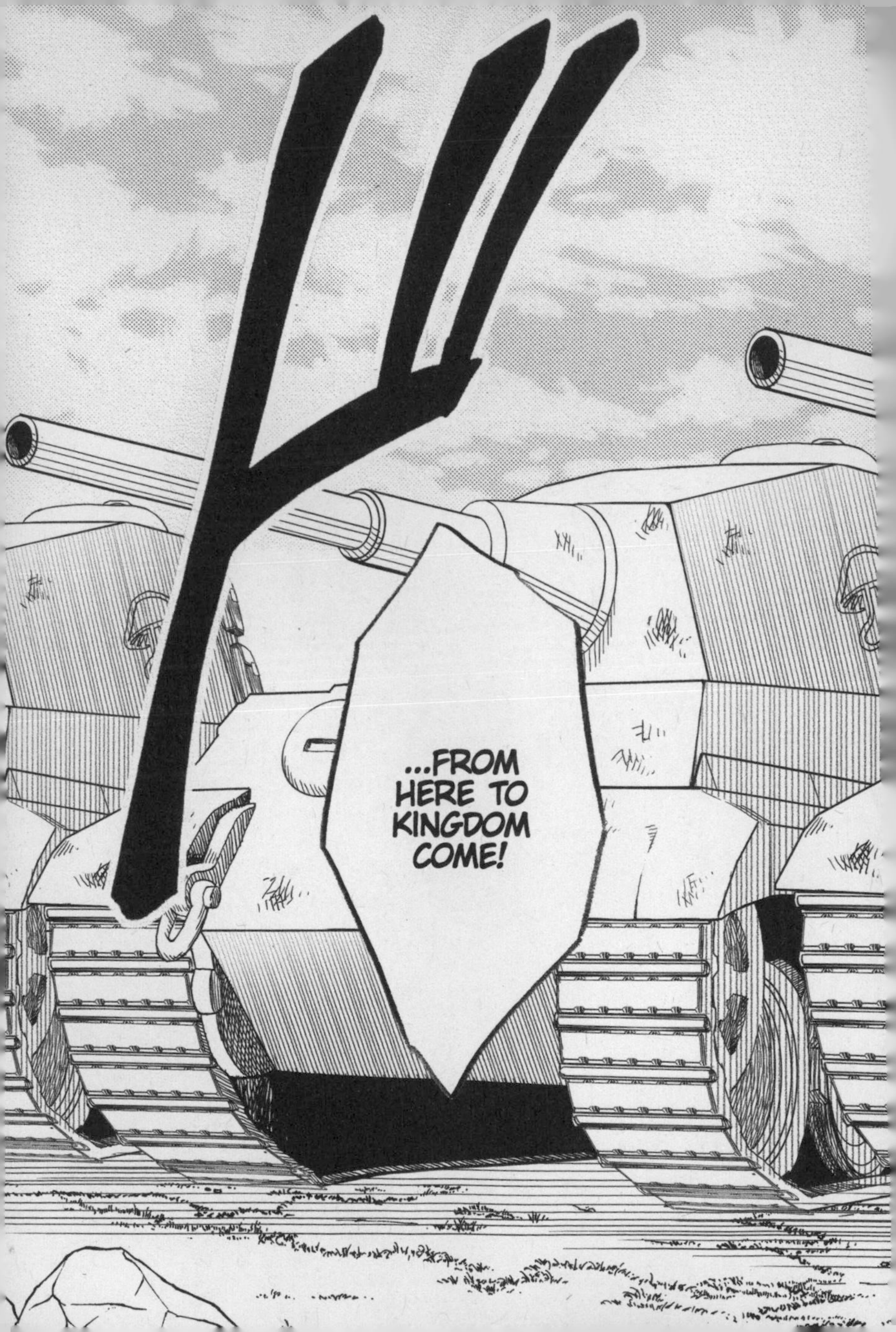
...FROM HERE TO KINGDOM COME!

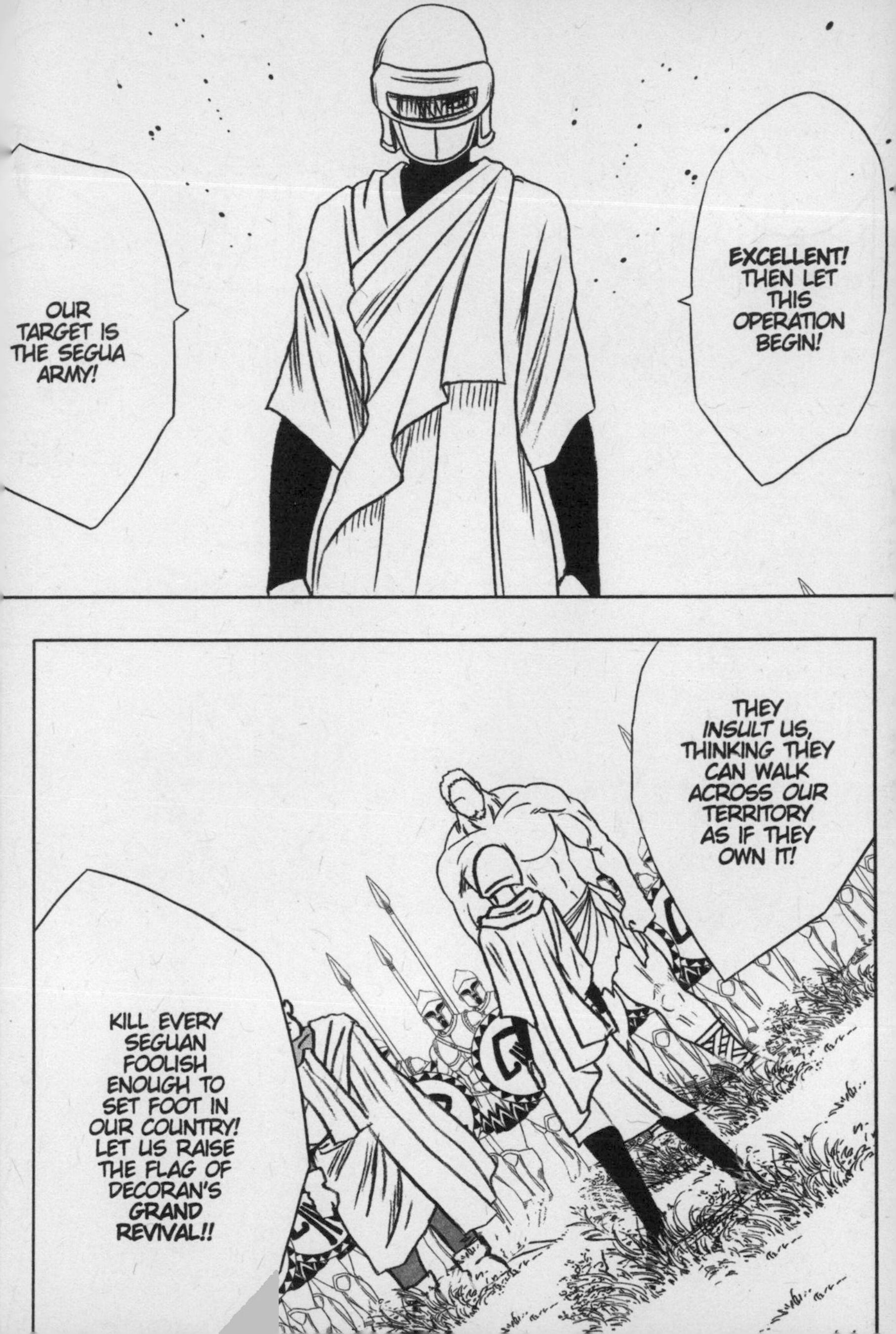
EXCELLENT! THEN LET THIS OPERATION BEGIN!
OUR TARGET IS THE SEGUA ARMY!
THEY INSULT US, THINKING THEY CAN WALK ACROSS OUR TERRITORY AS IF THEY OWN IT!
KILL EVERY SEGUAN FOOLISH ENOUGH TO SET FOOT IN OUR COUNTRY! LET US RAISE THE FLAG OF DECORAN'S GRAND REVIVAL!!

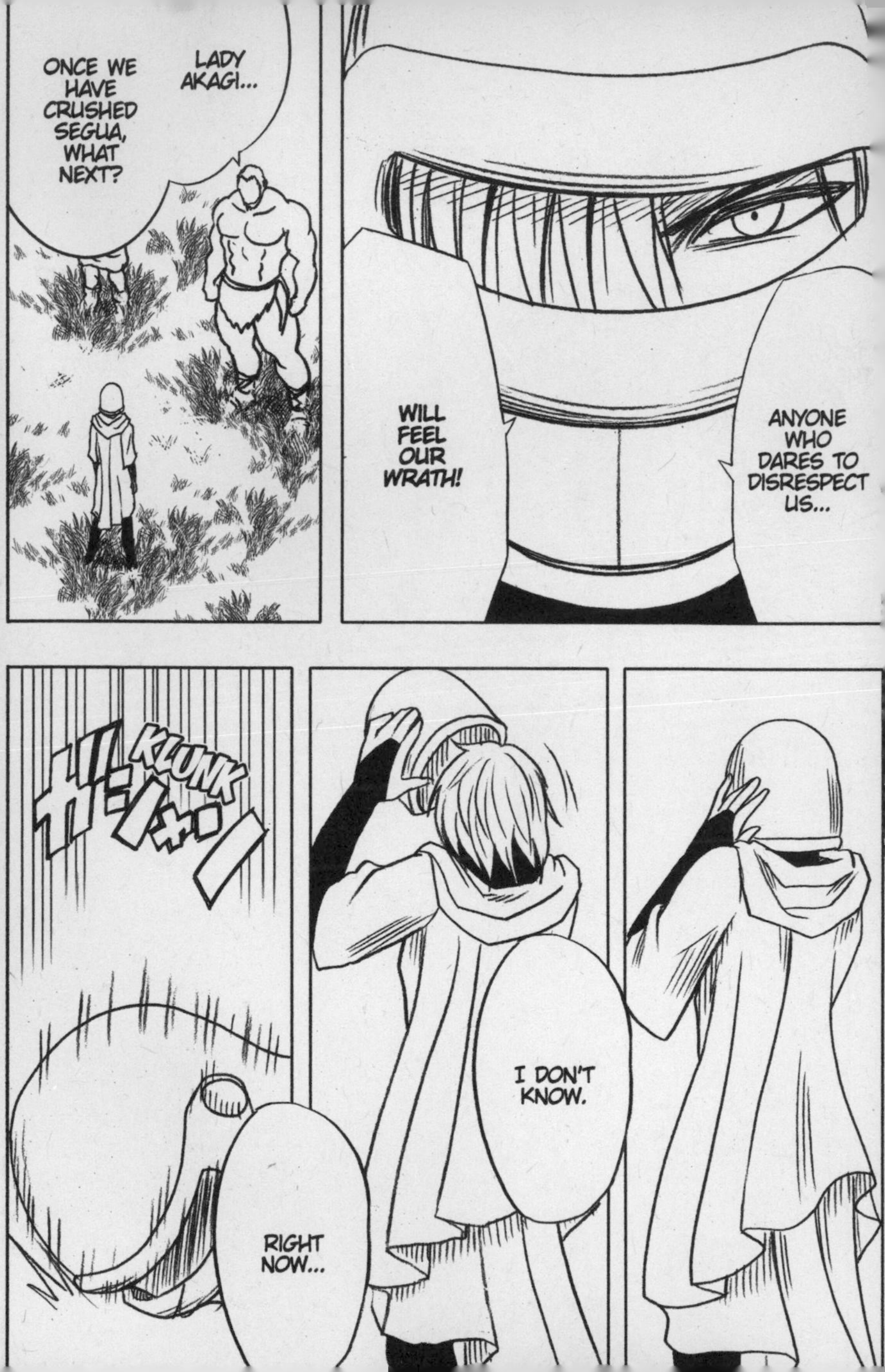
ANYONE WHO DARES TO DISRESPECT US...
WILL FEEL OUR WRATH!
LADY AKAGI...
ONCE WE HAVE CRUSHED SEGUA, WHAT NEXT?
I DON'T KNOW.
KLUNK
RIGHT NOW...

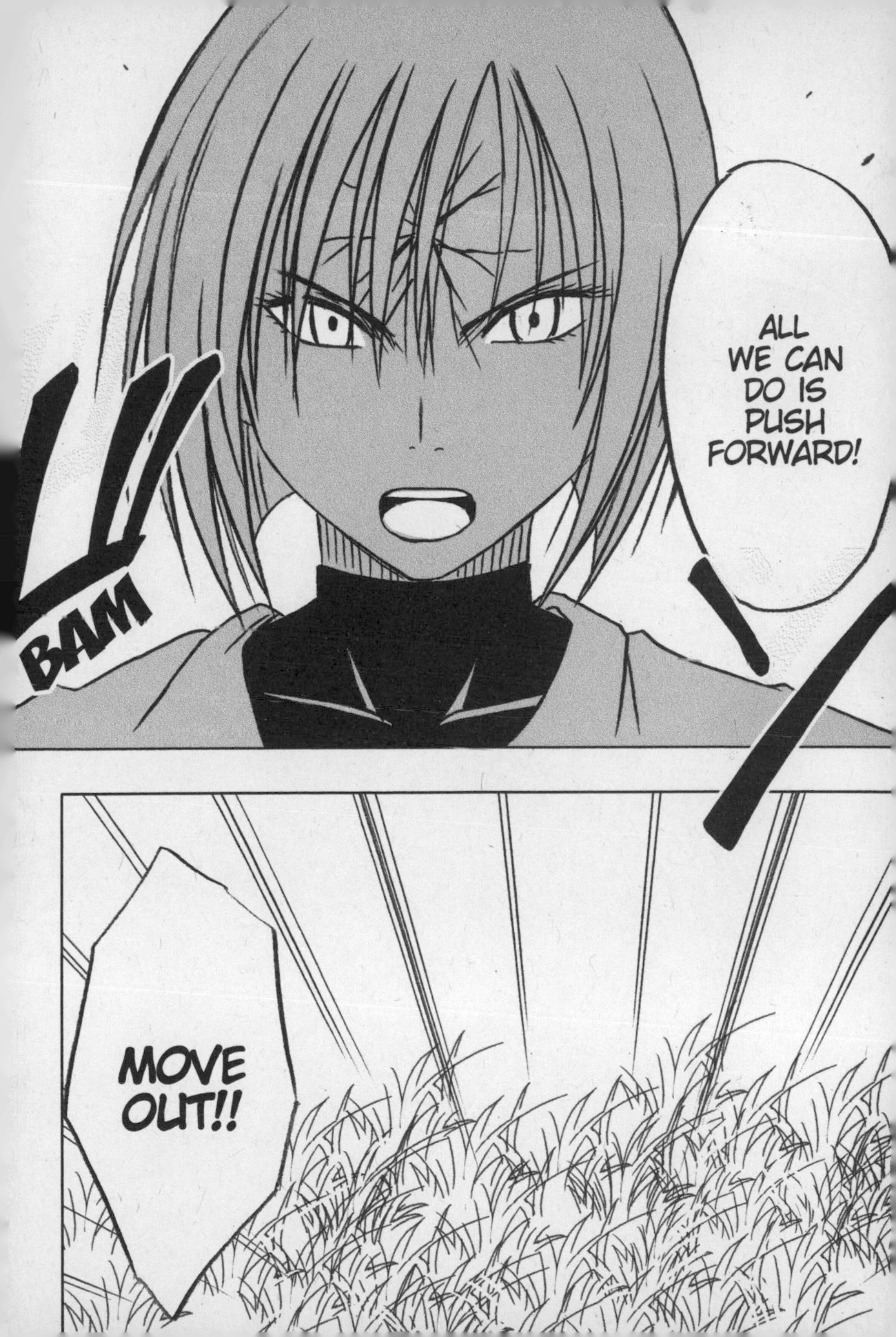
ALL WE CAN DO IS PUSH FORWARD!
BAM
MOVE OUT!!

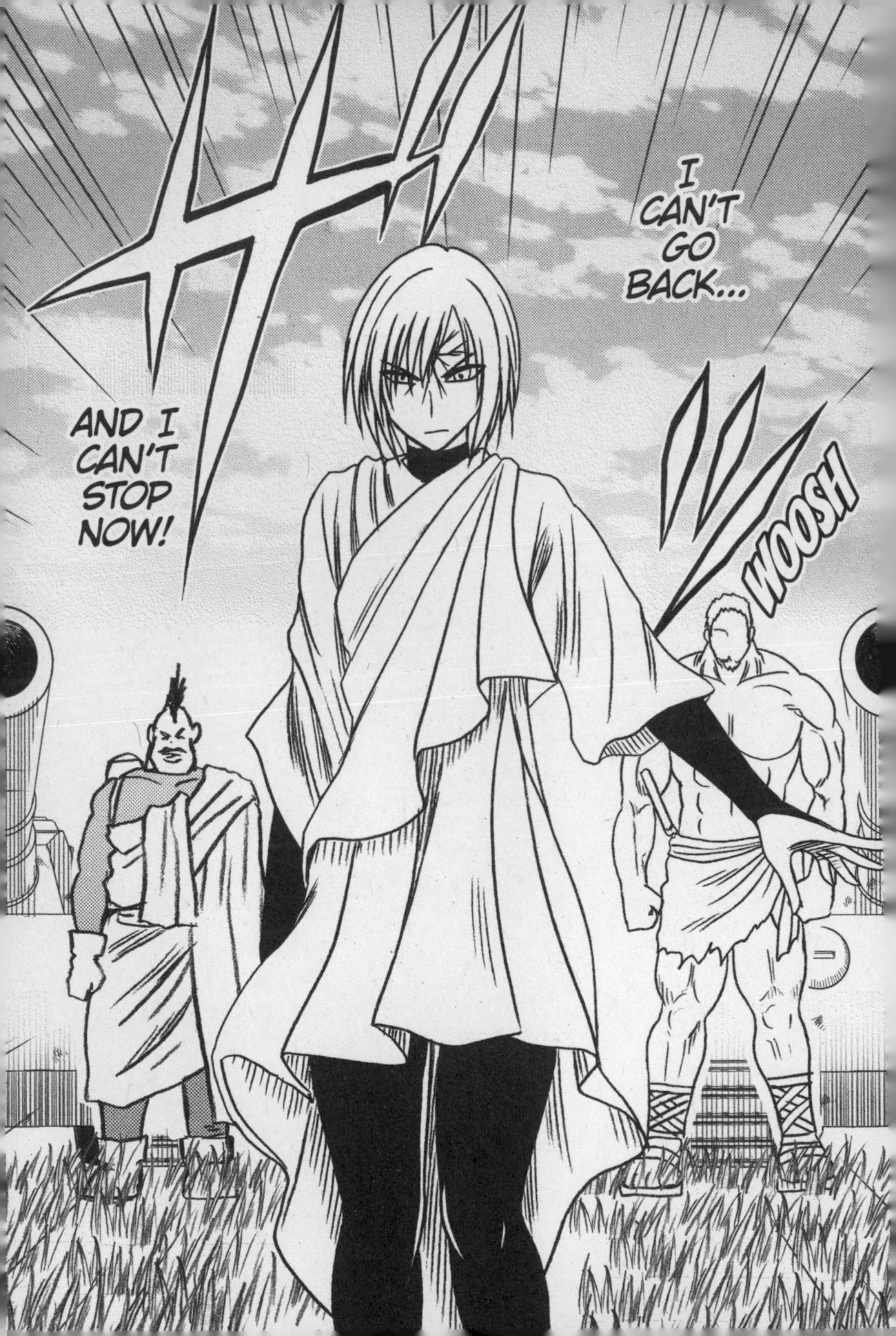
I CAN'T GO BACK...
WOOSH
AND I CAN'T STOP NOW!

Perusing Video Game History

ON THE EDGE OF THE BLUE WORLD

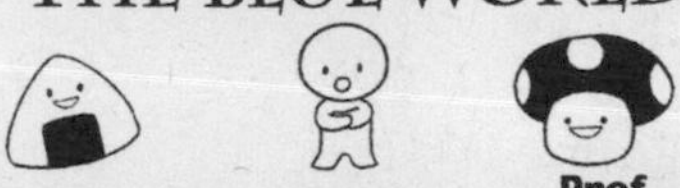

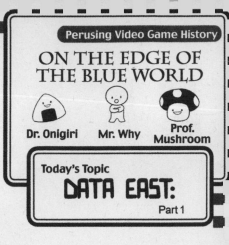

Dr. Onigiri Mr. Why Prof. Mushroom

Today's Topic

DATA EAST:

Part 1

Mr. Why: Right, so this time, we're going to talk about the software maker, Data East. We talked a little about them last volume, and I remember you saying they were an odd company.

Dr. Onigiri: Right. The Data East Corporation, also called "DECO," produced a lot of very unique games over the years. In fact, their slogan was "Leave the weird games to us!"

Prof. Mushroom: And their games weren't the only weird thing about them. They also sold offbeat products, such as dried mushrooms and gas masks.

Dr. Onigiri: They gave their games unique names to match the unique content. *Karnov*, *Bad Dudes vs. Ninja Dragon*, and *Skull Fang* just to name a few. But perhaps the strangest of them all was the action game *Atomic Runner Chelnov*.

Prof. Mushroom: It came out in 1988 as an arcade title. At first glance, it looks like any other side-scrolling action game, but there's one really big difference to it that most don't notice right away.

Dr. Onigiri: Correct. In *Chelnov*, you can't go backwards.

Mr. Why: Huh? You can't turn around and go back?

Prof. Mushroom: Think of it as the player always having no choice but to keep moving forward.

Mr. Why: Whoa, now that *is* pretty strange.

Dr. Onigiri: Maybe, but it was certainly a very complete, well-made game. Another big game for DECO was the tank-based *Metal Max*.

Prof. Mushroom: How about we talk more about *Metal Max* next time?

To Be Continued...

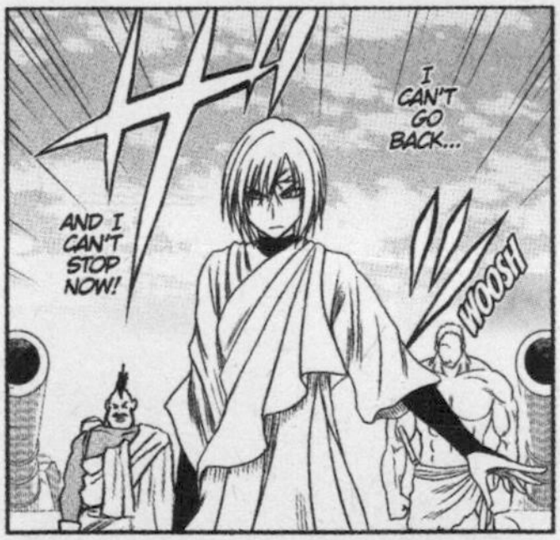
I CAN'T GO BACK...
AND I CAN'T STOP NOW!
WOOSH

Akagi never dwells on the past, always moving forward.

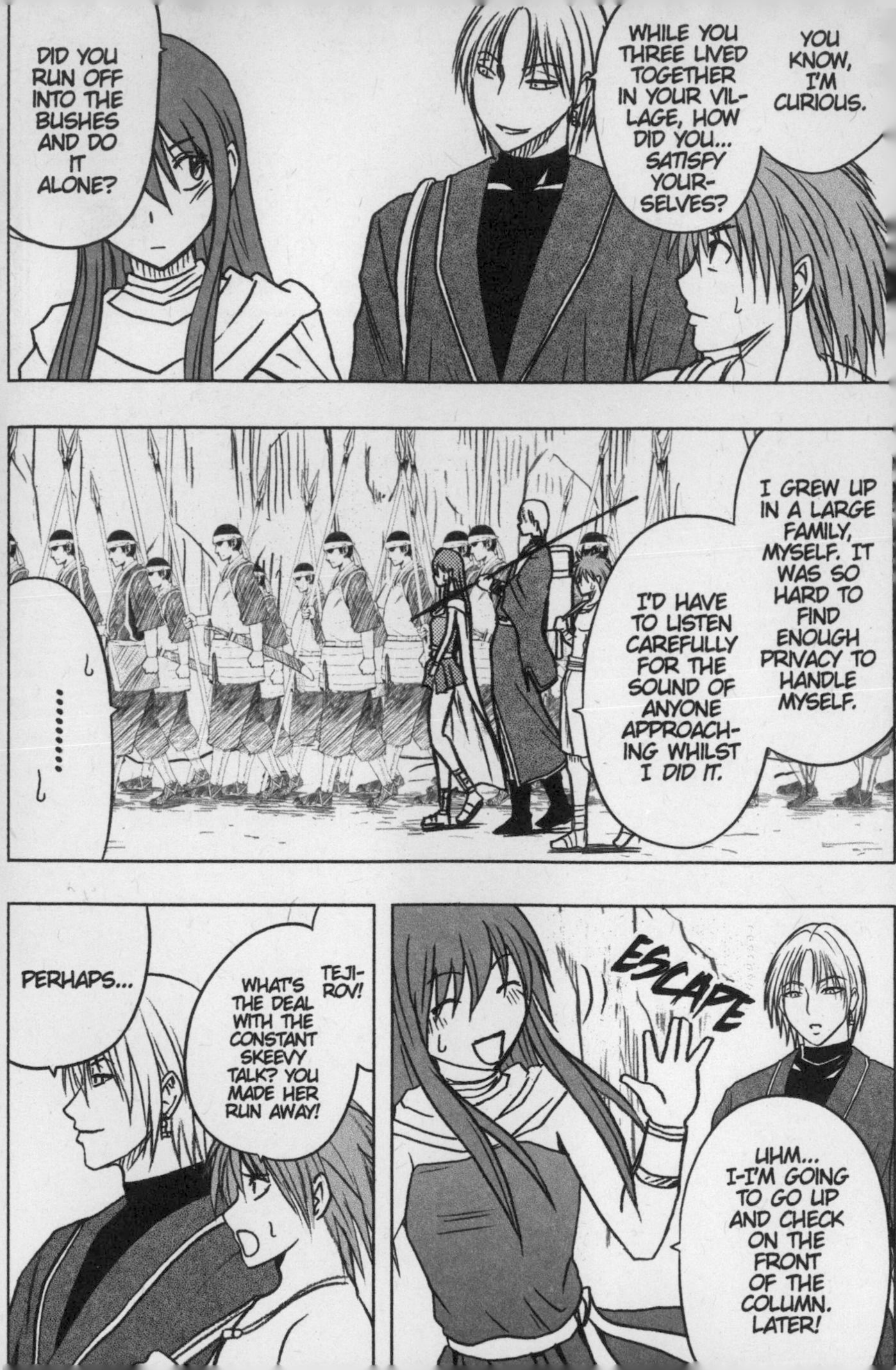

YOU KNOW, I'M CURIOUS.
WHILE YOU THREE LIVED TOGETHER IN YOUR VILLAGE, HOW DID YOU... SATISFY YOURSELVES?
DID YOU RUN OFF INTO THE BUSHES AND DO IT ALONE?
I GREW UP IN A LARGE FAMILY, MYSELF. IT WAS SO HARD TO FIND ENOUGH PRIVACY TO HANDLE MYSELF.
I'D HAVE TO LISTEN CAREFULLY FOR THE SOUND OF ANYONE APPROACHING WHILST I DID IT.
....
ESCAPE
UHM... I-I'M GOING TO GO UP AND CHECK ON THE FRONT OF THE COLUMN. LATER!
TEJIROV!
WHAT'S THE DEAL WITH THE CONSTANT SKEEVY TALK? YOU MADE HER RUN AWAY!
PERHAPS...

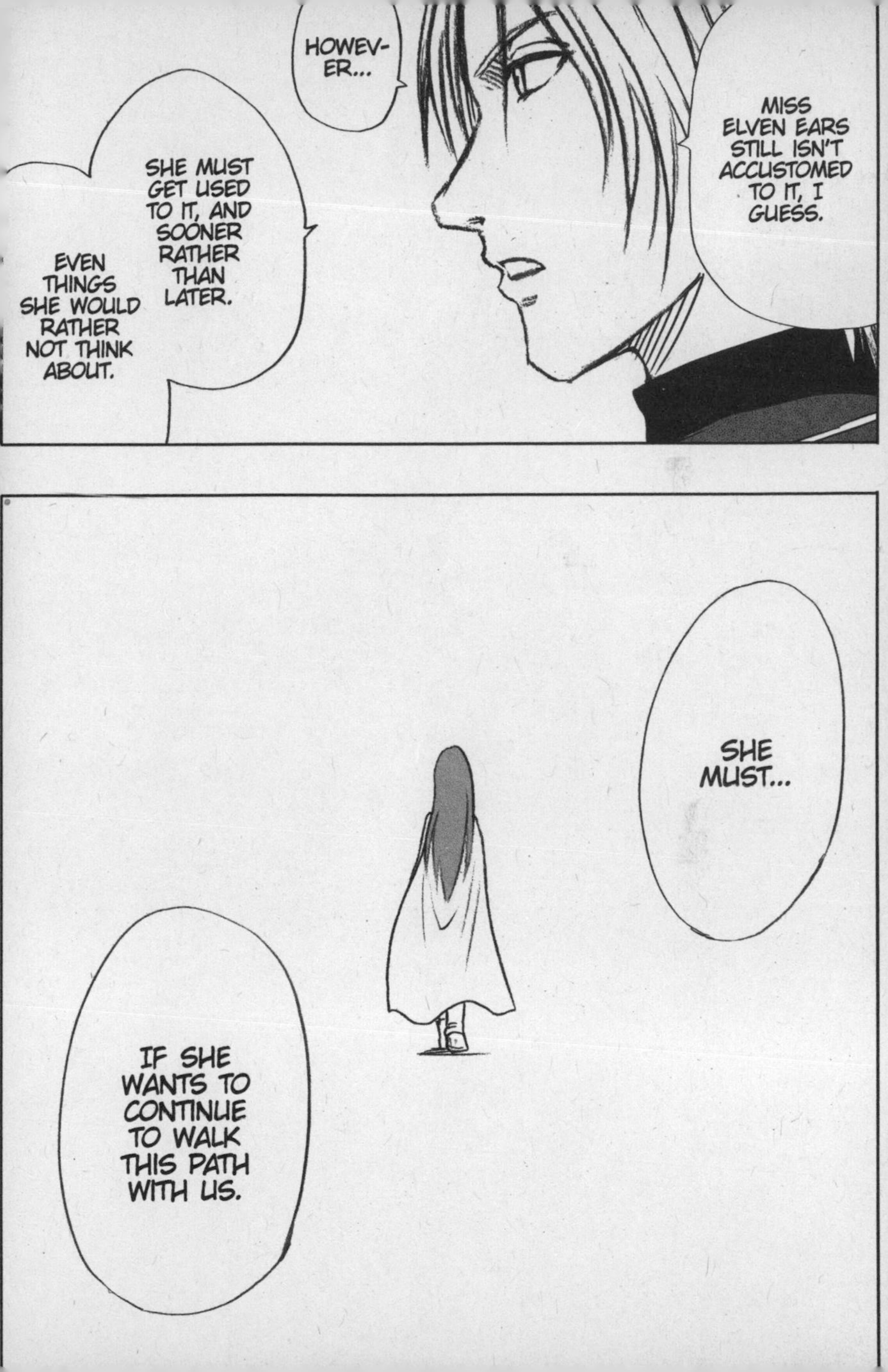
MISS ELVEN EARS STILL ISN'T ACCUSTOMED TO IT, I GUESS.
HOWEV-ER...
SHE MUST GET USED TO IT, AND SOONER RATHER THAN LATER.
EVEN THINGS SHE WOULD RATHER NOT THINK ABOUT.
SHE MUST...
IF SHE WANTS TO CONTINUE TO WALK THIS PATH WITH US.

Part 2

CHAPTER 5

OF TANKS
AND HUMANS

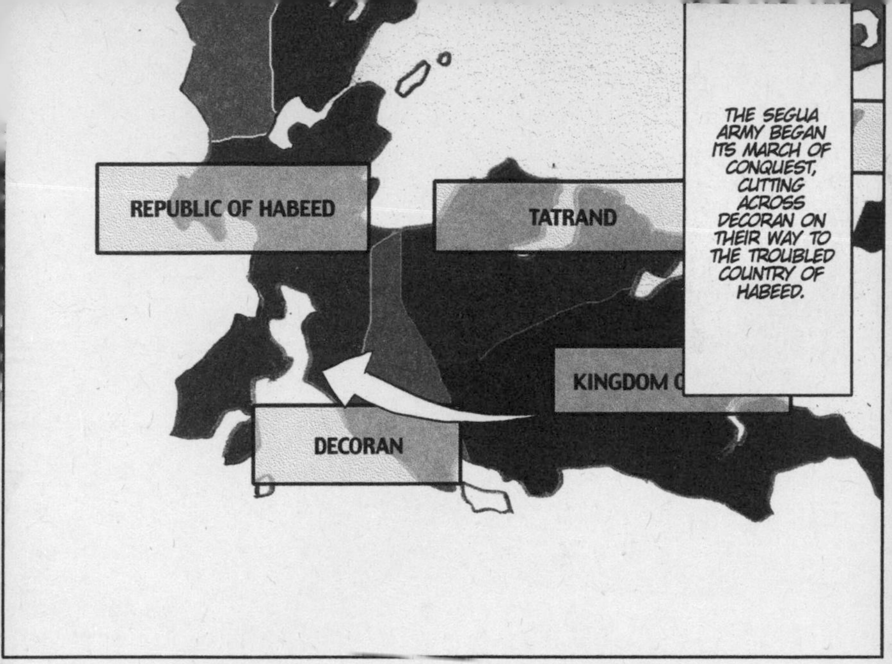
THE SEGUA ARMY BEGAN ITS MARCH OF CONQUEST, CUTTING ACROSS DECORAN ON THEIR WAY TO THE TROUBLED COUNTRY OF HABEED.
TATRAND
REPUBLIC OF HABEED
KINGDOM O
DECORAN

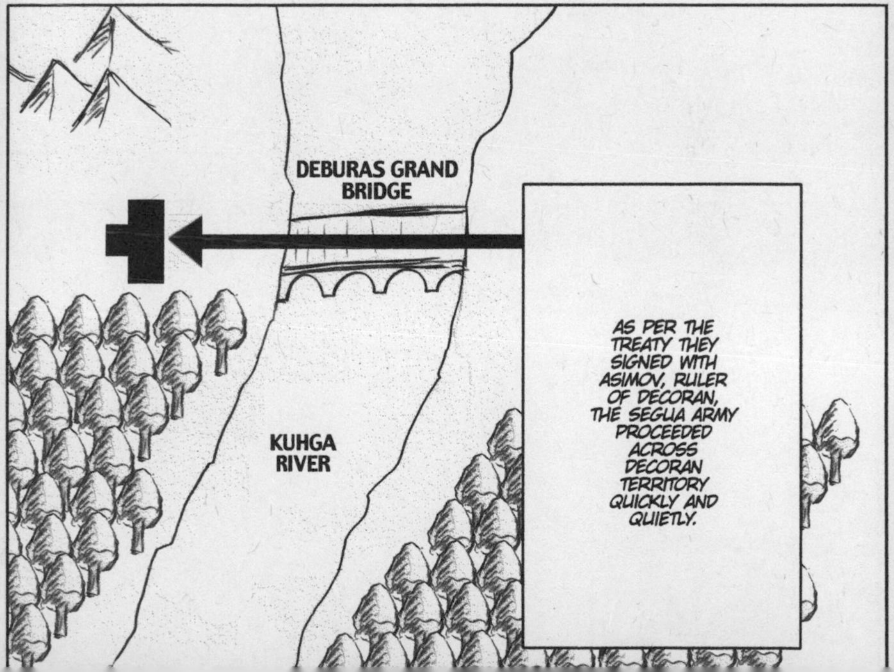
AS PER THE TREATY THEY SIGNED WITH ASIMOV, RULER OF DECORAN, THE SEGUA ARMY PROCEEDED ACROSS DECORAN TERRITORY QUICKLY AND QUIETLY.
DEBURAS GRAND BRIDGE
KUHGA RIVER

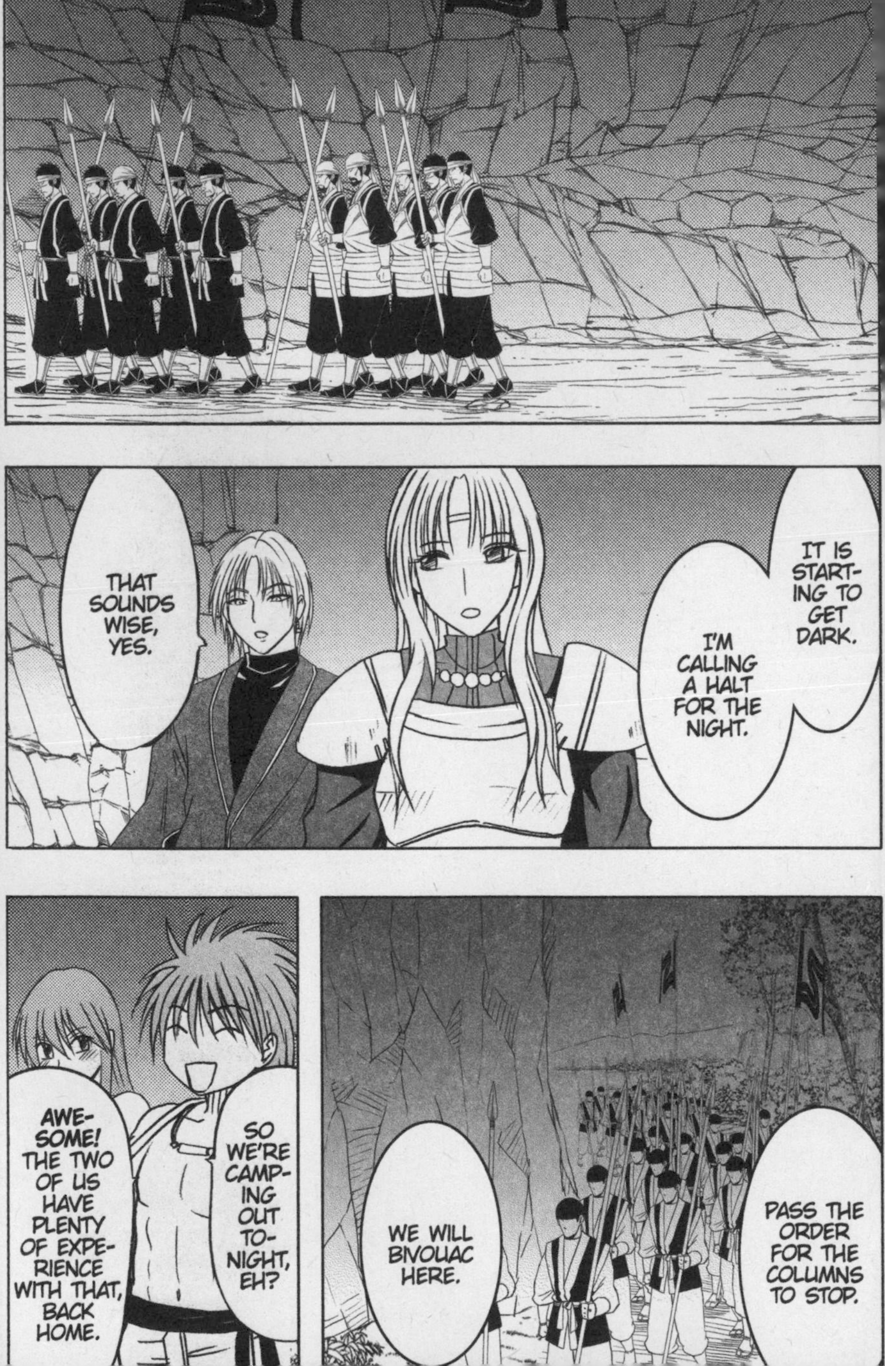
IT IS STARTING TO GET DARK.
I'M CALLING A HALT FOR THE NIGHT.
THAT SOUNDS WISE, YES.
PASS THE ORDER FOR THE COLUMNS TO STOP.
WE WILL BIVOUAC HERE.
SO WE'RE CAMPING OUT TONIGHT, EH?
AWESOME! THE TWO OF US HAVE PLENTY OF EXPERIENCE WITH THAT, BACK HOME.

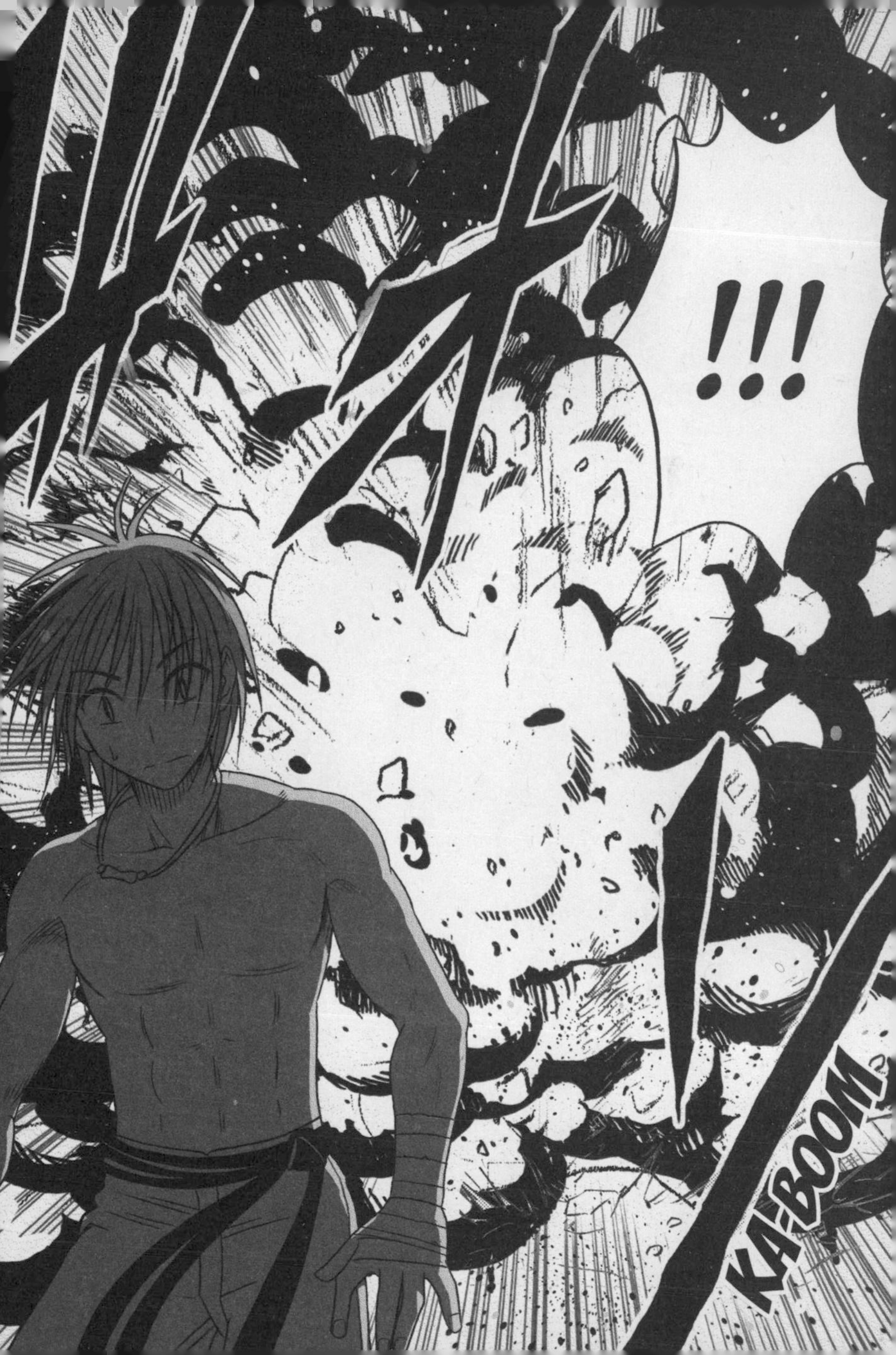
!!!
KA-BOOM

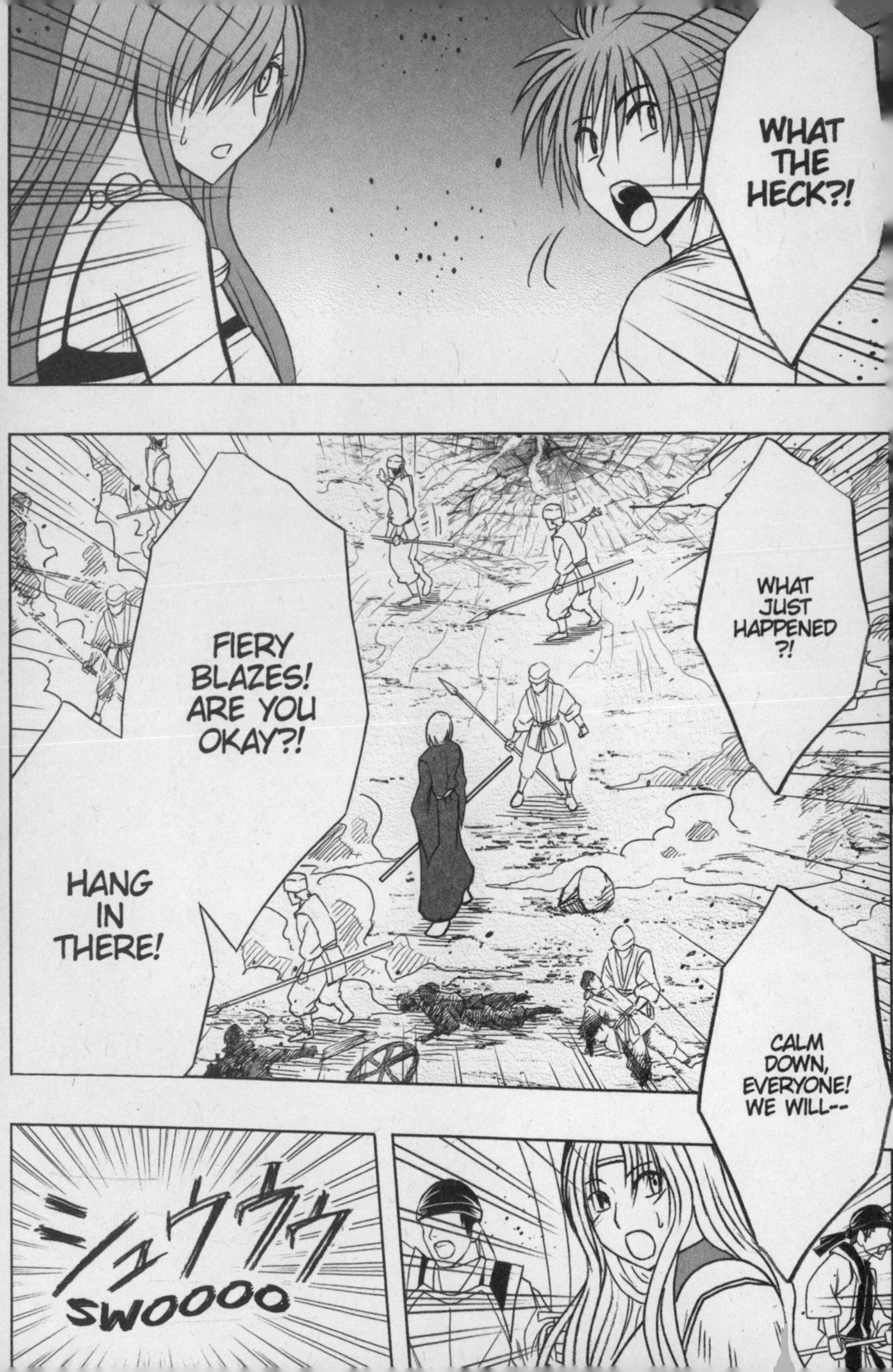
WHAT THE HECK?!
WHAT JUST HAPPENED?!
FIERY BLAZES! ARE YOU OKAY?!
HANG IN THERE!
CALM DOWN, EVERYONE! WE WILL--
シュウウウ
SWOOOO

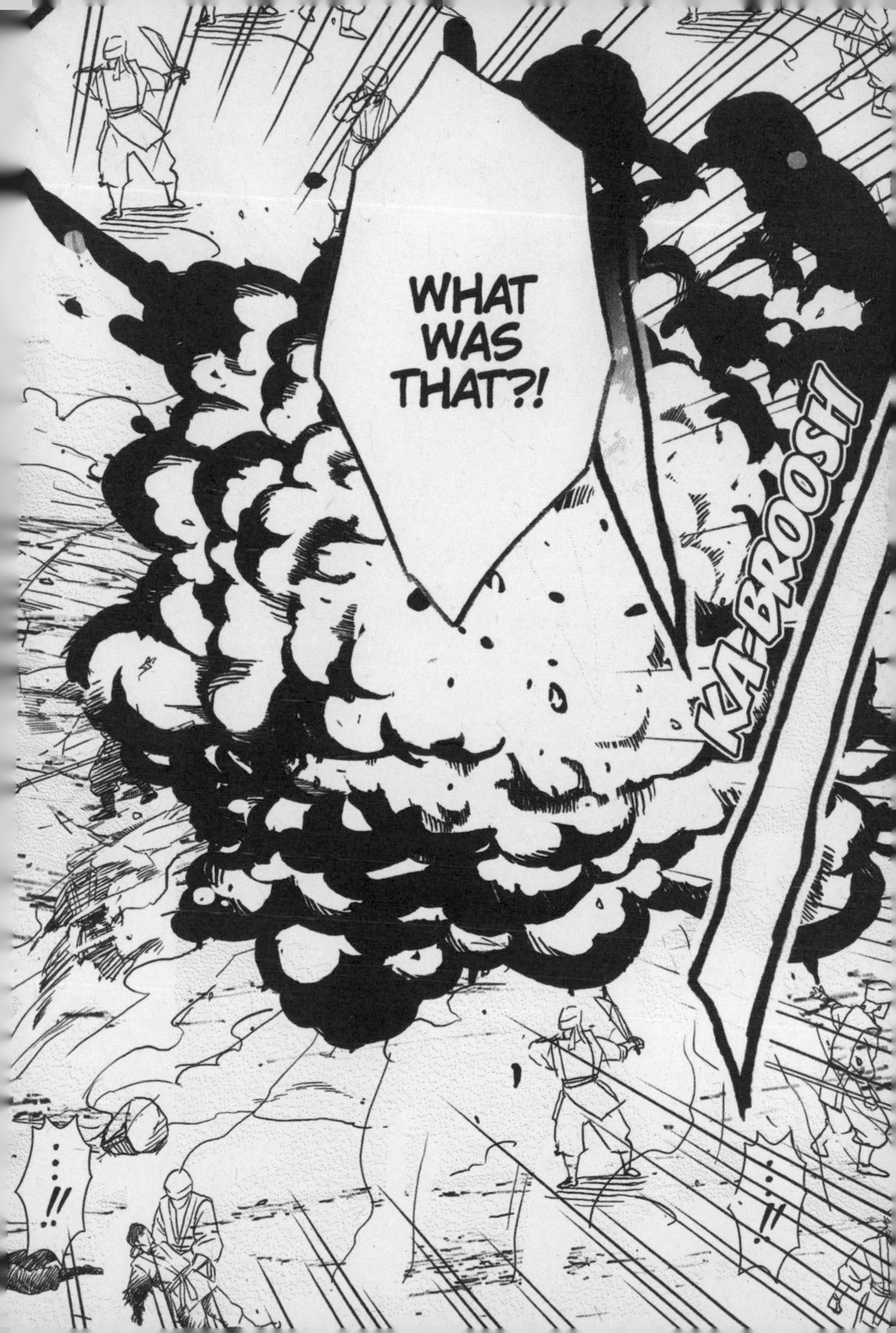
WHAT WAS THAT?!
KA-BROOSH
!!
...!!

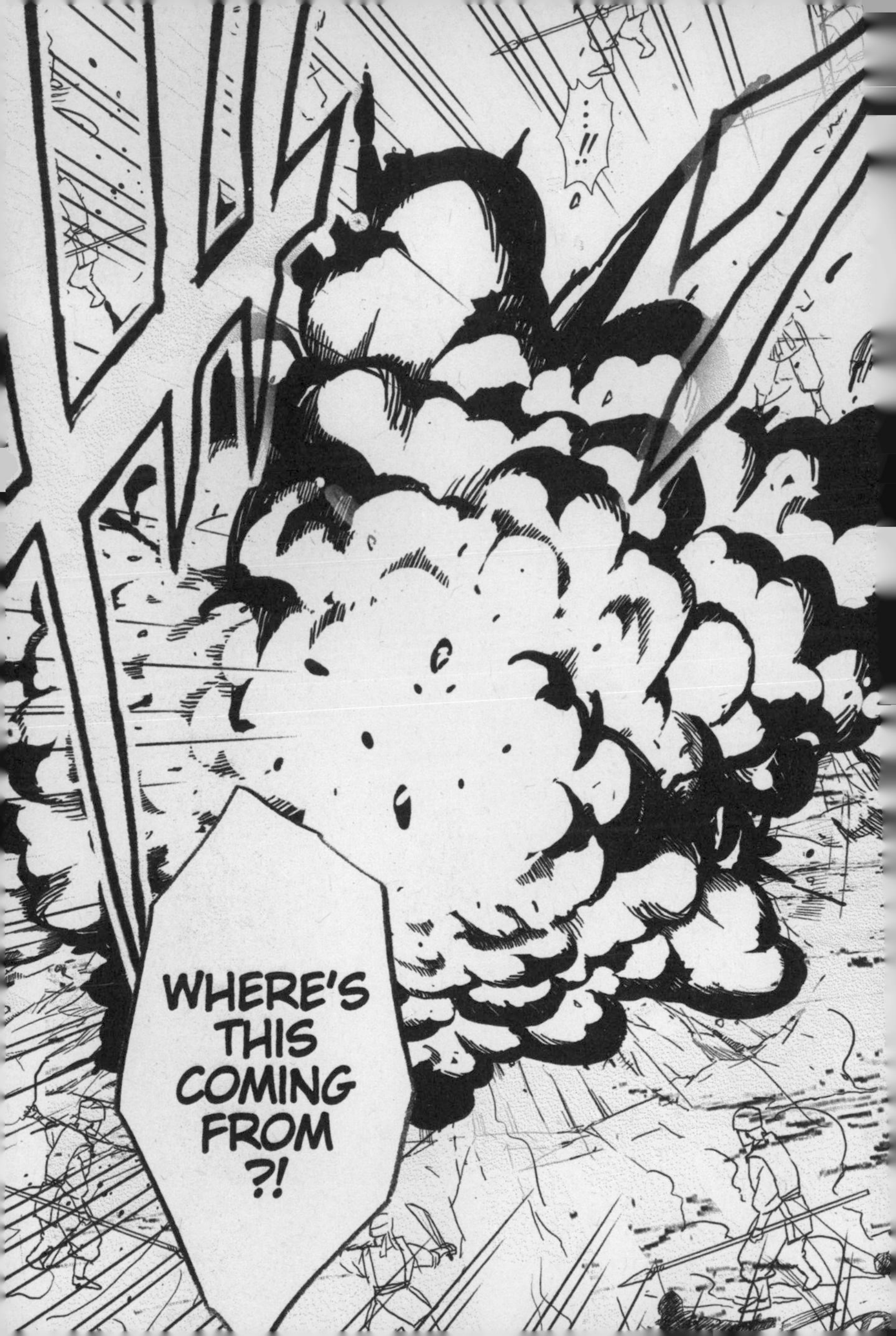
...!!
WHERE'S THIS COMING FROM ?!

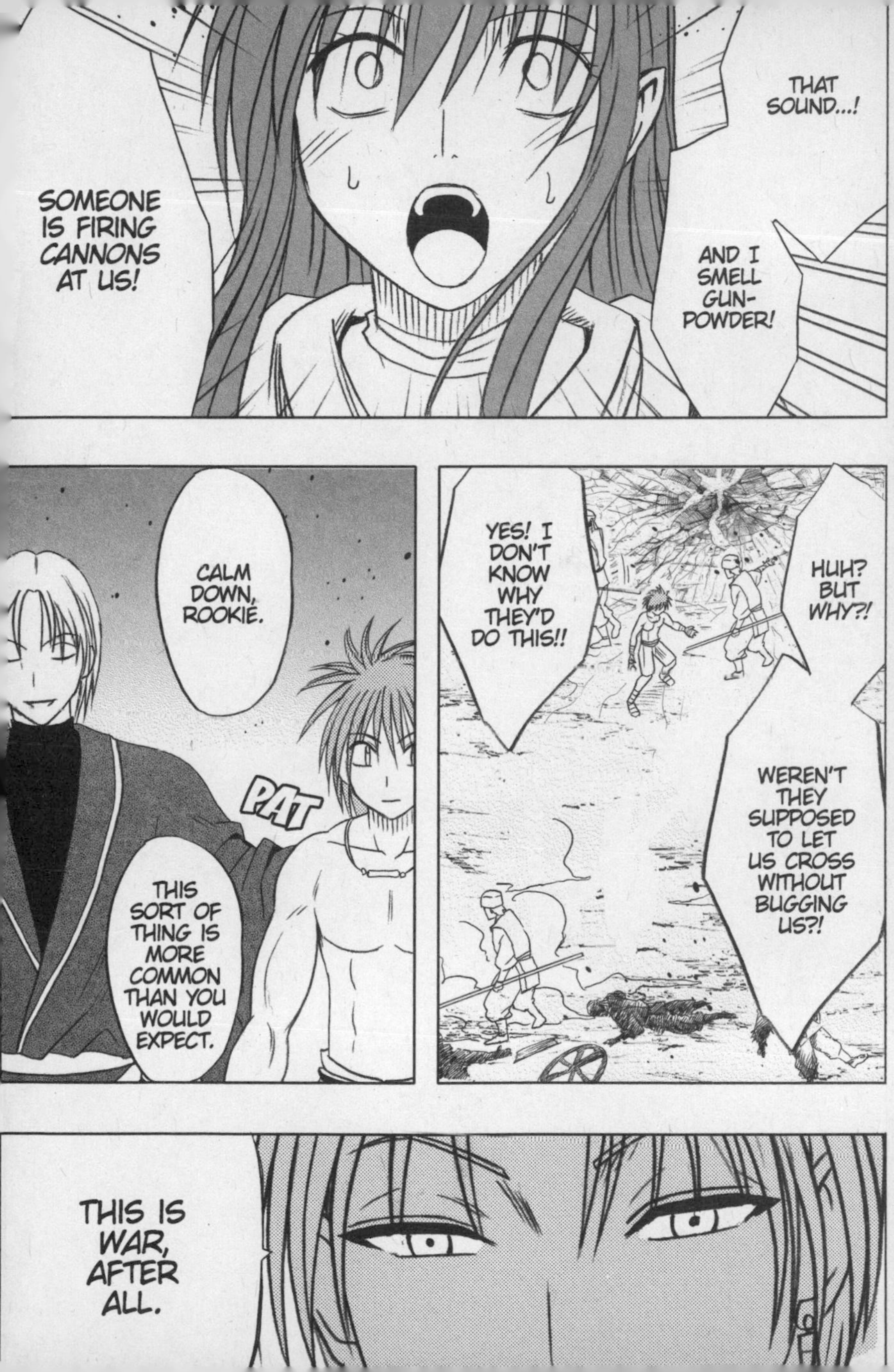
THAT SOUND...!
AND I SMELL GUN-POWDER!
SOMEONE IS FIRING CANNONS AT US!
HUH? BUT WHY?!
WEREN'T THEY SUPPOSED TO LET US CROSS WITHOUT BUGGING US?!
YES! I DON'T KNOW WHY THEY'D DO THIS!!
CALM DOWN, ROOKIE.
PAT
THIS SORT OF THING IS MORE COMMON THAN YOU WOULD EXPECT.
THIS IS WAR, AFTER ALL.

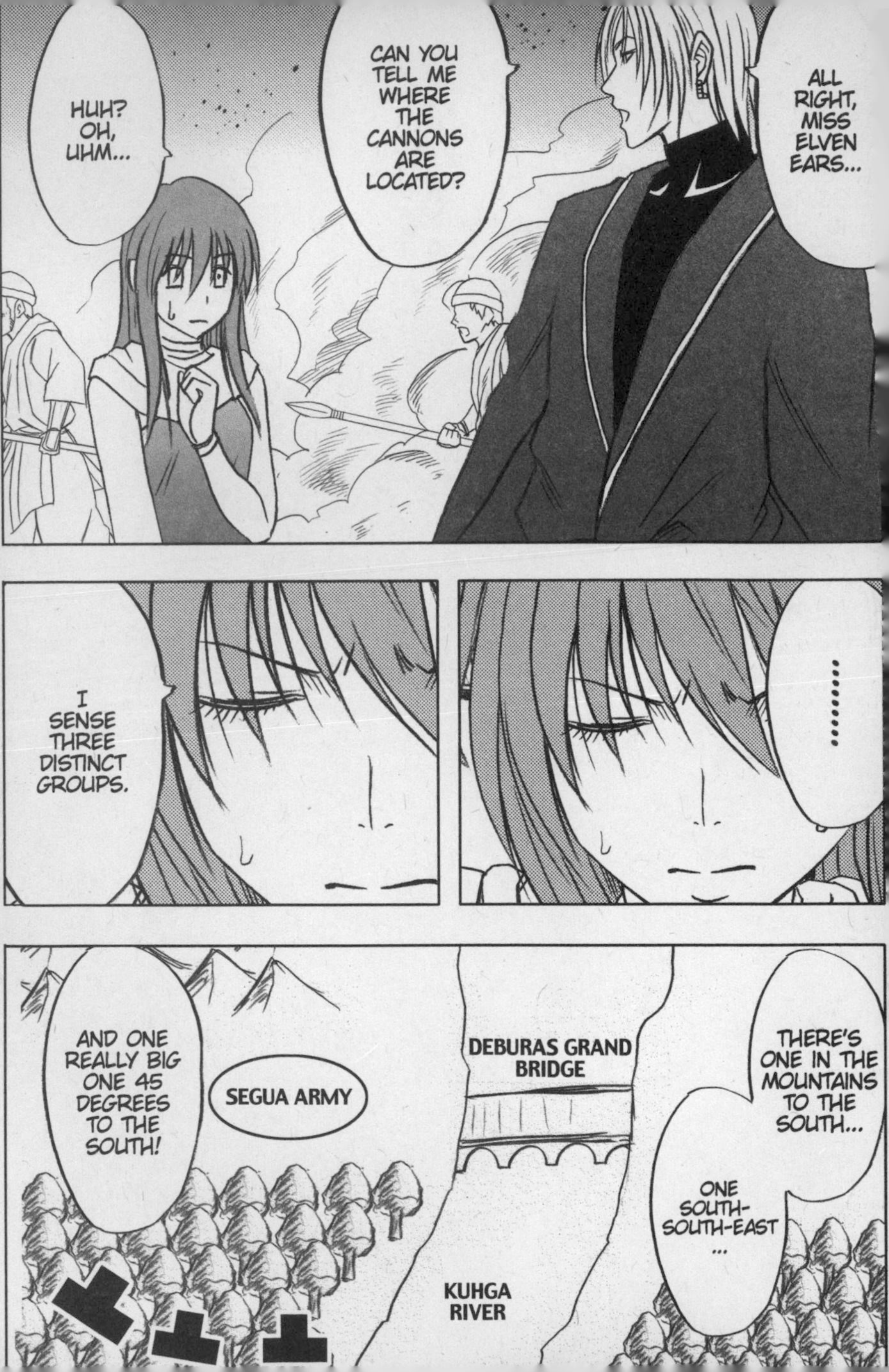
ALL RIGHT, MISS ELVEN EARS...
CAN YOU TELL ME WHERE THE CANNONS ARE LOCATED?
HUH? OH, UHM...
......
I SENSE THREE DISTINCT GROUPS.
THERE'S ONE IN THE MOUNTAINS TO THE SOUTH...
ONE SOUTH-SOUTH-EAST ...
DEBURAS GRAND BRIDGE
KUHGA RIVER
SEGUA ARMY
AND ONE REALLY BIG ONE 45 DEGREES TO THE SOUTH!

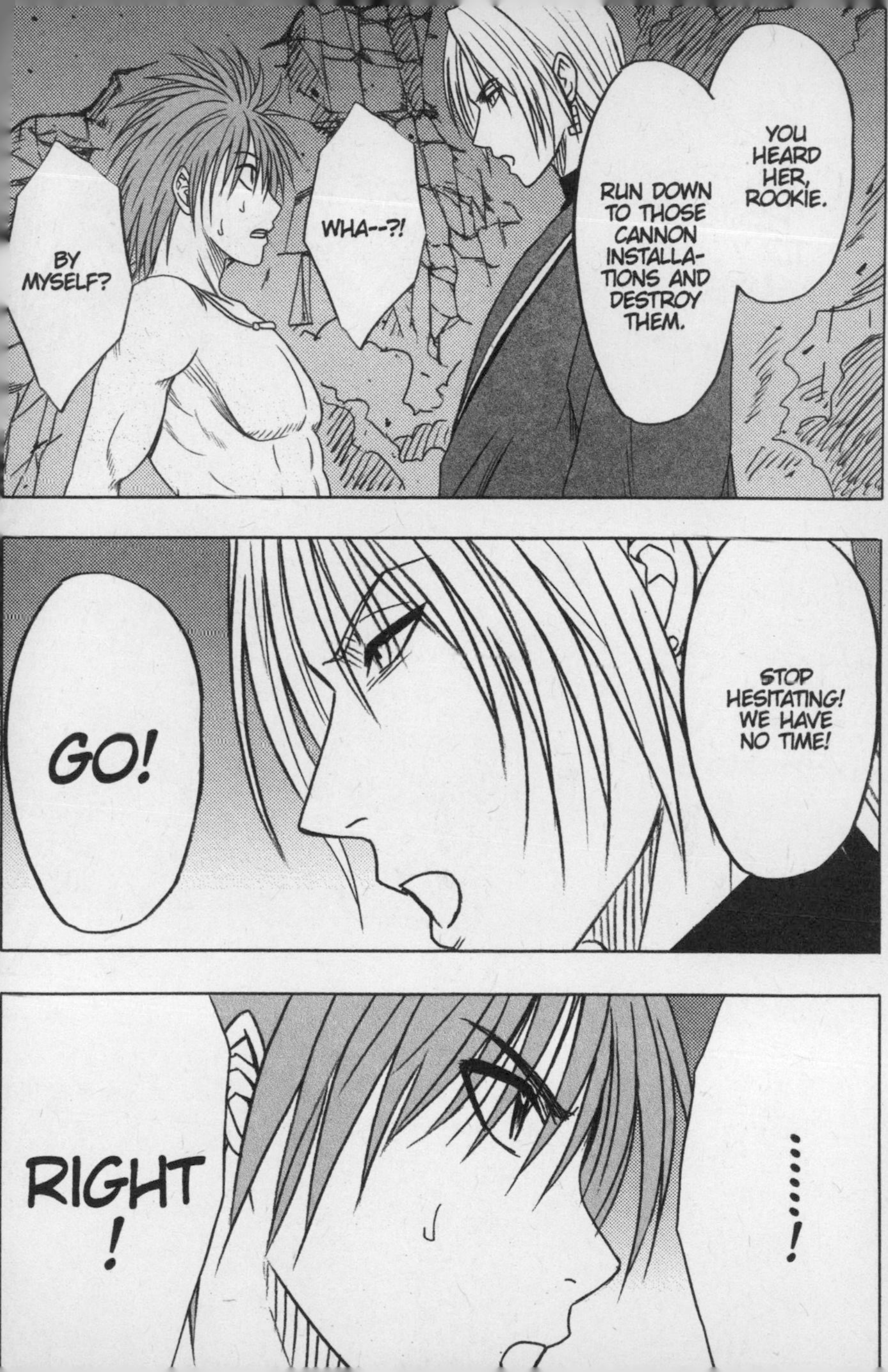
YOU HEARD HER, ROOKIE.
RUN DOWN TO THOSE CANNON INSTALLATIONS AND DESTROY THEM.
WHA--?!
BY MYSELF?
STOP HESITATING! WE HAVE NO TIME!
GO!
......!
RIGHT!

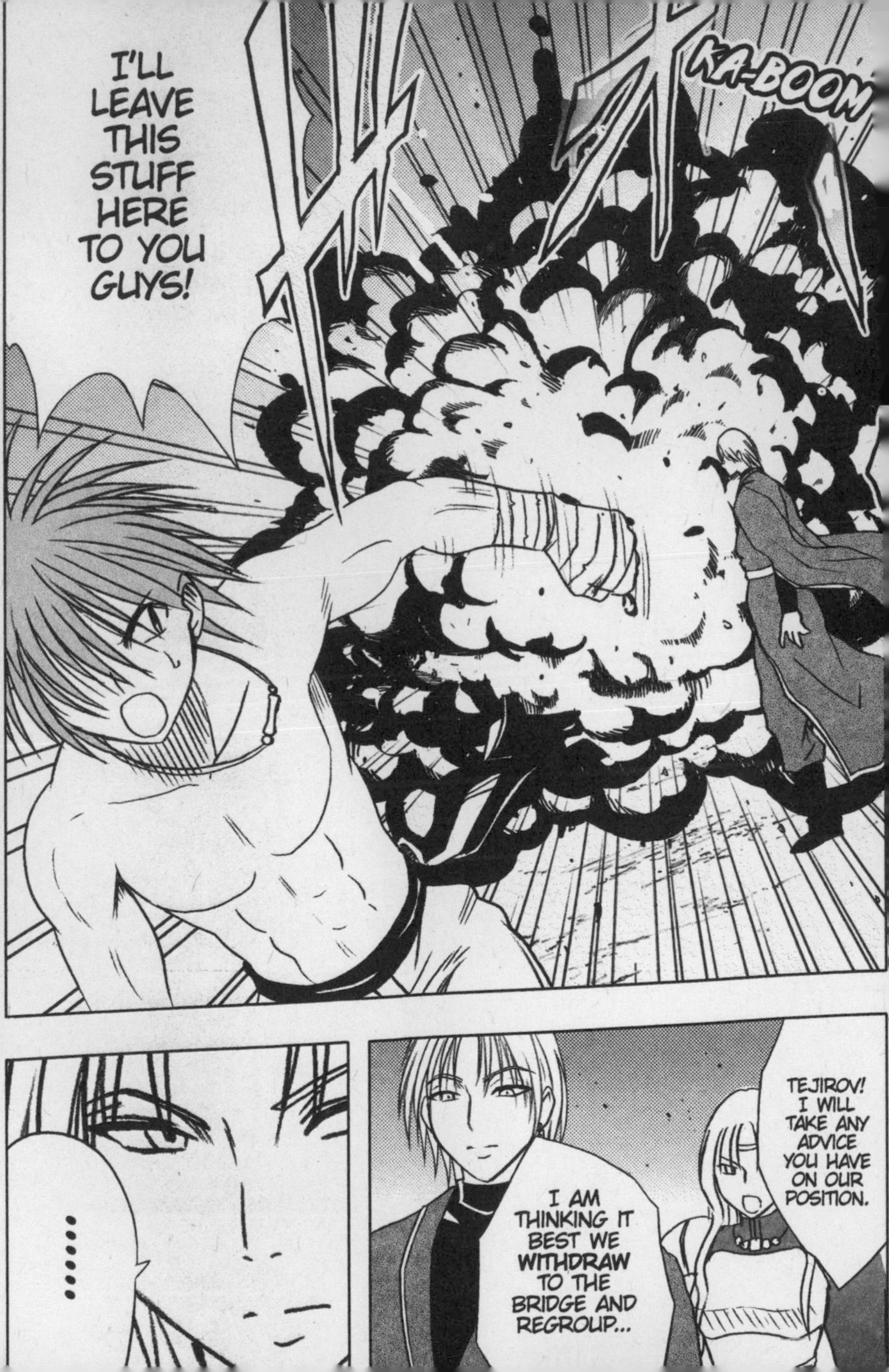
KA-BOOM
I'LL LEAVE THIS STUFF HERE TO YOU GUYS!
TEJIROV! I WILL TAKE ANY ADVICE YOU HAVE ON OUR POSITION.
I AM THINKING IT BEST WE WITHDRAW TO THE BRIDGE AND REGROUP...
......

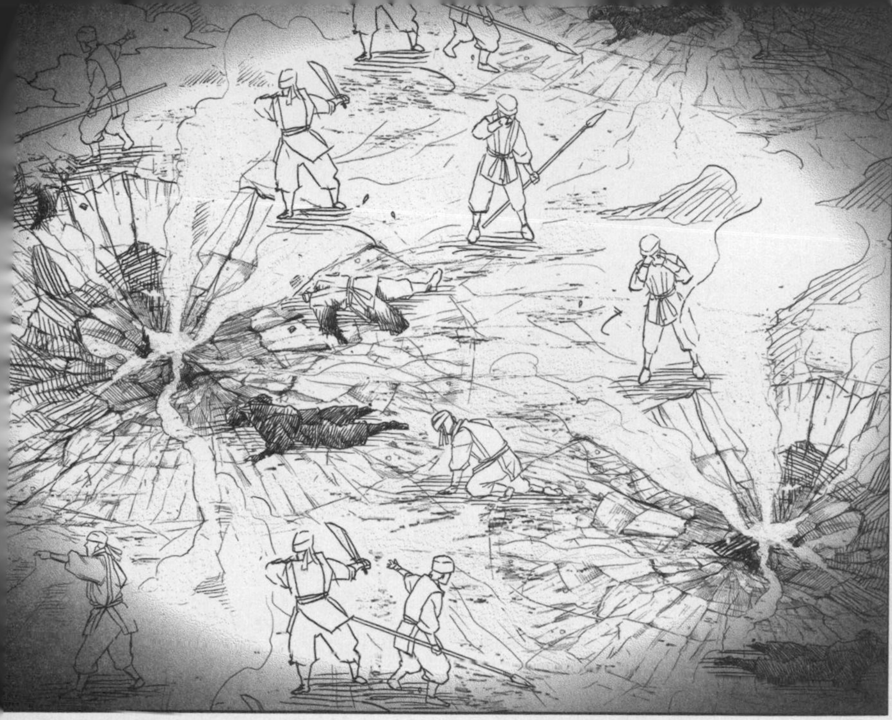

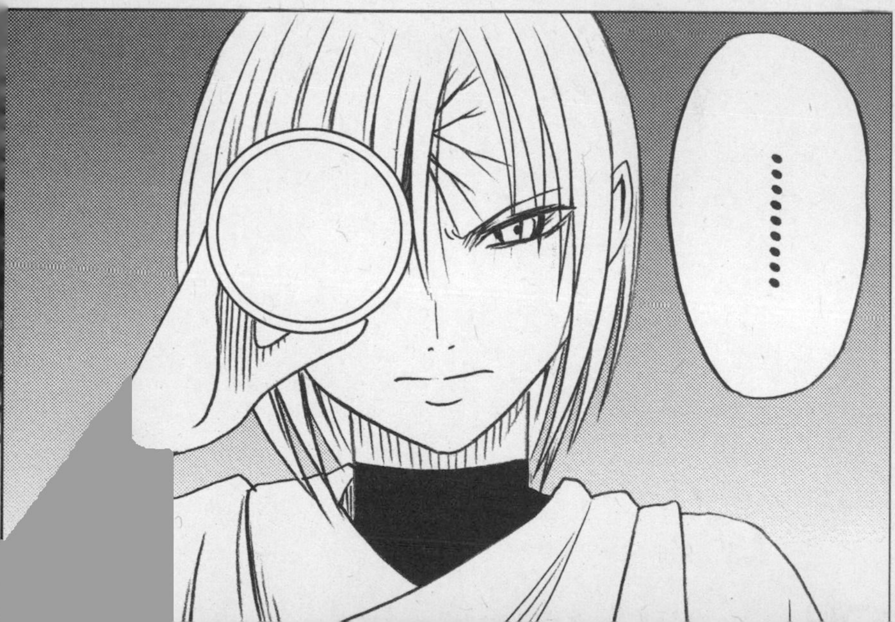
……..

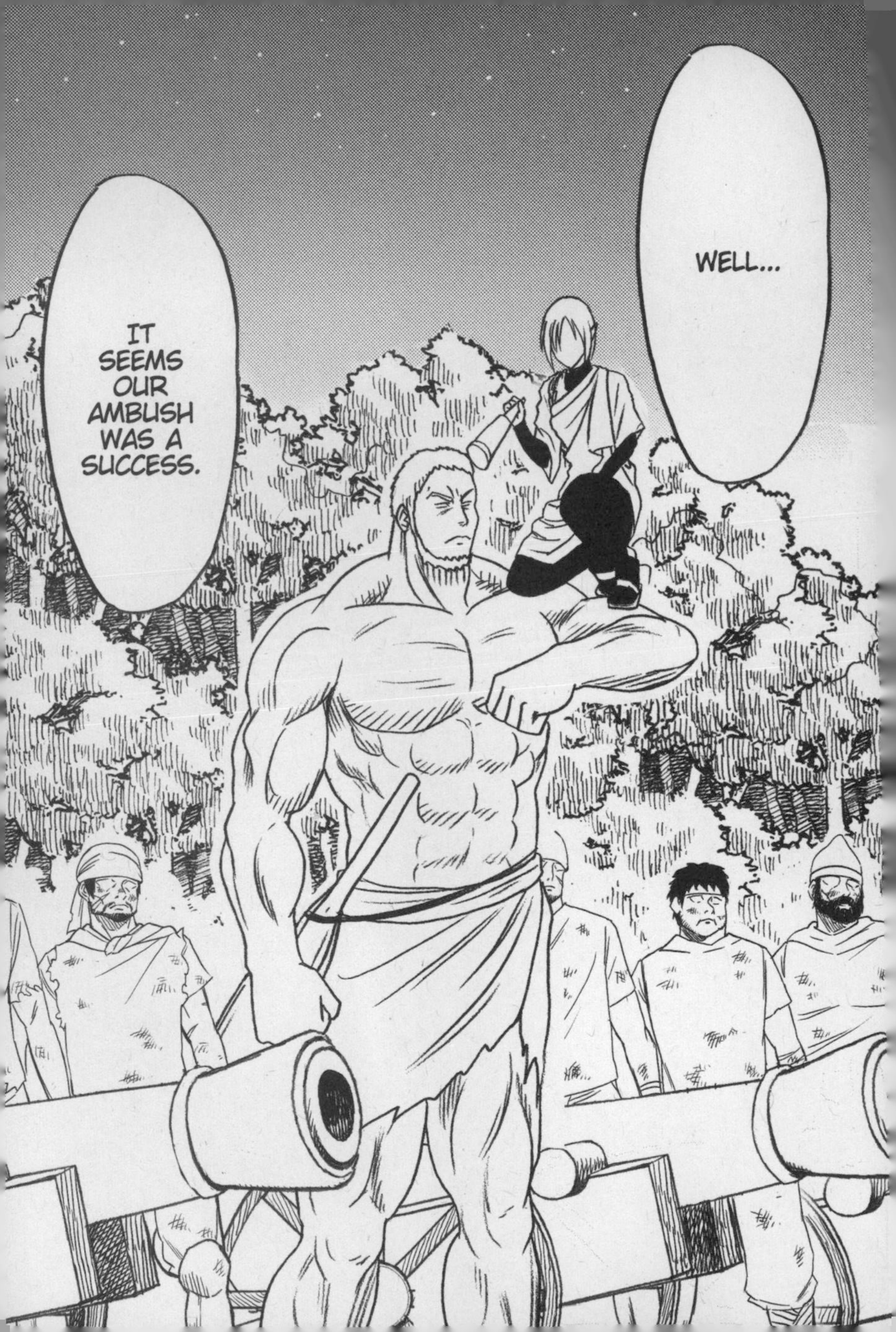
WELL...
IT SEEMS OUR AMBUSH WAS A SUCCESS.

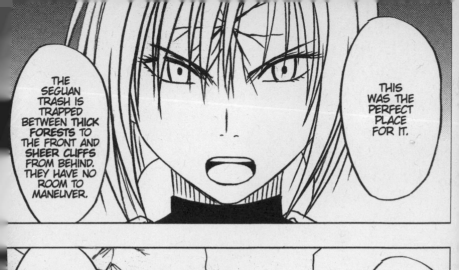

THIS WAS THE PERFECT PLACE FOR IT.
THE SEGUAN TRASH IS TRAPPED BETWEEN THICK FORESTS TO THE FRONT AND SHEER CLIFFS FROM BEHIND. THEY HAVE NO ROOM TO MANEUVER.
AND WHEN SUDDENLY ATTACKED AFTER A LONG DAY OF MARCHING...
DEBURAS GRAND BRIDGE
SEGUA ARMY
KUHGA RIVER
A COMMANDER'S FIRST INSTINCT IS TO PULL BACK ALONG THE ROAD THEY JUST TRAVELLED, THINKING IT "SAFE."
BUT WHEN THEY DO, THEY WILL RUN STRAIGHT INTO BLOX'S MOBILE TANK BATTALION, WHICH HAS MOVED TO CUT OFF THE BRIDGE.
DEBURAS GRAND BRIDGE
KUHGA RIVER
ASSAULTED FROM THE FRONT, WITH THEIR ESCAPE TO THE REAR BLOCKED, THE SEGUAN ARMY WILL CLUMP TOGETHER WHERE OUR CANNONS CAN CUT THEM TO PIECES!

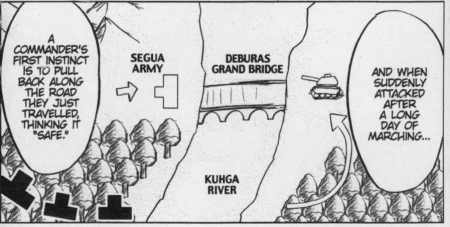

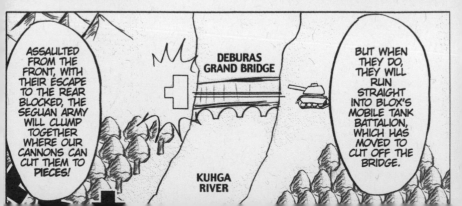

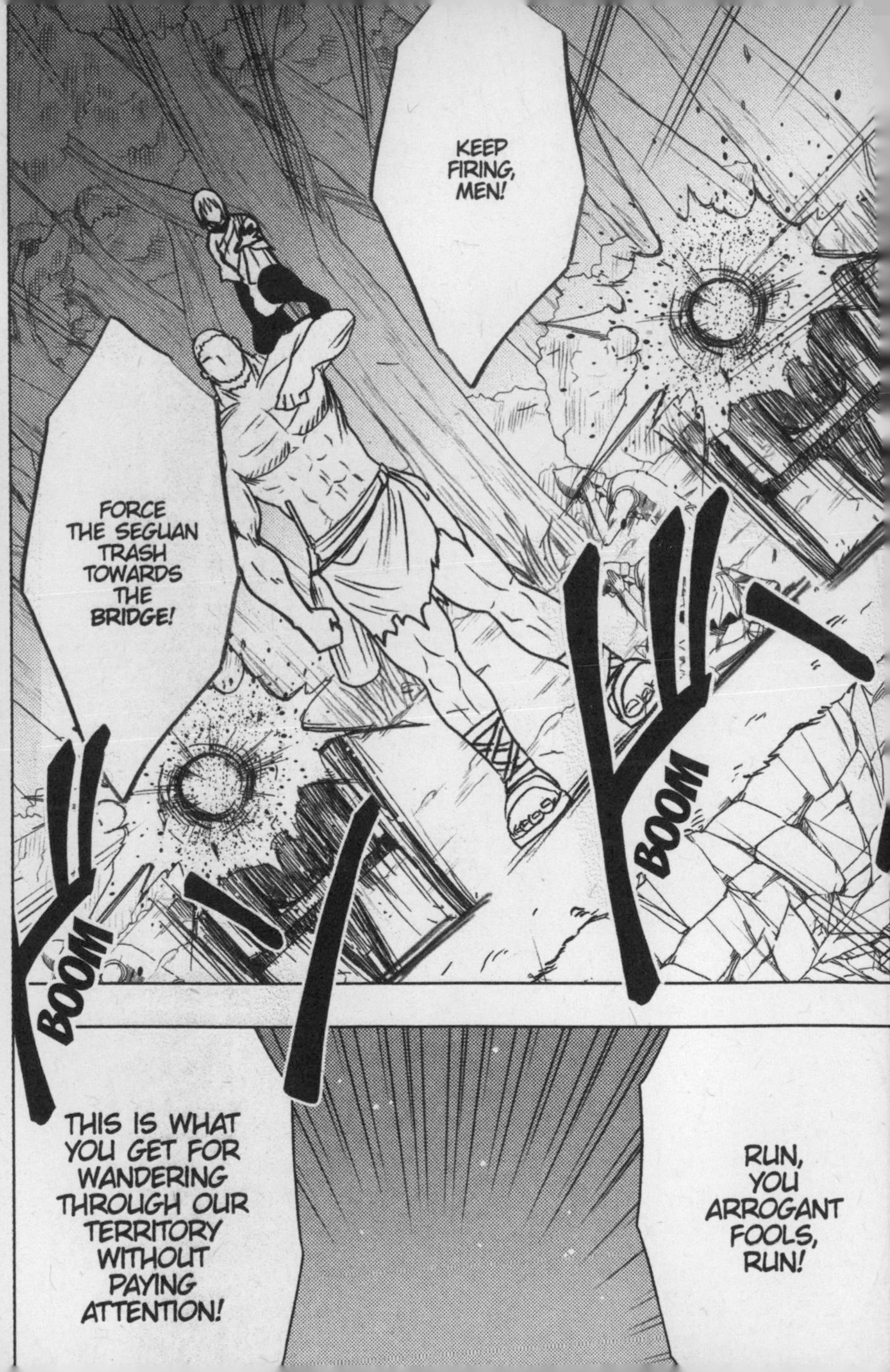
KEEP FIRING, MEN!
FORCE THE SEGUAN TRASH TOWARDS THE BRIDGE!
BOOM
BOOM
RUN, YOU ARROGANT FOOLS, RUN!
THIS IS WHAT YOU GET FOR WANDERING THROUGH OUR TERRITORY WITHOUT PAYING ATTENTION!

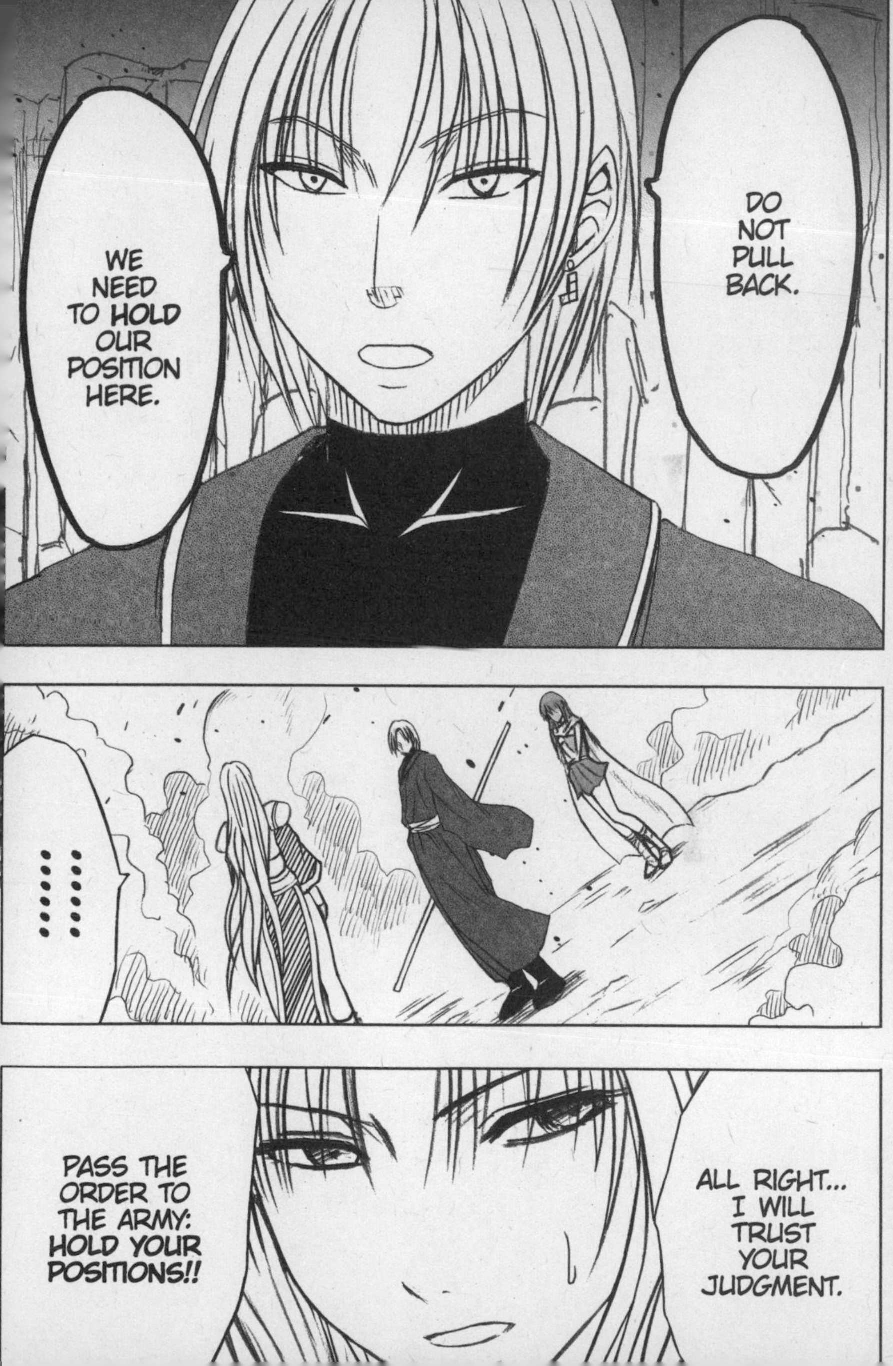
DO NOT PULL BACK.
WE NEED TO HOLD OUR POSITION HERE.
......
ALL RIGHT... I WILL TRUST YOUR JUDGMENT.
PASS THE ORDER TO THE ARMY: HOLD YOUR POSITIONS!!

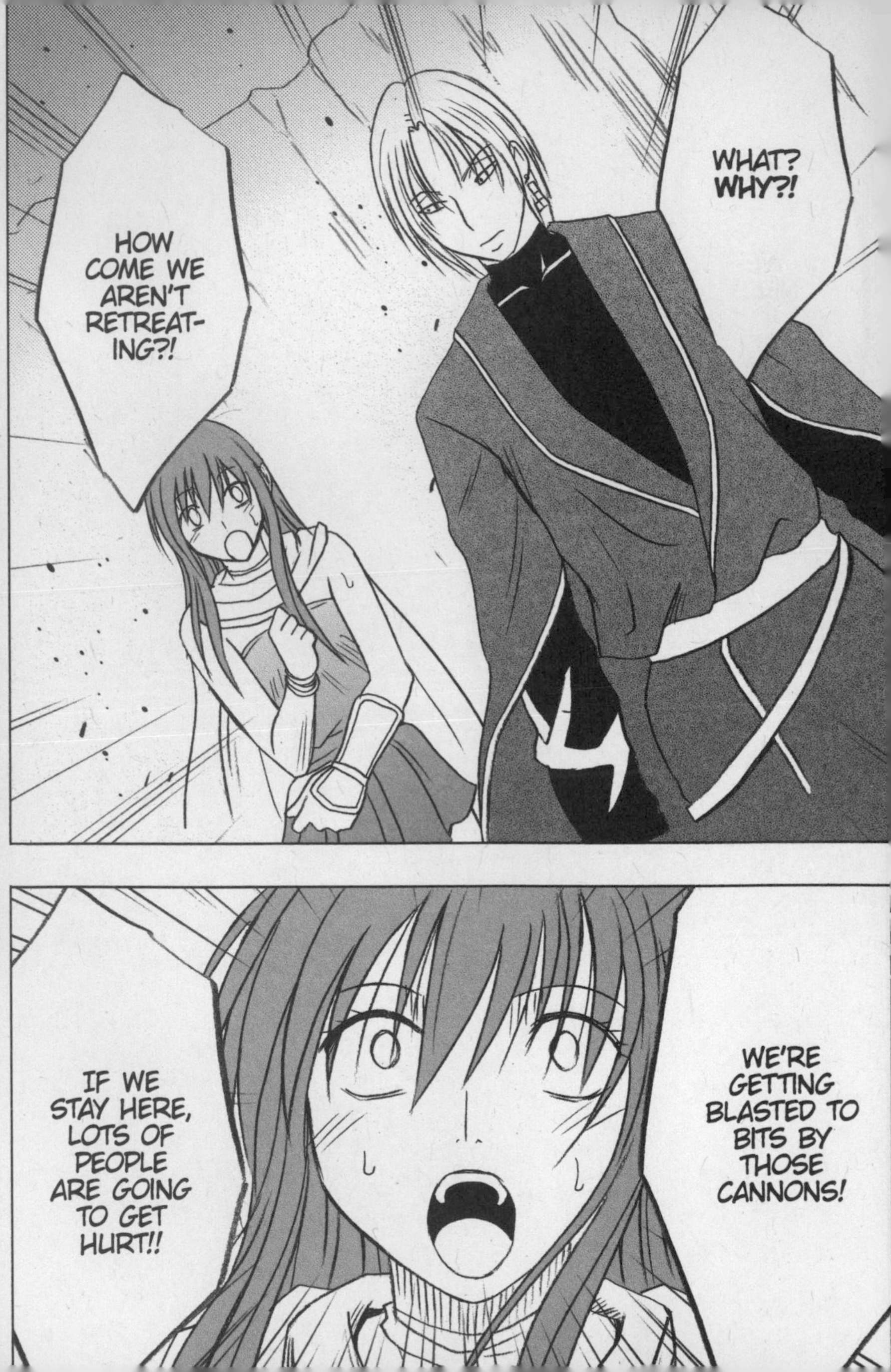
WHAT? WHY?!
HOW COME WE AREN'T RETREATING?!
WE'RE GETTING BLASTED TO BITS BY THOSE CANNONS!
IF WE STAY HERE, LOTS OF PEOPLE ARE GOING TO GET HURT!!

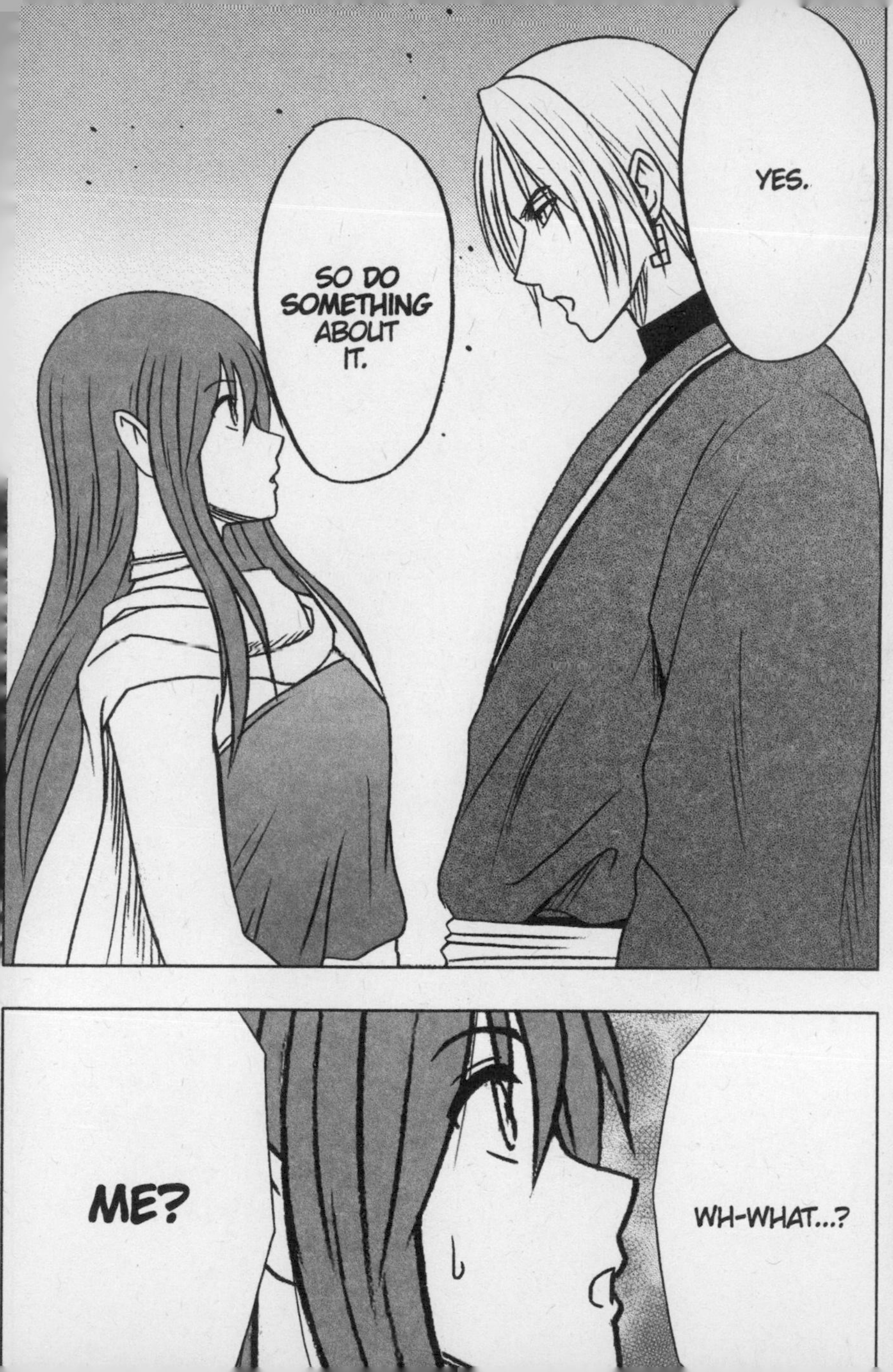
YES.
SO DO SOMETHING ABOUT IT.
WH-WHAT...?
ME?

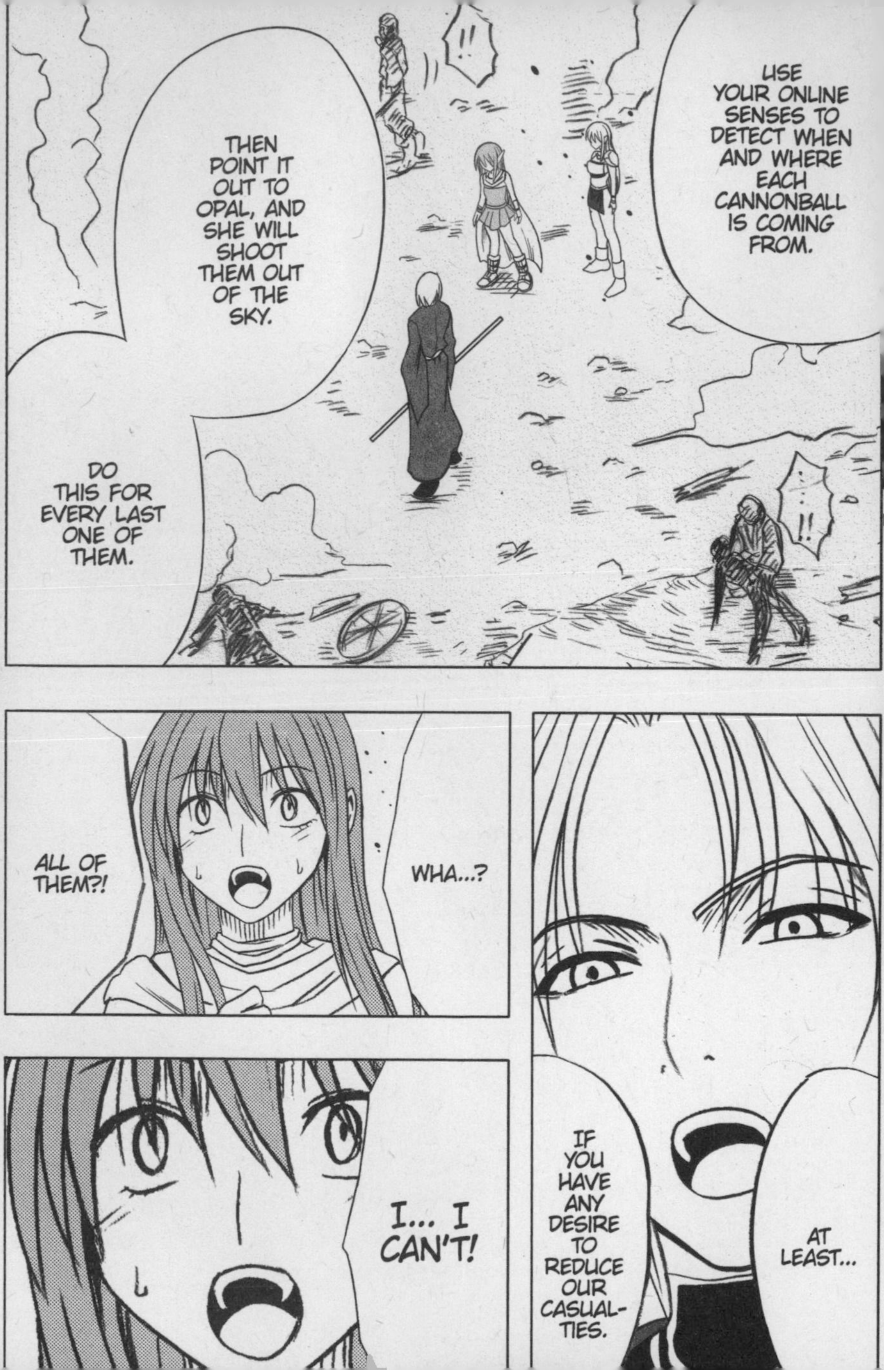
!!
USE YOUR ONLINE SENSES TO DETECT WHEN AND WHERE EACH CANNONBALL IS COMING FROM.
THEN POINT IT OUT TO OPAL, AND SHE WILL SHOOT THEM OUT OF THE SKY.
DO THIS FOR EVERY LAST ONE OF THEM.
...!!
AT LEAST...
IF YOU HAVE ANY DESIRE TO REDUCE OUR CASUAL-TIES.
WHA...?
ALL OF THEM?!
I... I CAN'T!

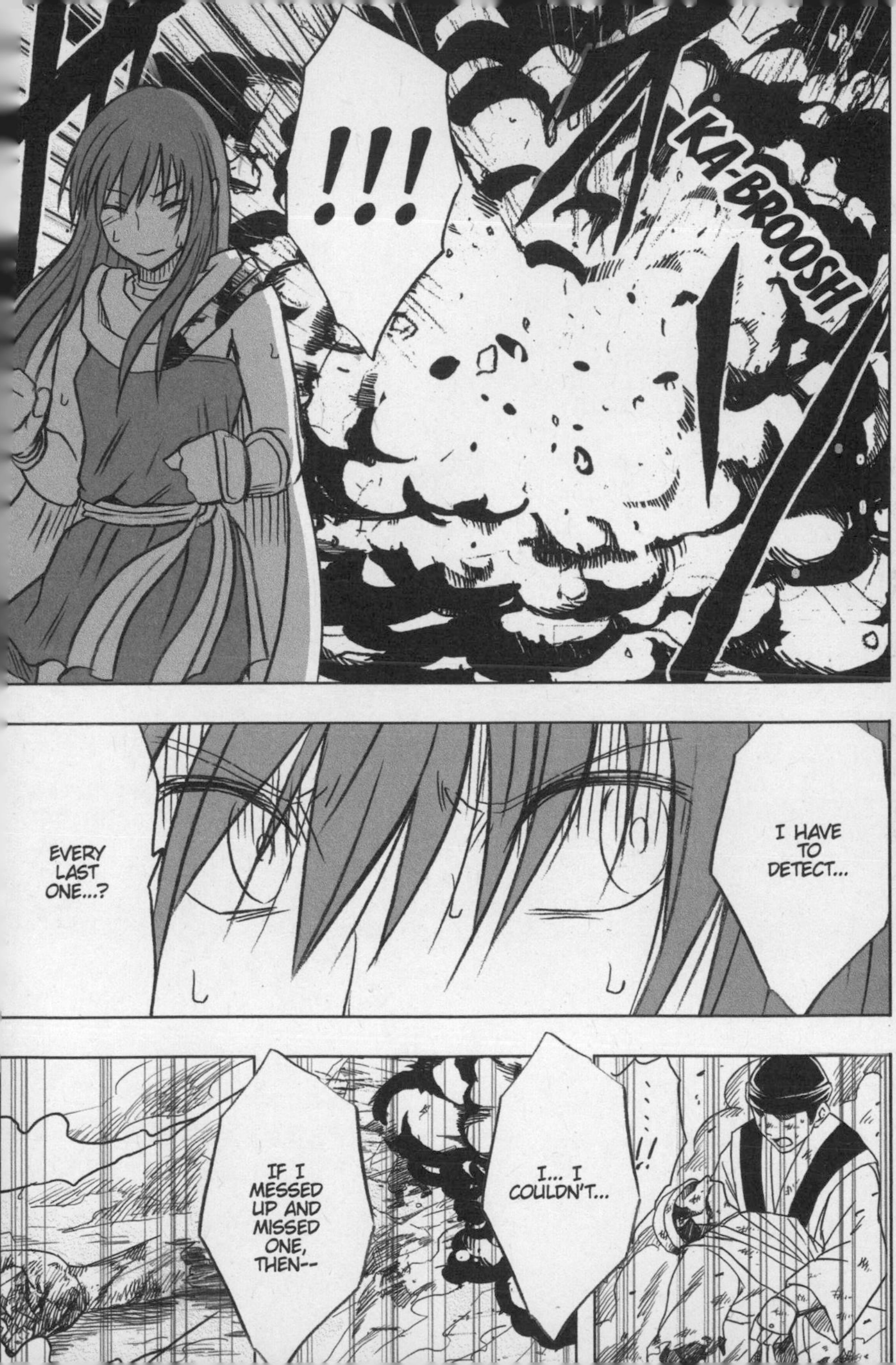
KA-BROOSH
!!!
I HAVE TO DETECT...
EVERY LAST ONE...?
!!
I... I COULDN'T...
IF I MESSED UP AND MISSED ONE, THEN--

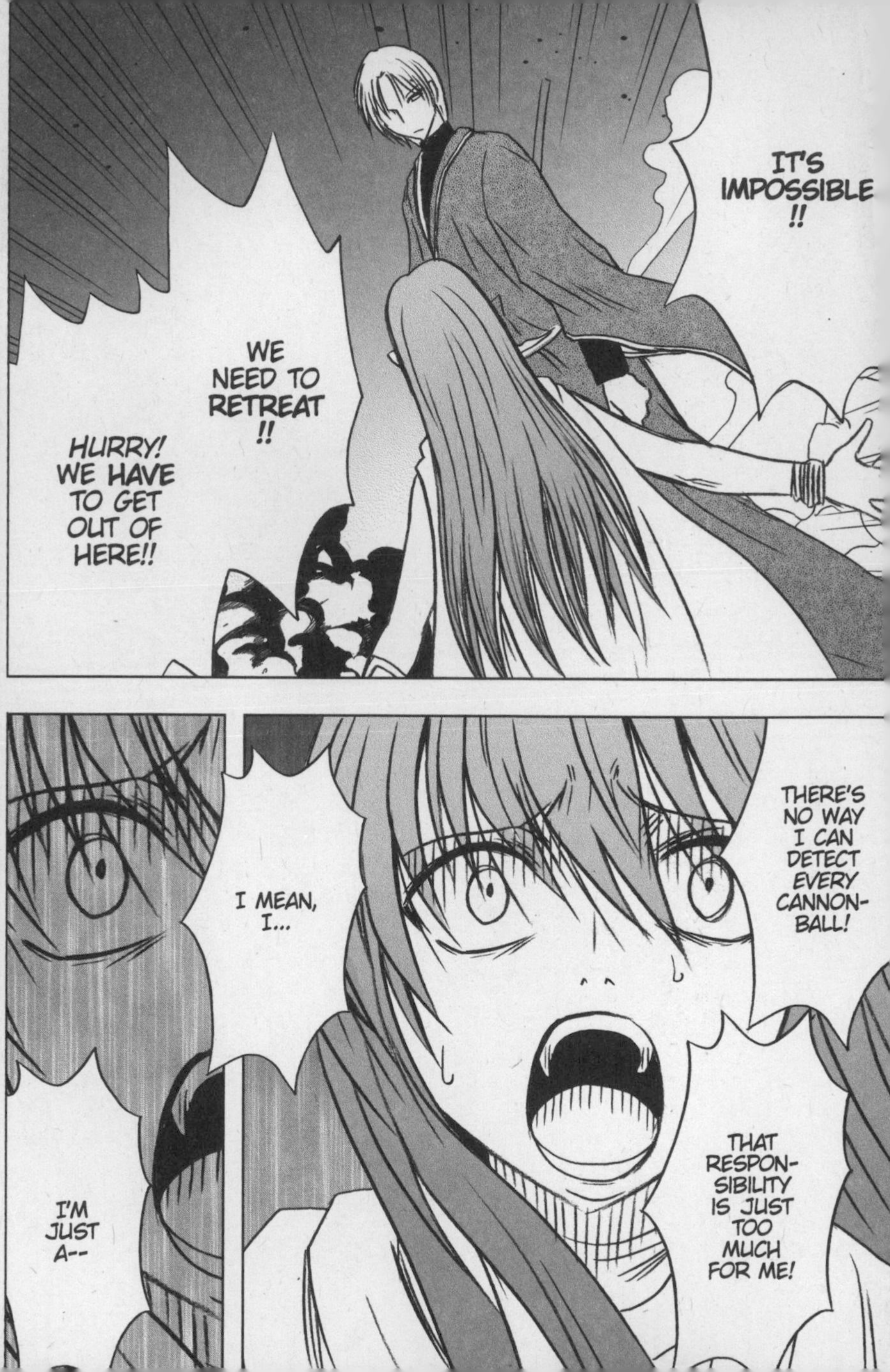
IT'S IMPOSSIBLE!!
WE NEED TO RETREAT!!
HURRY! WE HAVE TO GET OUT OF HERE!!
THERE'S NO WAY I CAN DETECT EVERY CANNON-BALL!
THAT RESPON-SIBILITY IS JUST TOO MUCH FOR ME!
I MEAN, I...
I'M JUST A--

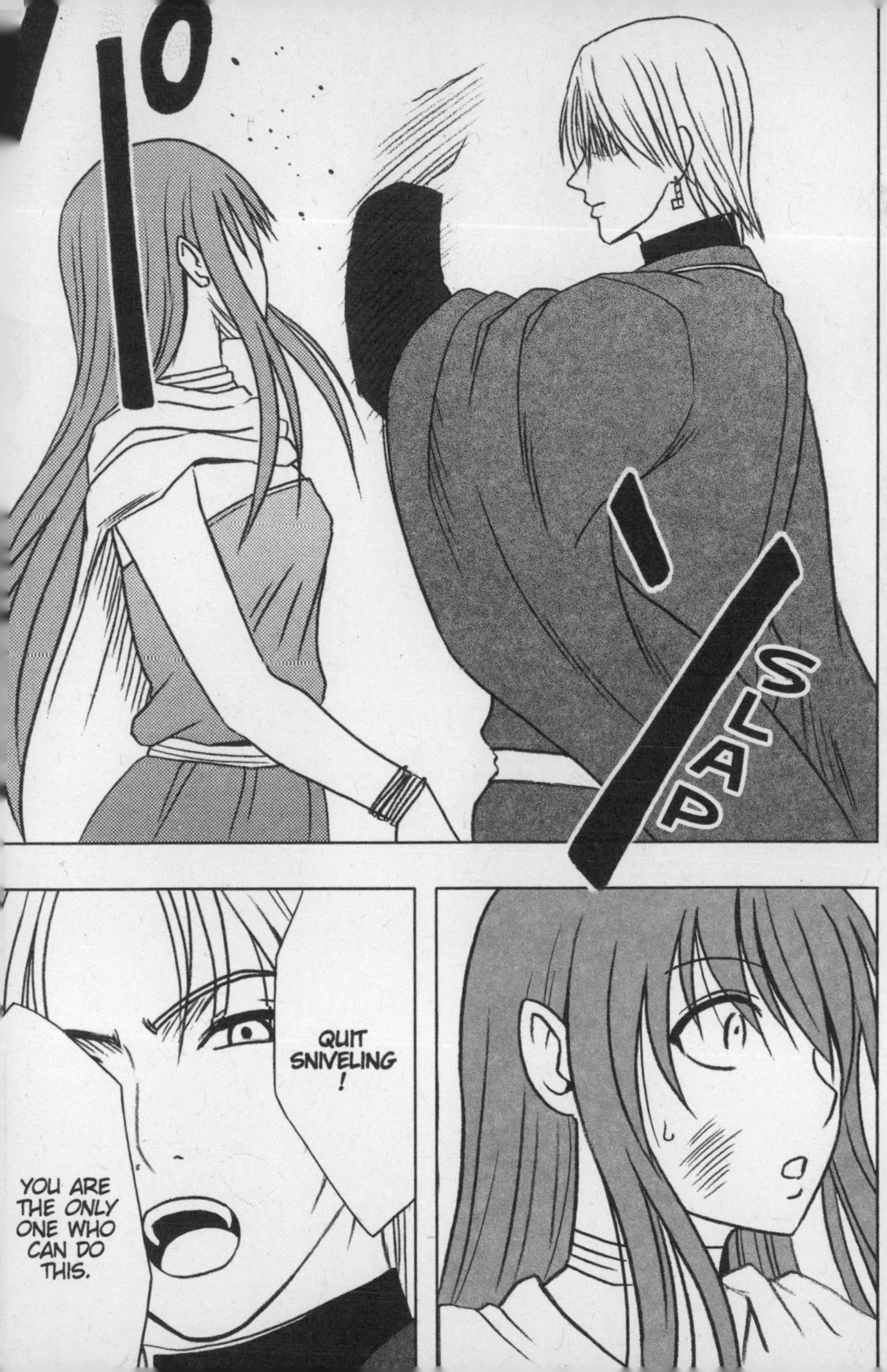
SLAP
QUIT SNIVELING!
YOU ARE THE ONLY ONE WHO CAN DO THIS.

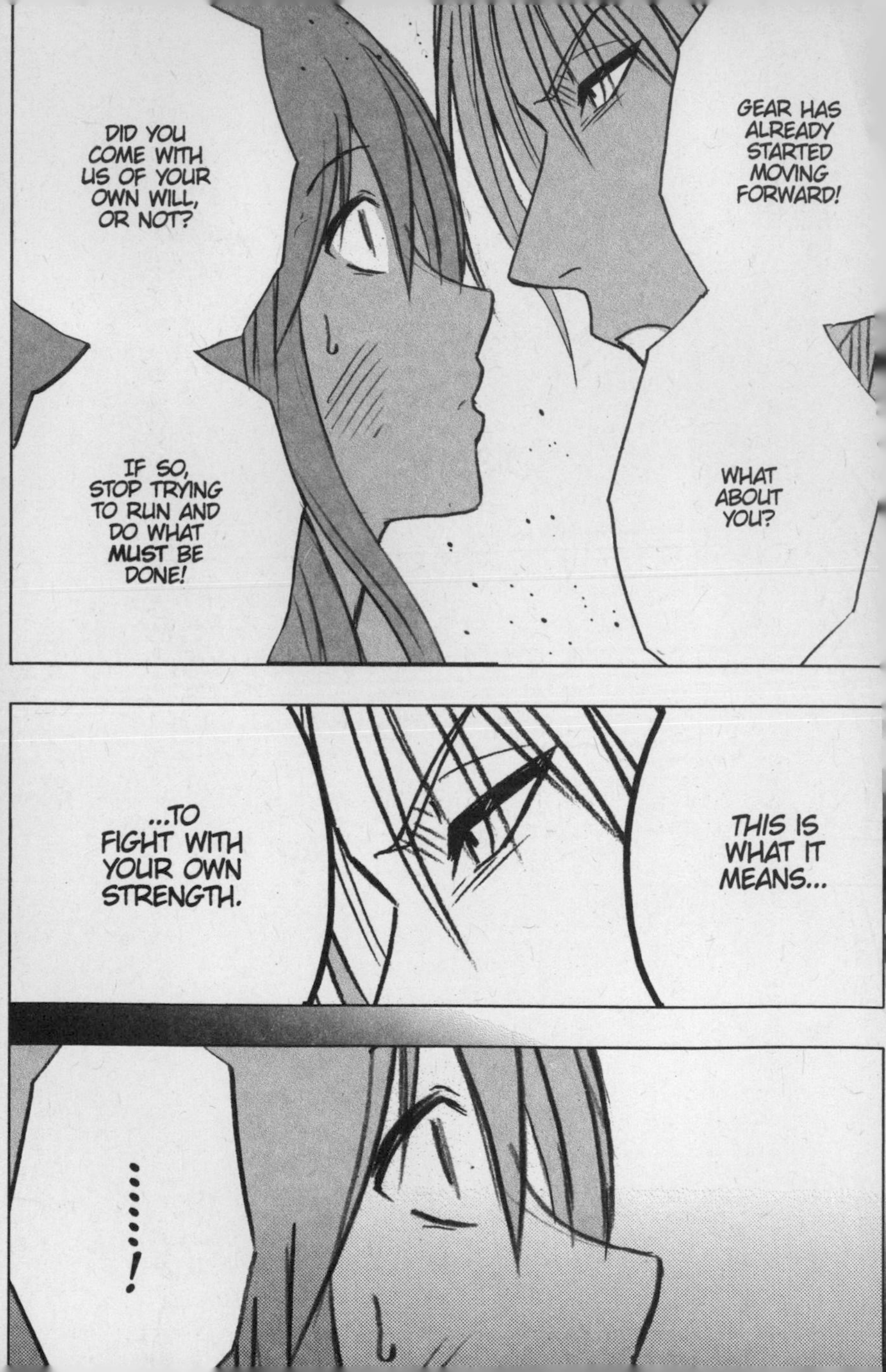
GEAR HAS ALREADY STARTED MOVING FORWARD!
WHAT ABOUT YOU?
DID YOU COME WITH US OF YOUR OWN WILL, OR NOT?
IF SO, STOP TRYING TO RUN AND DO WHAT MUST BE DONE!
THIS IS WHAT IT MEANS...
...TO FIGHT WITH YOUR OWN STRENGTH.
......!

GEAR!

HELP TIAL!!

THAT DAY...

I COULDN'T DO ANYTHING.

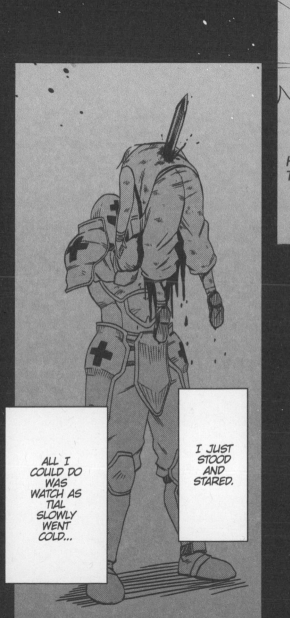

I JUST STOOD AND STARED.

ALL I COULD DO WAS WATCH AS TIAL SLOWLY WENT COLD...

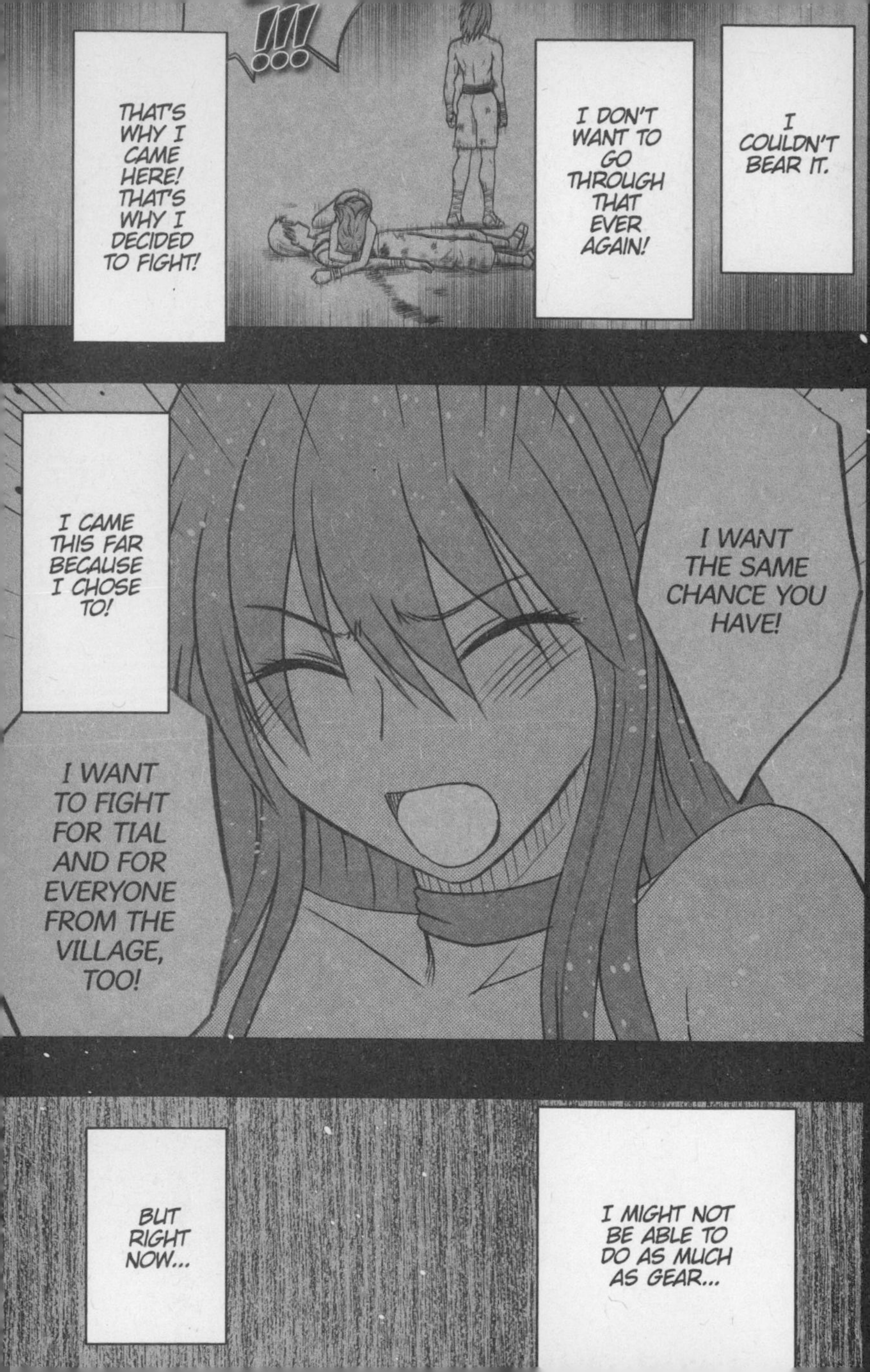
I COULDN'T BEAR IT.
I DON'T WANT TO GO THROUGH THAT EVER AGAIN!
!!!
THAT'S WHY I CAME HERE! THAT'S WHY I DECIDED TO FIGHT!
I WANT THE SAME CHANCE YOU HAVE!
I CAME THIS FAR BECAUSE I CHOSE TO!
I WANT TO FIGHT FOR TIAL AND FOR EVERYONE FROM THE VILLAGE, TOO!
I MIGHT NOT BE ABLE TO DO AS MUCH AS GEAR...
BUT RIGHT NOW...

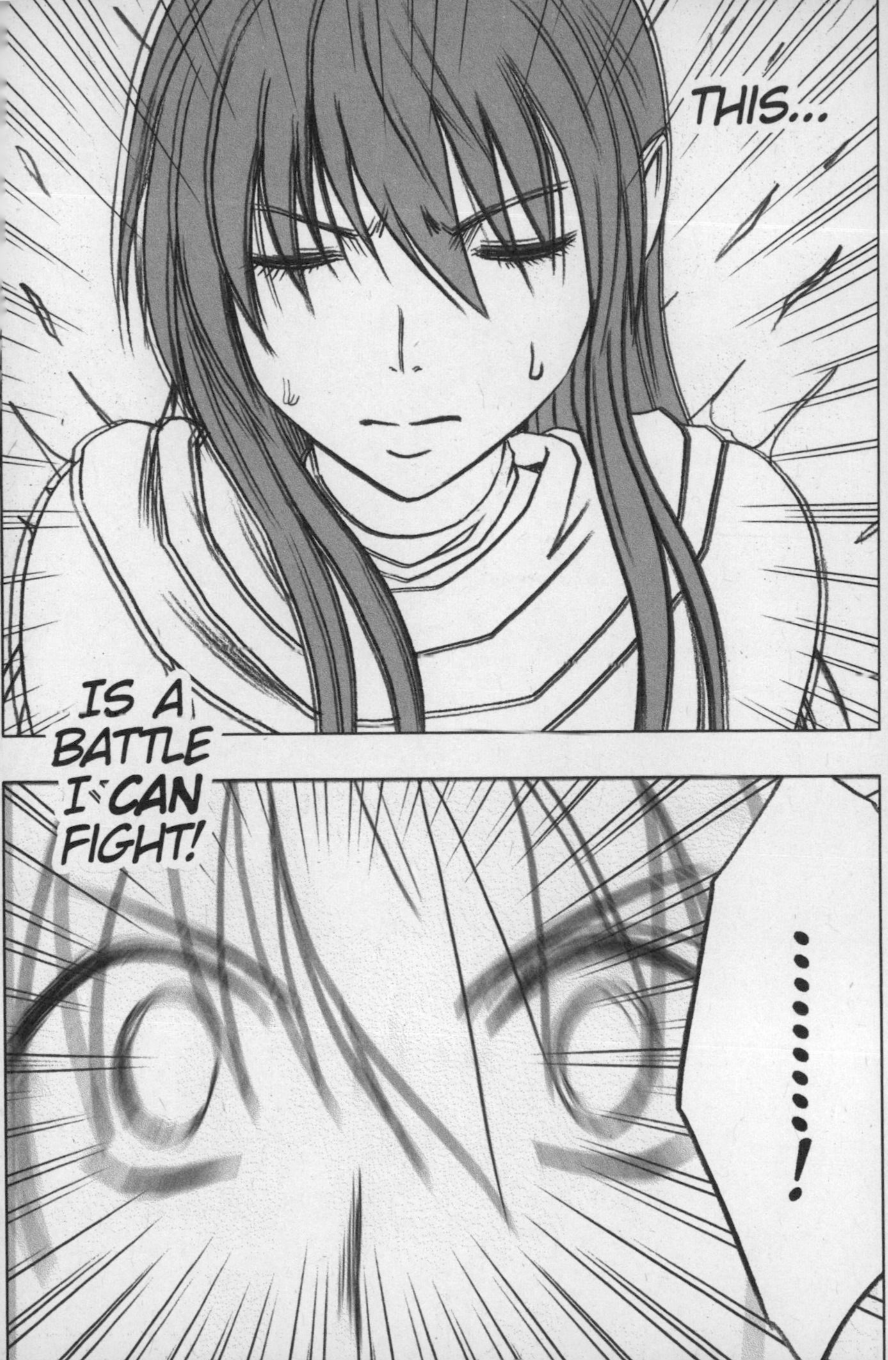
THIS...
IS A BATTLE I CAN FIGHT!
........!

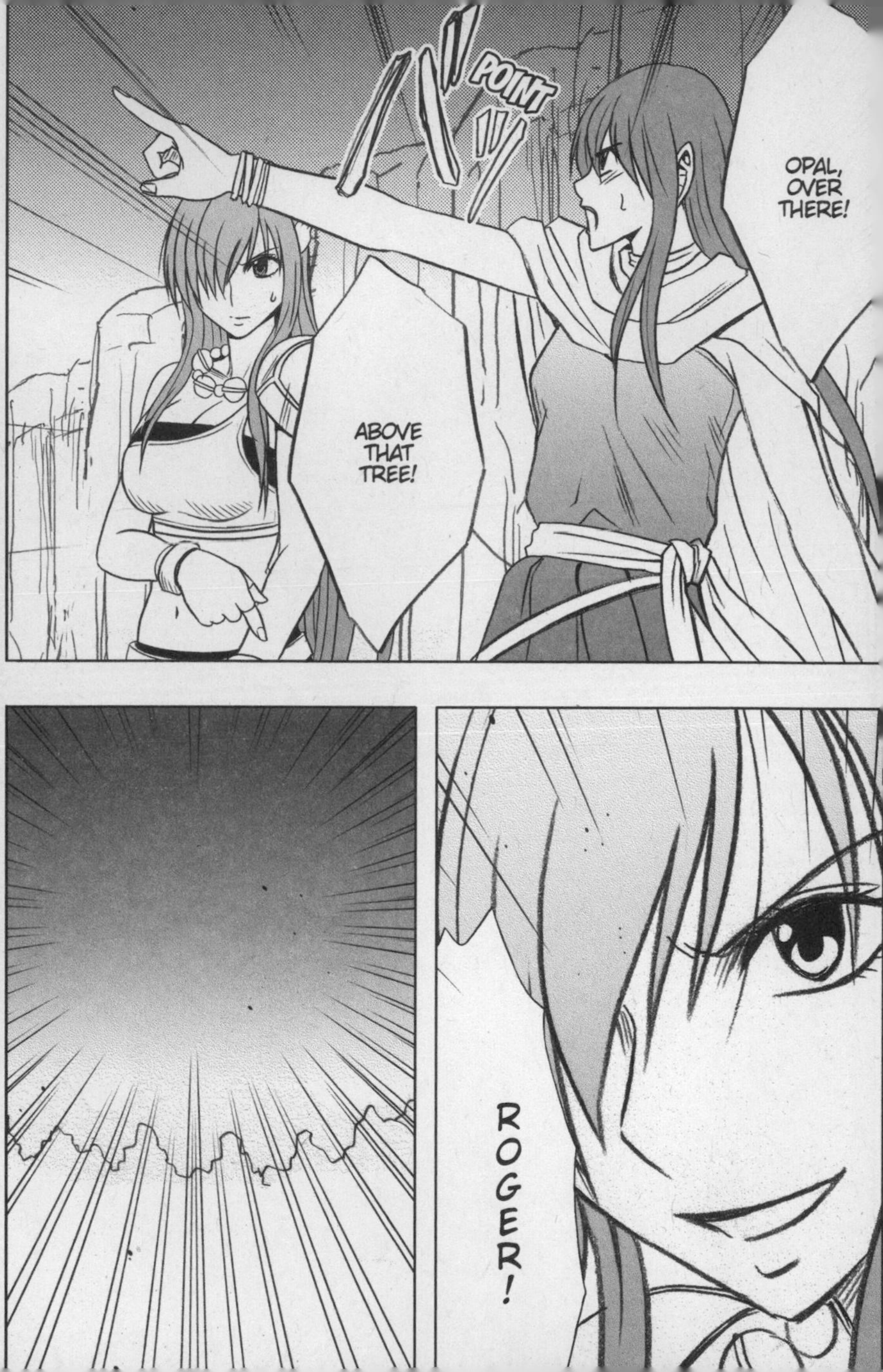
OPAL, OVER THERE!
POINT
ABOVE THAT TREE!
ROGER!

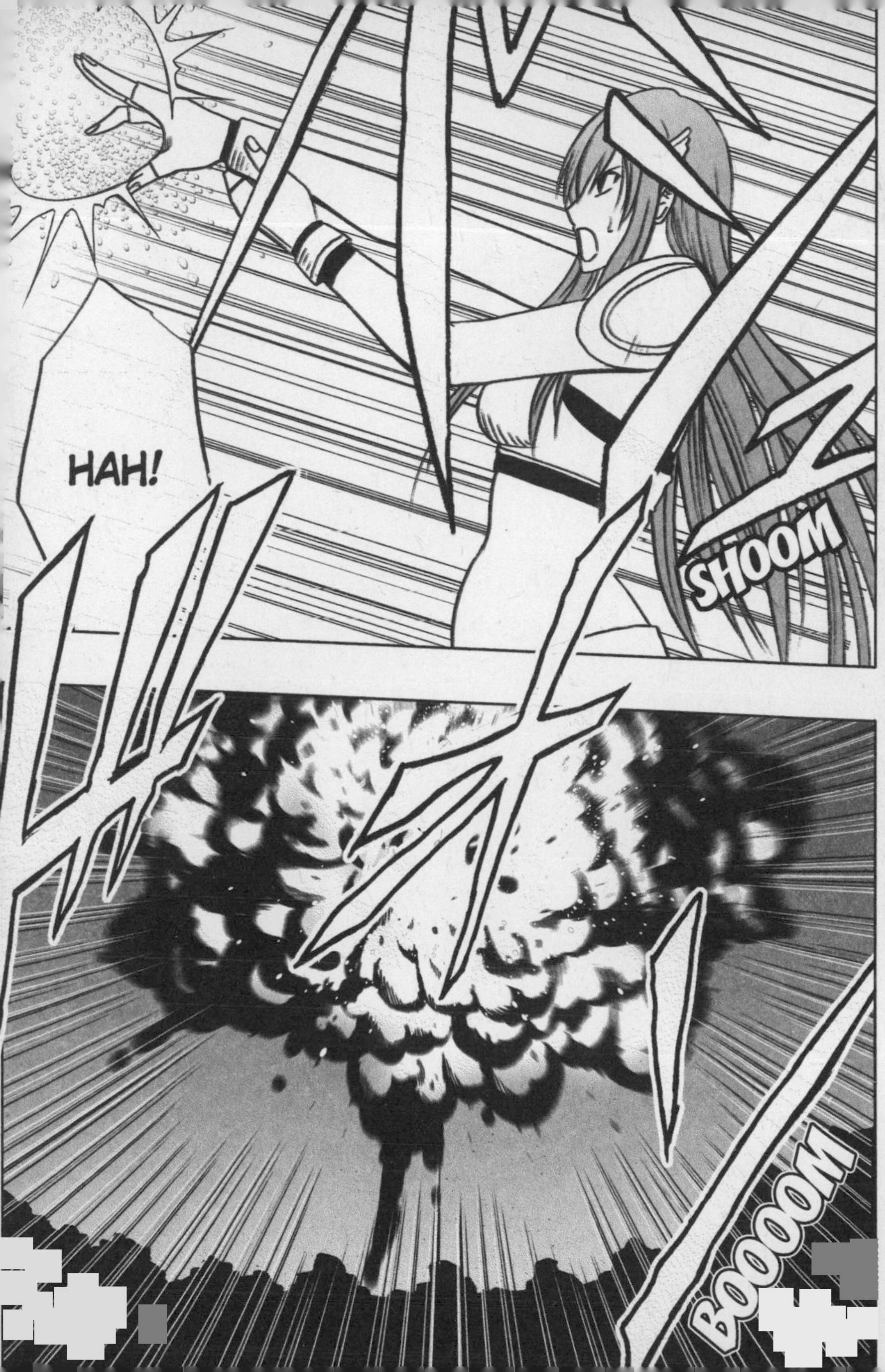
SHOOM
HAH!
BOOOOM

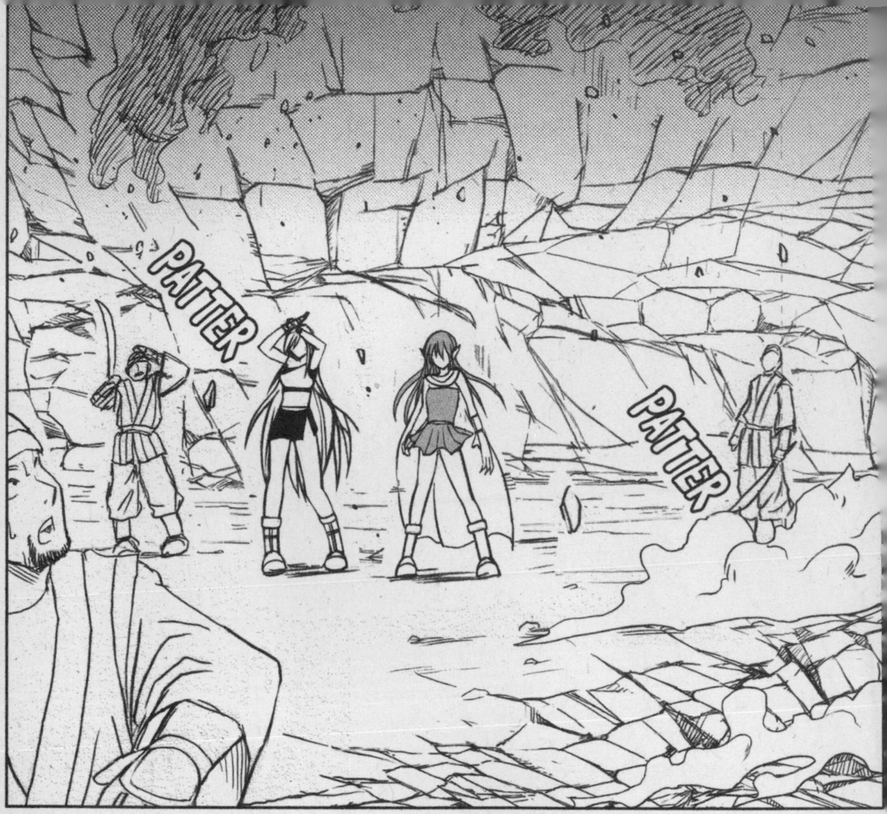
PATTER
PATTER
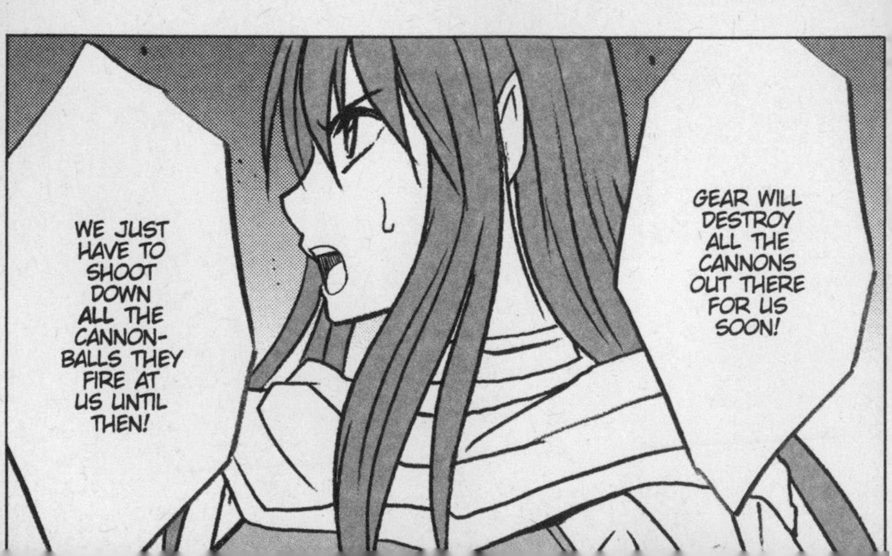
GEAR WILL DESTROY ALL THE CANNONS OUT THERE FOR US SOON!
WE JUST HAVE TO SHOOT DOWN ALL THE CANNON-BALLS THEY FIRE AT US UNTIL THEN!

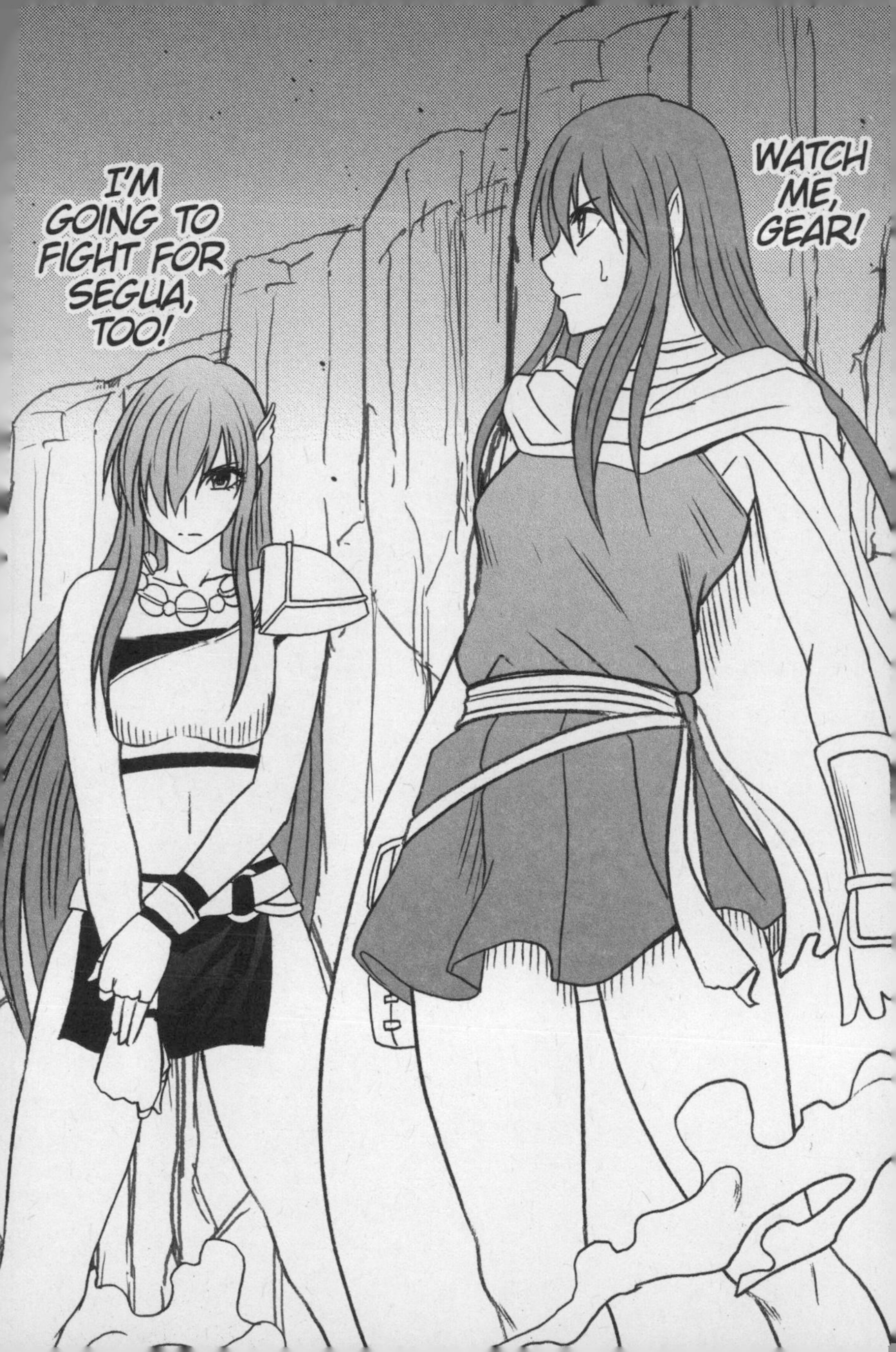
WATCH ME, GEAR!
I'M GOING TO FIGHT FOR SEGUA, TOO!

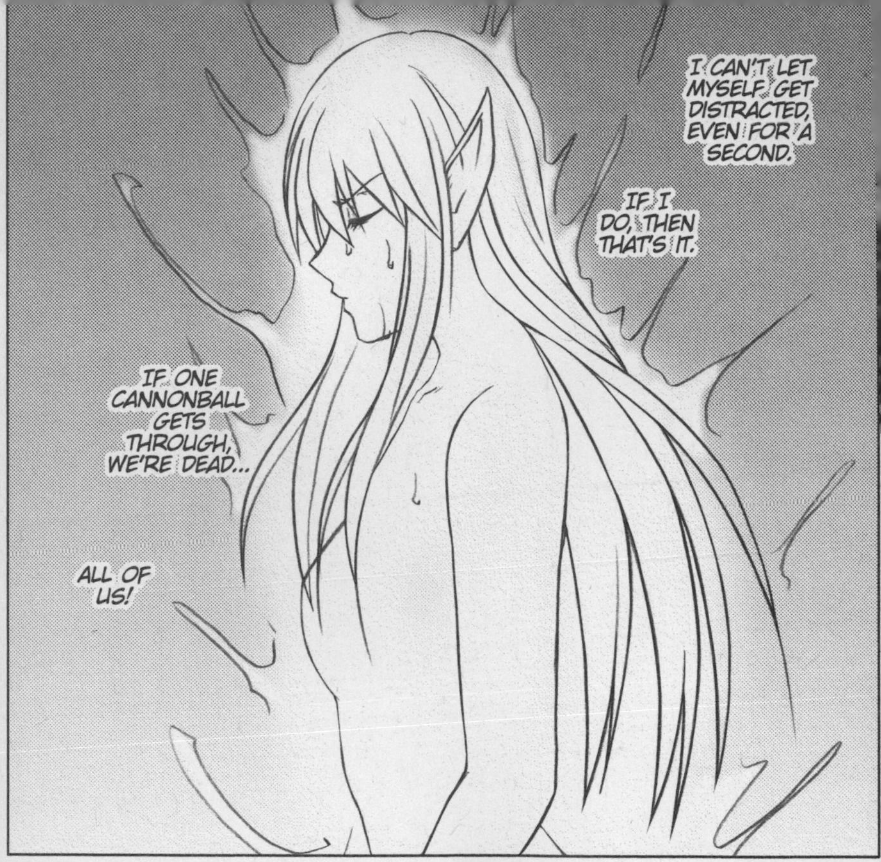
I CAN'T LET MYSELF GET DISTRACTED, EVEN FOR A SECOND.
IF I DO, THEN THAT'S IT.
IF ONE CANNONBALL GETS THROUGH, WE'RE DEAD...
ALL OF US!
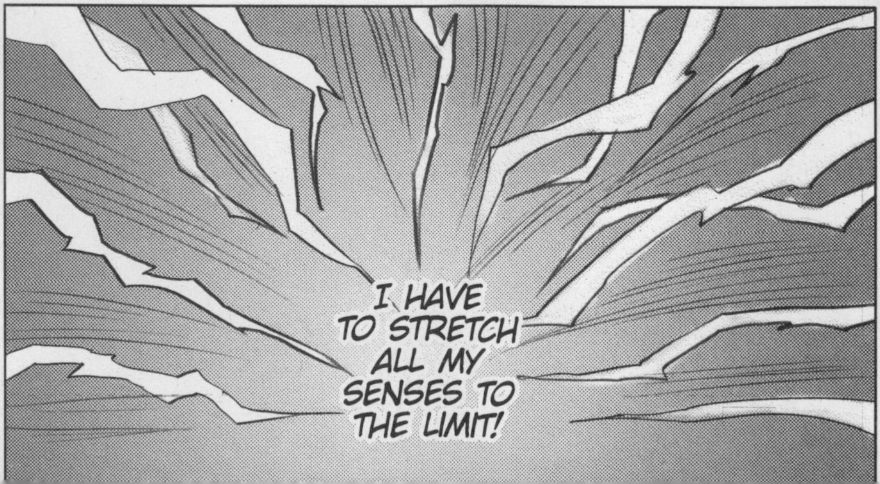
I HAVE TO STRETCH ALL MY SENSES TO THE LIMIT!

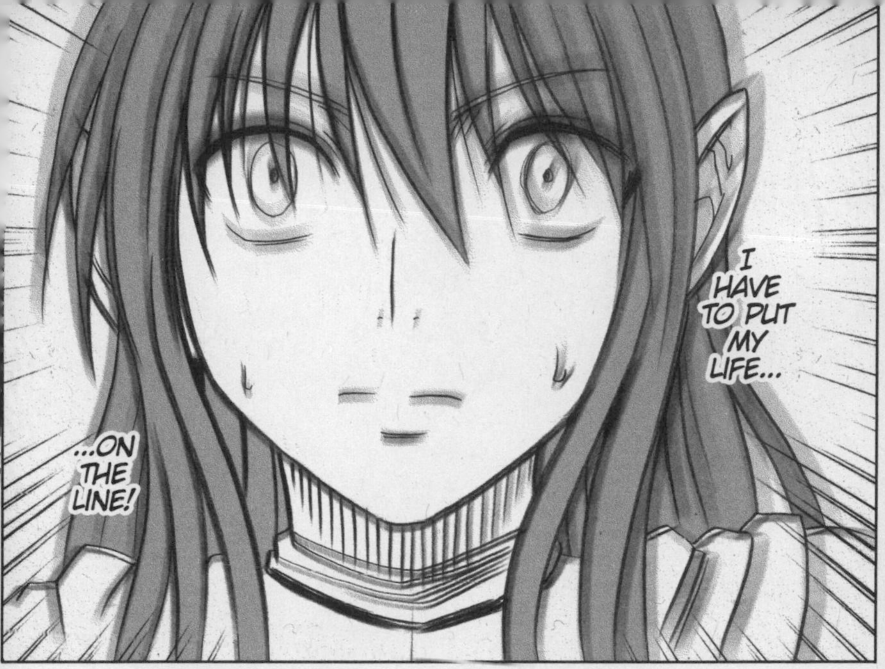
I HAVE TO PUT MY LIFE...
...ON THE LINE!
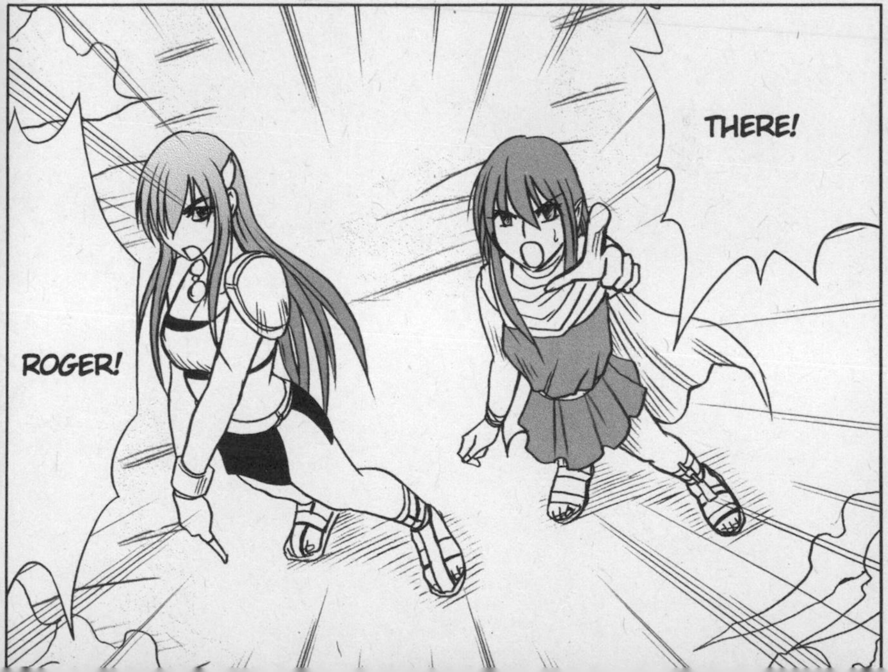
THERE!
ROGER!

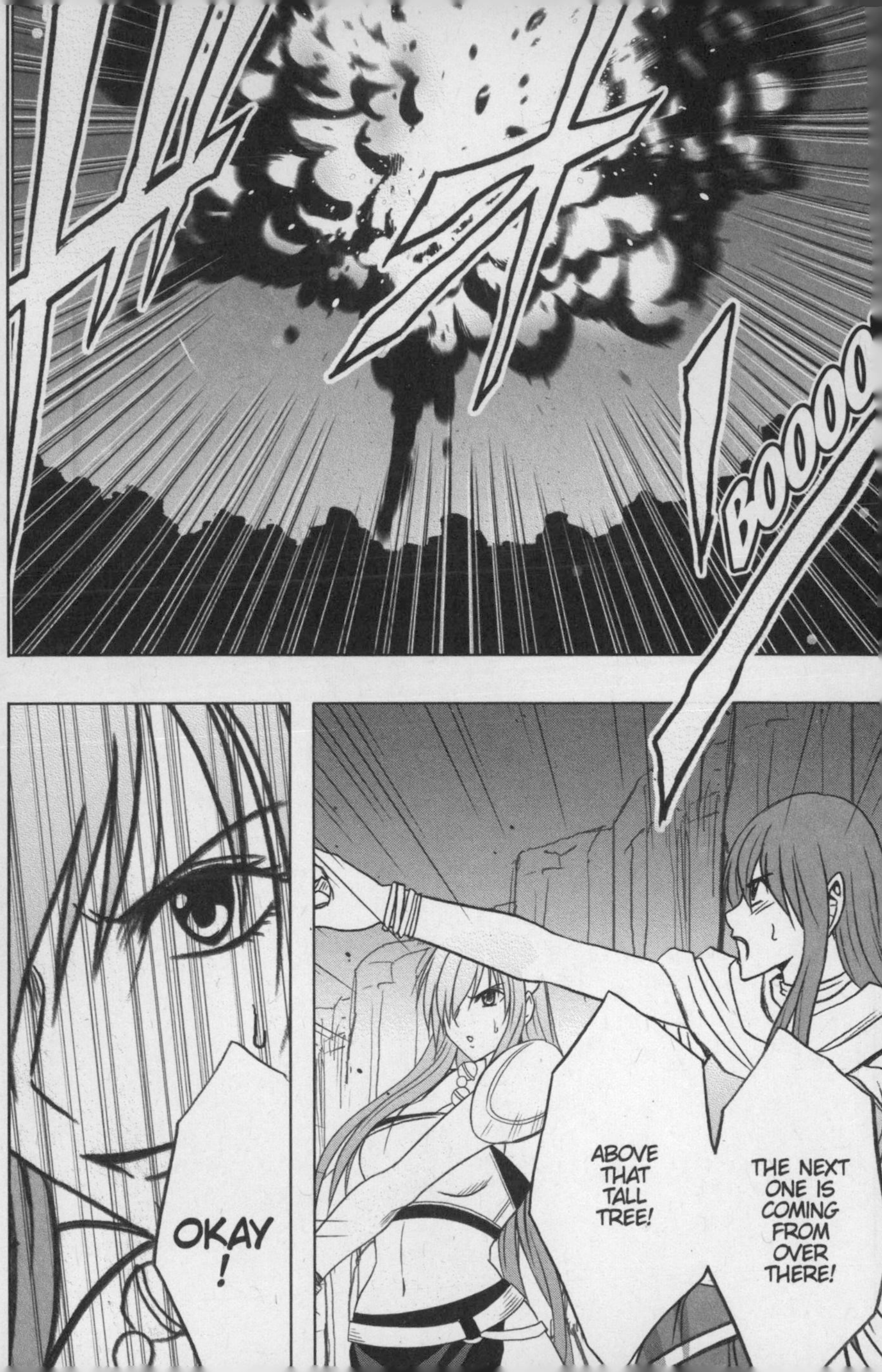
BOOOO
THE NEXT ONE IS COMING FROM OVER THERE!
ABOVE THAT TALL TREE!
OKAY!

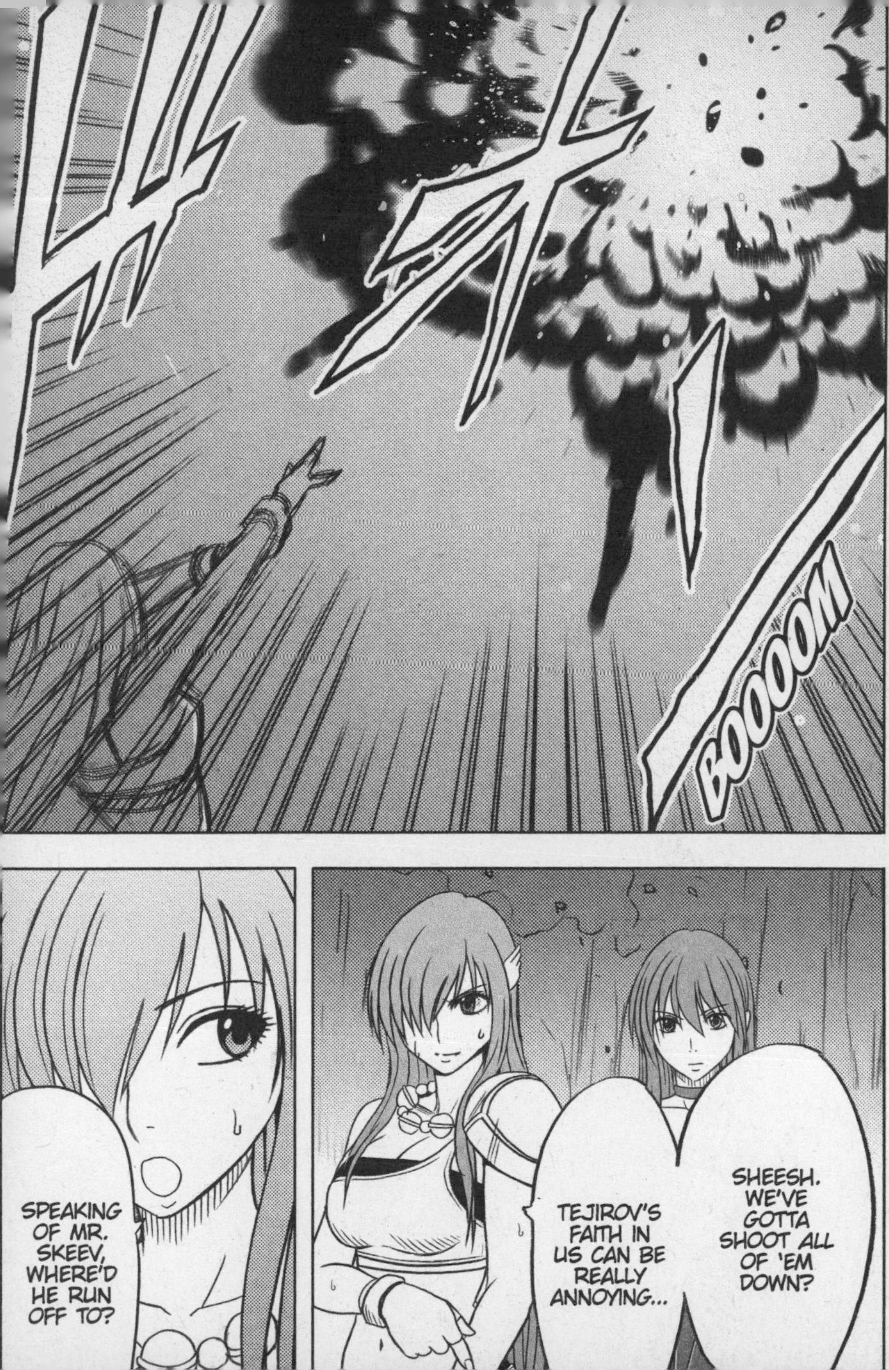
BOOOOM
SHEESH. WE'VE GOTTA SHOOT ALL OF 'EM DOWN?
TEJIROV'S FAITH IN US CAN BE REALLY ANNOYING...
SPEAKING OF MR. SKEEV, WHERE'D HE RUN OFF TO?

CHAPTER 6

A DANGEROUS PAIR

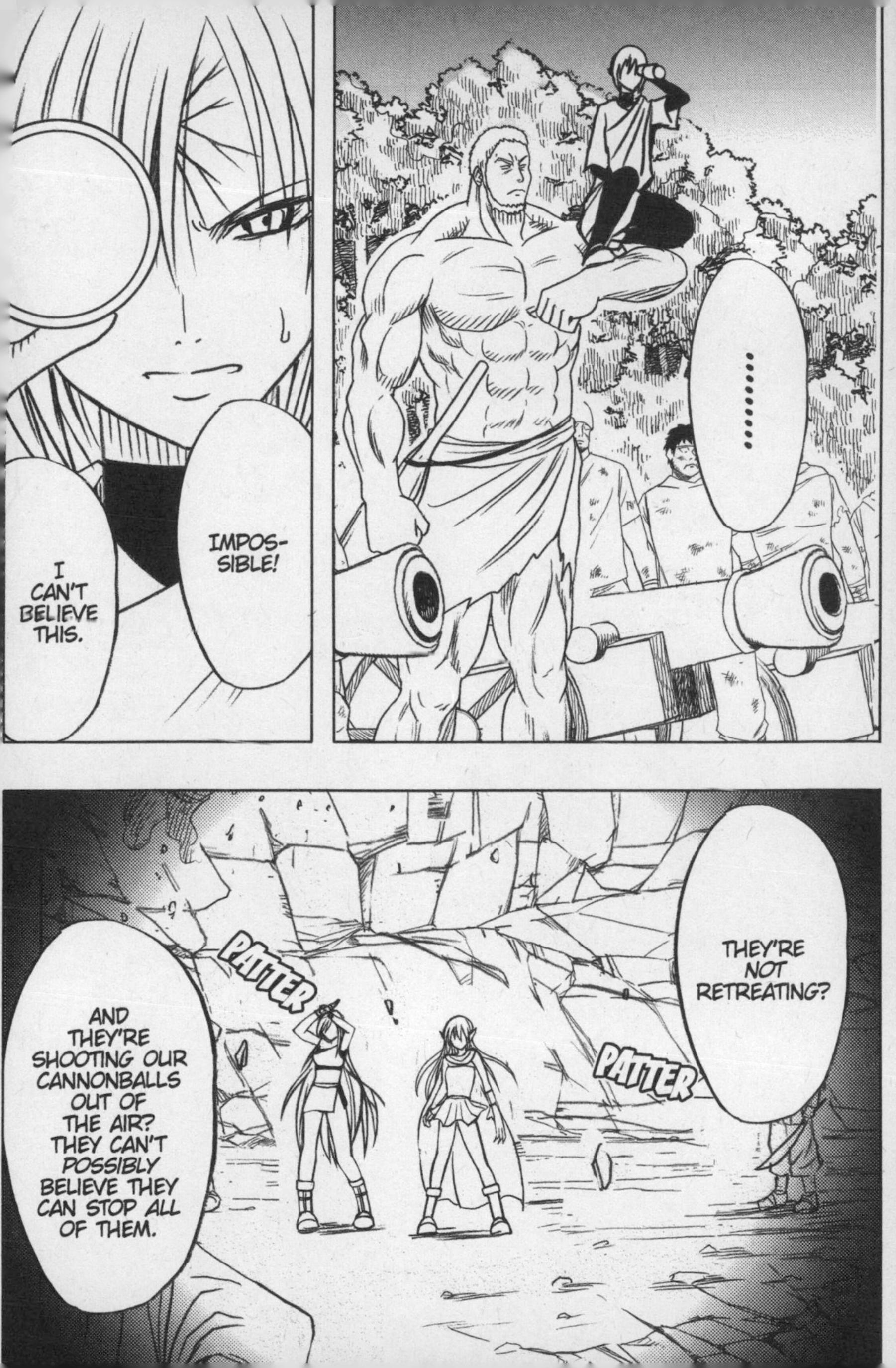
......
IMPOSSIBLE!
I CAN'T BELIEVE THIS.
THEY'RE NOT RETREATING?
PATTER
PATTER
!
AND THEY'RE SHOOTING OUR CANNONBALLS OUT OF THE AIR? THEY CAN'T POSSIBLY BELIEVE THEY CAN STOP ALL OF THEM.

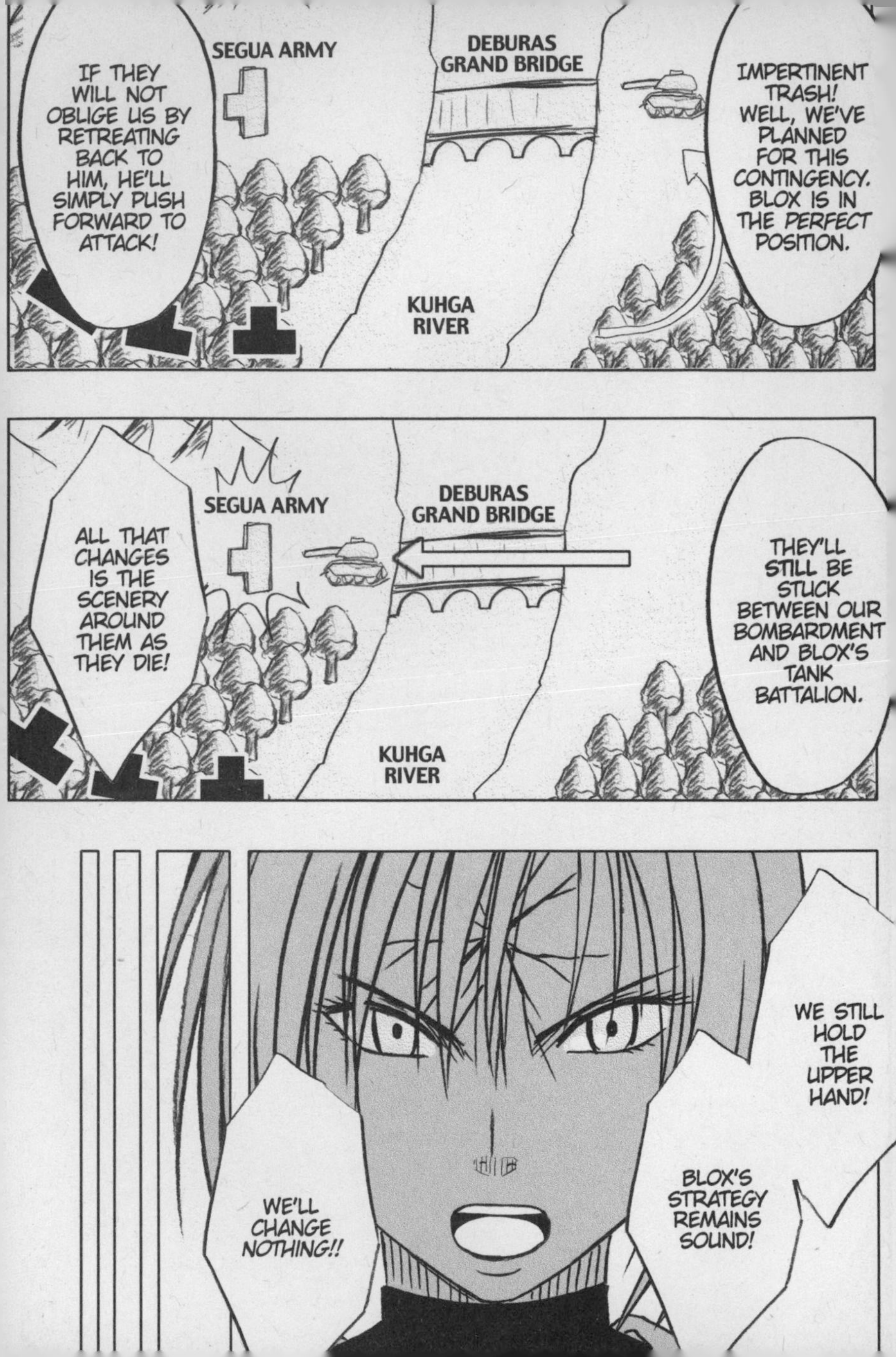
IMPERTINENT TRASH! WELL, WE'VE PLANNED FOR THIS CONTINGENCY. BLOX IS IN THE PERFECT POSITION.
DEBURAS GRAND BRIDGE
SEGUA ARMY
KUHGA RIVER
IF THEY WILL NOT OBLIGE US BY RETREATING BACK TO HIM, HE'LL SIMPLY PUSH FORWARD TO ATTACK!
THEY'LL STILL BE STUCK BETWEEN OUR BOMBARDMENT AND BLOX'S TANK BATTALION.
DEBURAS GRAND BRIDGE
SEGUA ARMY
KUHGA RIVER
ALL THAT CHANGES IS THE SCENERY AROUND THEM AS THEY DIE!
WE STILL HOLD THE UPPER HAND!
BLOX'S STRATEGY REMAINS SOUND!
WE'LL CHANGE NOTHING!!

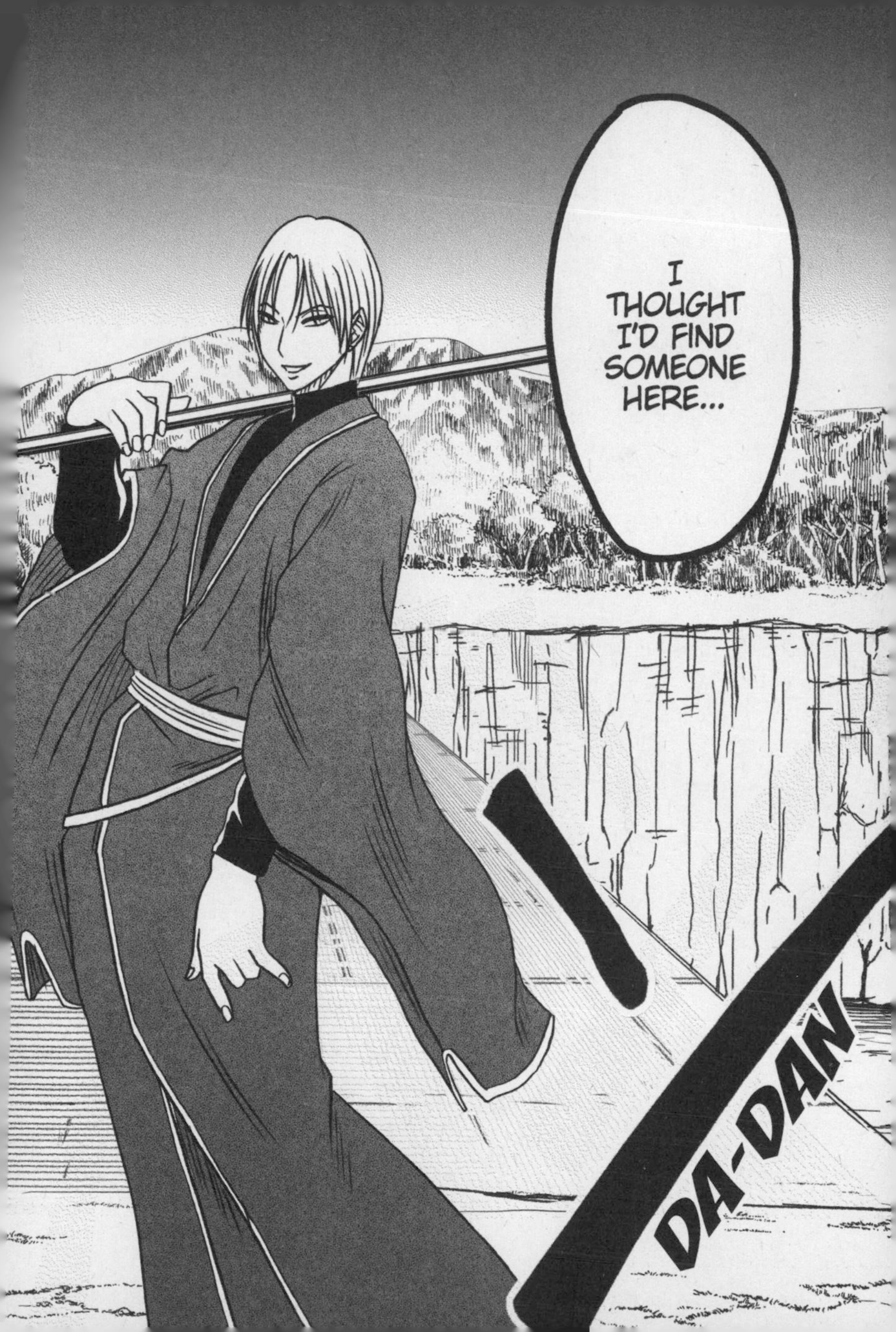
I THOUGHT I'D FIND SOMEONE HERE...
DA-DAN

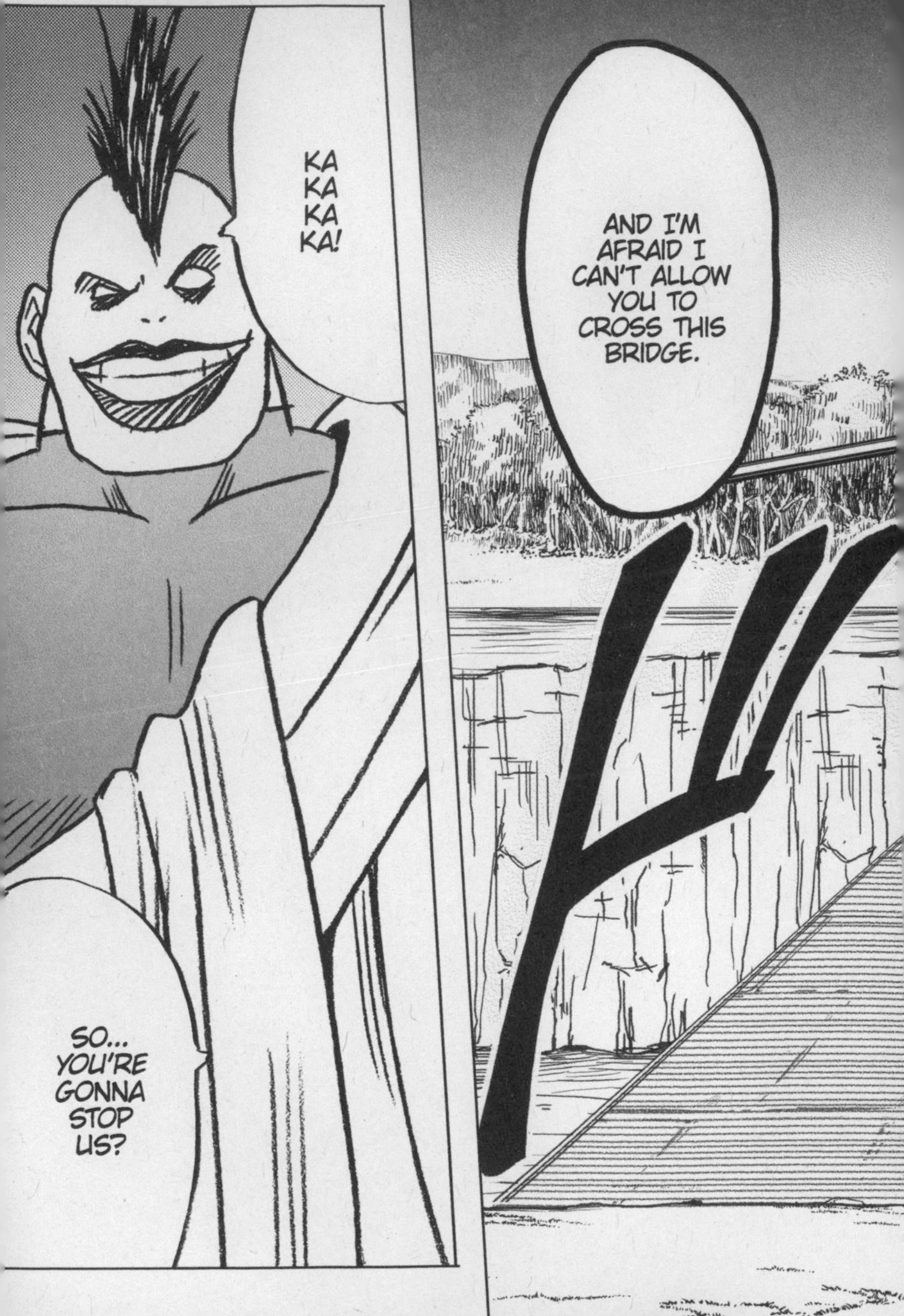
AND I'M AFRAID I CAN'T ALLOW YOU TO CROSS THIS BRIDGE.
KA KA KA KA KA!
SO... YOU'RE GONNA STOP US?

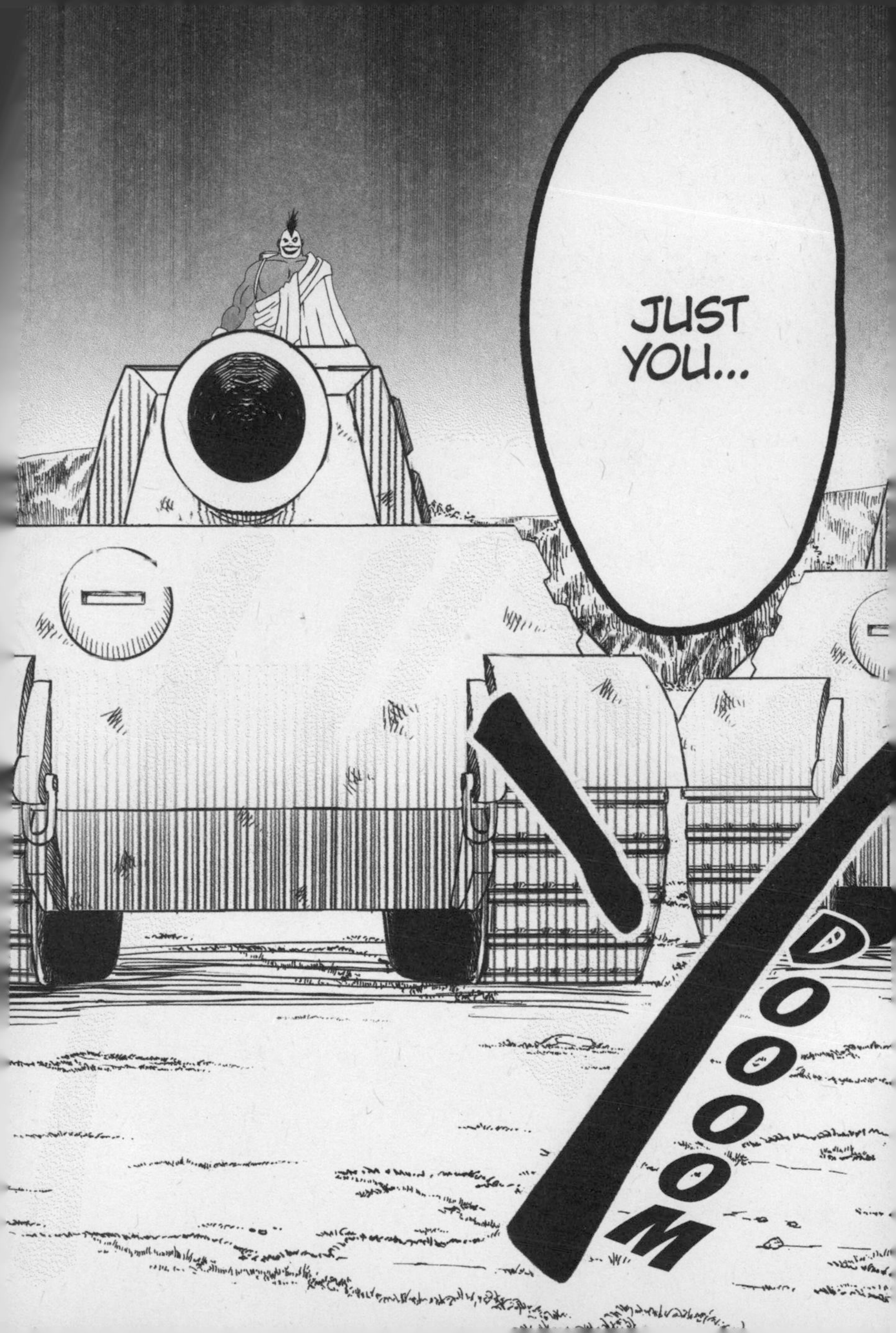
JUST YOU...
DOOOOOM

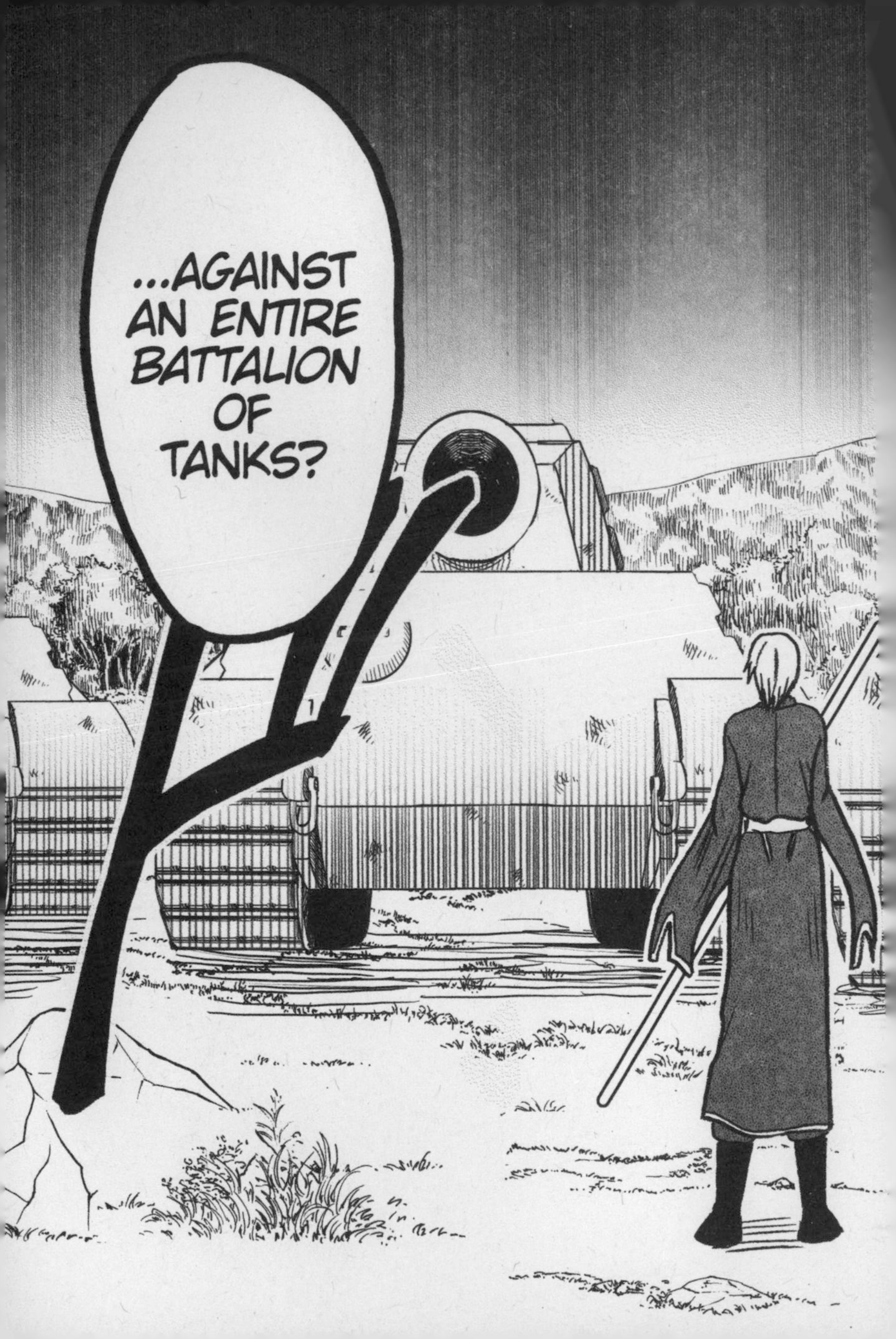
...AGAINST AN ENTIRE BATTALION OF TANKS?

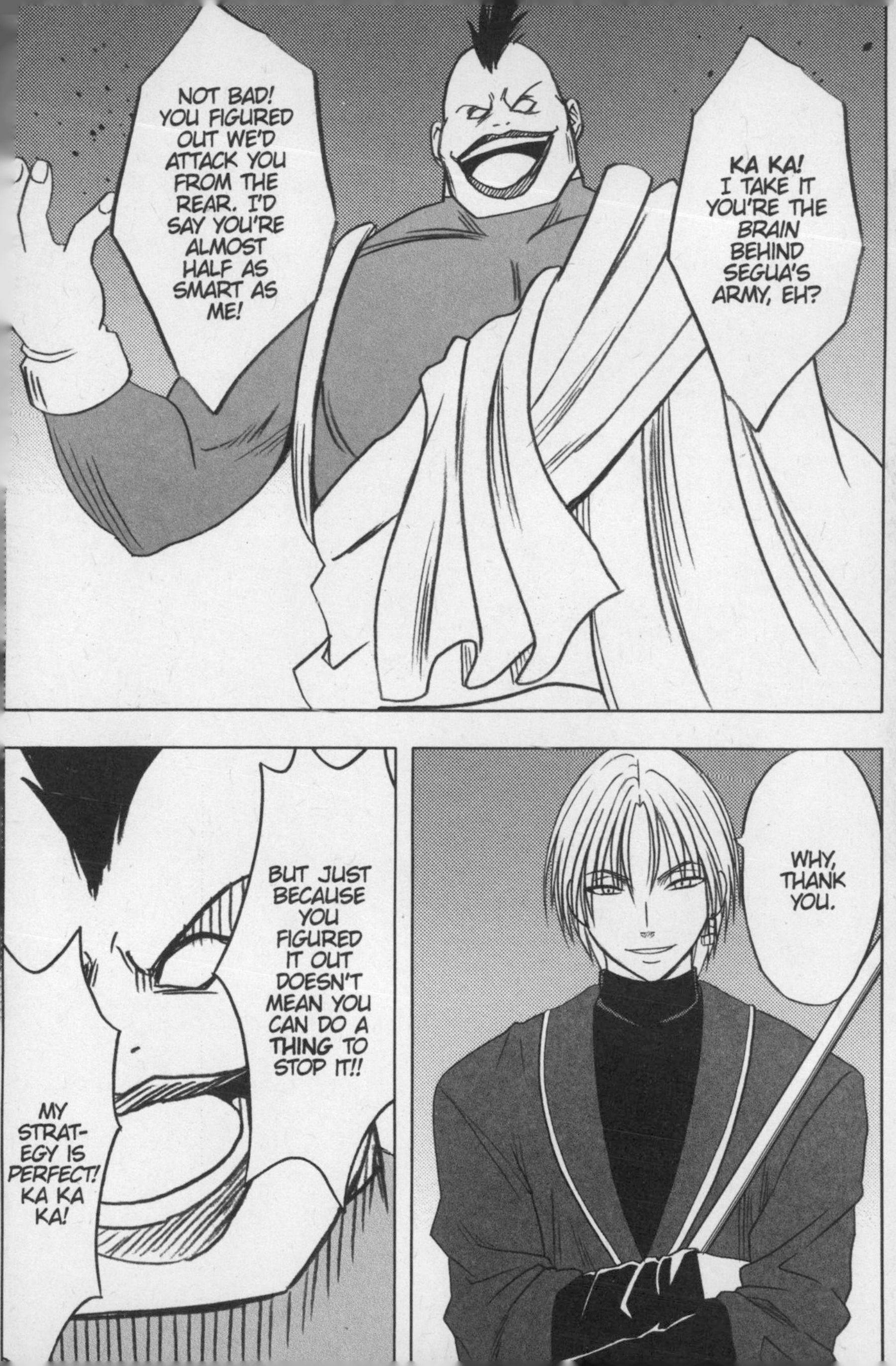
KA KA! I TAKE IT YOU'RE THE BRAIN BEHIND SEGUA'S ARMY, EH?
NOT BAD! YOU FIGURED OUT WE'D ATTACK YOU FROM THE REAR. I'D SAY YOU'RE ALMOST HALF AS SMART AS ME!
WHY, THANK YOU.
BUT JUST BECAUSE YOU FIGURED IT OUT DOESN'T MEAN YOU CAN DO A THING TO STOP IT!!
MY STRAT-EGY IS PERFECT! KA KA KA!

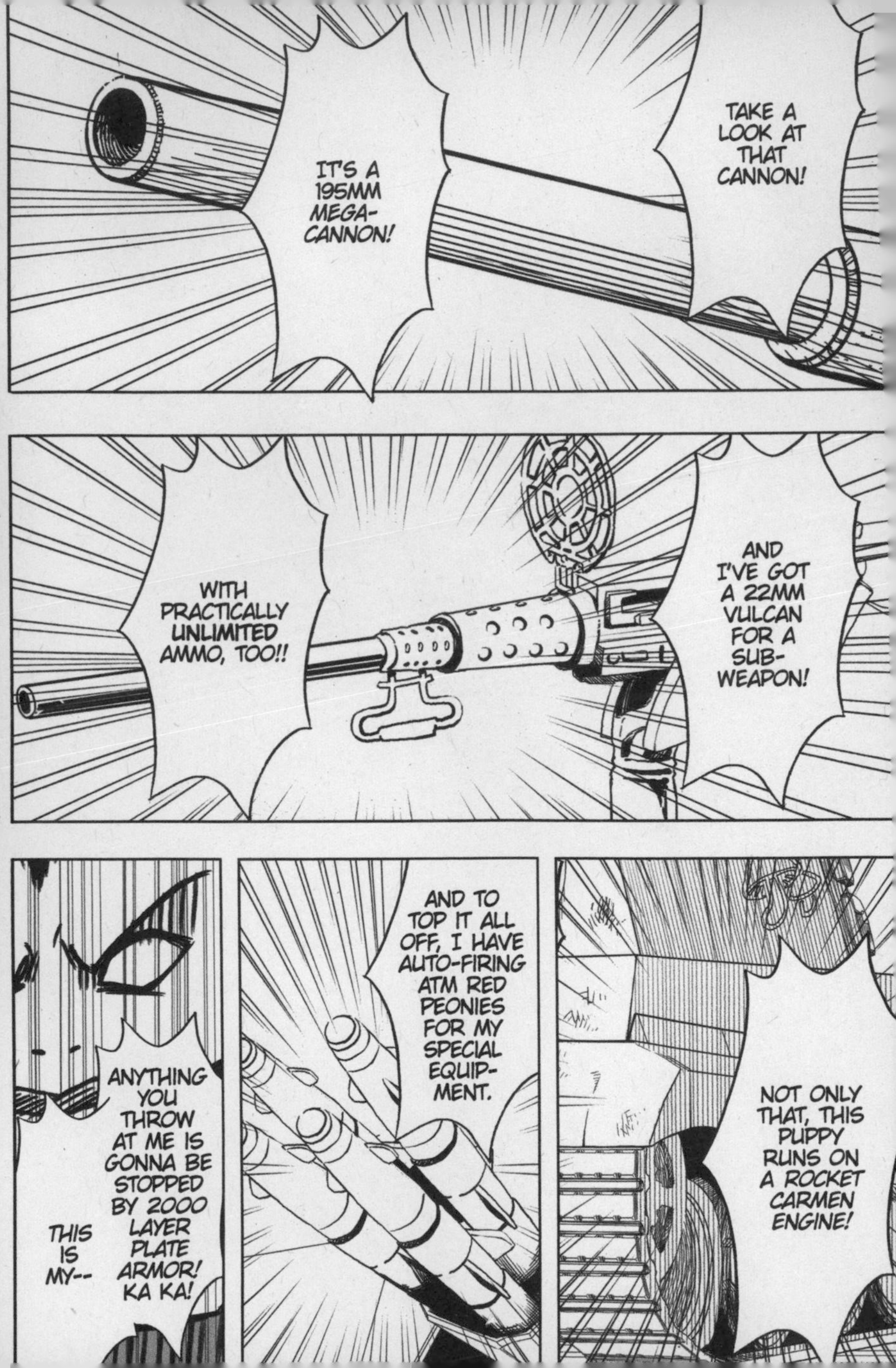
TAKE A LOOK AT THAT CANNON!
IT'S A 195MM MEGA-CANNON!
AND I'VE GOT A 22MM VULCAN FOR A SUB-WEAPON!
WITH PRACTICALLY UNLIMITED AMMO, TOO!!
NOT ONLY THAT, THIS PUPPY RUNS ON A ROCKET CARMEN ENGINE!
AND TO TOP IT ALL OFF, I HAVE AUTO-FIRING ATM RED PEONIES FOR MY SPECIAL EQUIP-MENT.
ANYTHING YOU THROW AT ME IS GONNA BE STOPPED BY 2000 LAYER PLATE ARMOR! KA KA!
THIS IS MY--

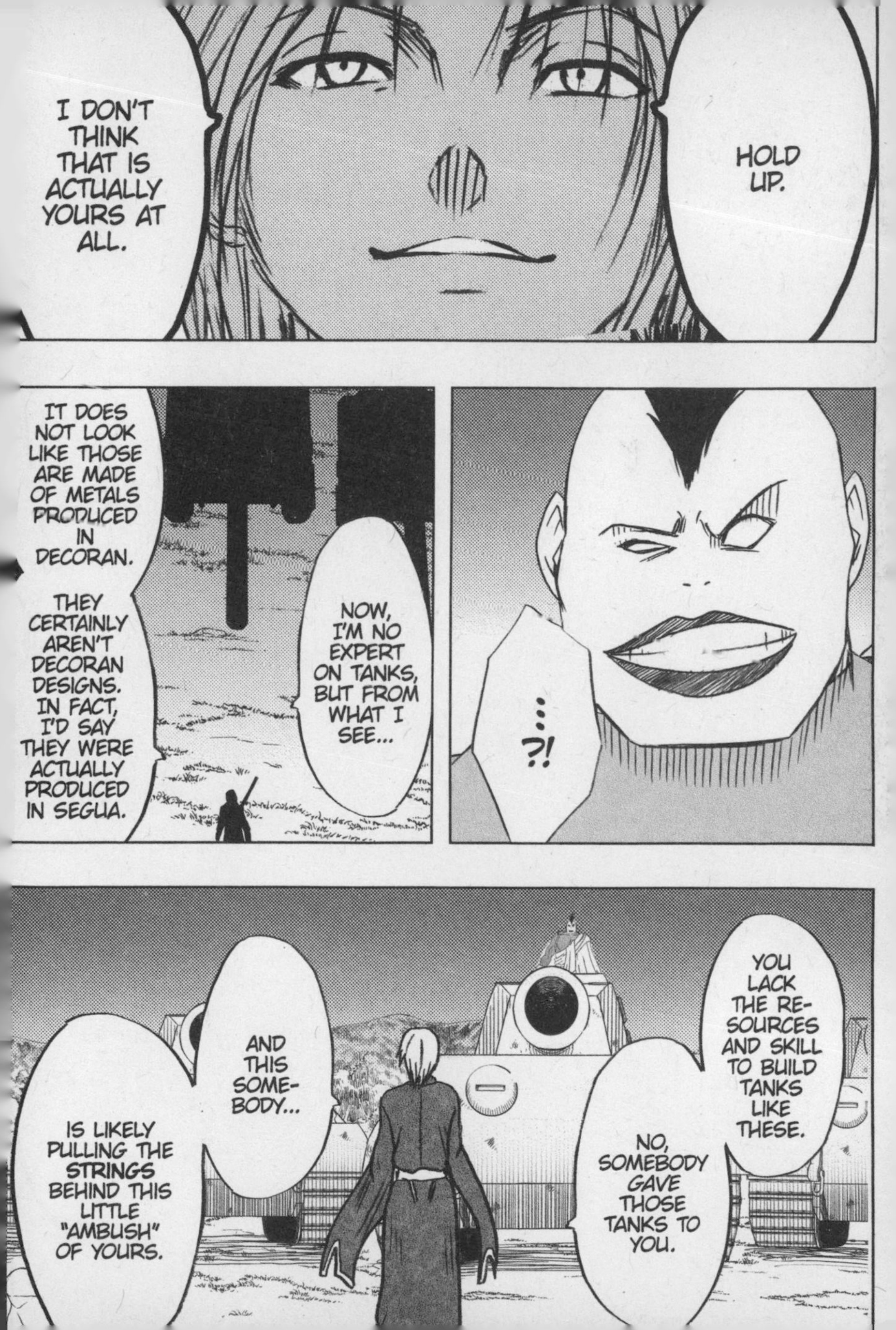
HOLD UP.
I DON'T THINK THAT IS ACTUALLY YOURS AT ALL.
...?!
NOW, I'M NO EXPERT ON TANKS, BUT FROM WHAT I SEE...
IT DOES NOT LOOK LIKE THOSE ARE MADE OF METALS PRODUCED IN DECORAN.
THEY CERTAINLY AREN'T DECORAN DESIGNS. IN FACT, I'D SAY THEY WERE ACTUALLY PRODUCED IN SEGUA.
YOU LACK THE RE-SOURCES AND SKILL TO BUILD TANKS LIKE THESE.
NO, SOMEBODY GAVE THOSE TANKS TO YOU.
AND THIS SOME-BODY...
IS LIKELY PULLING THE STRINGS BEHIND THIS LITTLE "AMBUSH" OF YOURS.

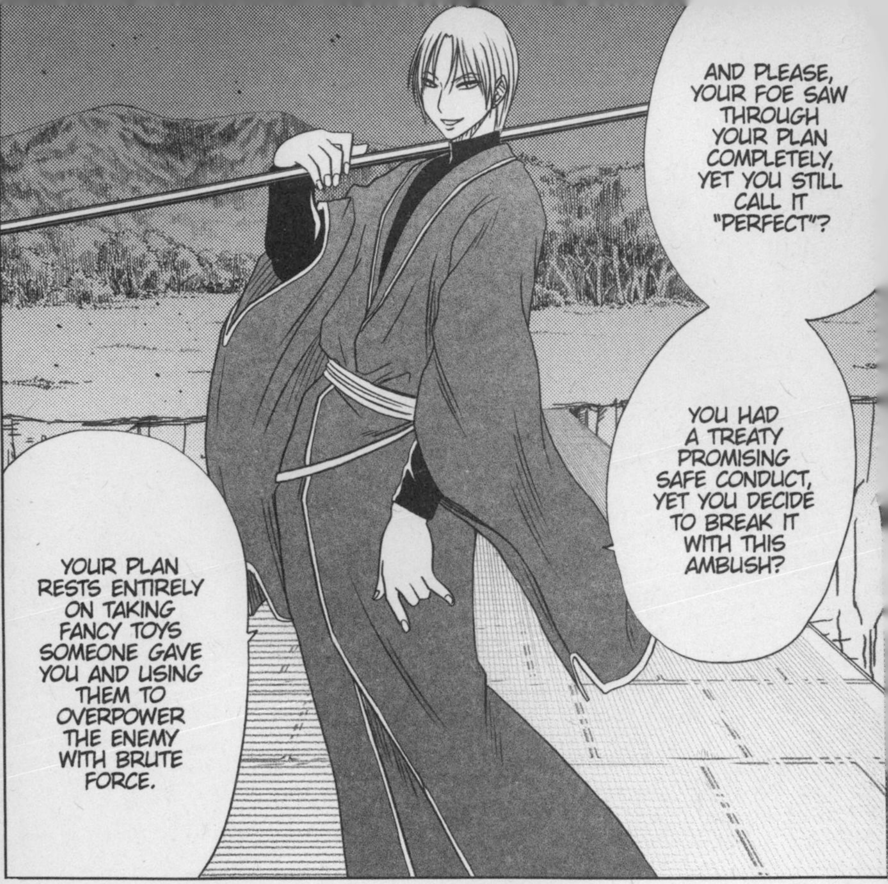
AND PLEASE, YOUR FOE SAW THROUGH YOUR PLAN COMPLETELY, YET YOU STILL CALL IT "PERFECT"?
YOU HAD A TREATY PROMISING SAFE CONDUCT, YET YOU DECIDE TO BREAK IT WITH THIS AMBUSH?
YOUR PLAN RESTS ENTIRELY ON TAKING FANCY TOYS SOMEONE GAVE YOU AND USING THEM TO OVERPOWER THE ENEMY WITH BRUTE FORCE.

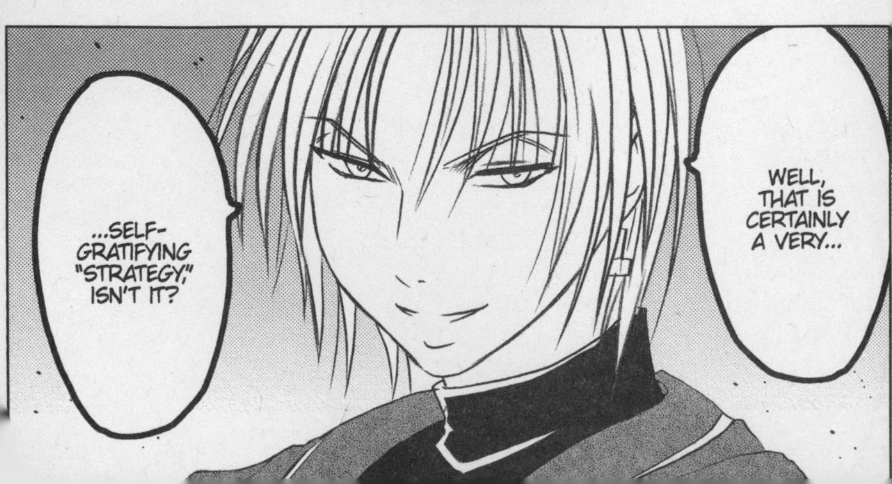
WELL, THAT IS CERTAINLY A VERY...
...SELF-GRATIFYING "STRATEGY," ISN'T IT?

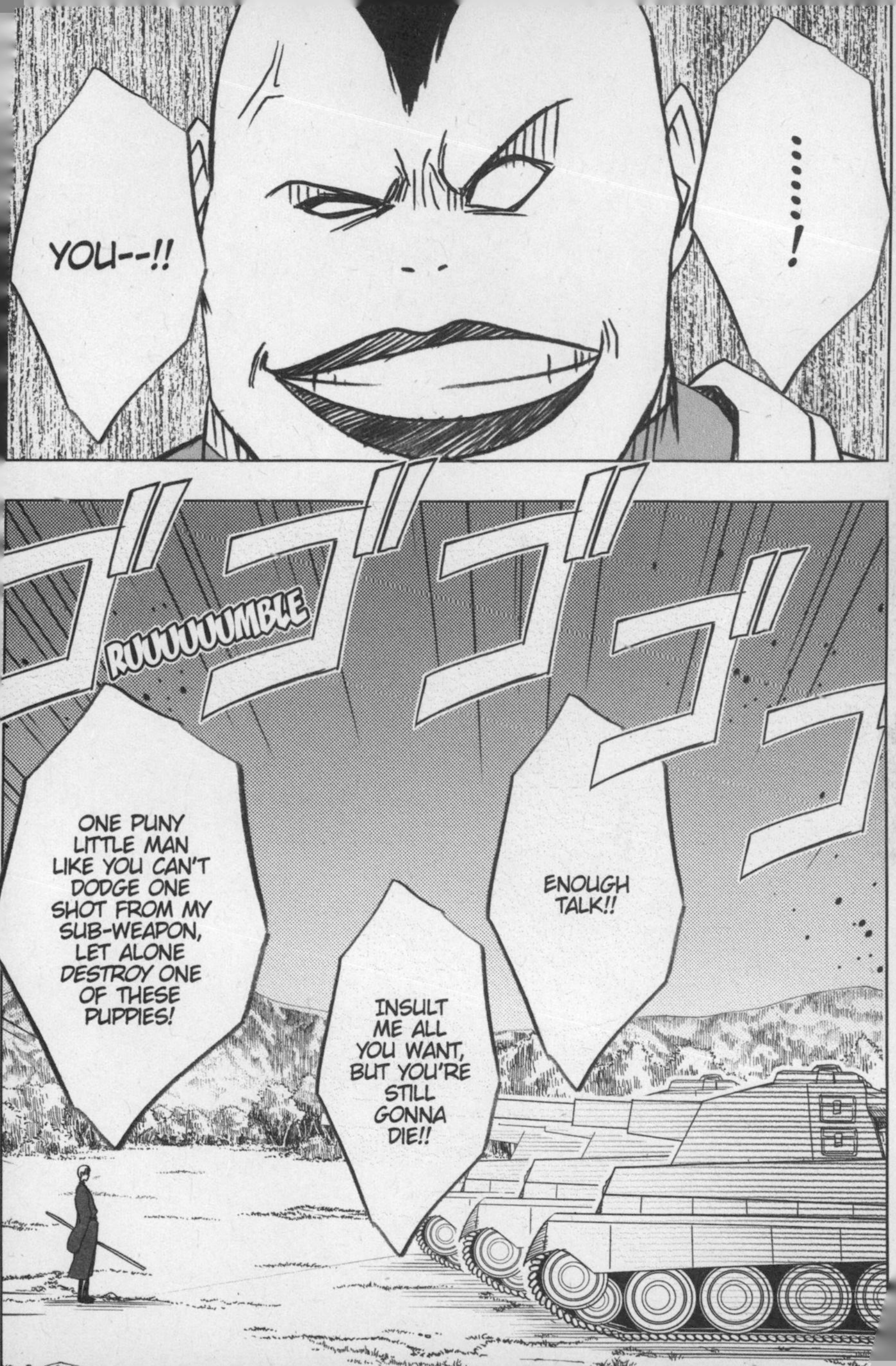
......!
YOU--!!
RUUUUUUMBLE
ENOUGH TALK!!
ONE PUNY LITTLE MAN LIKE YOU CAN'T DODGE ONE SHOT FROM MY SUB-WEAPON, LET ALONE DESTROY ONE OF THESE PUPPIES!
INSULT ME ALL YOU WANT, BUT YOU'RE STILL GONNA DIE!!

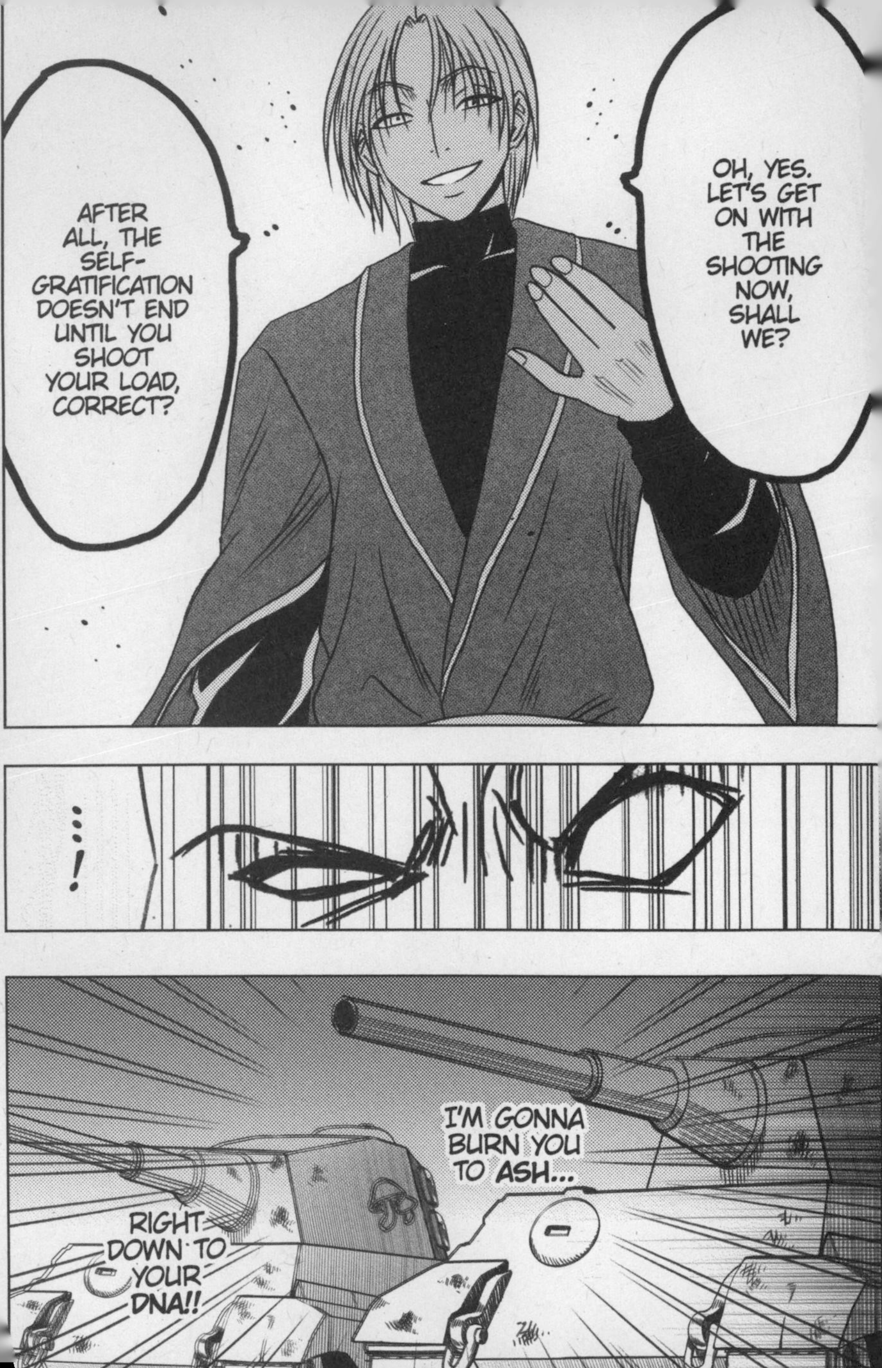
OH, YES. LET'S GET ON WITH THE SHOOTING NOW, SHALL WE?
AFTER ALL, THE SELF-GRATIFICATION DOESN'T END UNTIL YOU SHOOT YOUR LOAD, CORRECT?
...!
I'M GONNA BURN YOU TO ASH...
RIGHT DOWN TO YOUR DNA!!

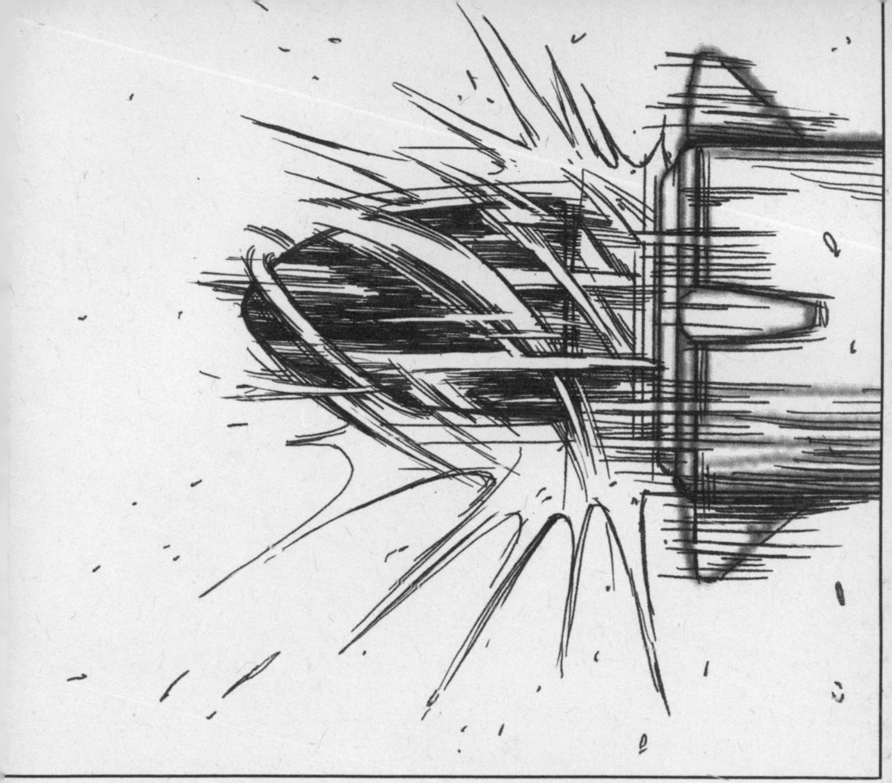
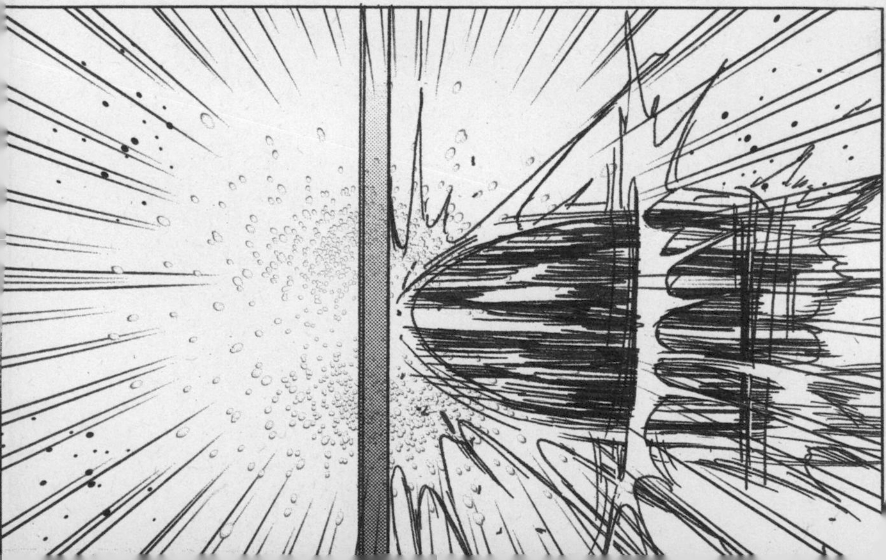

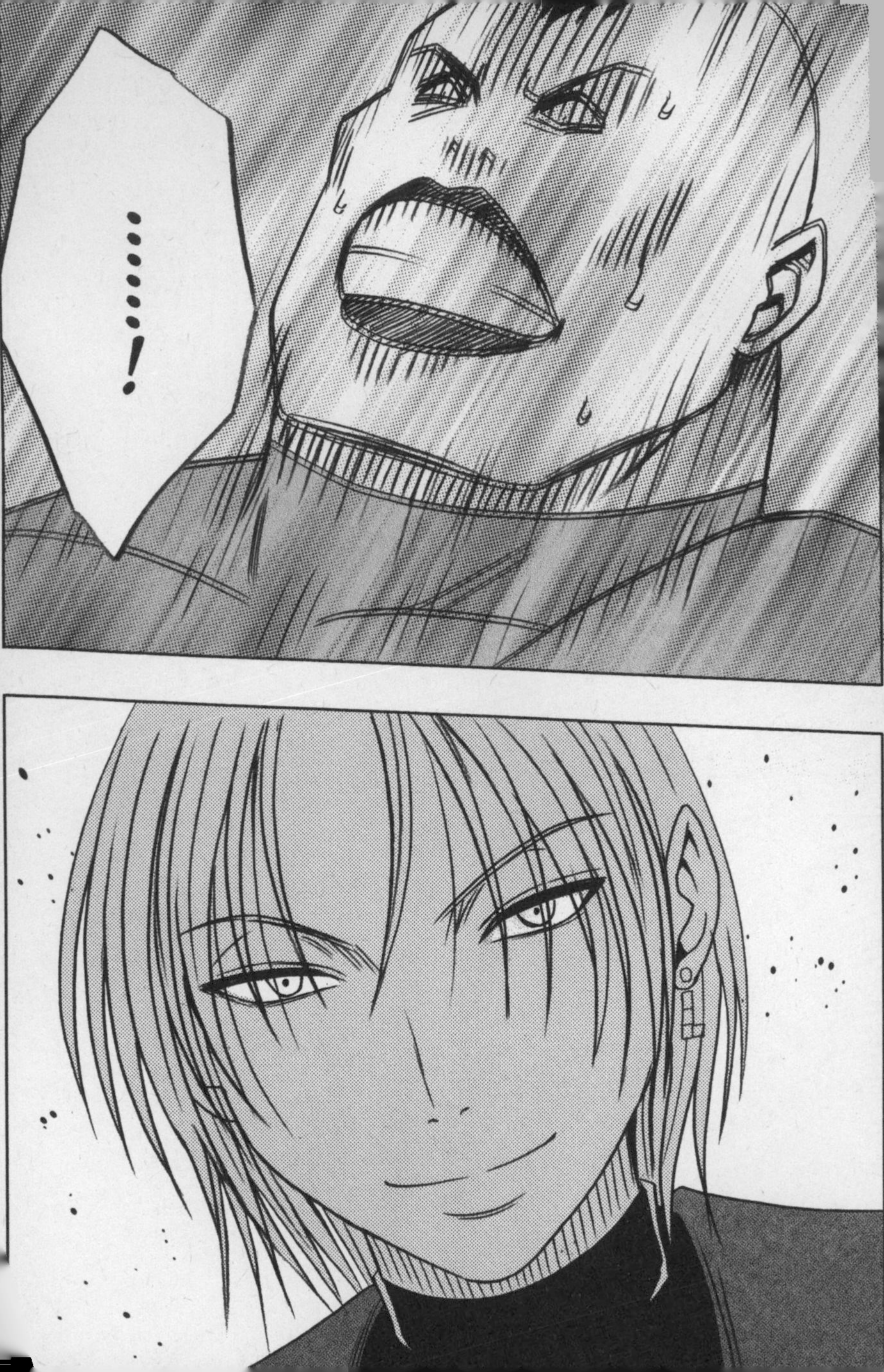
......!

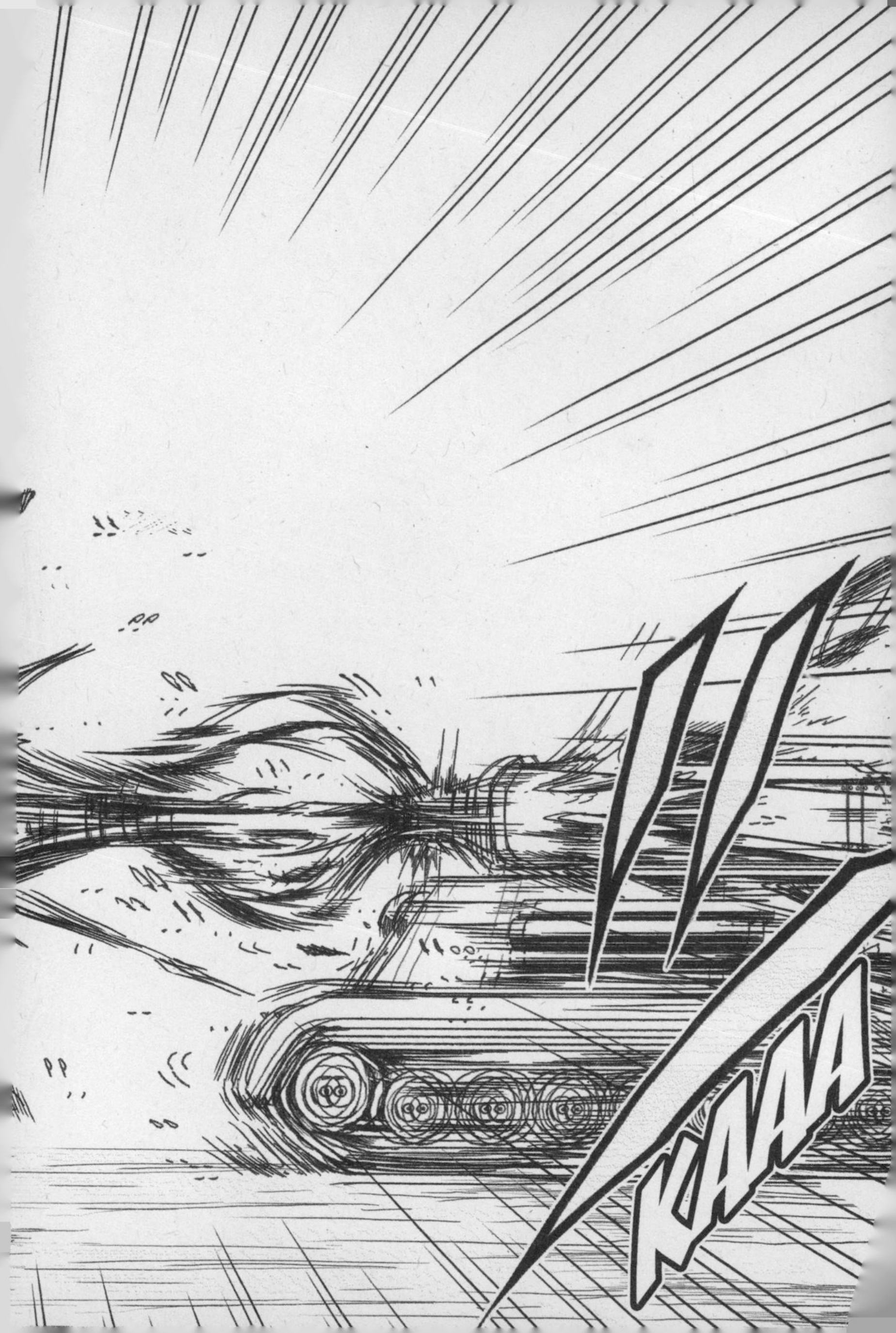
KAAA

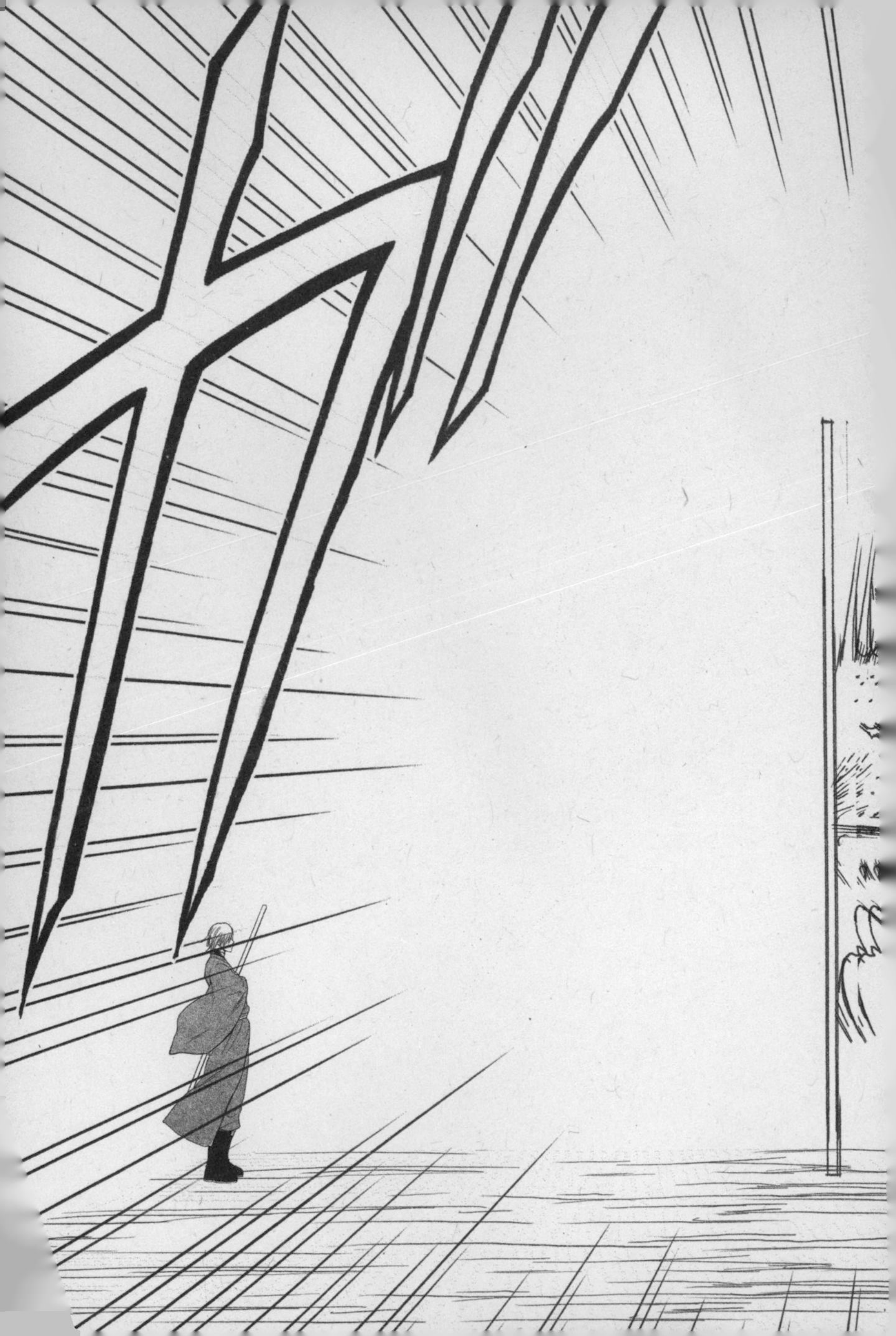

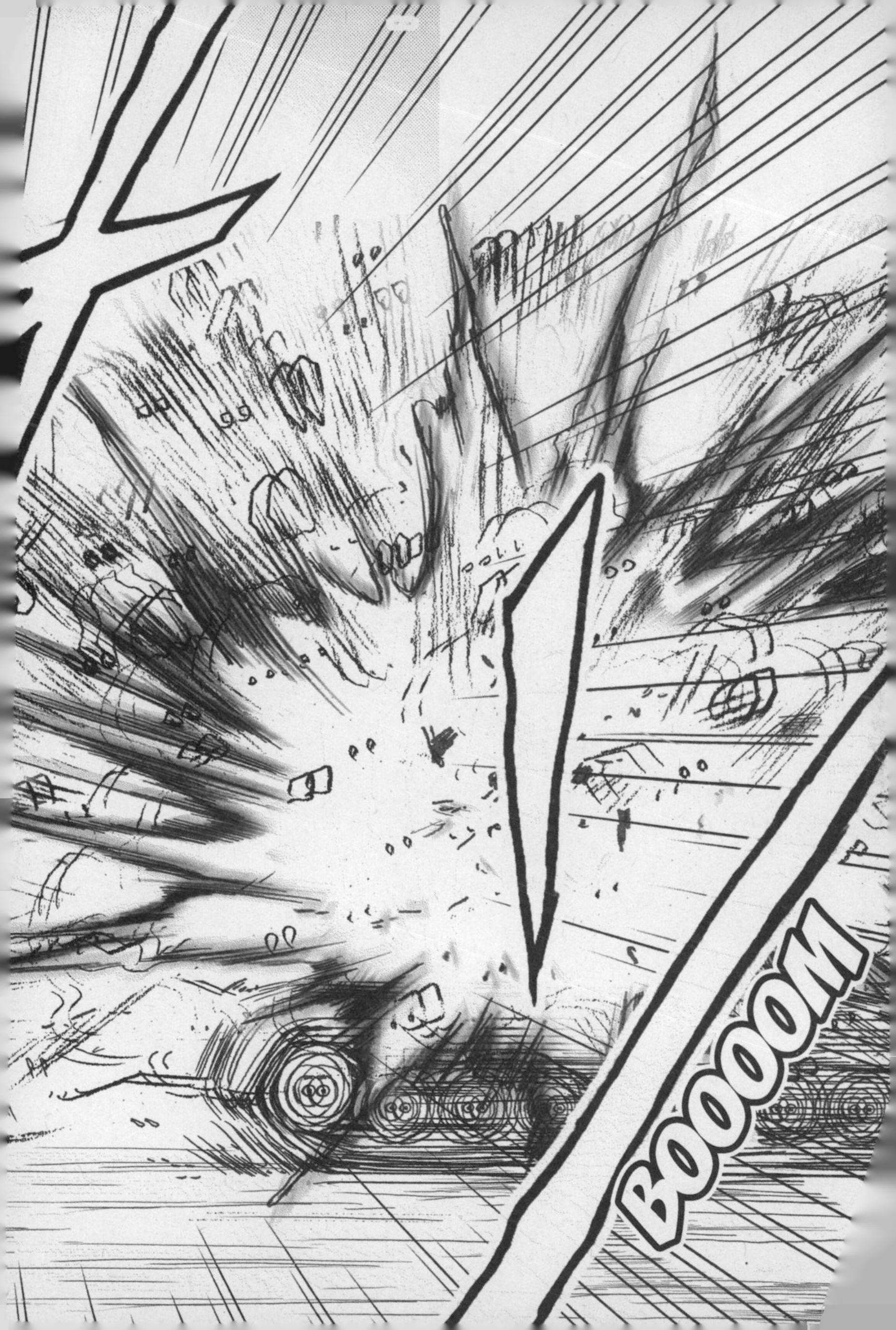
BOOOOOM

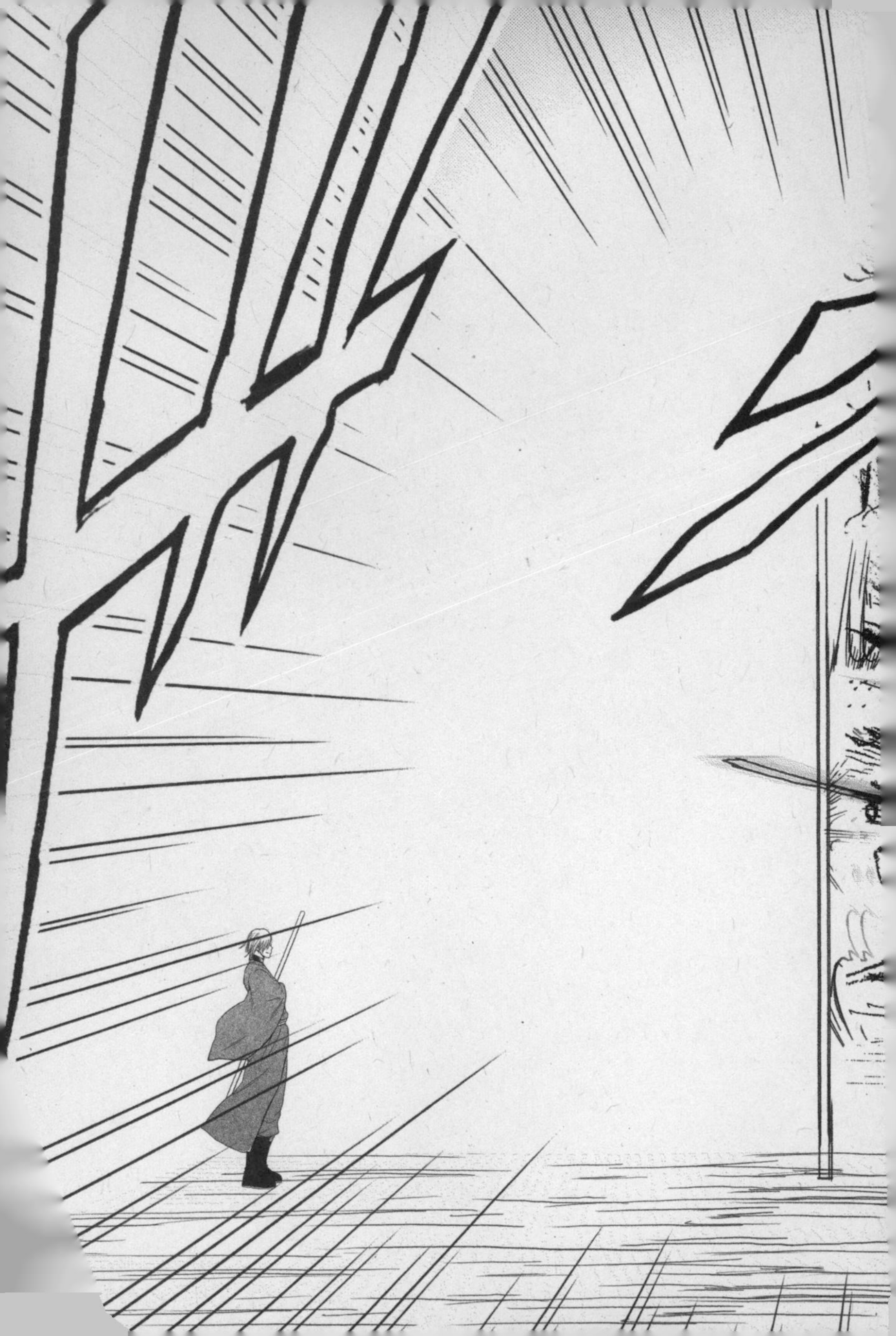

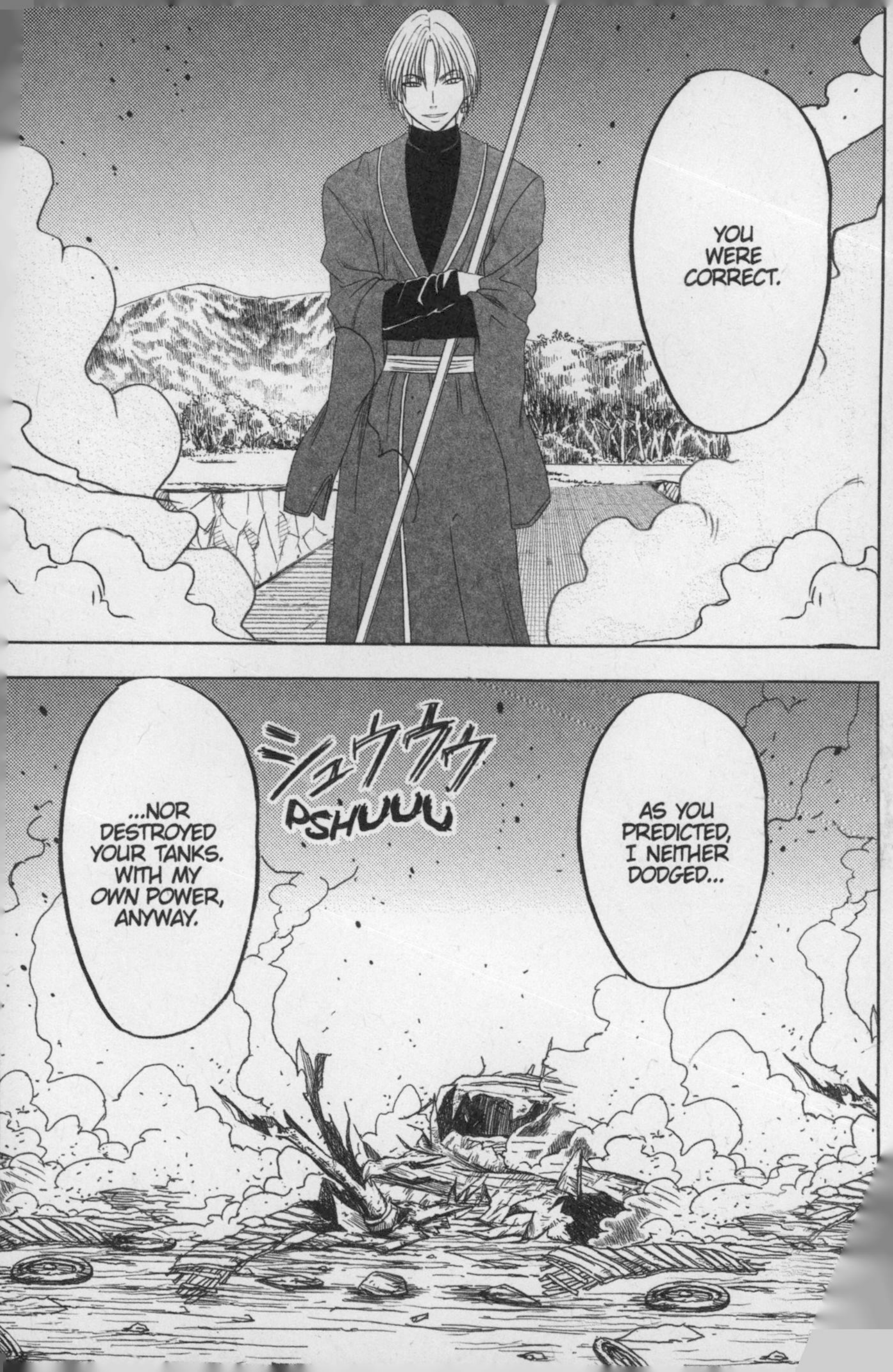
YOU WERE CORRECT.
AS YOU PREDICTED, I NEITHER DODGED...
シュウウウ
PSHUUU
...NOR DESTROYED YOUR TANKS. WITH MY OWN POWER, ANYWAY.

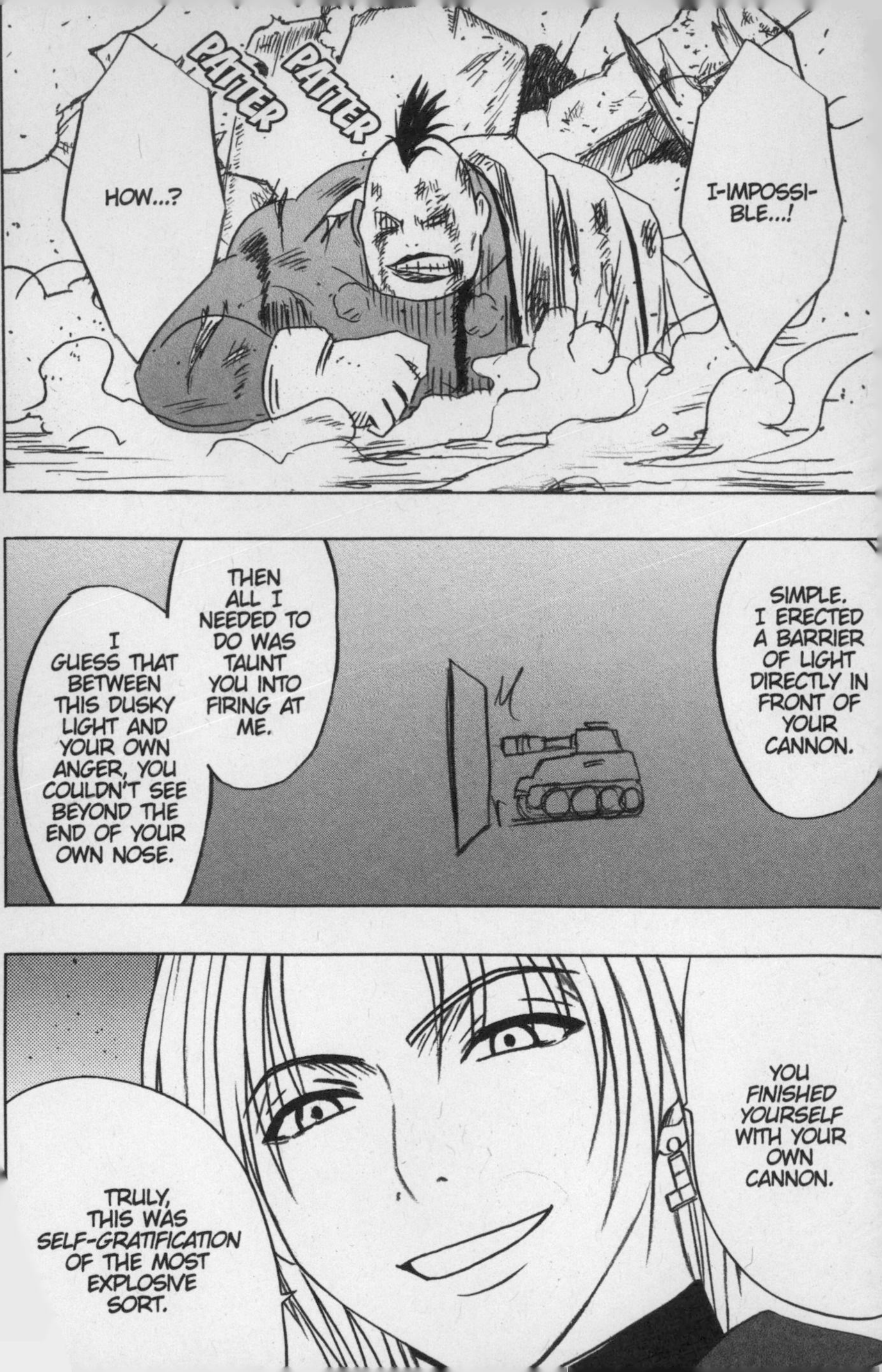
I-IMPOSSIBLE...!
PATTER PATTER
HOW...?
SIMPLE. I ERECTED A BARRIER OF LIGHT DIRECTLY IN FRONT OF YOUR CANNON.
THEN ALL I NEEDED TO DO WAS TAUNT YOU INTO FIRING AT ME.
I GUESS THAT BETWEEN THIS DUSKY LIGHT AND YOUR OWN ANGER, YOU COULDN'T SEE BEYOND THE END OF YOUR OWN NOSE.
YOU FINISHED YOURSELF WITH YOUR OWN CANNON.
TRULY, THIS WAS SELF-GRATIFICATION OF THE MOST EXPLOSIVE SORT.

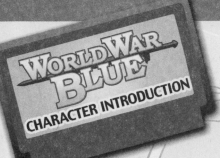

WORLD WAR BLUE

CHARACTER INTRODUCTION

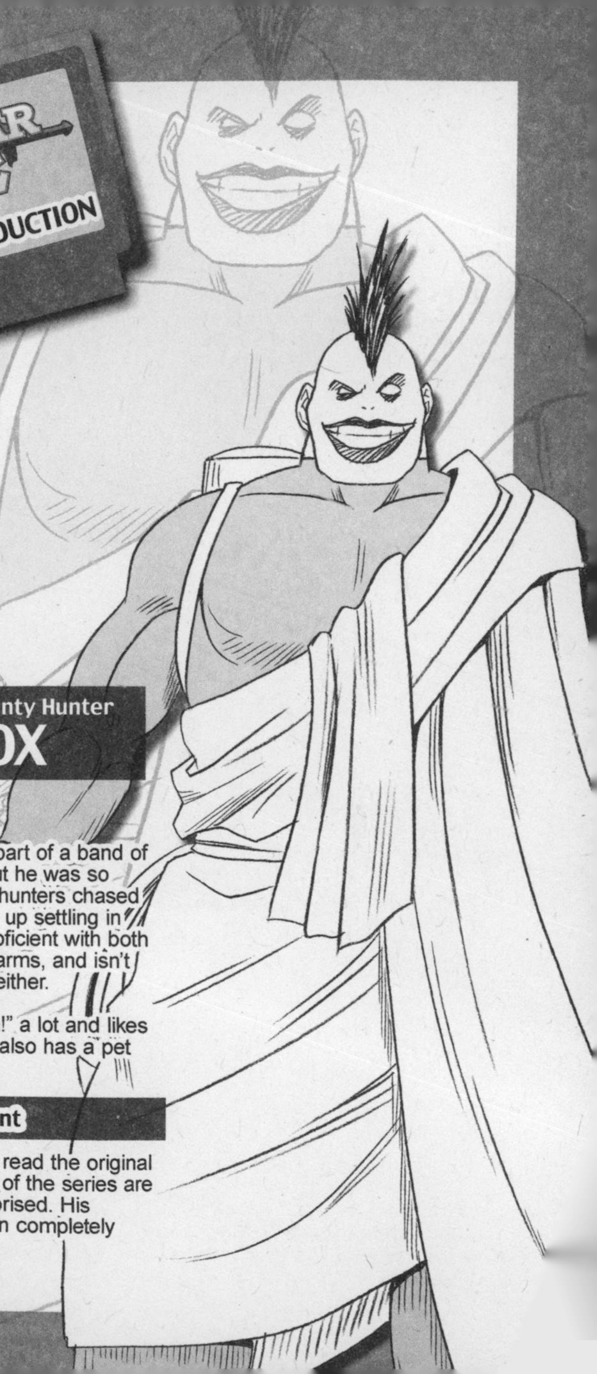

The Steel Bounty Hunter

BLOX

BLOX

Unknown origin.

He was originally part of a band of bounty-hunters, but he was so disliked, the other hunters chased him off. He wound up settling in Decoran. He is proficient with both machines and firearms, and isn't bad in a fist-fight, either.

He says "Ka ka ka!" a lot and likes energy drinks. He also has a pet dog.

Author Comment

Those of you who read the original webcomic version of the series are probably very surprised. His character has been completely revamped.

Perusing Video Game History

ON THE EDGE OF THE BLUE WORLD

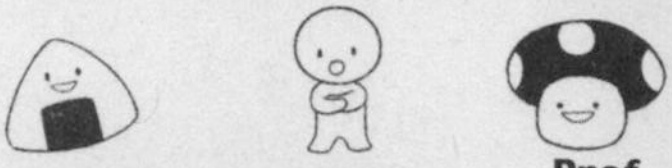

Dr. Onigiri   Mr. Why   Prof. Mushroom

Today's Topic

METAL MAX

Mr. Why: So what kind of game is *Metal Max?*

Dr. Onigiri: Data East released *Metal Max* in 1991. It's an RPG where you play as a bounty-hunter who drives his own tank around, collecting bounties.

Prof. Mushroom: It's a series of games, too. In each title, you have the ability to modify your tank as much as you want.

Dr. Onigiri: There are lots of different tank types, too, with cool names like "Abyssinian" and "Stradovari." You get to add three different types of weapons to them--main cannons, special equipment, and sub-weapons with unlimited ammo. You can layer up on armor, which functions as HP, and switch out your engine for a more powerful one. I had a lot of fun customizing my tank. The most powerful equipment was called the "Red Peony," which was awesome despite the weird name. Lots of players found themselves wandering around looking for more stuff to customize their tank with instead of following the story.

Prof. Mushroom: Don't forget Ted Broiler, the boss from *Metal Max 2.*

Dr. Onigiri: Right. He was huge, had a flaming red Mohawk, enormous lips and a really distinct speech style. But the biggest thing about him was his really powerful flame attack. Players learned to shudder every time he said, "I'll burn you to ash, right down to your DNA! Ka ka ka!"

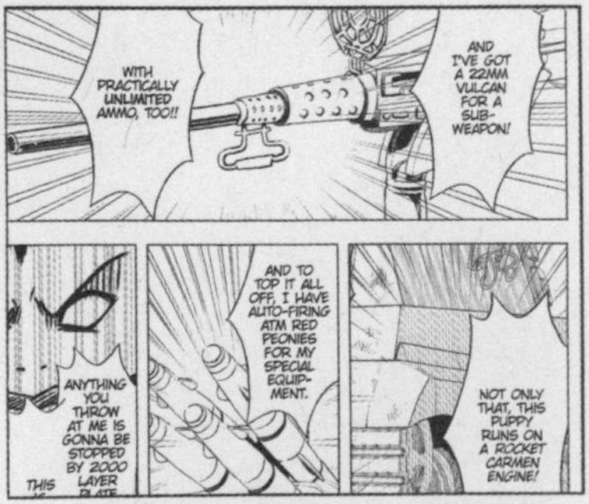
AND I'VE GOT A 22MM VULCAN FOR A SUB-WEAPON!
WITH PRACTICALLY UNLIMITED AMMO, TOO!!
NOT ONLY THAT, THIS PUPPY RUNS ON A ROCKET CARMEN ENGINE!
AND TO TOP IT ALL OFF, I HAVE AUTO-FIRING ATM RED PEONIES FOR MY SPECIAL EQUIP-MENT.
ANYTHING YOU THROW AT ME IS GONNA BE STOPPED BY 2000 LAYER
THIS

Blox's tank battalion is equipped with a wide variety of powerful weapons.

Prof. Mushroom: Right when you thought you had him dead to rights, he'd heal himself back to full health with a healing item. Plus, if you went into that fight without heat-shields, you were, well... *toast.* He was famous as a really nasty boss, back in the day.

To Be Continued...

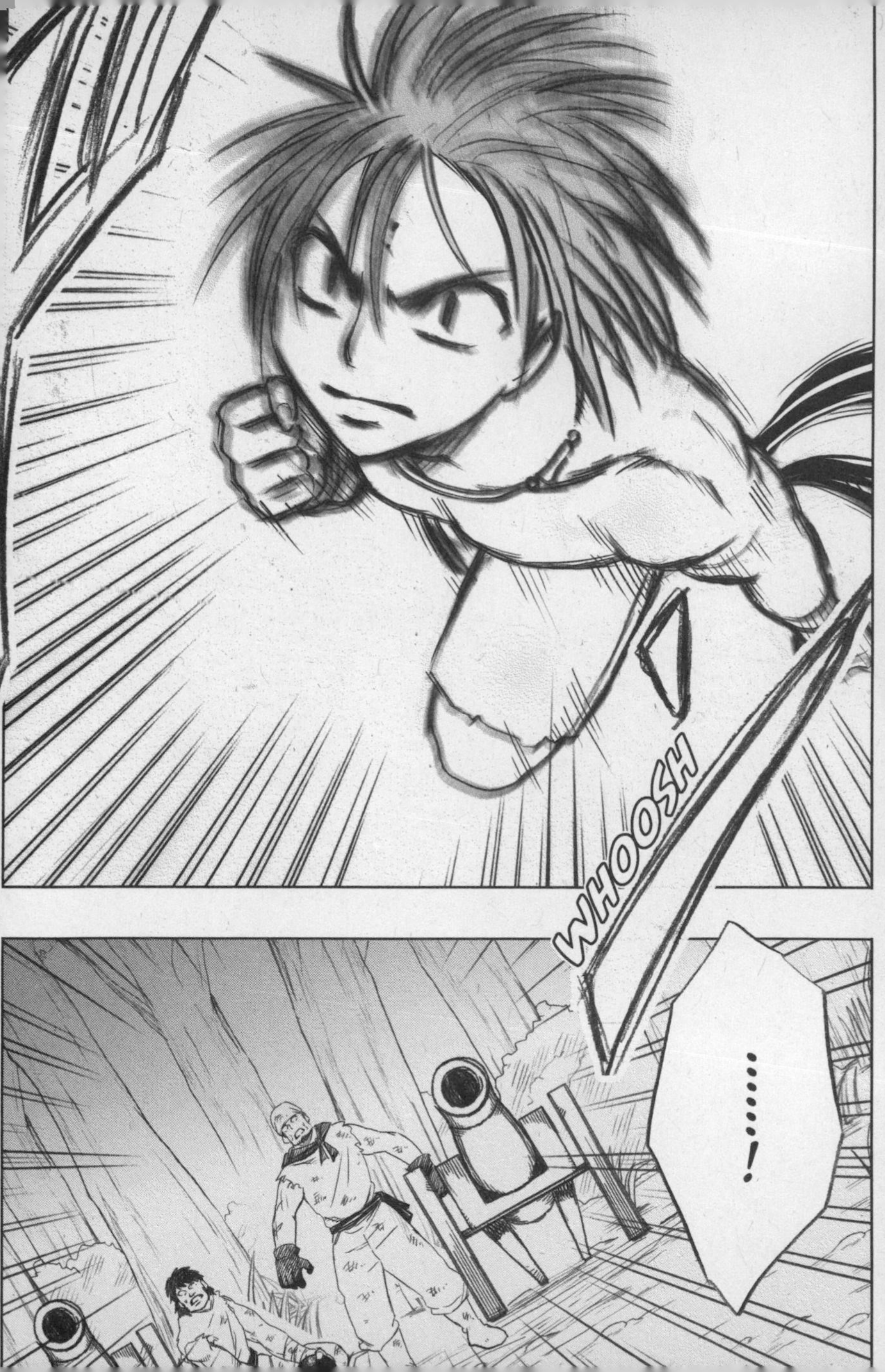
WHOOSH
......!

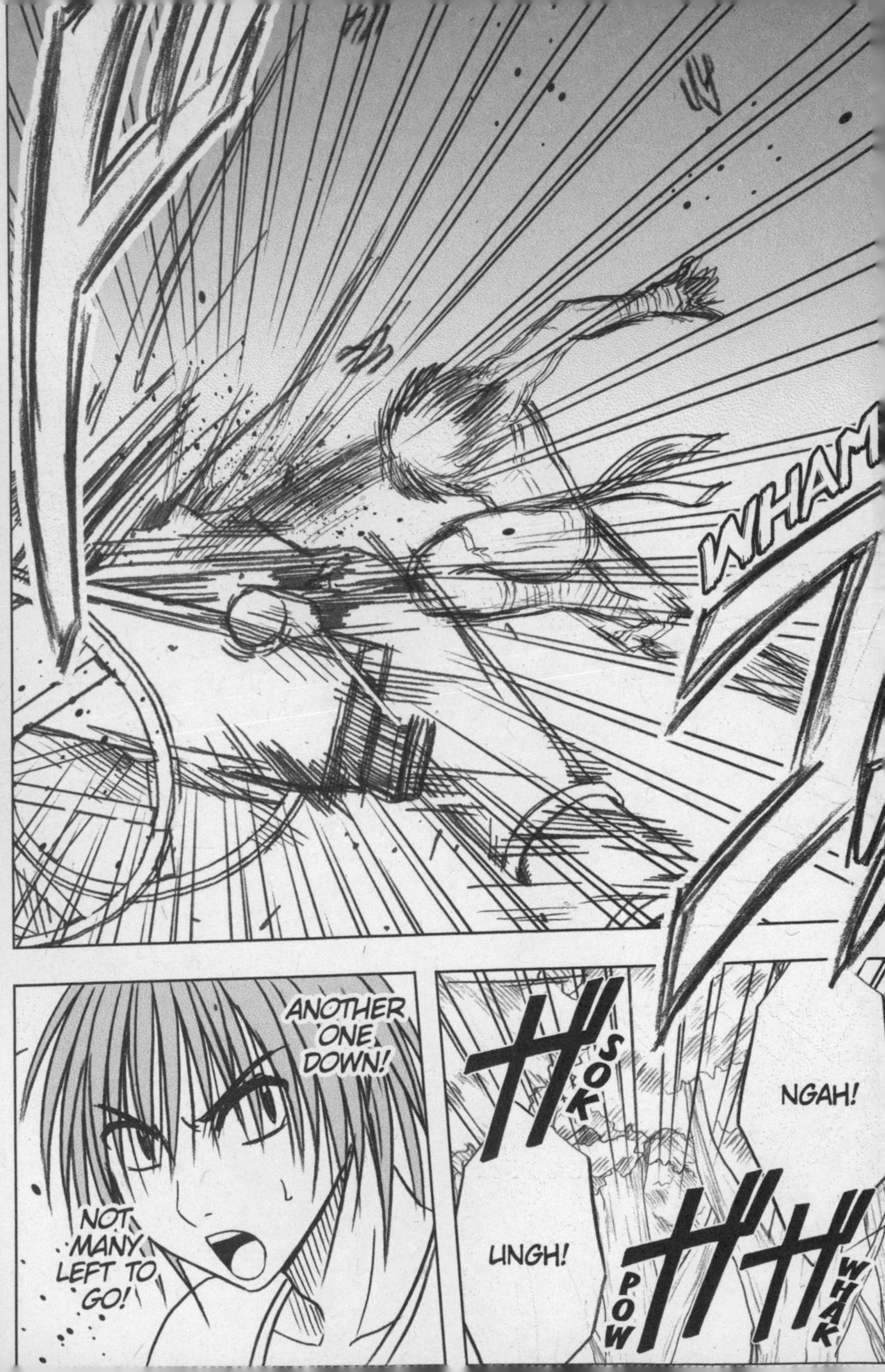
WHAM
SOK
NGAH!
UNGH!
WHAK
POW
ANOTHER ONE DOWN!
NOT MANY LEFT TO GO!

CHAPTER 7

THE GODS'
SILENCE

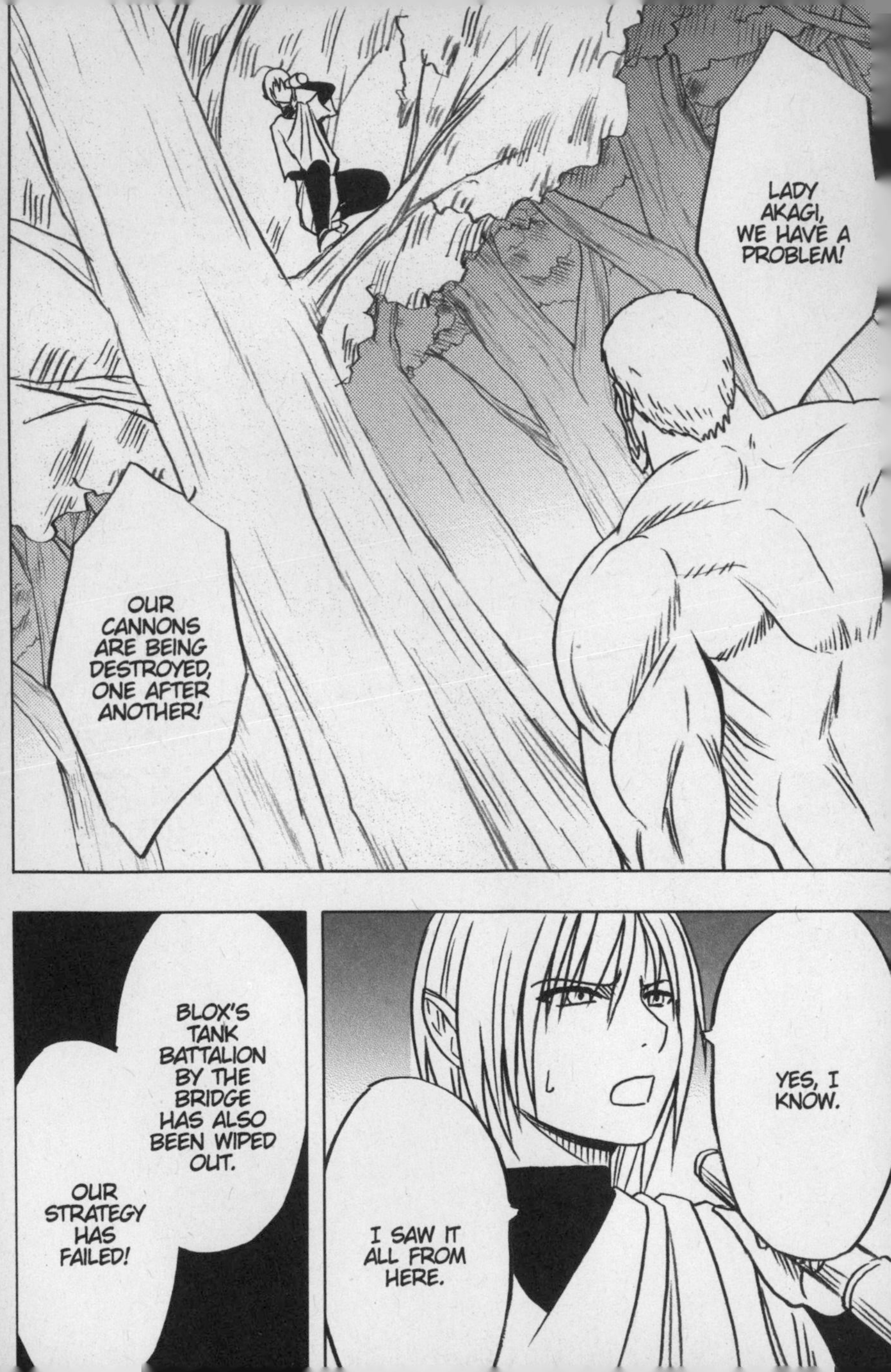
LADY AKAGI, WE HAVE A PROBLEM!
OUR CANNONS ARE BEING DESTROYED, ONE AFTER ANOTHER!
YES, I KNOW.
I SAW IT ALL FROM HERE.
BLOX'S TANK BATTALION BY THE BRIDGE HAS ALSO BEEN WIPED OUT.
OUR STRATEGY HAS FAILED!

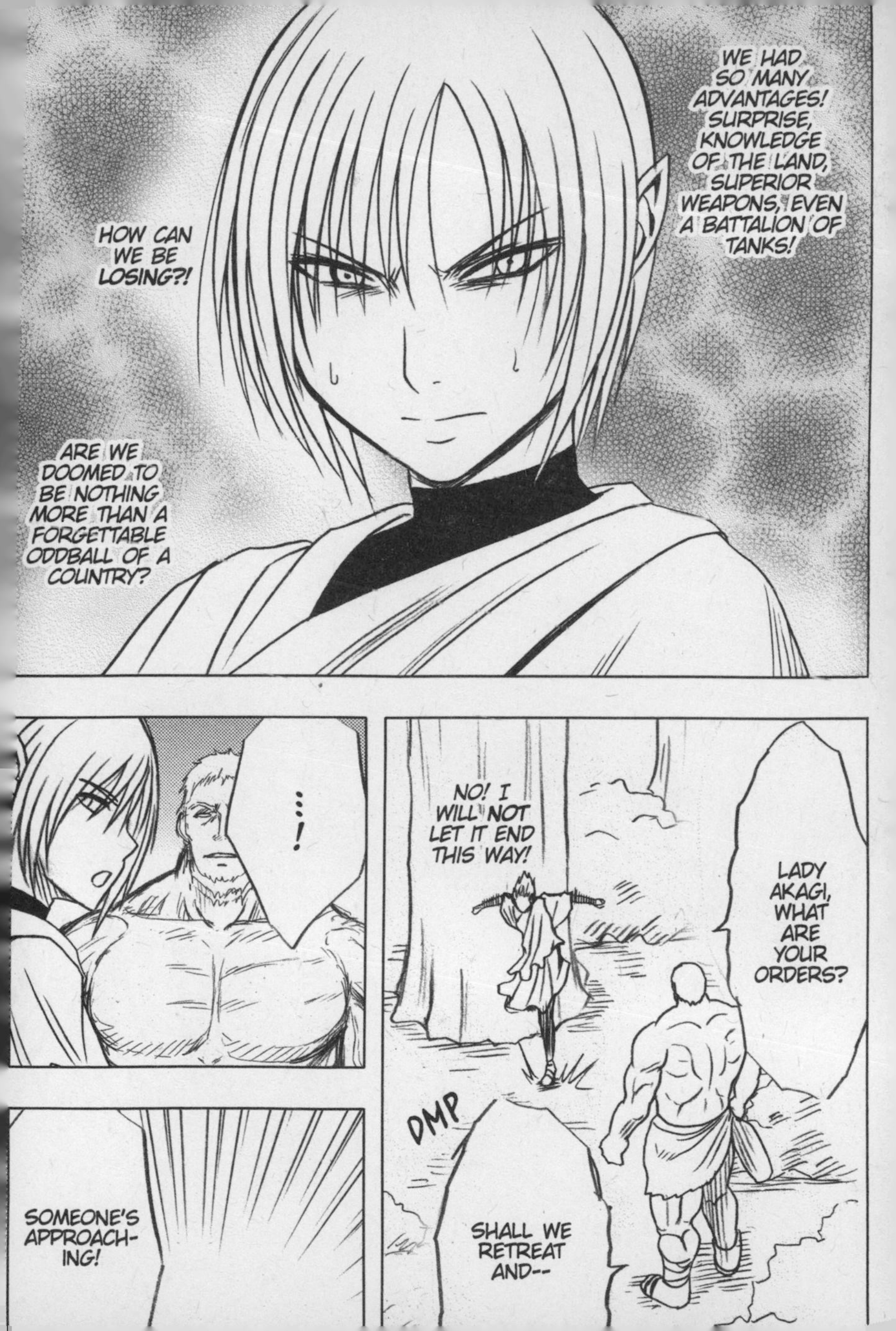
WE HAD SO MANY ADVANTAGES! SURPRISE, KNOWLEDGE OF THE LAND, SUPERIOR WEAPONS, EVEN A BATTALION OF TANKS!
HOW CAN WE BE LOSING?!
ARE WE DOOMED TO BE NOTHING MORE THAN A FORGETTABLE ODDBALL OF A COUNTRY?
LADY AKAGI, WHAT ARE YOUR ORDERS?
NO! I WILL NOT LET IT END THIS WAY!
DMP
SHALL WE RETREAT AND--
...!
SOMEONE'S APPROACH-ING!

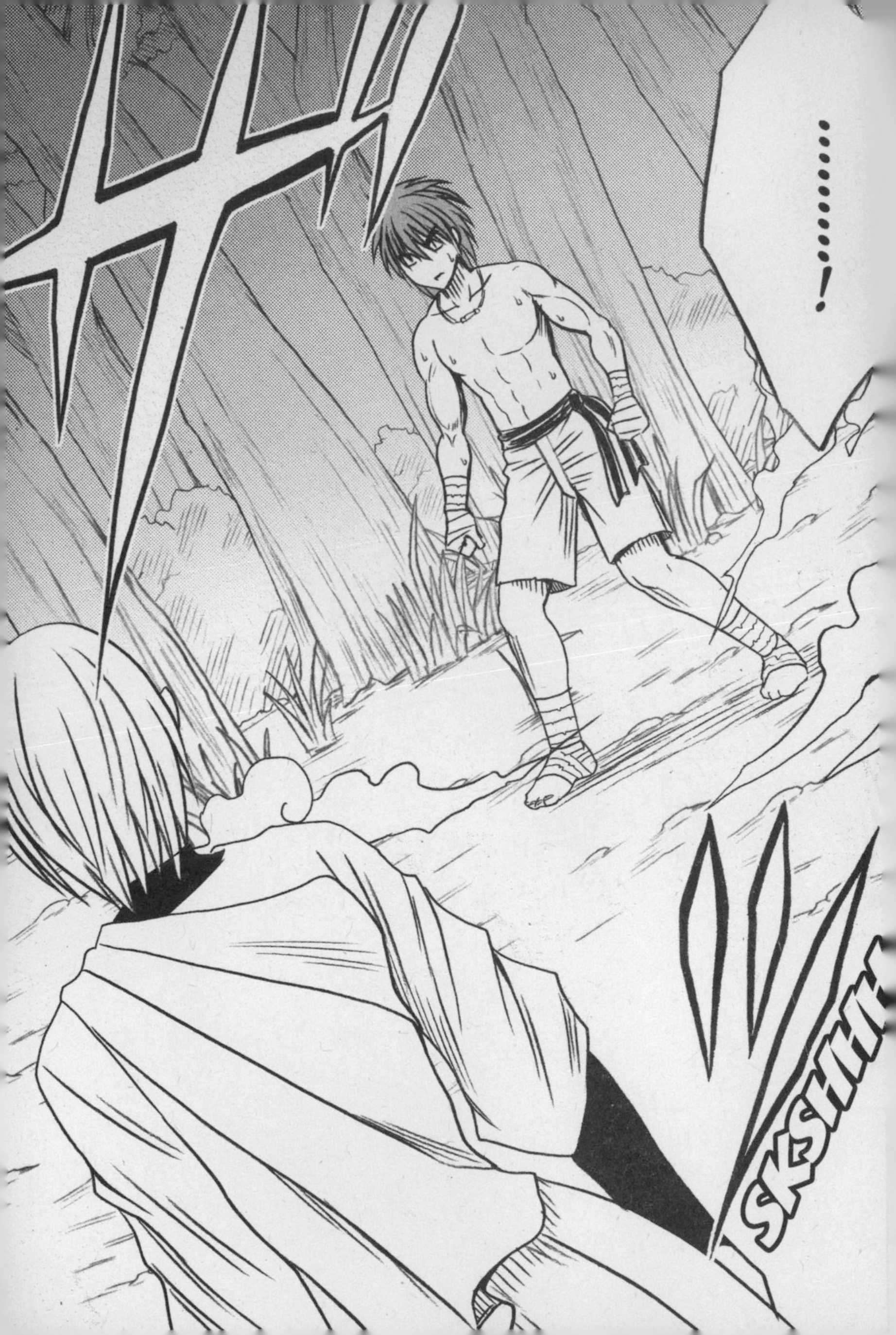
......!
SKSHHH

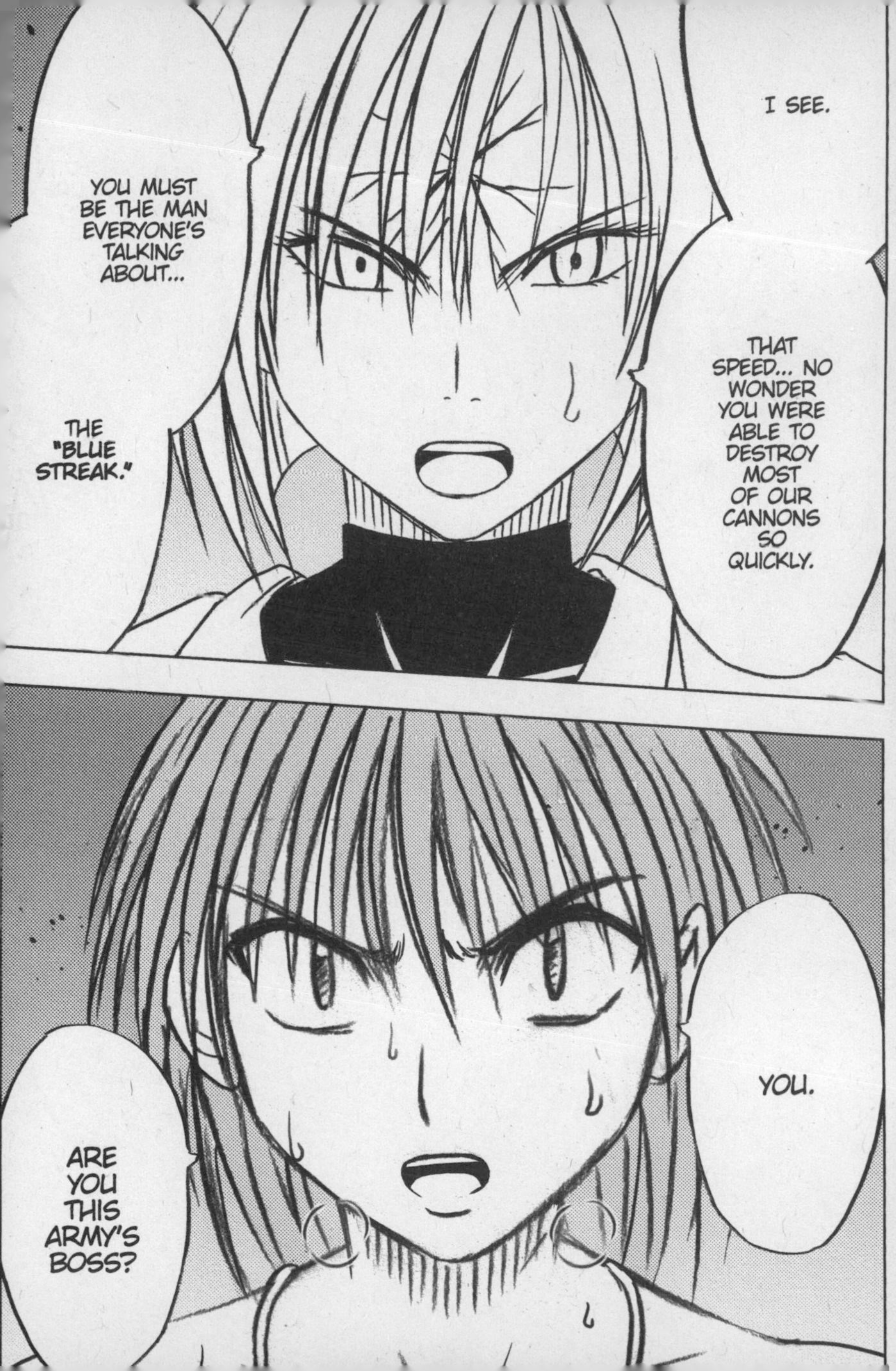
I SEE.
THAT SPEED... NO WONDER YOU WERE ABLE TO DESTROY MOST OF OUR CANNONS SO QUICKLY.
YOU MUST BE THE MAN EVERYONE'S TALKING ABOUT...
THE "BLUE STREAK."
YOU.
ARE YOU THIS ARMY'S BOSS?

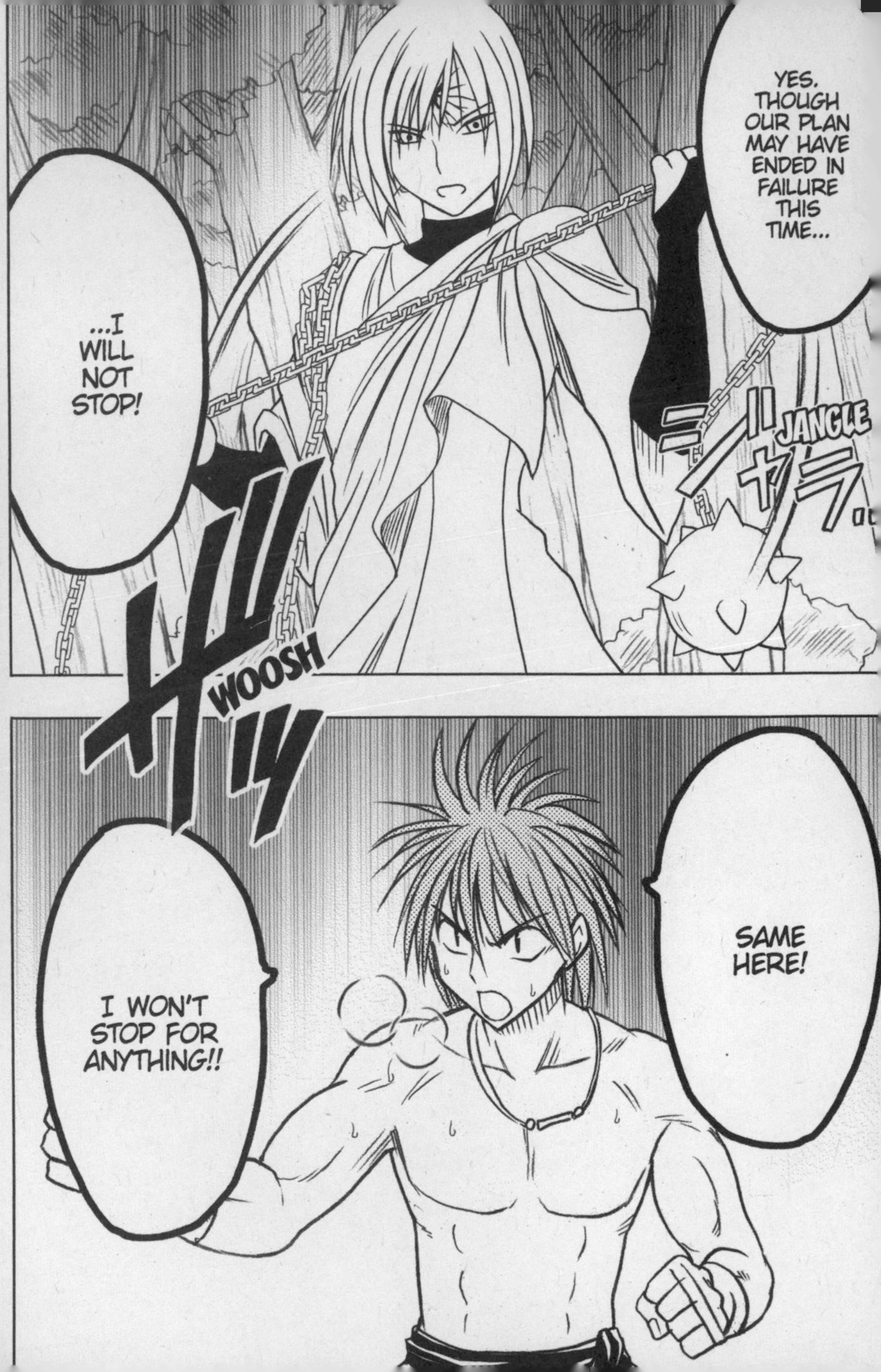
YES. THOUGH OUR PLAN MAY HAVE ENDED IN FAILURE THIS TIME...
JANGLE
...I WILL NOT STOP!
WOOSH
SAME HERE!
I WON'T STOP FOR ANYTHING!!

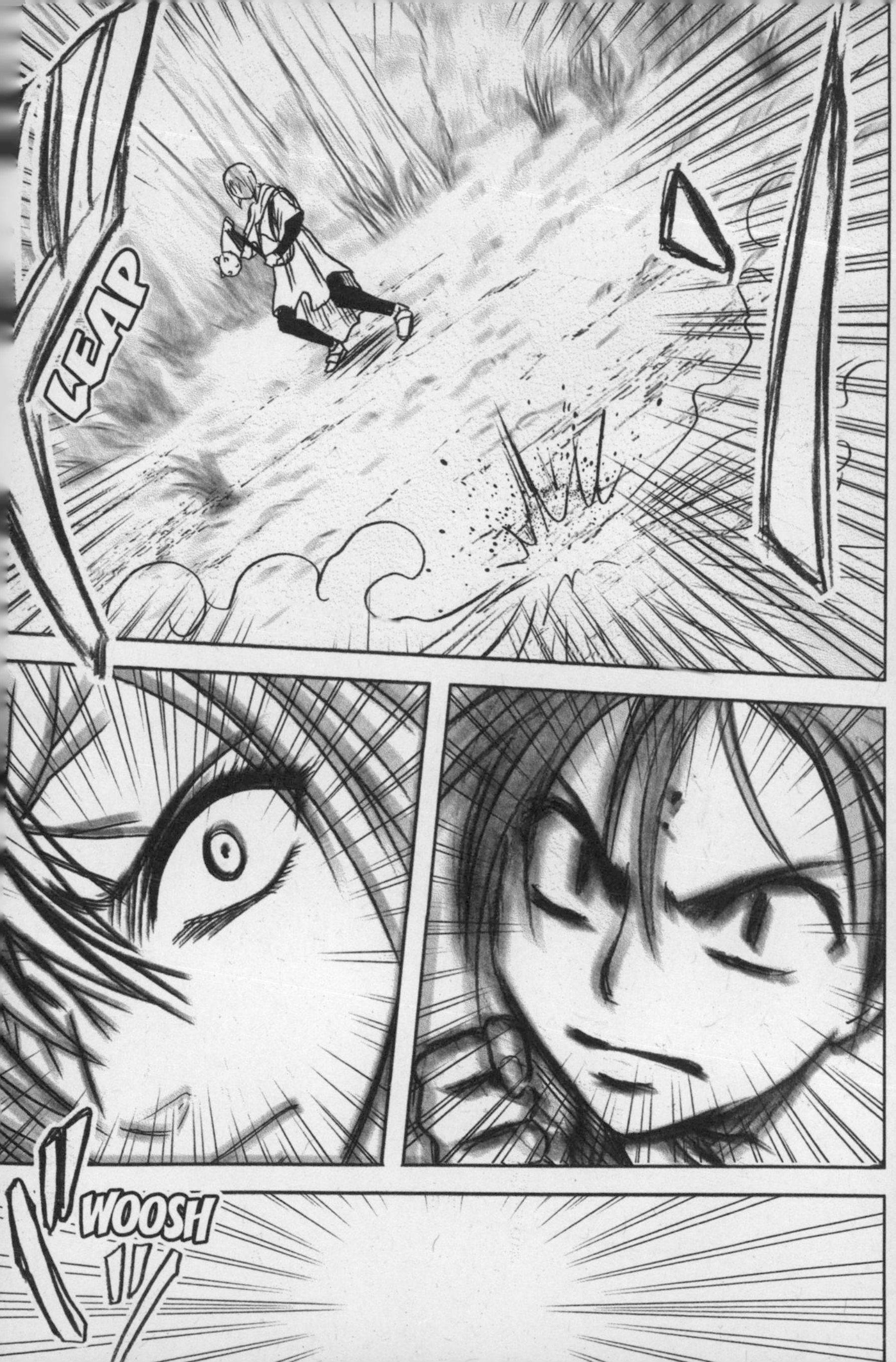
LEAP
WOOSH

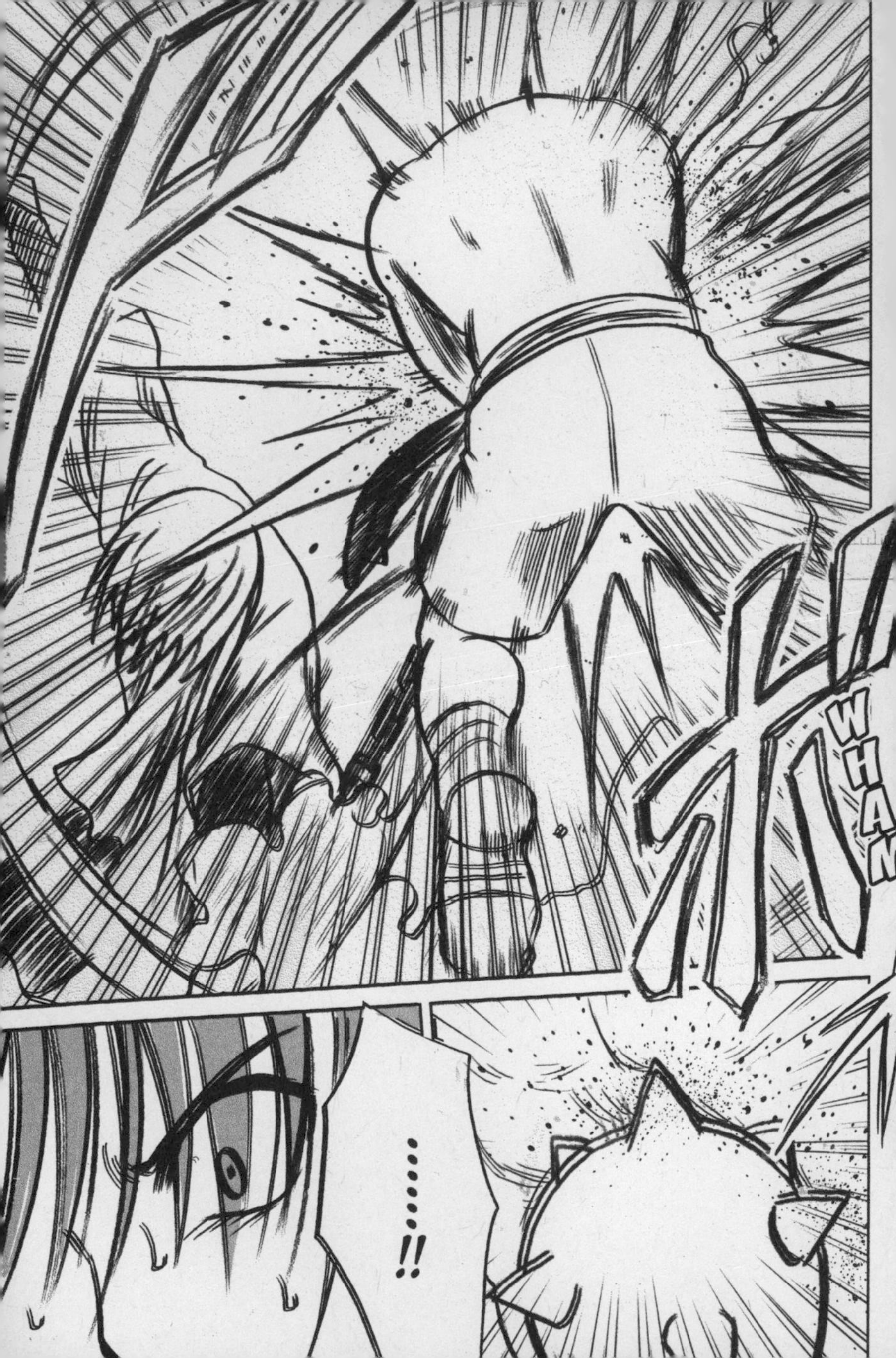
WHAM
......!!

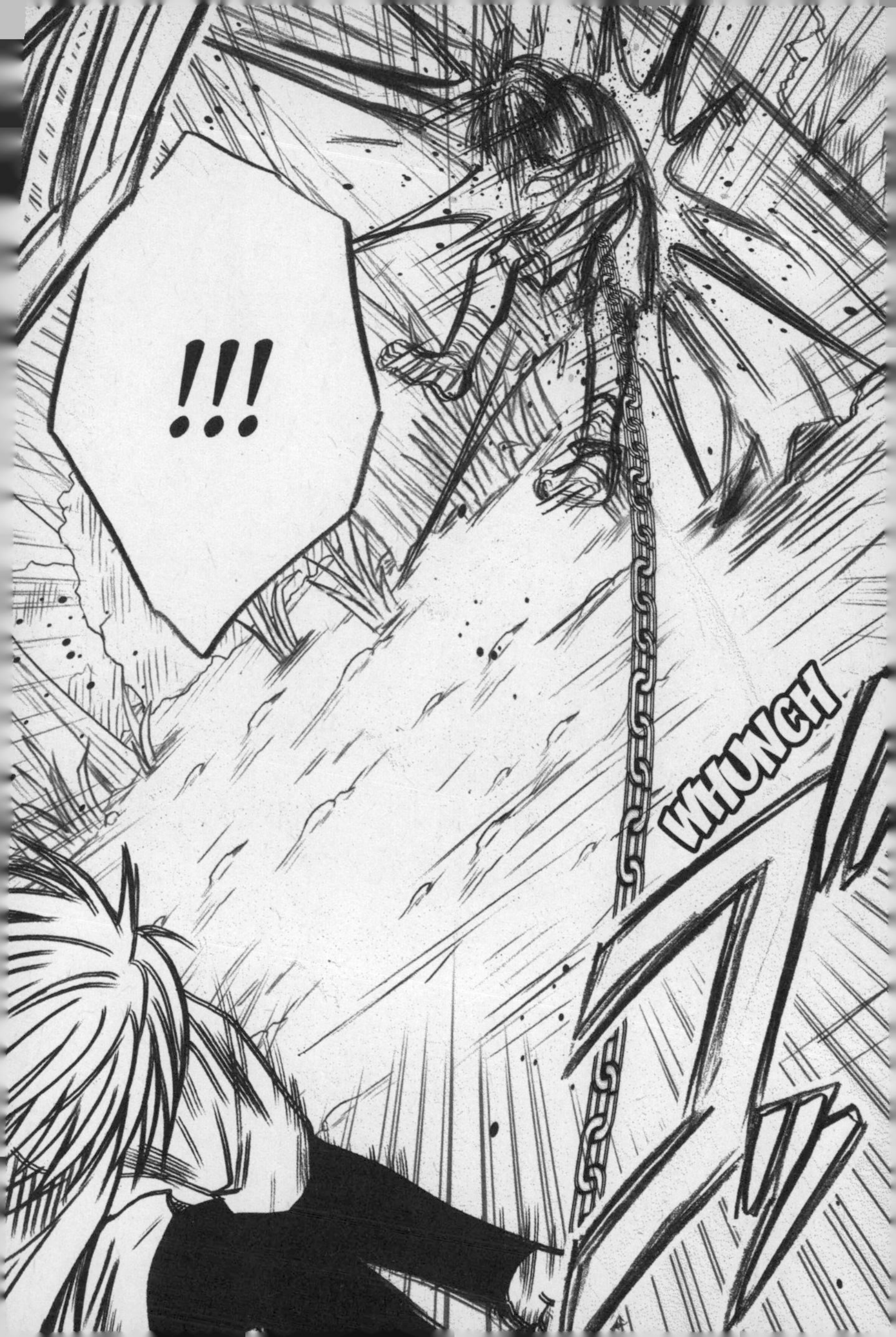
!!!
WHUNCH

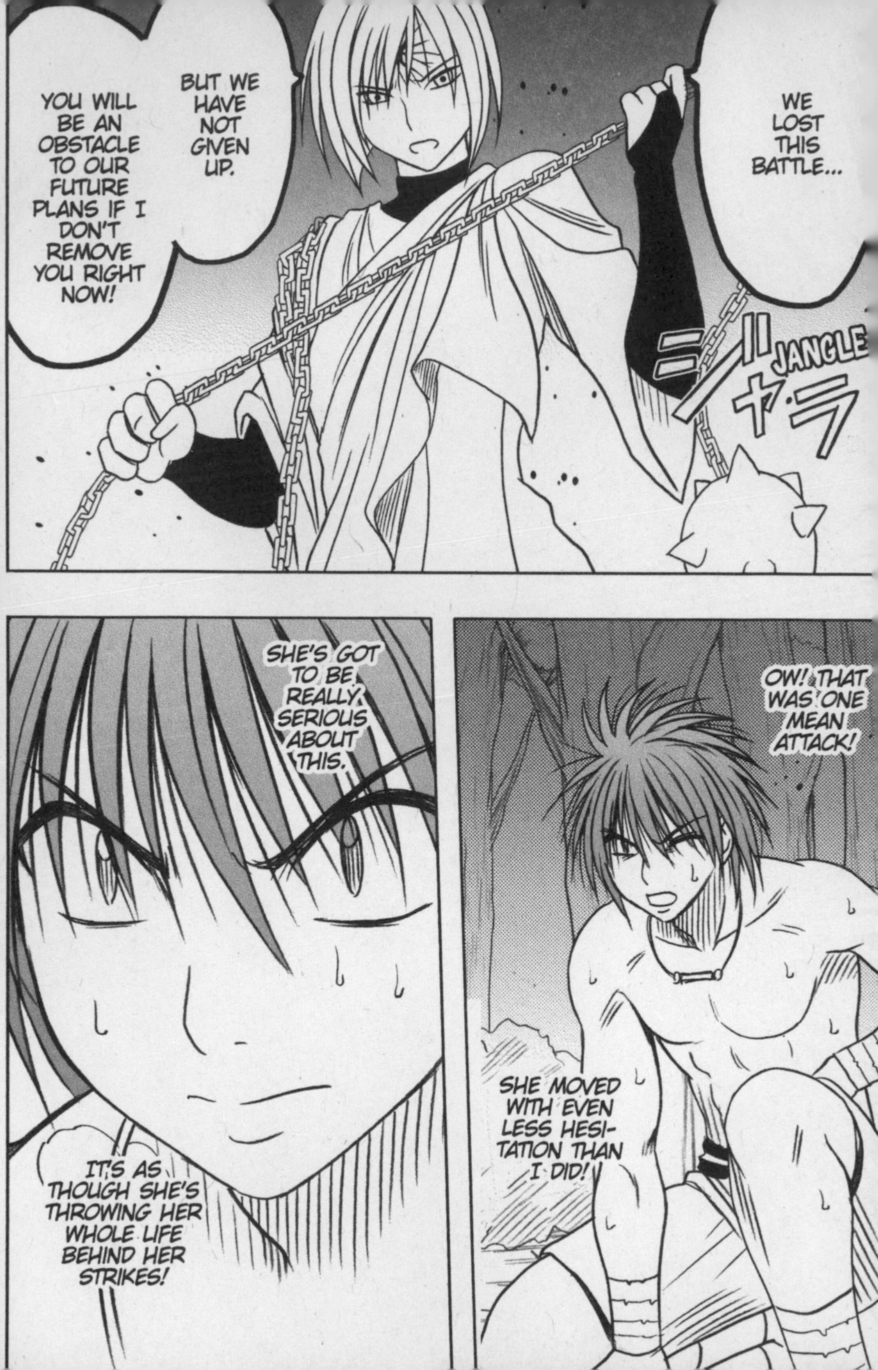
WE LOST THIS BATTLE...
BUT WE HAVE NOT GIVEN UP.
YOU WILL BE AN OBSTACLE TO OUR FUTURE PLANS IF I DON'T REMOVE YOU RIGHT NOW!
JANGLE
OW! THAT WAS ONE MEAN ATTACK!
SHE MOVED WITH EVEN LESS HESITATION THAN I DID!
SHE'S GOT TO BE REALLY SERIOUS ABOUT THIS.
IT'S AS THOUGH SHE'S THROWING HER WHOLE LIFE BEHIND HER STRIKES!

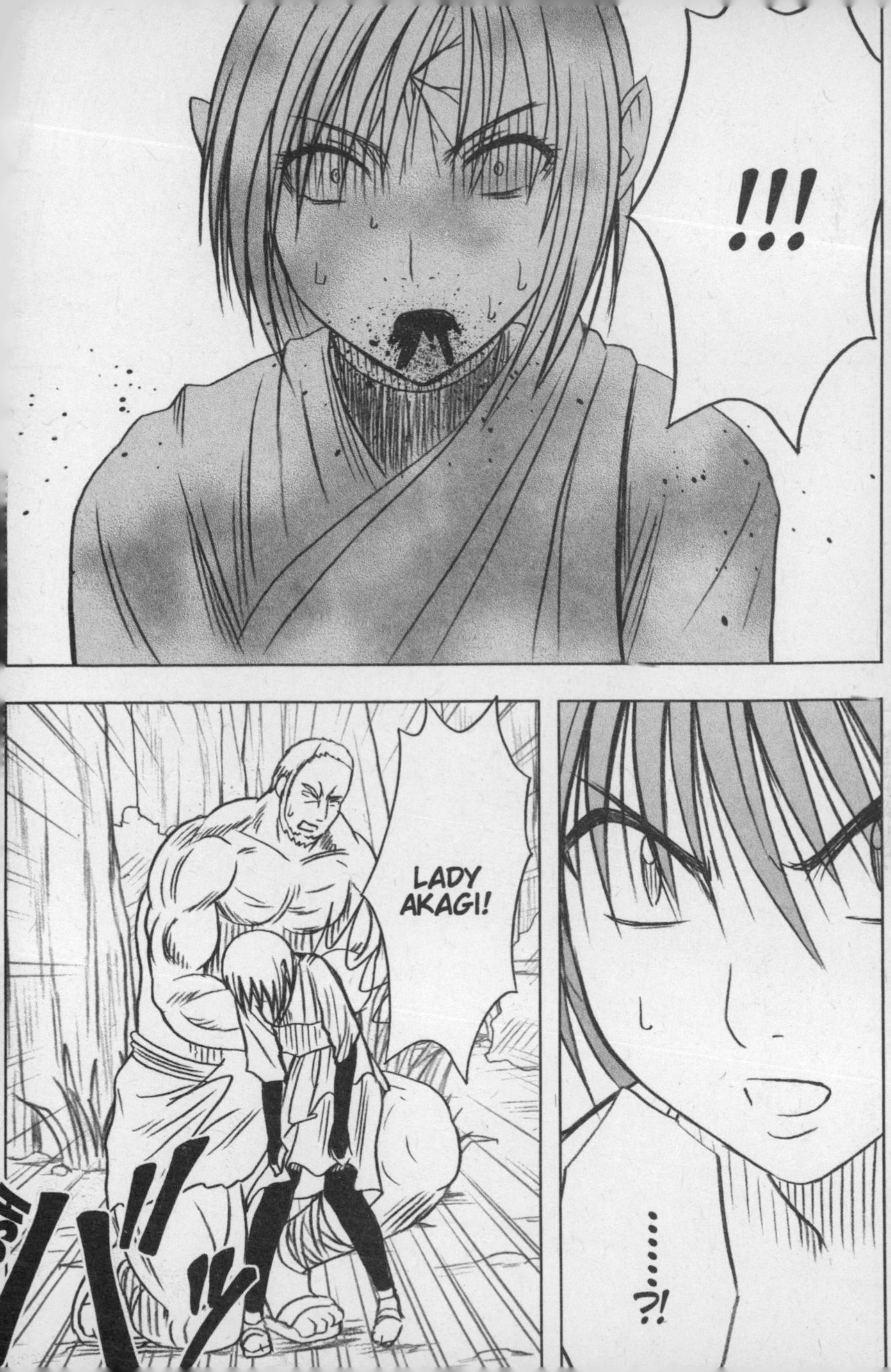
!!!
......?!
LADY AKAGI!

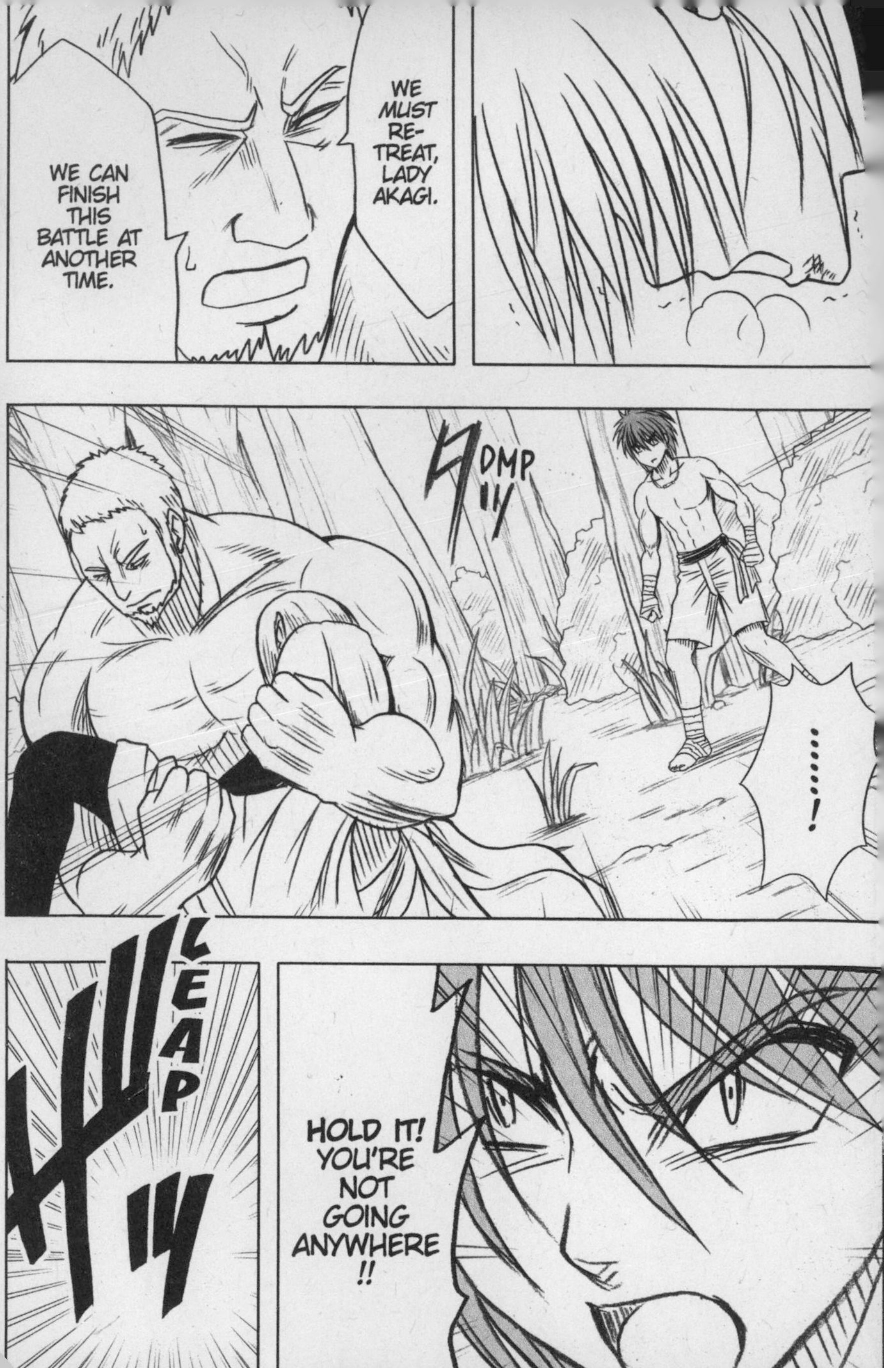
WE MUST RE-TREAT, LADY AKAGI.
WE CAN FINISH THIS BATTLE AT ANOTHER TIME.
SDMP
......!
HOLD IT! YOU'RE NOT GOING ANYWHERE!!
LEAP

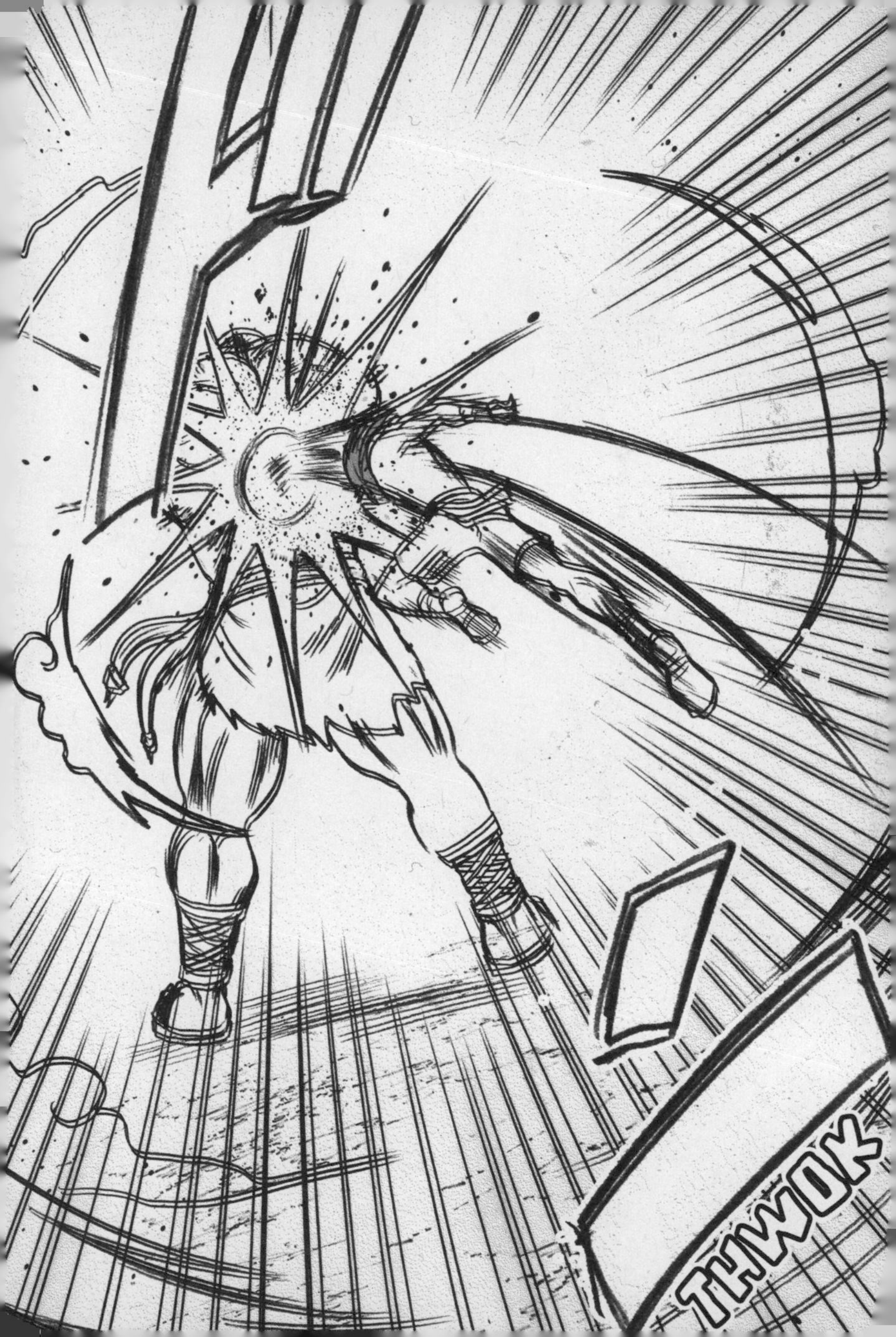
THWOK

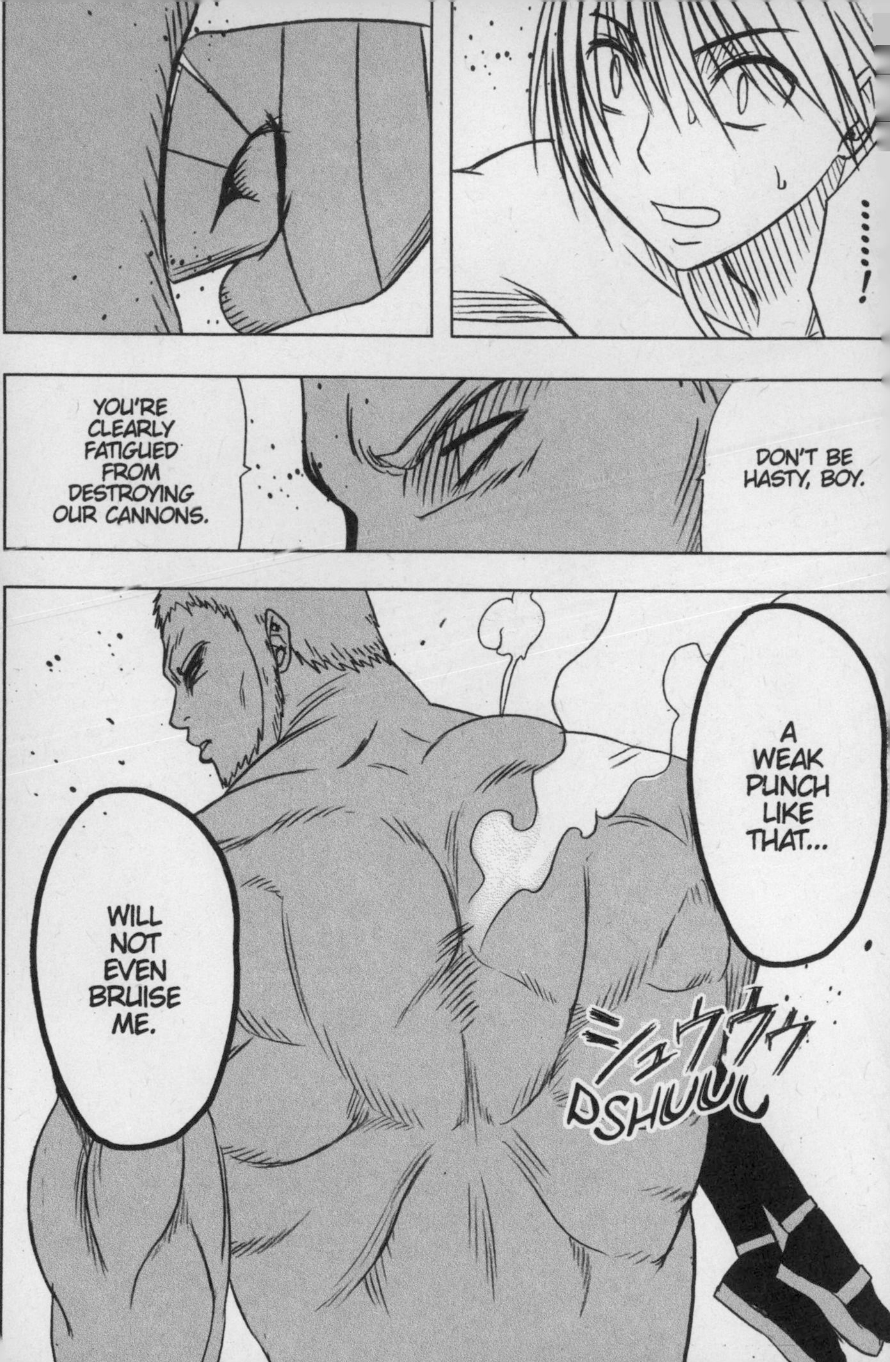
....!
DON'T BE HASTY, BOY.
YOU'RE CLEARLY FATIGUED FROM DESTROYING OUR CANNONS.
A WEAK PUNCH LIKE THAT...
シュウウウ
DSHUUU
WILL NOT EVEN BRUISE ME.

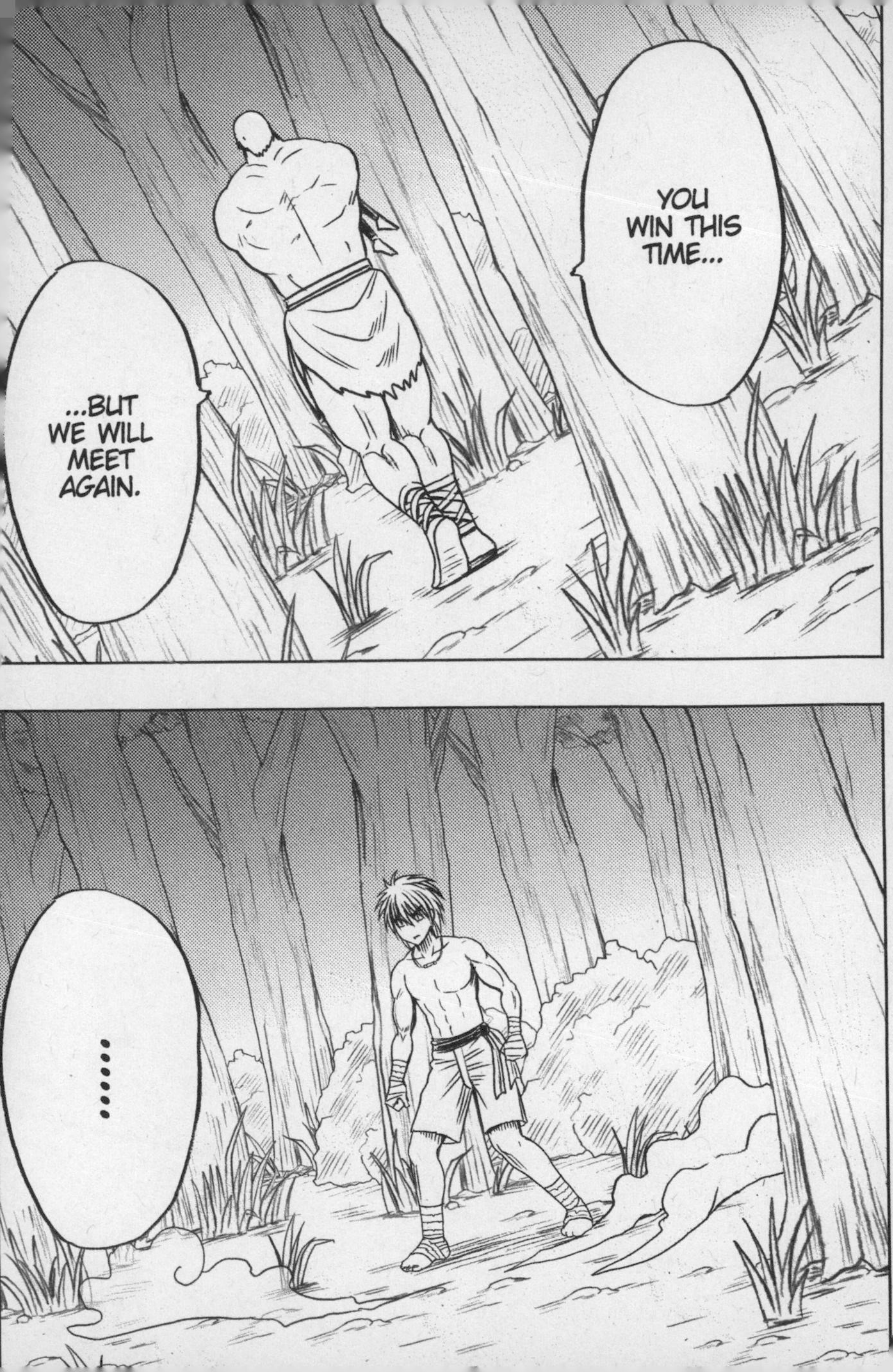
YOU WIN THIS TIME...
...BUT WE WILL MEET AGAIN.
......

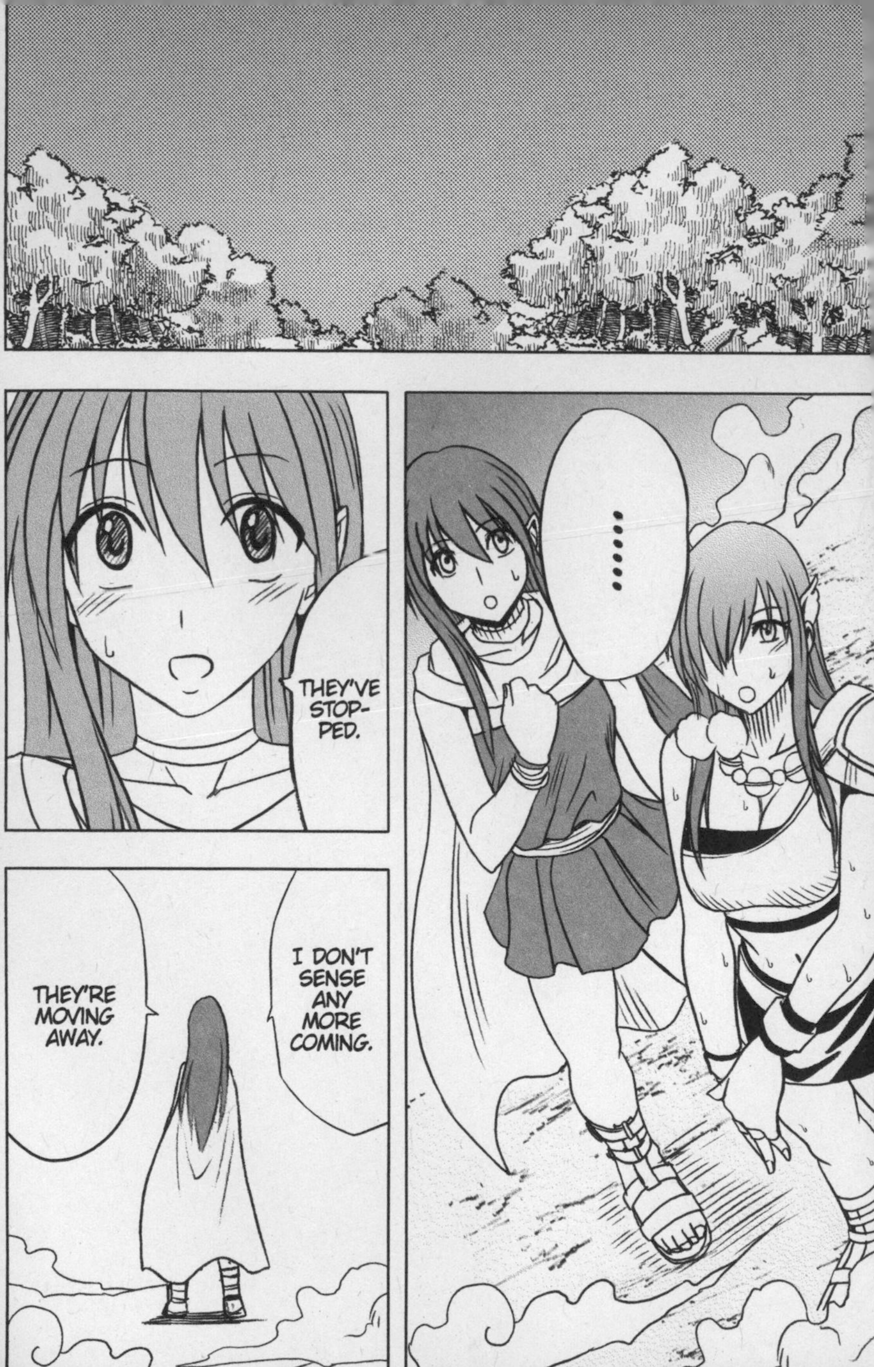
......
THEY'VE STOP-PED.
I DON'T SENSE ANY MORE COMING.
THEY'RE MOVING AWAY.

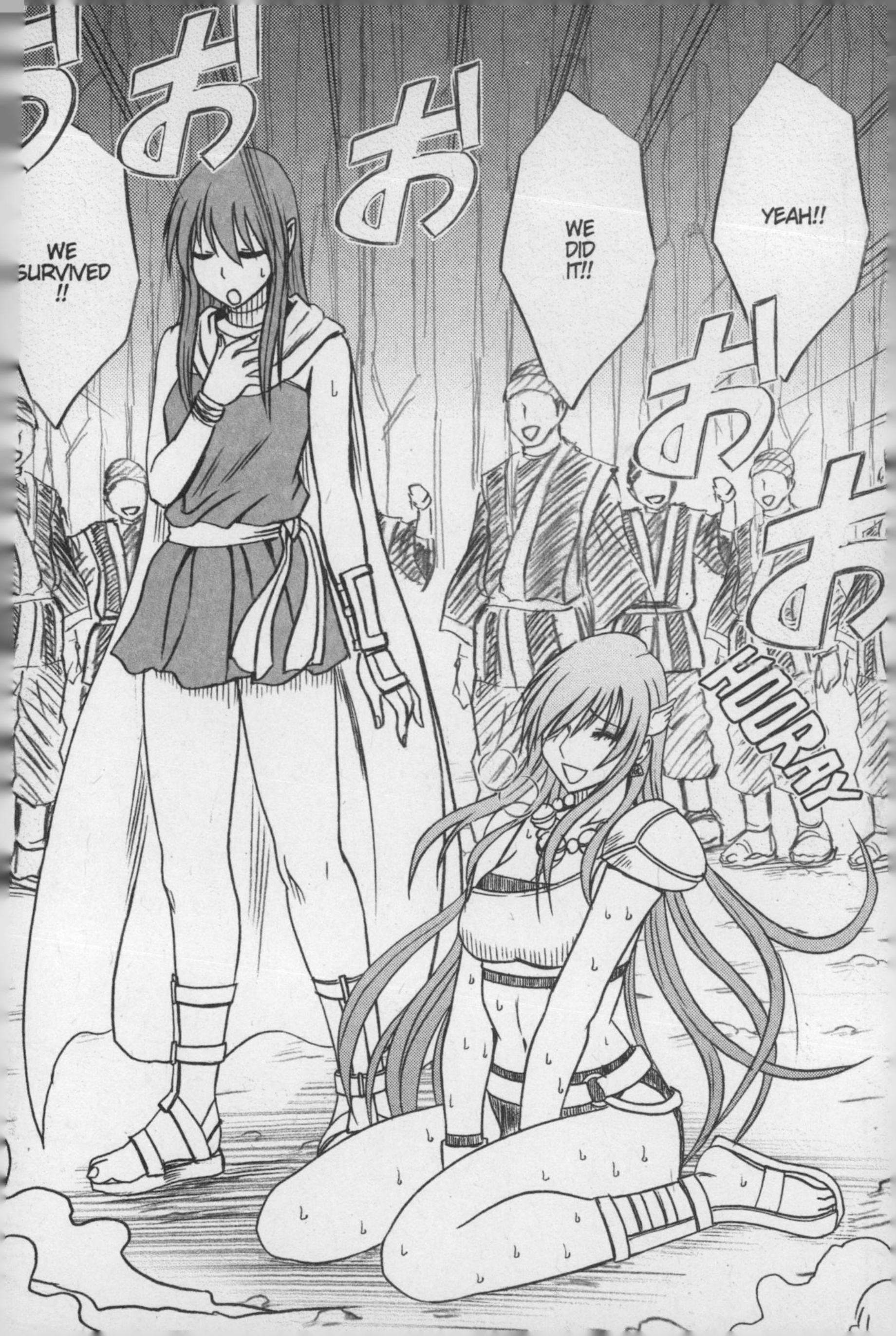
YEAH!!
WE DID IT!!
HOORAY
WE SURVIVED!!

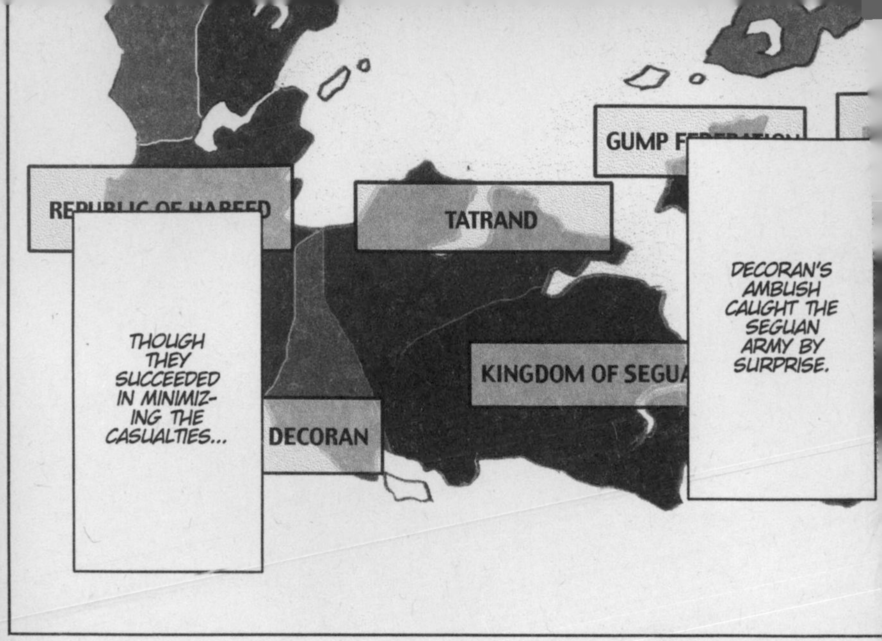
DECORAN'S AMBUSH CAUGHT THE SEGUAN ARMY BY SURPRISE.
TATRAND
DECORAN
THOUGH THEY SUCCEEDED IN MINIMIZ-ING THE CASUALTIES...

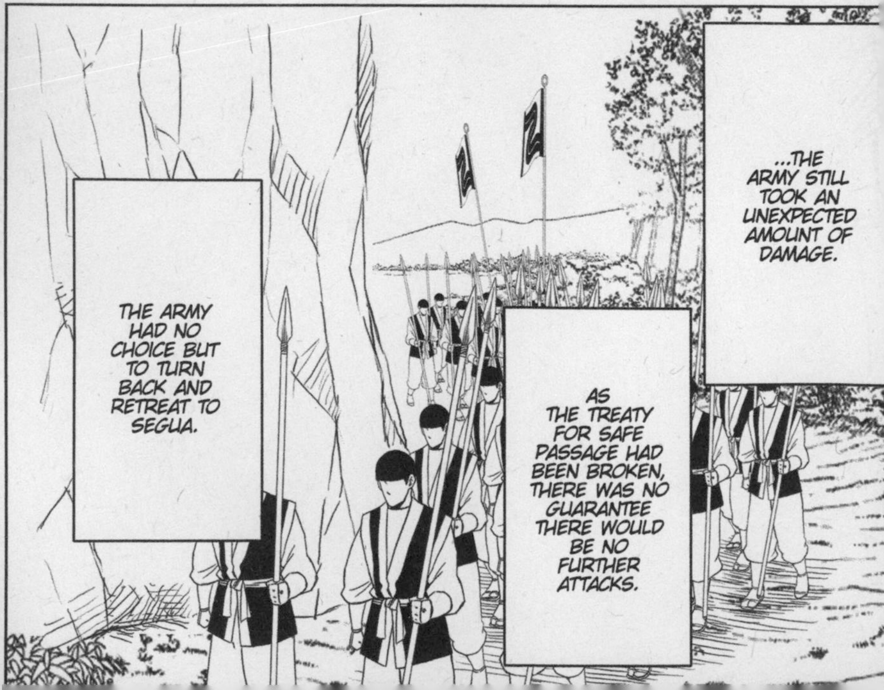
...THE ARMY STILL TOOK AN UNEXPECTED AMOUNT OF DAMAGE.
AS THE TREATY FOR SAFE PASSAGE HAD BEEN BROKEN, THERE WAS NO GUARANTEE THERE WOULD BE NO FURTHER ATTACKS.
THE ARMY HAD NO CHOICE BUT TO TURN BACK AND RETREAT TO SEGUA.

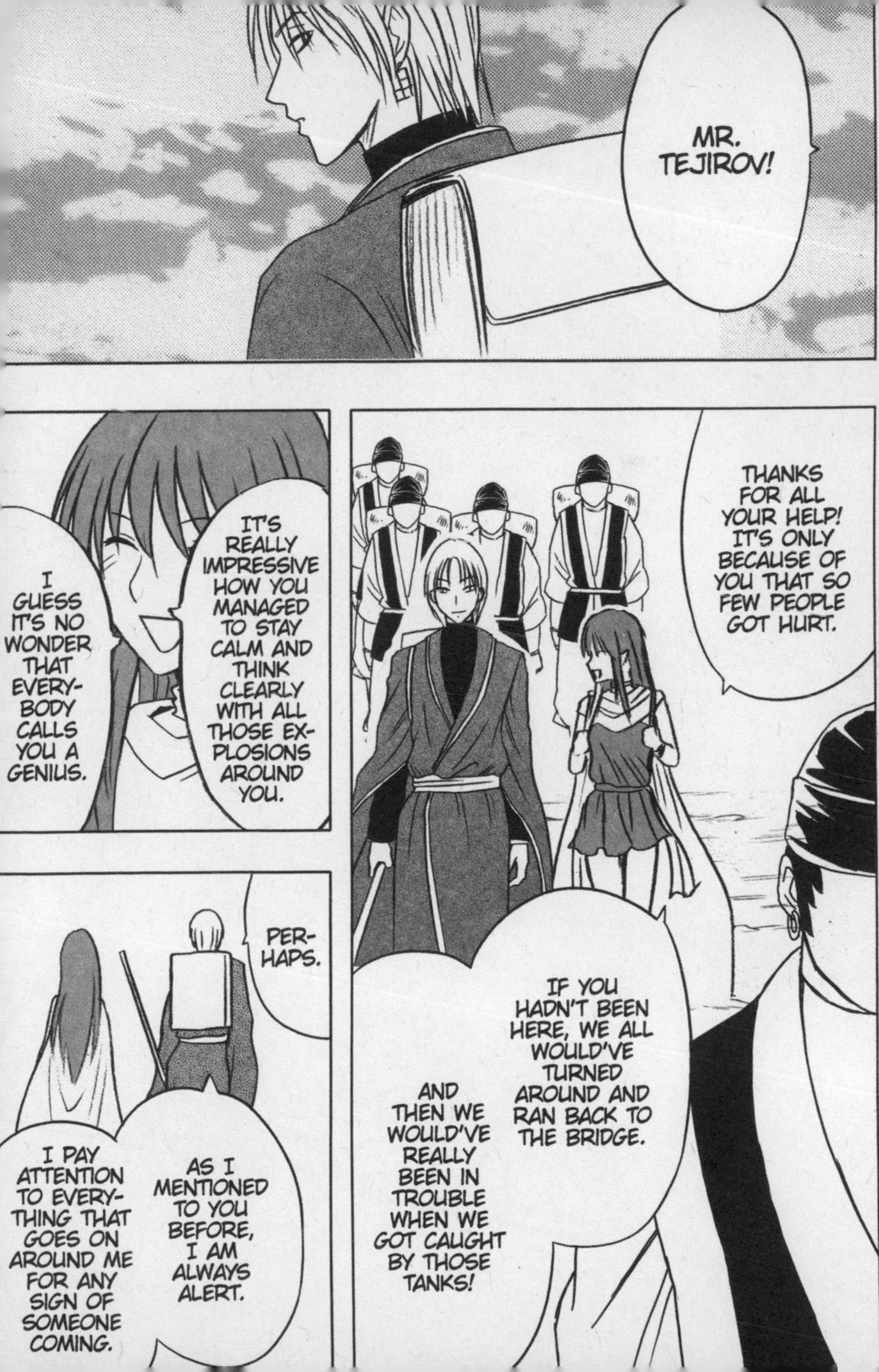
MR. TEJIROV!
THANKS FOR ALL YOUR HELP! IT'S ONLY BECAUSE OF YOU THAT SO FEW PEOPLE GOT HURT.
IF YOU HADN'T BEEN HERE, WE ALL WOULD'VE TURNED AROUND AND RAN BACK TO THE BRIDGE.
AND THEN WE WOULD'VE REALLY BEEN IN TROUBLE WHEN WE GOT CAUGHT BY THOSE TANKS!
IT'S REALLY IMPRESSIVE HOW YOU MANAGED TO STAY CALM AND THINK CLEARLY WITH ALL THOSE EX-PLOSIONS AROUND YOU.
I GUESS IT'S NO WONDER THAT EVERY-BODY CALLS YOU A GENIUS.
PER-HAPS.
AS I MENTIONED TO YOU BEFORE, I AM ALWAYS ALERT.
I PAY ATTENTION TO EVERY-THING THAT GOES ON AROUND ME FOR ANY SIGN OF SOMEONE COMING.

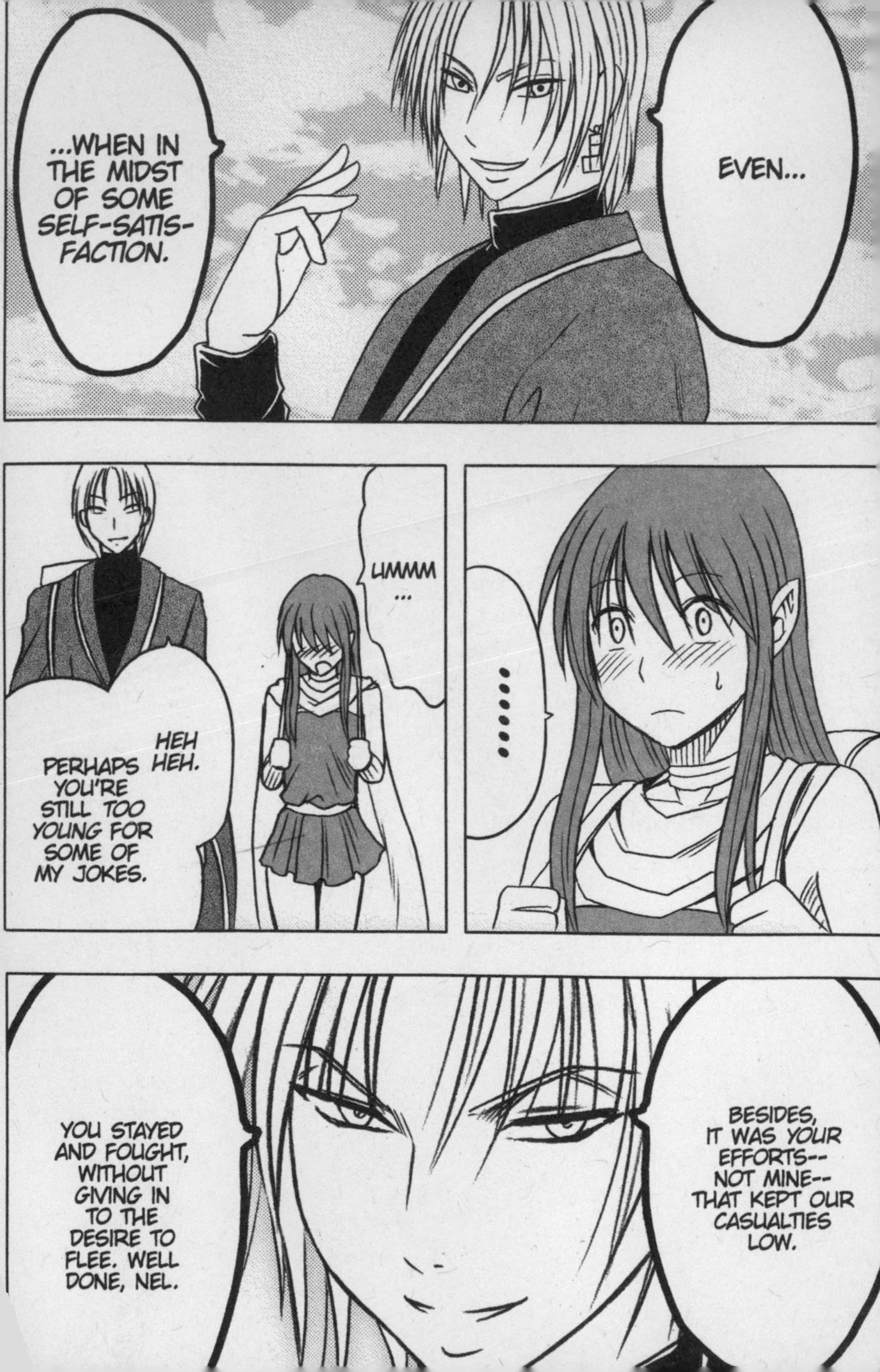
EVEN...
...WHEN IN THE MIDST OF SOME SELF-SATIS-FACTION.
......
UMMM ...
HEH HEH. PERHAPS YOU'RE STILL TOO YOUNG FOR SOME OF MY JOKES.
BESIDES, IT WAS YOUR EFFORTS-- NOT MINE-- THAT KEPT OUR CASUALTIES LOW.
YOU STAYED AND FOUGHT, WITHOUT GIVING IN TO THE DESIRE TO FLEE. WELL DONE, NEL.

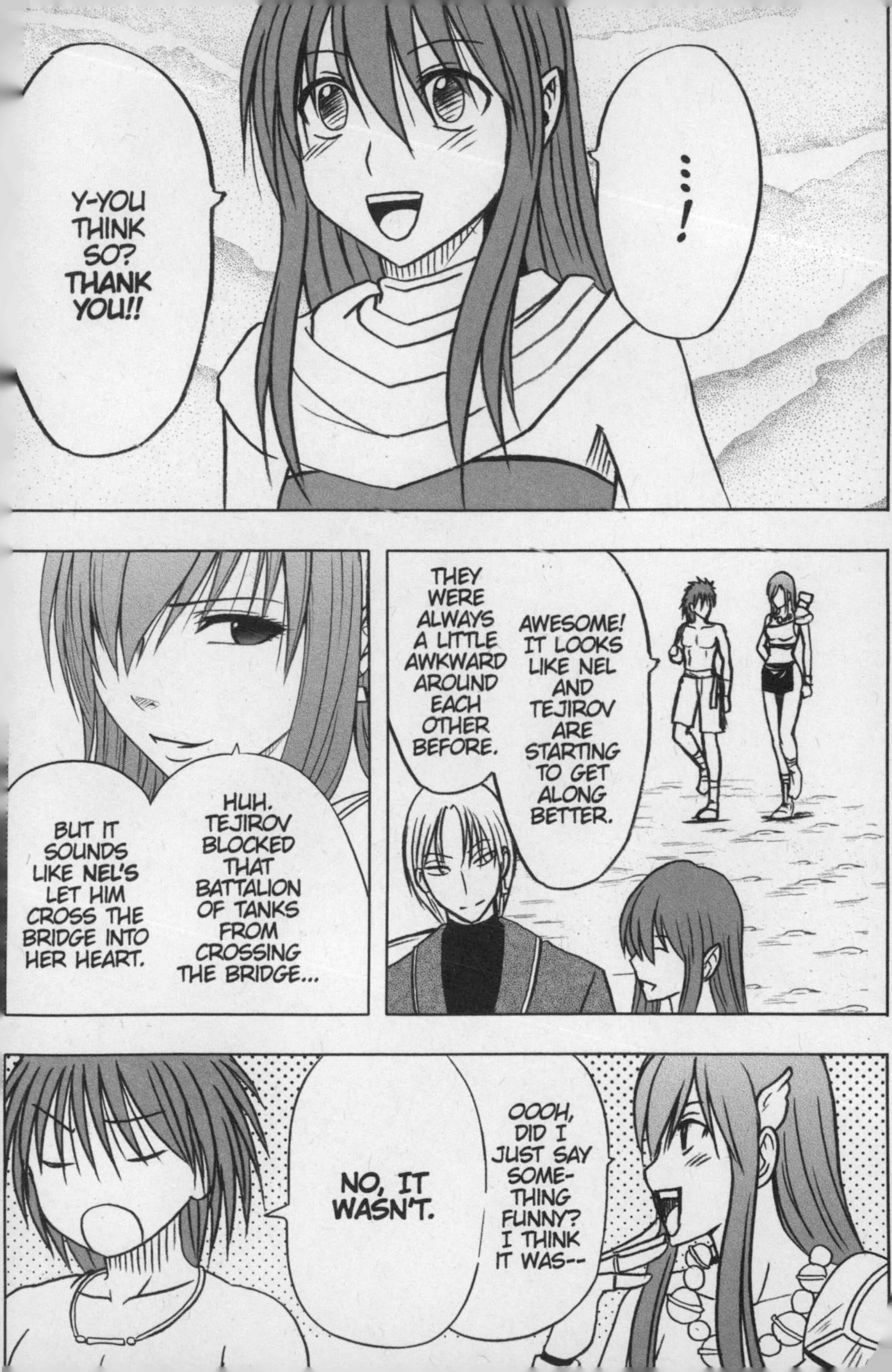
...!
Y-YOU THINK SO? THANK YOU!!
AWESOME! IT LOOKS LIKE NEL AND TEJIROV ARE STARTING TO GET ALONG BETTER.
THEY WERE ALWAYS A LITTLE AWKWARD AROUND EACH OTHER BEFORE.
HUH. TEJIROV BLOCKED THAT BATTALION OF TANKS FROM CROSSING THE BRIDGE...
BUT IT SOUNDS LIKE NEL'S LET HIM CROSS THE BRIDGE INTO HER HEART.
OOOH, DID I JUST SAY SOME-THING FUNNY? I THINK IT WAS--
NO, IT WASN'T.

ME AND
OPAL AND
NEL AND
TEJIROV.

WE WERE
A TEAM. I
BELIEVED AS
LONG AS THE
FOUR OF
US WERE
TOGETHER...

...EVEN
NINTELDO
ITSELF
WOULDN'T
STAND A
CHANCE.

BACK THEN
I DIDN'T
KNOW...

...IT WAS TO
BE THE LAST
TIME WE'D BE
TOGETHER IN
BATTLE.

THE FOUR OF
US WOULD
NEVER FIGHT
SIDE-BY-SIDE
AGAIN.

WORLD WAR BLUE
CHARACTER INTRODUCTION

Nonstop Runner
AKAGI

Decoran native.

Younger sister of Asimov, Lord of Decoran. She used to be a quiet and gentle person, but after a life-changing event, she became obsessed with only pushing forward. Once she picks a path, she never, ever turns back.

She is skilled with whips, boomerangs, and weighted chains.

Author Comment

I've changed her outfit from the original webcomic version to look more like the flowing robes worn by the Statue of Liberty. Also unlike the webcomic run, she doesn't have online senses like Nel.

WORLD WAR BLUE

CHARACTER INTRODUCTION

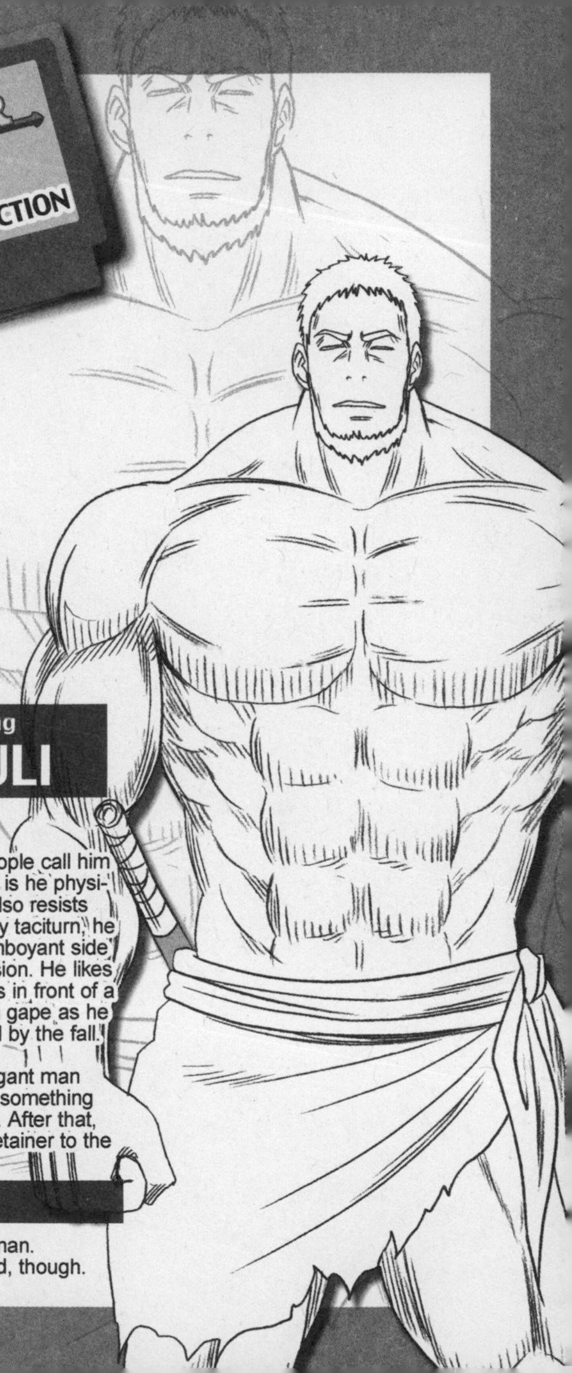

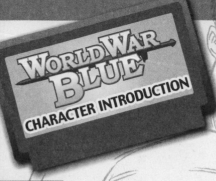

The Undying

HERCULI

Decoran native.

He is so tough that people call him The Undying. Not only is he physically tough, his body also resists aging. Though normally taciturn, he does have a more flamboyant side that surfaces on occasion. He likes to jump off of high cliffs in front of a crowd and watch them gape as he walks away, unscathed by the fall.

He used to be an arrogant man who loved to fight, but something changed him long ago. After that, he became a faithful retainer to the Decoran royal family.

Author Comment

The standard macho-man. He's over 100 years old, though.

Perusing Video Game History

ON THE EDGE OF THE BLUE WORLD

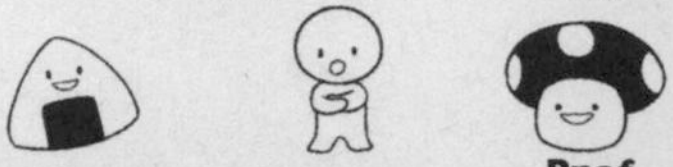

Dr. Onigiri Mr. Why Prof. Mushroom

Today's Topic

DATA EAST: PART 2

Mr. Why: Okay, so now I know about *Chelnov* and *Metal Max*. What other games did Data East produce?

Dr. Onigiri: Well, there was the *Glory of Hercules* RPG series. That was just about as popular as *Metal Max*.

Prof. Mushroom: Originally released for the Famicom in 1987, the *Glory of Hercules* was a series of RPGs with a mythical flavor, where Hercules went on adventures to save Venus from the grasp of Hades.

Dr. Onigiri: Four games were released in total, but the most popular of them was the third, *Glory of Hercules*: *Silence of the Gods*. It was released for the Super Famicom in 1992.

Prof. Mushroom: Yeah. In that one, Hercules had become completely immortal, but had lost all his memories. On his adventures to regain them, he got involved in some shenanigans between humans and gods. Its close resemblance to the *Final Fantasy* series won it a lot of fans.

Mr. Why: That sounds interesting! I thought Data East made only weird and wacky titles, but I guess they had some more mainstream games, as well!

Prof. Mushroom: Indeed. Their catchphrase was "leave the weird games to us," but it's not like they aimed to make everything weird, right from the get-go.

Dr. Onigiri: Yeah.

To Be Continued...

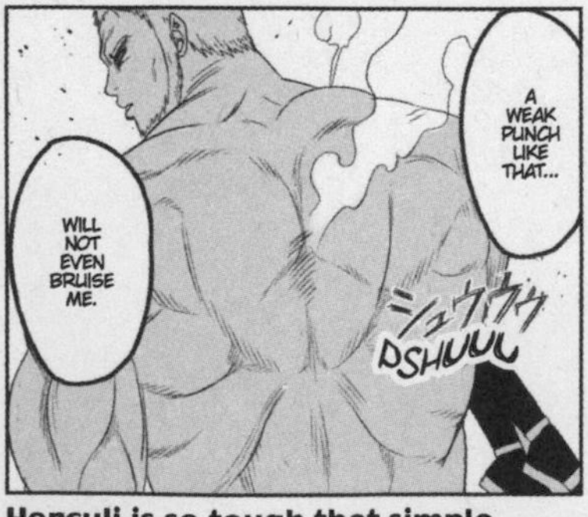
A WEAK PUNCH LIKE THAT...
WILL NOT EVEN BRUISE ME.
シュウウウ
DSHUUU

Herculi is so tough that simple physical attacks don't hurt him. It's no wonder people call him the Undying.

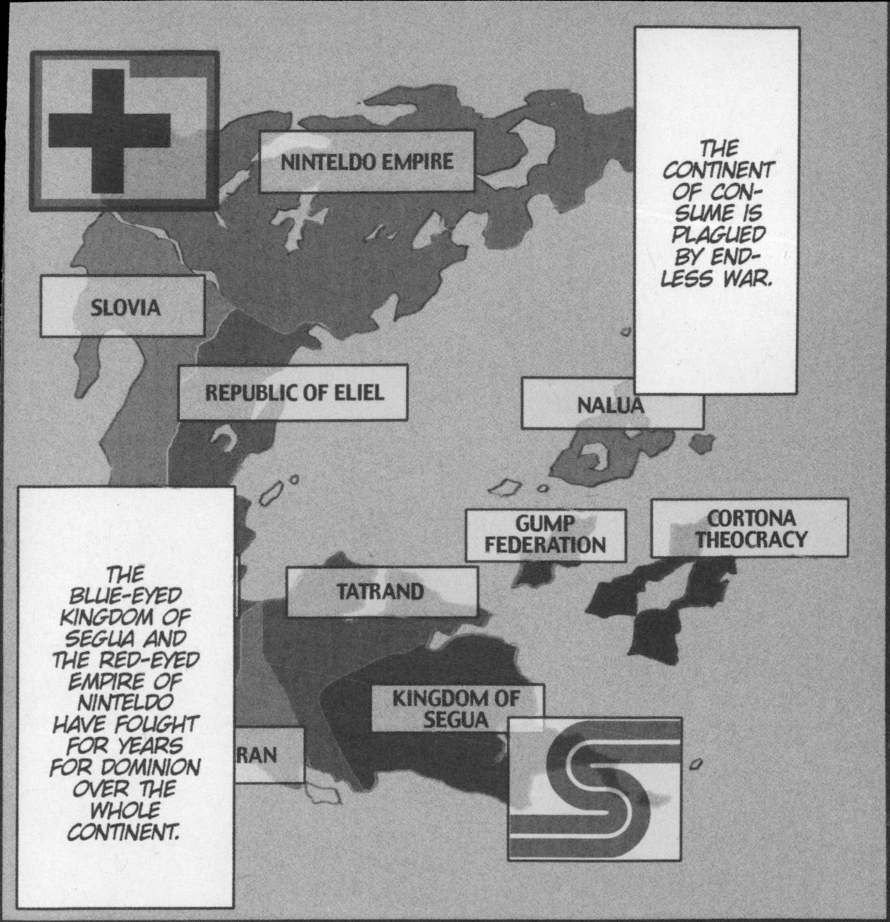
THE CONTINENT OF CONSUME IS PLAGUED BY ENDLESS WAR.
NINTELDO EMPIRE
SLOVIA
REPUBLIC OF ELIEL
NALUA
CORTONA THEOCRACY
GUMP FEDERATION
TATRAND
KINGDOM OF SEGUA
RAN
THE BLUE-EYED KINGDOM OF SEGUA AND THE RED-EYED EMPIRE OF NINTELDO HAVE FOUGHT FOR YEARS FOR DOMINION OVER THE WHOLE CONTINENT.

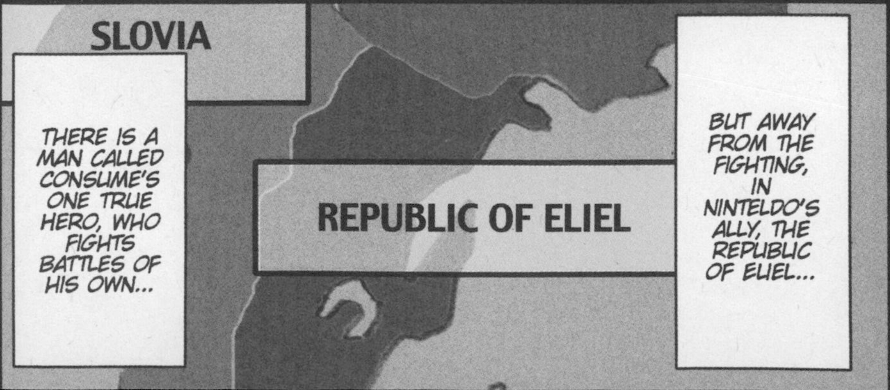
BUT AWAY FROM THE FIGHTING, IN NINTELDO'S ALLY, THE REPUBLIC OF ELIEL...
SLOVIA
REPUBLIC OF ELIEL
THERE IS A MAN CALLED CONSUME'S ONE TRUE HERO, WHO FIGHTS BATTLES OF HIS OWN...

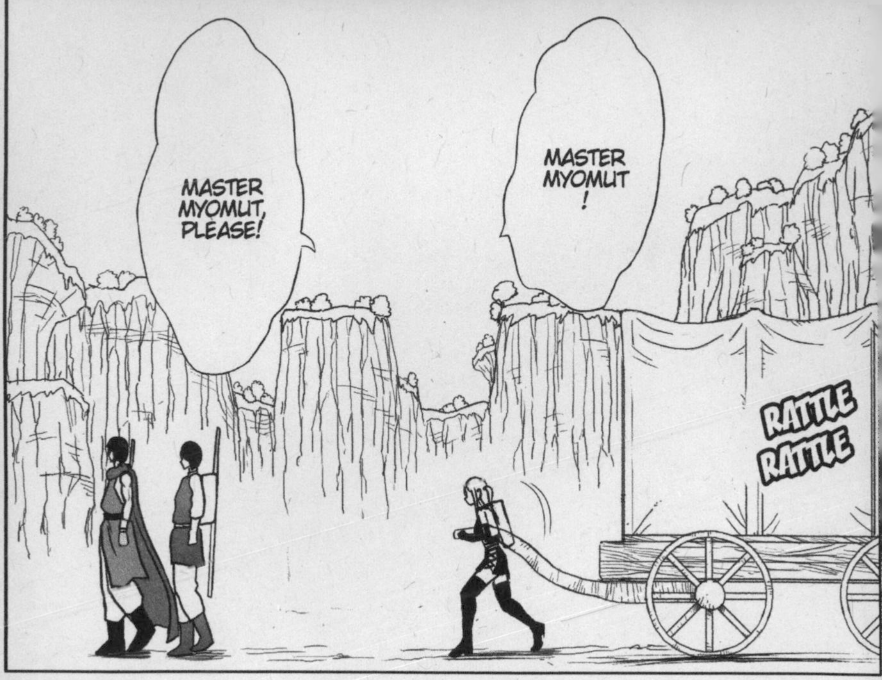
MASTER MYOMUT!
MASTER MYOMUT, PLEASE!
RATTLE RATTLE
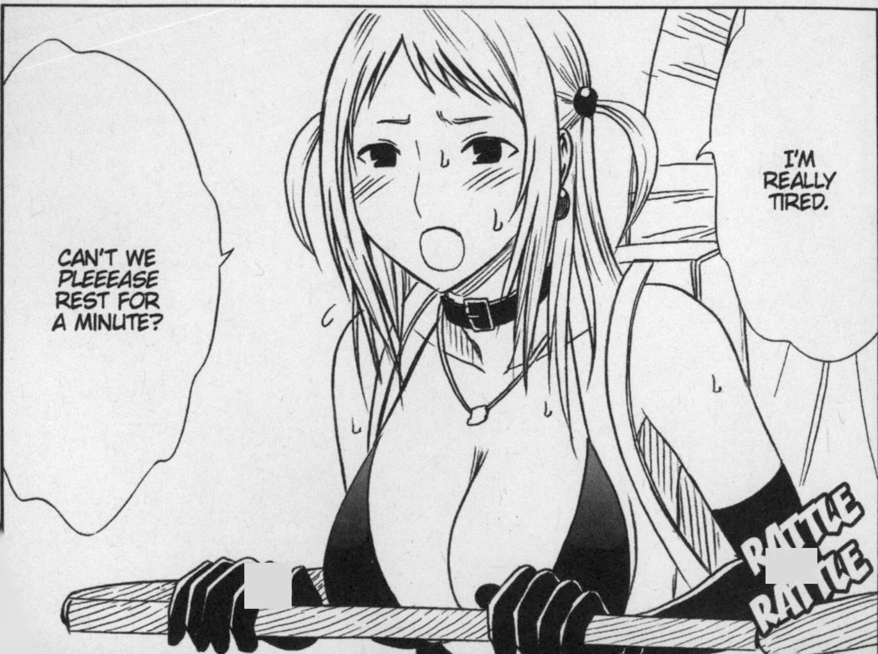
I'M REALLY TIRED.
CAN'T WE PLEEEASE REST FOR A MINUTE?
RATTLE RATTLE

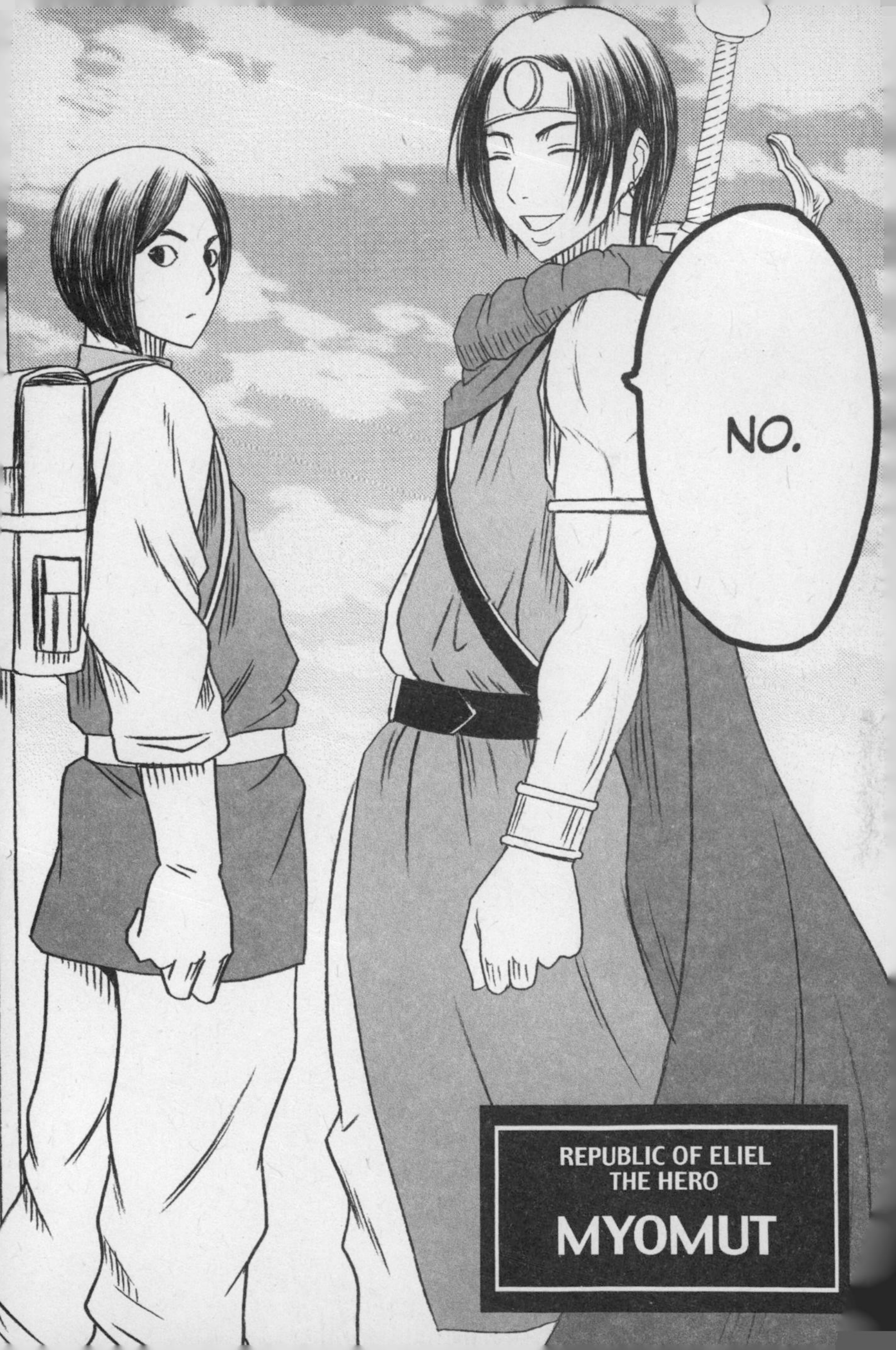
NO.
REPUBLIC OF ELIEL
THE HERO
MYOMUT

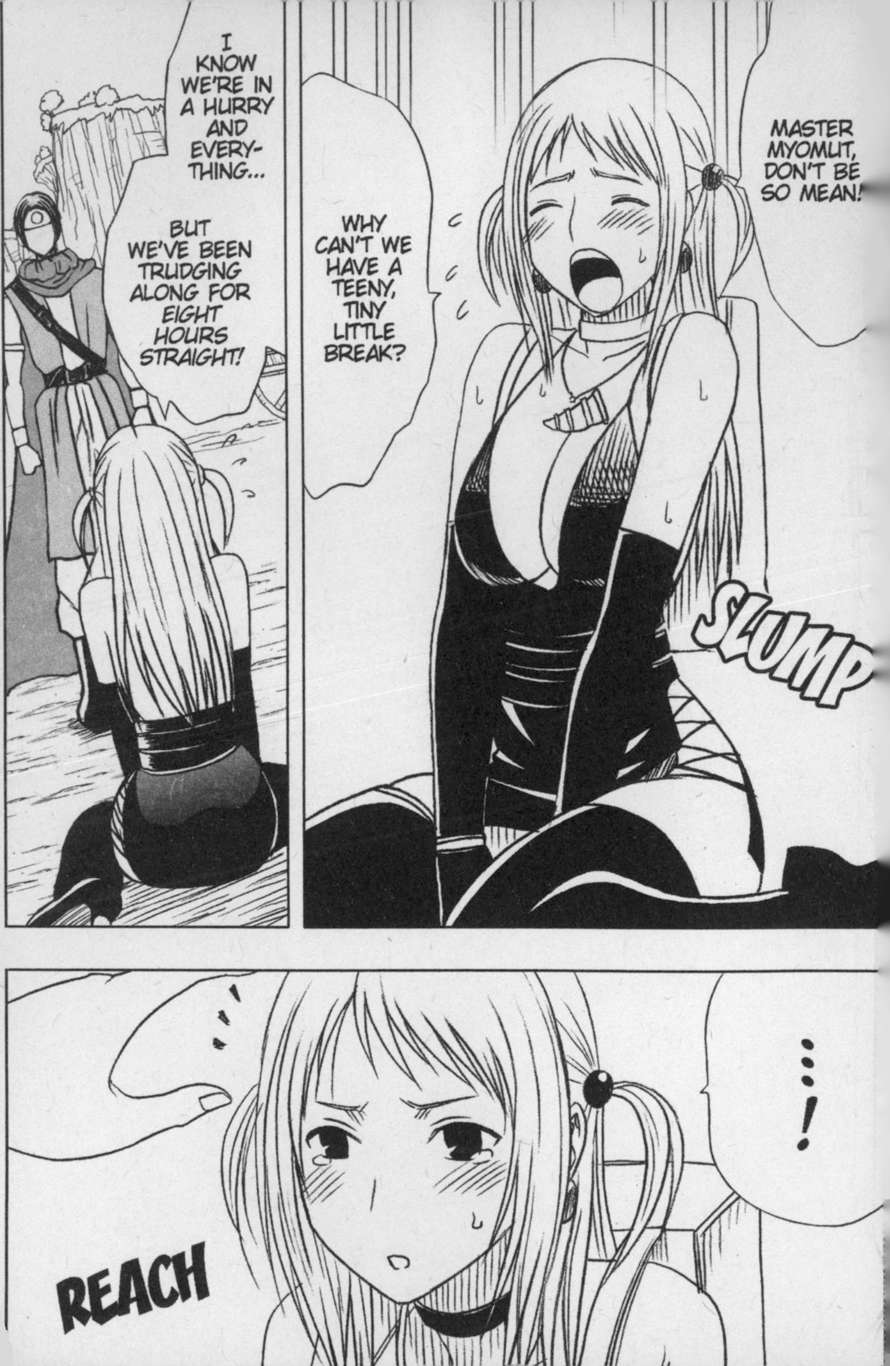
MASTER MYOMUT, DON'T BE SO MEAN!
WHY CAN'T WE HAVE A TEENY, TINY LITTLE BREAK?
SLUMP
I KNOW WE'RE IN A HURRY AND EVERYTHING...
BUT WE'VE BEEN TRUDGING ALONG FOR EIGHT HOURS STRAIGHT!
...!
REACH

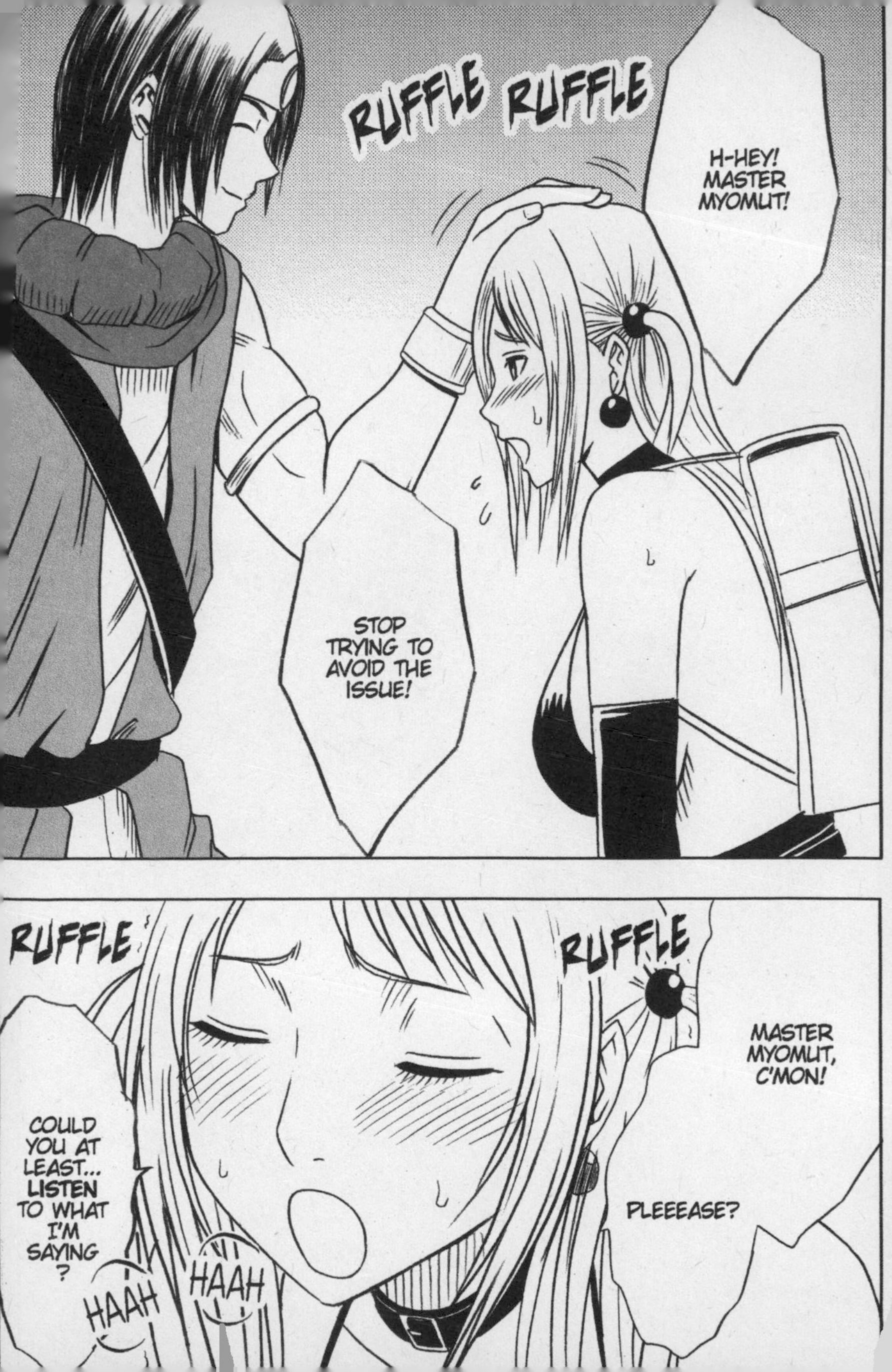
H-HEY! MASTER MYOMUT!
RUFFLE RUFFLE
STOP TRYING TO AVOID THE ISSUE!
RUFFLE
MASTER MYOMUT, C'MON!
PLEEEASE?
RUFFLE
COULD YOU AT LEAST... LISTEN TO WHAT I'M SAYING?
HAAH
HAAH

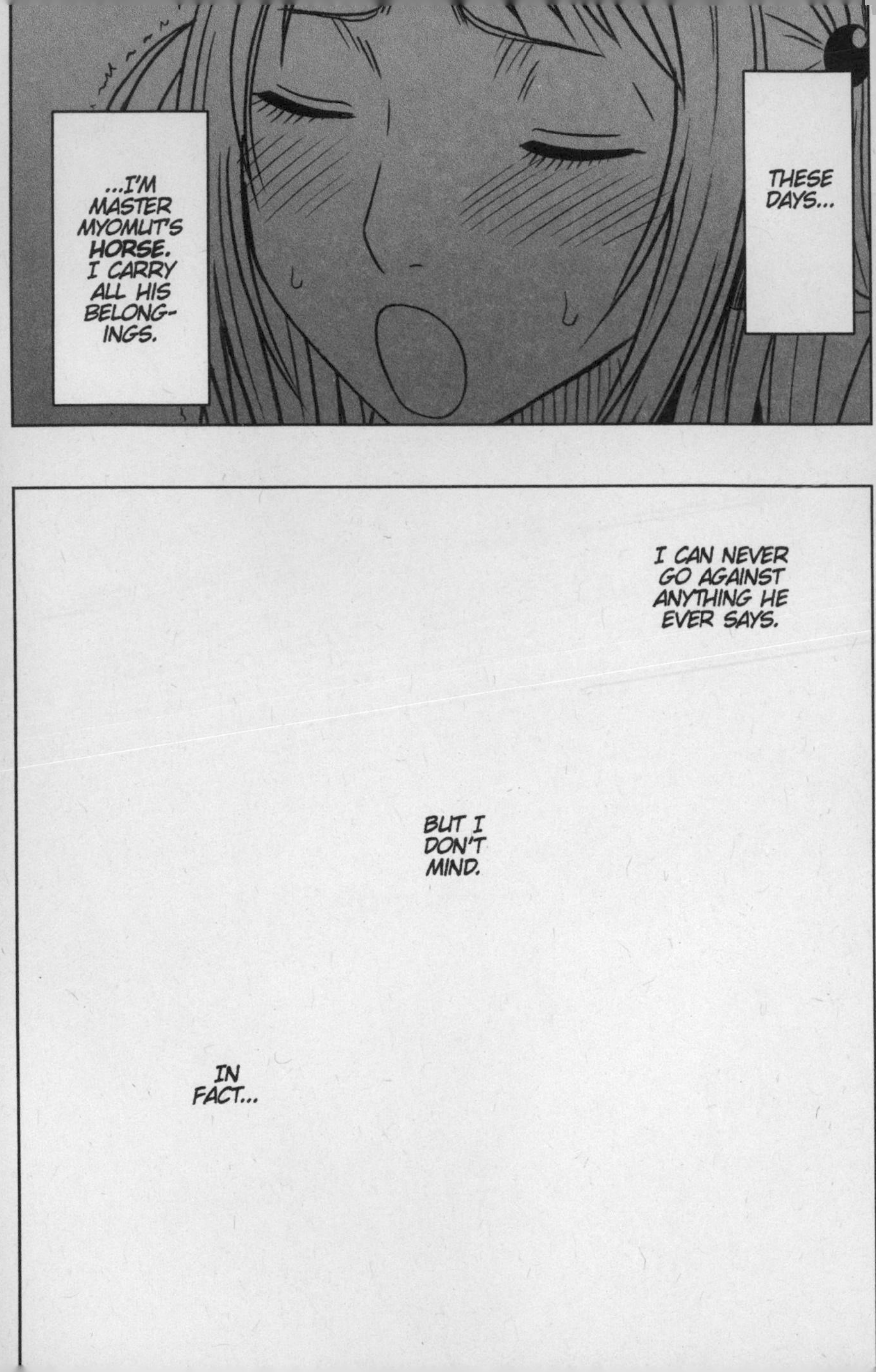
THESE DAYS...
...I'M MASTER MYOMUT'S HORSE. I CARRY ALL HIS BELONG-INGS.
I CAN NEVER GO AGAINST ANYTHING HE EVER SAYS.
BUT I DON'T MIND.
IN FACT...

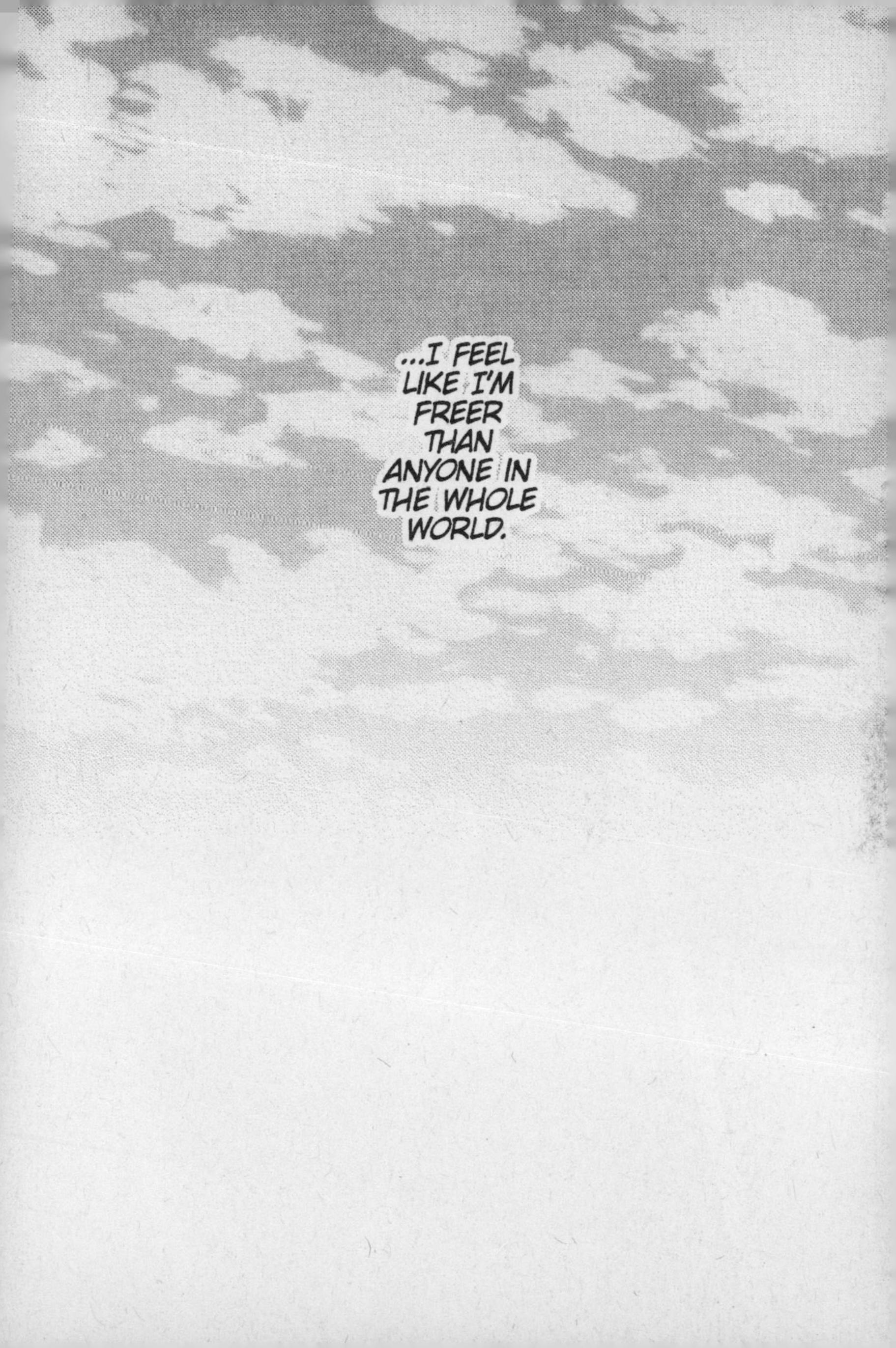
...I FEEL LIKE I'M FREER THAN ANYONE IN THE WHOLE WORLD.

SIDE STORY

THE HERO MYOMUT

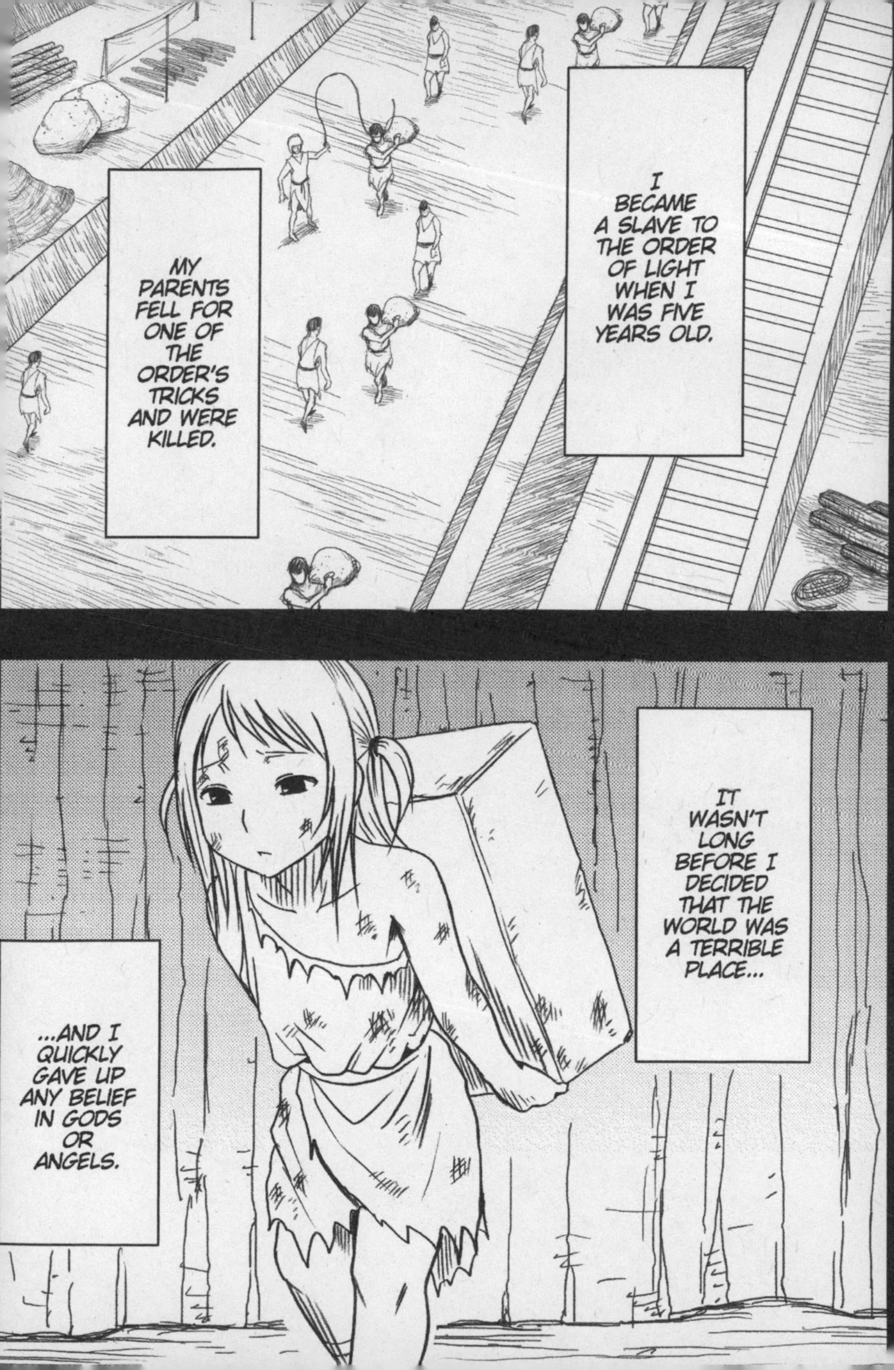
I BECAME A SLAVE TO THE ORDER OF LIGHT WHEN I WAS FIVE YEARS OLD.
MY PARENTS FELL FOR ONE OF THE ORDER'S TRICKS AND WERE KILLED.
IT WASN'T LONG BEFORE I DECIDED THAT THE WORLD WAS A TERRIBLE PLACE...
...AND I QUICKLY GAVE UP ANY BELIEF IN GODS OR ANGELS.

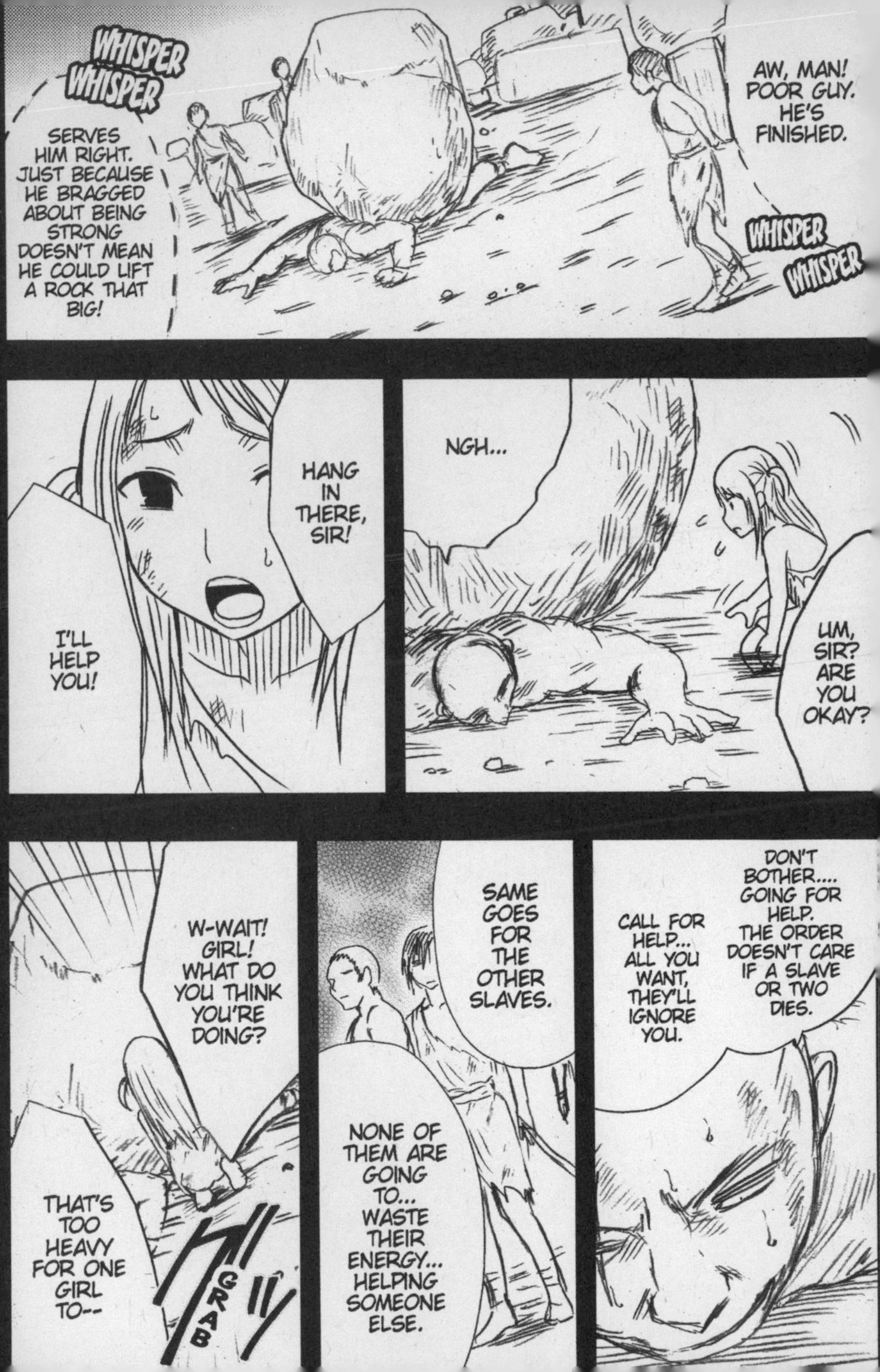
AW, MAN! POOR GUY. HE'S FINISHED.
WHISPER WHISPER
WHISPER WHISPER
SERVES HIM RIGHT. JUST BECAUSE HE BRAGGED ABOUT BEING STRONG DOESN'T MEAN HE COULD LIFT A ROCK THAT BIG!
NGH...
UM, SIR? ARE YOU OKAY?
HANG IN THERE, SIR!
I'LL HELP YOU!
DON'T BOTHER.... GOING FOR HELP. THE ORDER DOESN'T CARE IF A SLAVE OR TWO DIES.
CALL FOR HELP... ALL YOU WANT, THEY'LL IGNORE YOU.
SAME GOES FOR THE OTHER SLAVES.
NONE OF THEM ARE GOING TO... WASTE THEIR ENERGY... HELPING SOMEONE ELSE.
W-WAIT! GIRL! WHAT DO YOU THINK YOU'RE DOING?
THAT'S TOO HEAVY FOR ONE GIRL TO--
GRAB

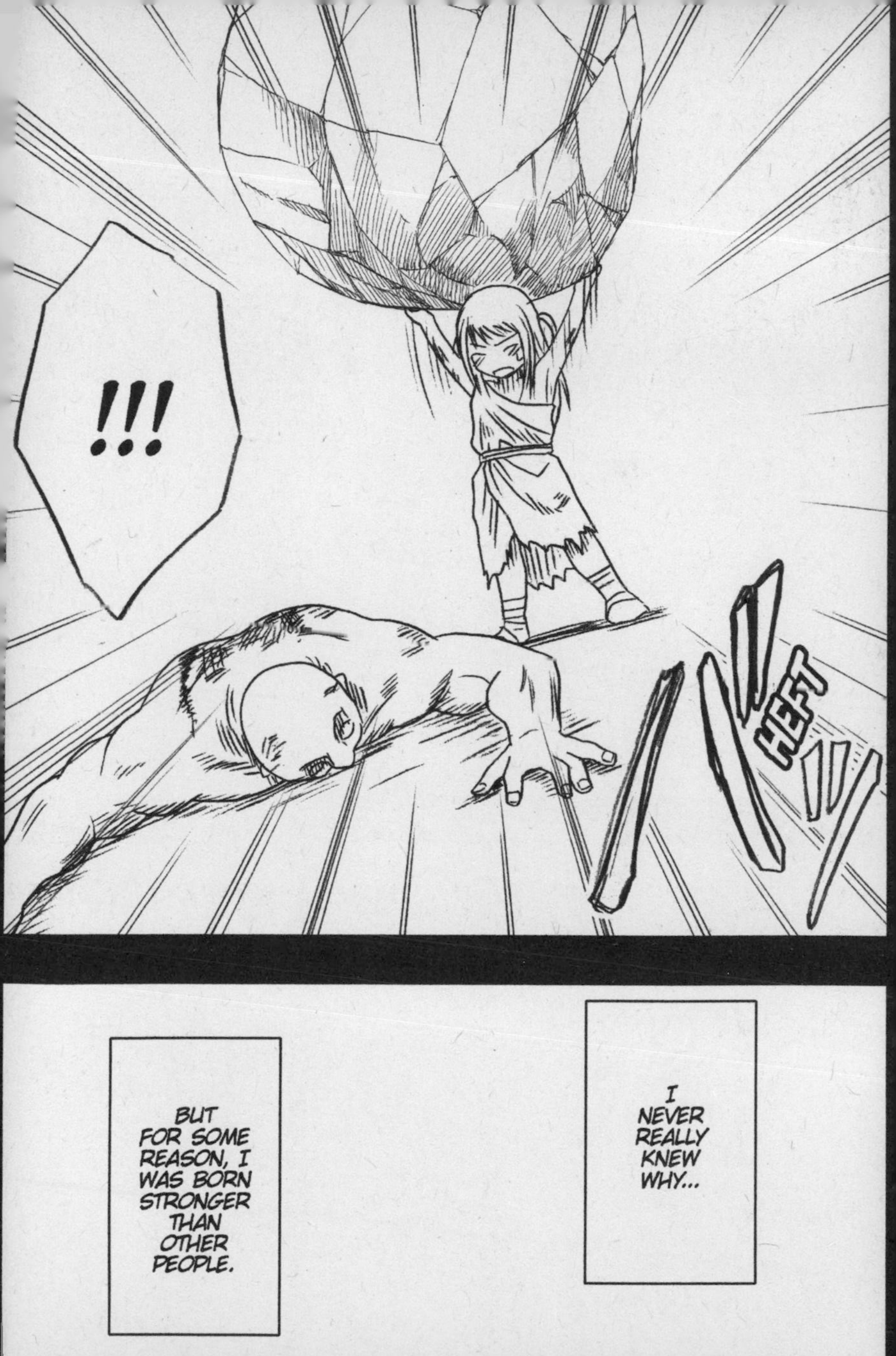
HEFT
!!!
I NEVER REALLY KNEW WHY...
BUT FOR SOME REASON, I WAS BORN STRONGER THAN OTHER PEOPLE.

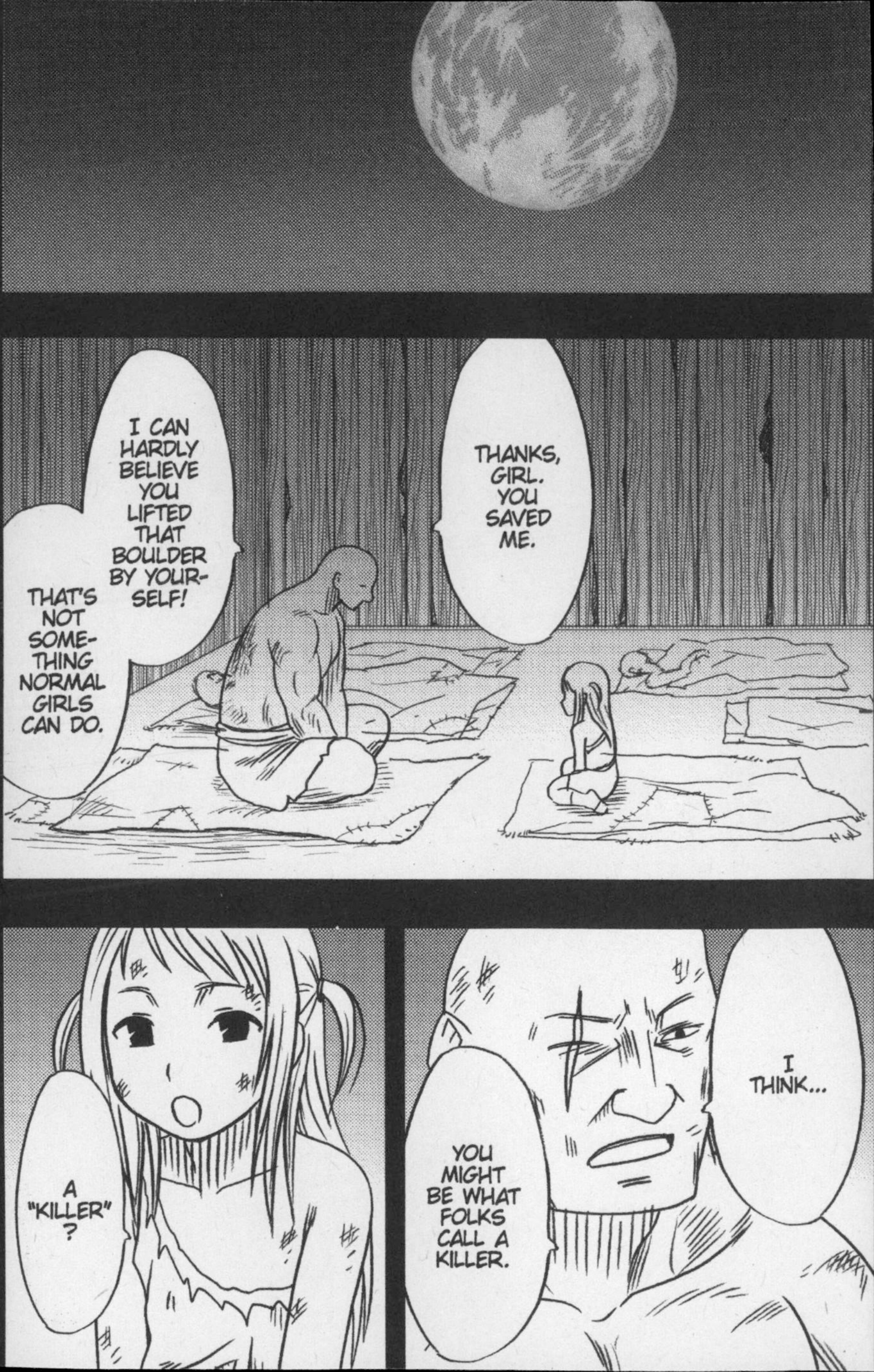
THANKS, GIRL. YOU SAVED ME.
I CAN HARDLY BELIEVE YOU LIFTED THAT BOULDER BY YOUR-SELF!
THAT'S NOT SOME-THING NORMAL GIRLS CAN DO.
I THINK...
YOU MIGHT BE WHAT FOLKS CALL A KILLER.
A "KILLER"?

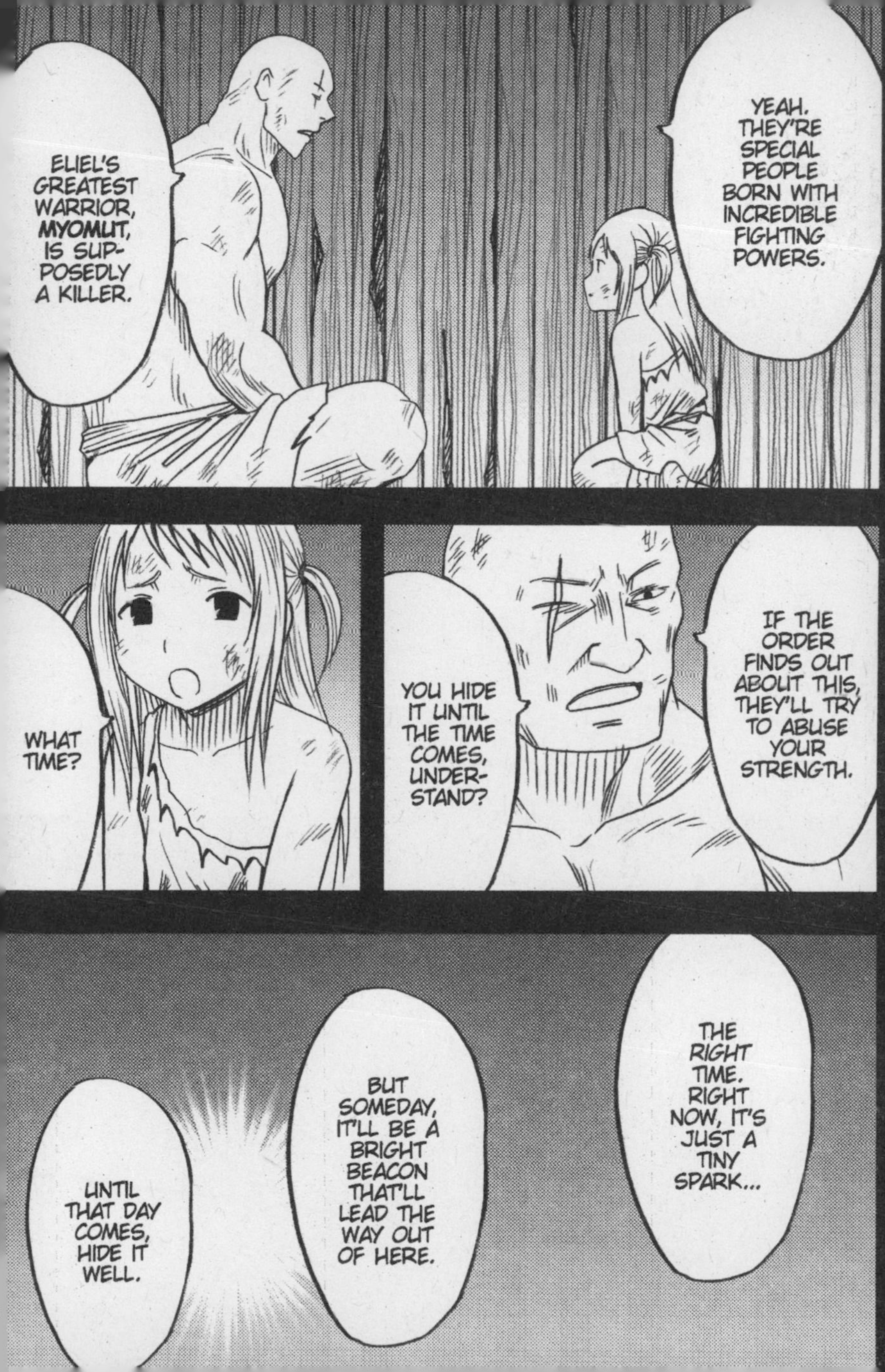
YEAH. THEY'RE SPECIAL PEOPLE BORN WITH INCREDIBLE FIGHTING POWERS.
ELIEL'S GREATEST WARRIOR, MYOMUT, IS SUP-POSEDLY A KILLER.
IF THE ORDER FINDS OUT ABOUT THIS, THEY'LL TRY TO ABUSE YOUR STRENGTH.
YOU HIDE IT UNTIL THE TIME COMES, UNDER-STAND?
WHAT TIME?
THE RIGHT TIME. RIGHT NOW, IT'S JUST A TINY SPARK...
BUT SOMEDAY, IT'LL BE A BRIGHT BEACON THAT'LL LEAD THE WAY OUT OF HERE.
UNTIL THAT DAY COMES, HIDE IT WELL.

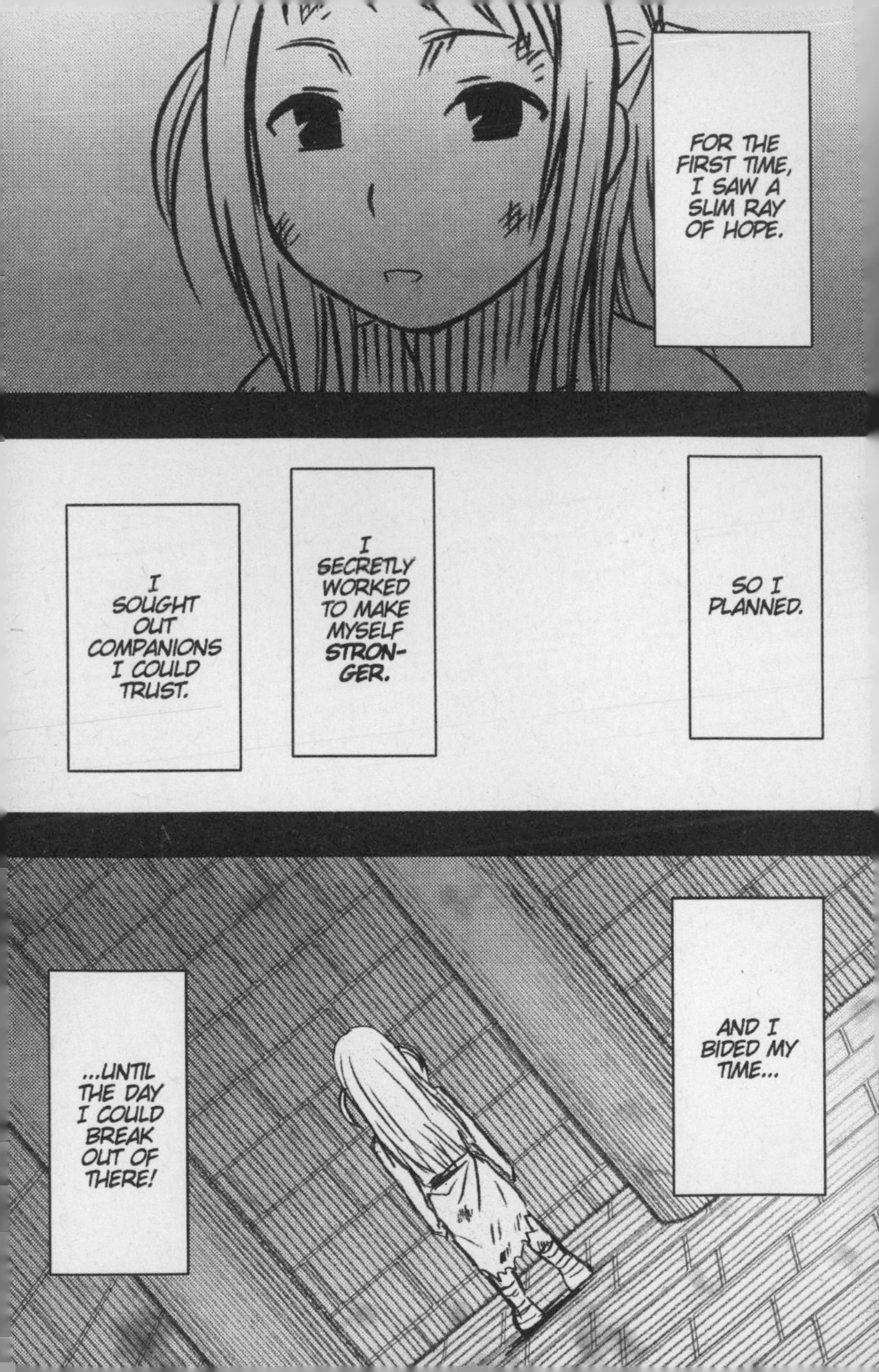
FOR THE FIRST TIME, I SAW A SLIM RAY OF HOPE.
SO I PLANNED.
I SECRETLY WORKED TO MAKE MYSELF STRON-GER.
I SOUGHT OUT COMPANIONS I COULD TRUST.
AND I BIDED MY TIME...
...UNTIL THE DAY I COULD BREAK OUT OF THERE!

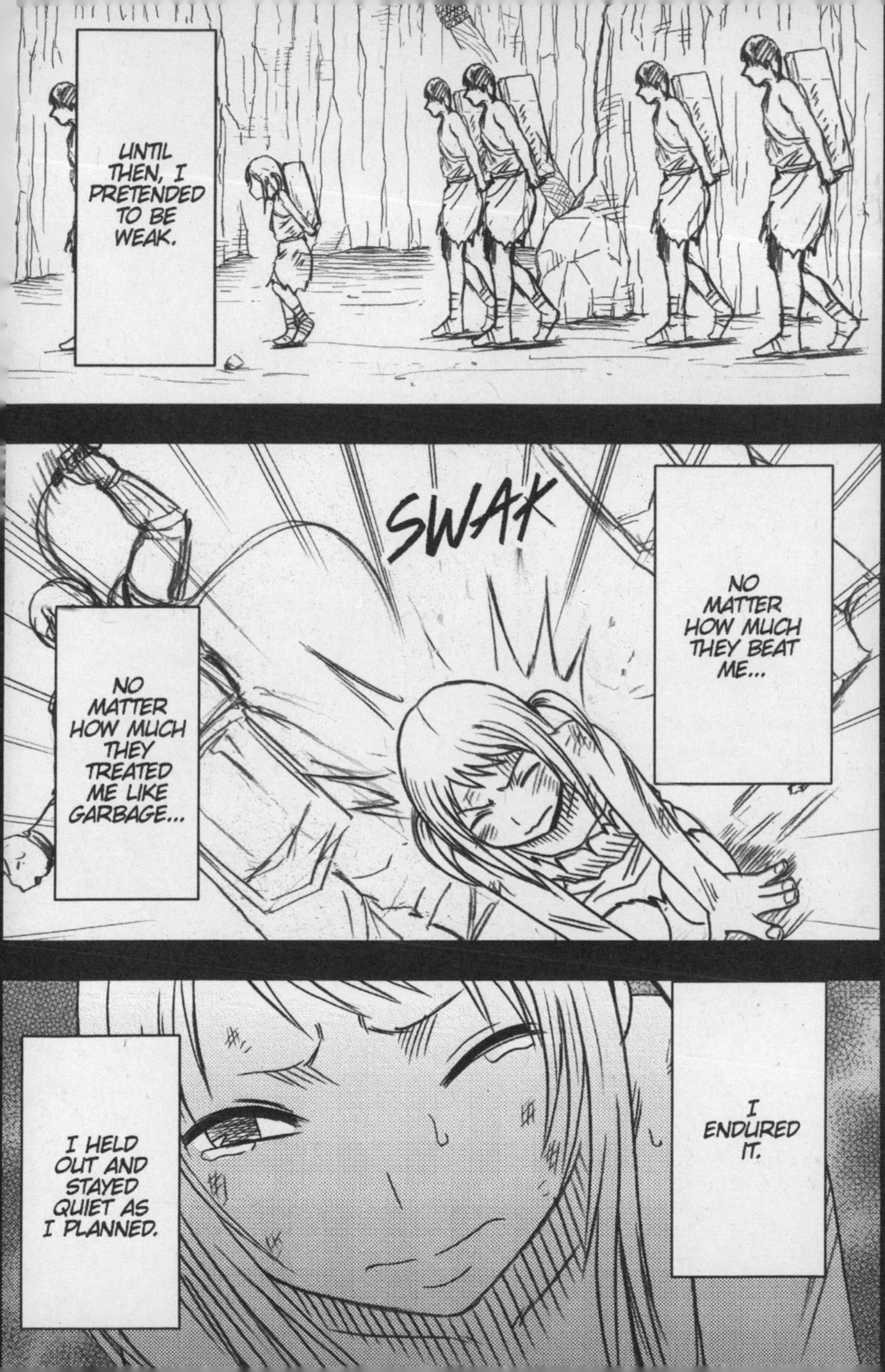
UNTIL THEN, I PRETENDED TO BE WEAK.
NO MATTER HOW MUCH THEY BEAT ME...
SWAK
NO MATTER HOW MUCH THEY TREATED ME LIKE GARBAGE...
I ENDURED IT.
I HELD OUT AND STAYED QUIET AS I PLANNED.

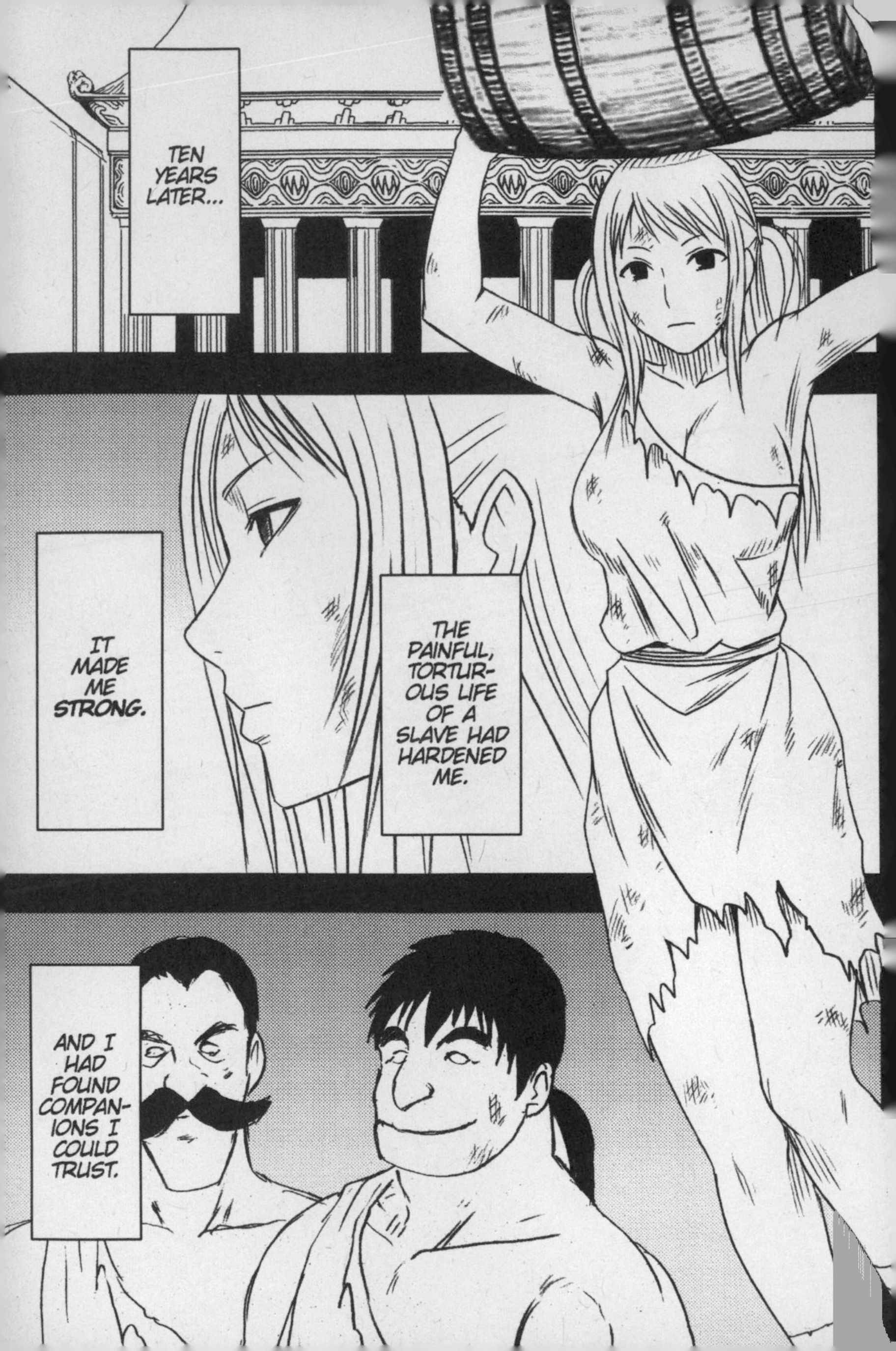
TEN YEARS LATER...
THE PAINFUL, TORTUROUS LIFE OF A SLAVE HAD HARDENED ME.
IT MADE ME STRONG.
AND I HAD FOUND COMPANIONS I COULD TRUST.

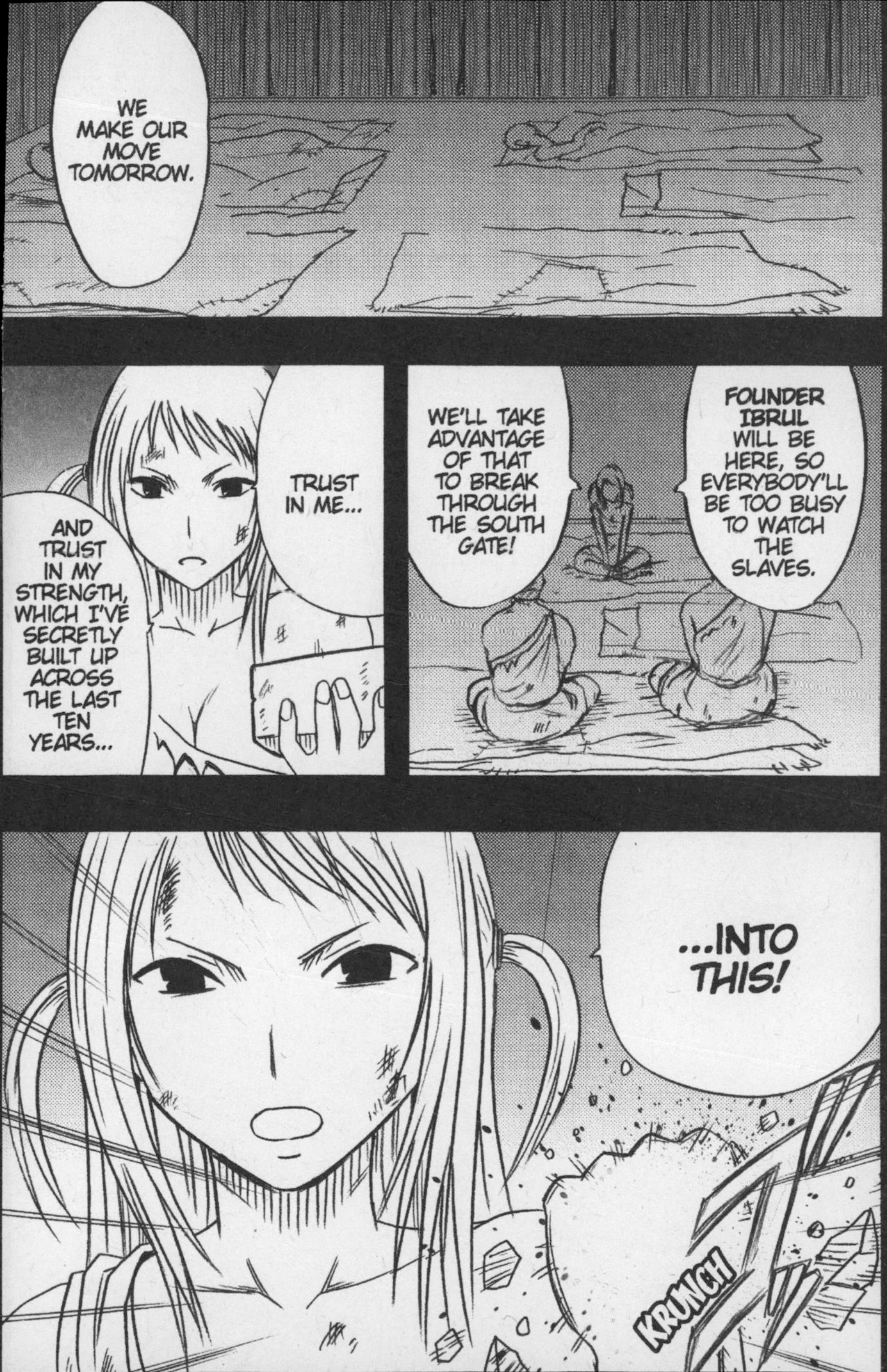
WE MAKE OUR MOVE TOMORROW.
FOUNDER IBRUL WILL BE HERE, SO EVERYBODY'LL BE TOO BUSY TO WATCH THE SLAVES.
WE'LL TAKE ADVANTAGE OF THAT TO BREAK THROUGH THE SOUTH GATE!
TRUST IN ME...
AND TRUST IN MY STRENGTH, WHICH I'VE SECRETLY BUILT UP ACROSS THE LAST TEN YEARS...
...INTO THIS!
KRUNCH

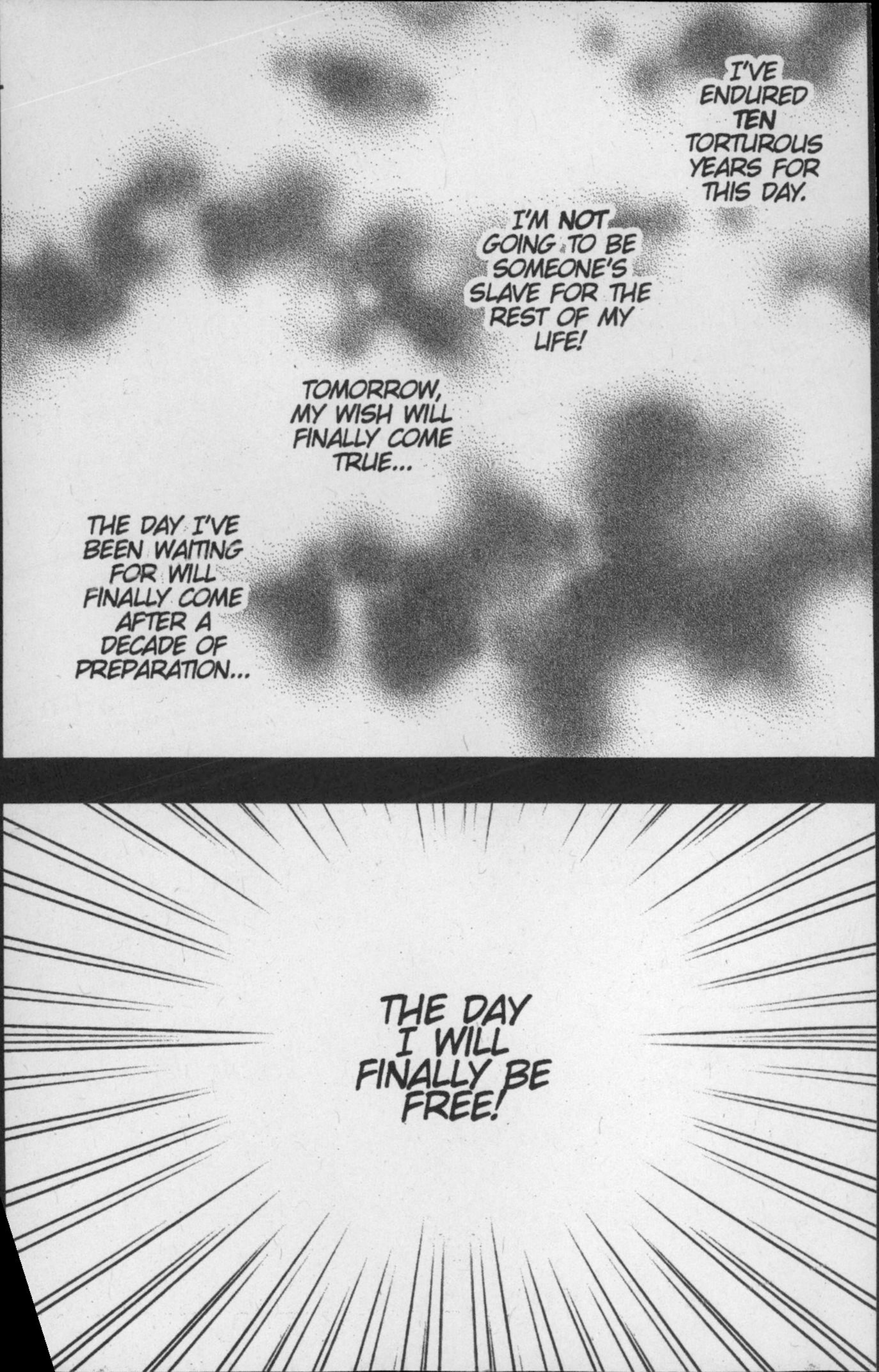
I'VE ENDURED TEN TORTUROUS YEARS FOR THIS DAY.
I'M NOT GOING TO BE SOMEONE'S SLAVE FOR THE REST OF MY LIFE!
TOMORROW, MY WISH WILL FINALLY COME TRUE...
THE DAY I'VE BEEN WAITING FOR WILL FINALLY COME AFTER A DECADE OF PREPARATION...
THE DAY I WILL FINALLY BE FREE!

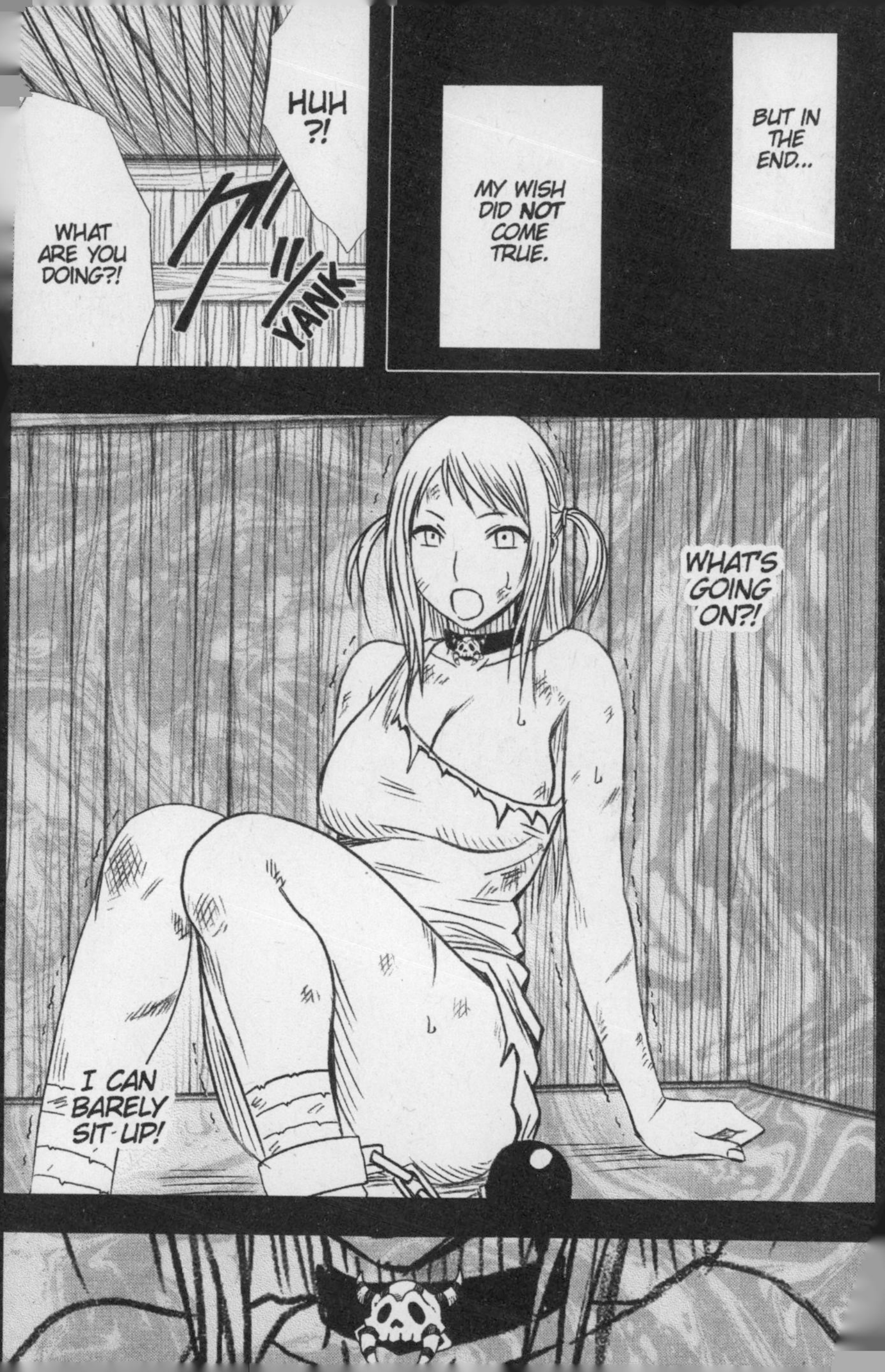
BUT IN THE END...
MY WISH DID NOT COME TRUE.
HUH ?!
YANK
WHAT ARE YOU DOING?!
WHAT'S GOING ON?!
I CAN BARELY SIT-UP!

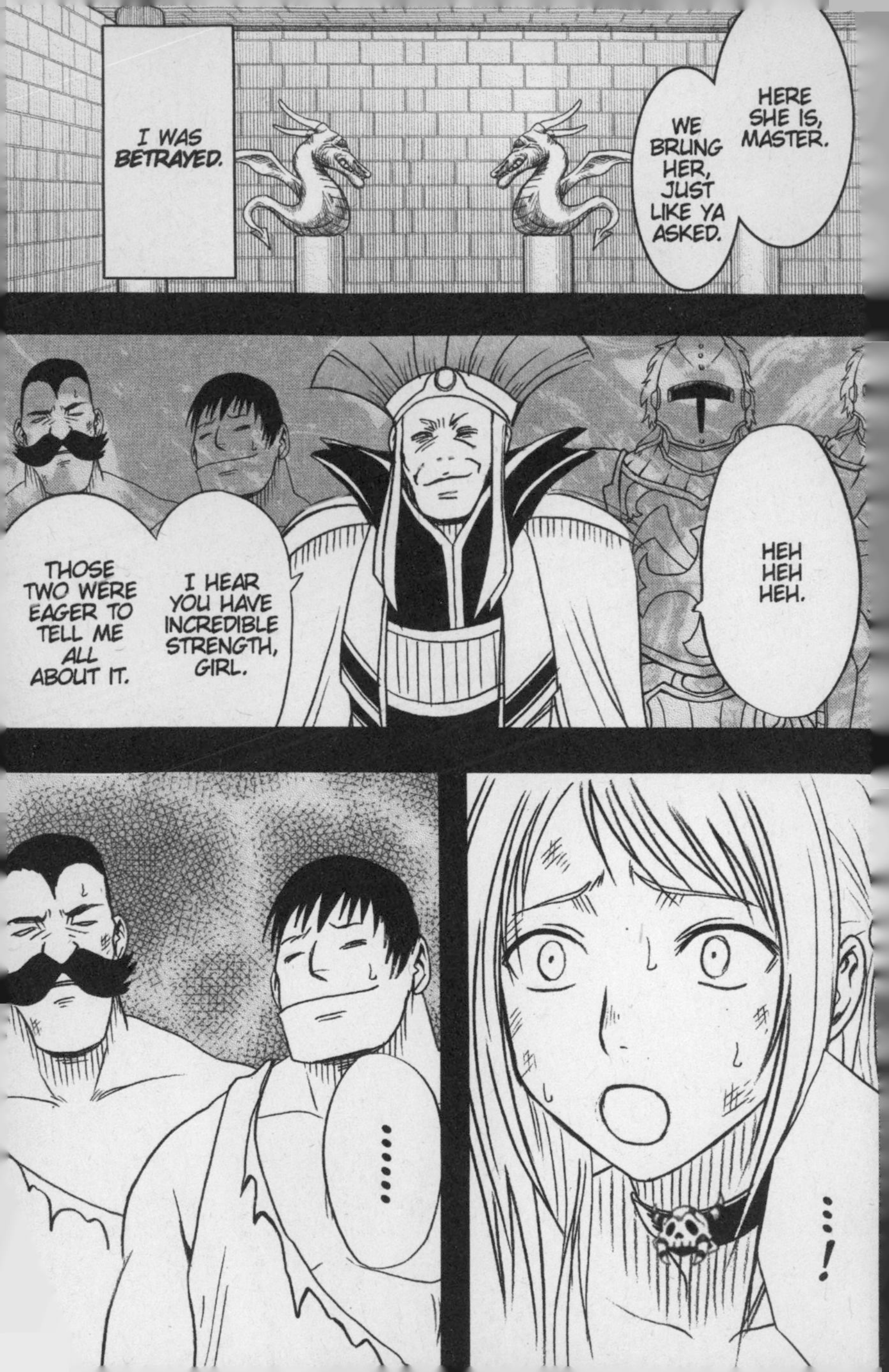
HERE SHE IS, MASTER.
WE BRUNG HER, JUST LIKE YA ASKED.
I WAS BETRAYED.
HEH HEH HEH.
I HEAR YOU HAVE INCREDIBLE STRENGTH, GIRL.
THOSE TWO WERE EAGER TO TELL ME ALL ABOUT IT.
...!
......

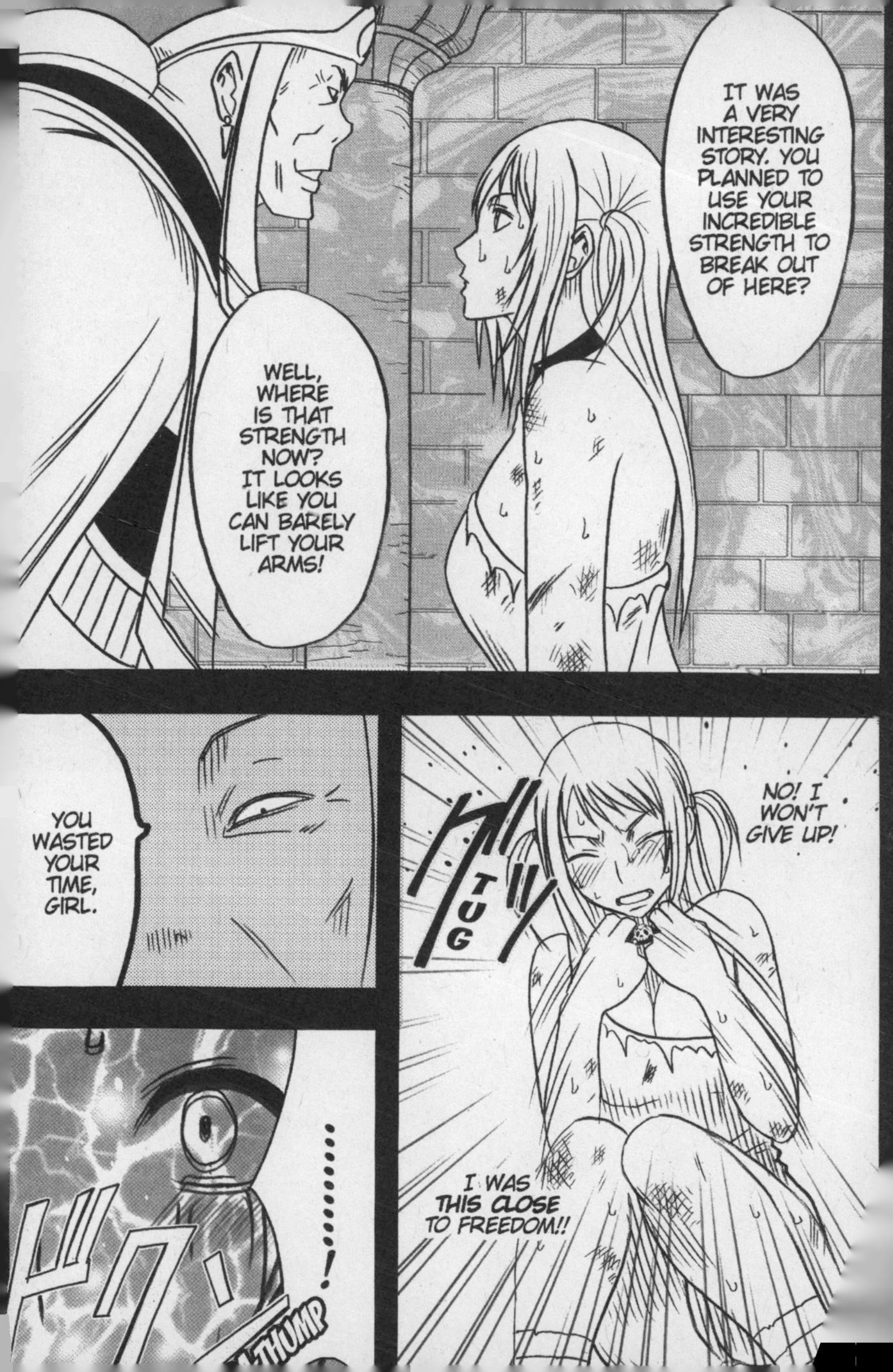
IT WAS A VERY INTERESTING STORY. YOU PLANNED TO USE YOUR INCREDIBLE STRENGTH TO BREAK OUT OF HERE?
WELL, WHERE IS THAT STRENGTH NOW? IT LOOKS LIKE YOU CAN BARELY LIFT YOUR ARMS!
NO! I WON'T GIVE UP!
TUG
I WAS THIS CLOSE TO FREEDOM!!
YOU WASTED YOUR TIME, GIRL.
......!
THUMP

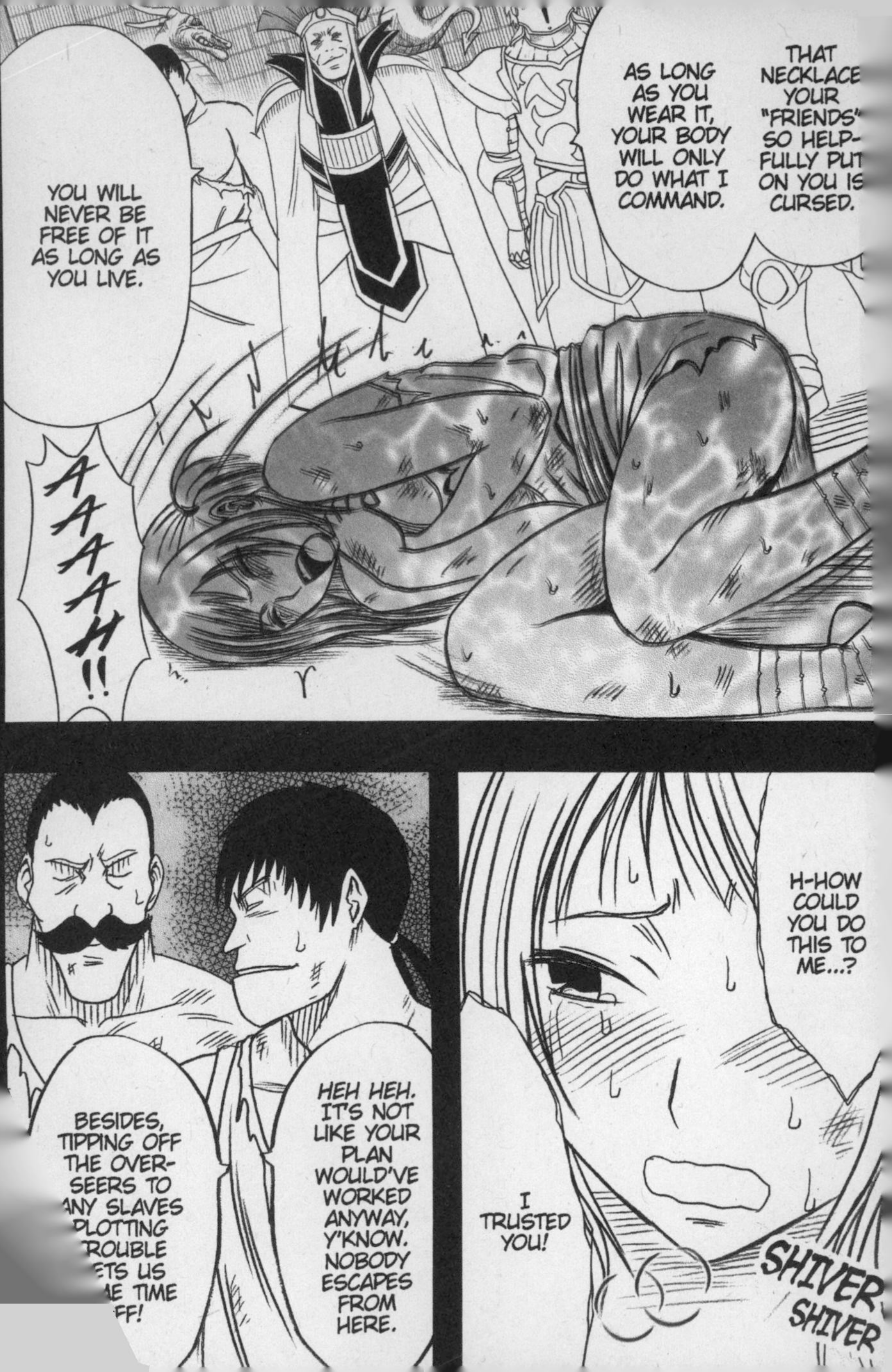
THAT NECKLACE YOUR "FRIENDS" SO HELPFULLY PUT ON YOU IS CURSED.
AS LONG AS YOU WEAR IT, YOUR BODY WILL ONLY DO WHAT I COMMAND.
YOU WILL NEVER BE FREE OF IT AS LONG AS YOU LIVE.
AAAAAH!!
H-HOW COULD YOU DO THIS TO ME...?
I TRUSTED YOU!
SHIVER SHIVER
HEH HEH. IT'S NOT LIKE YOUR PLAN WOULD'VE WORKED ANYWAY, Y'KNOW. NOBODY ESCAPES FROM HERE.
BESIDES, TIPPING OFF THE OVER-SEERS TO ANY SLAVES PLOTTING TROUBLE ETS US ME TIME FF!

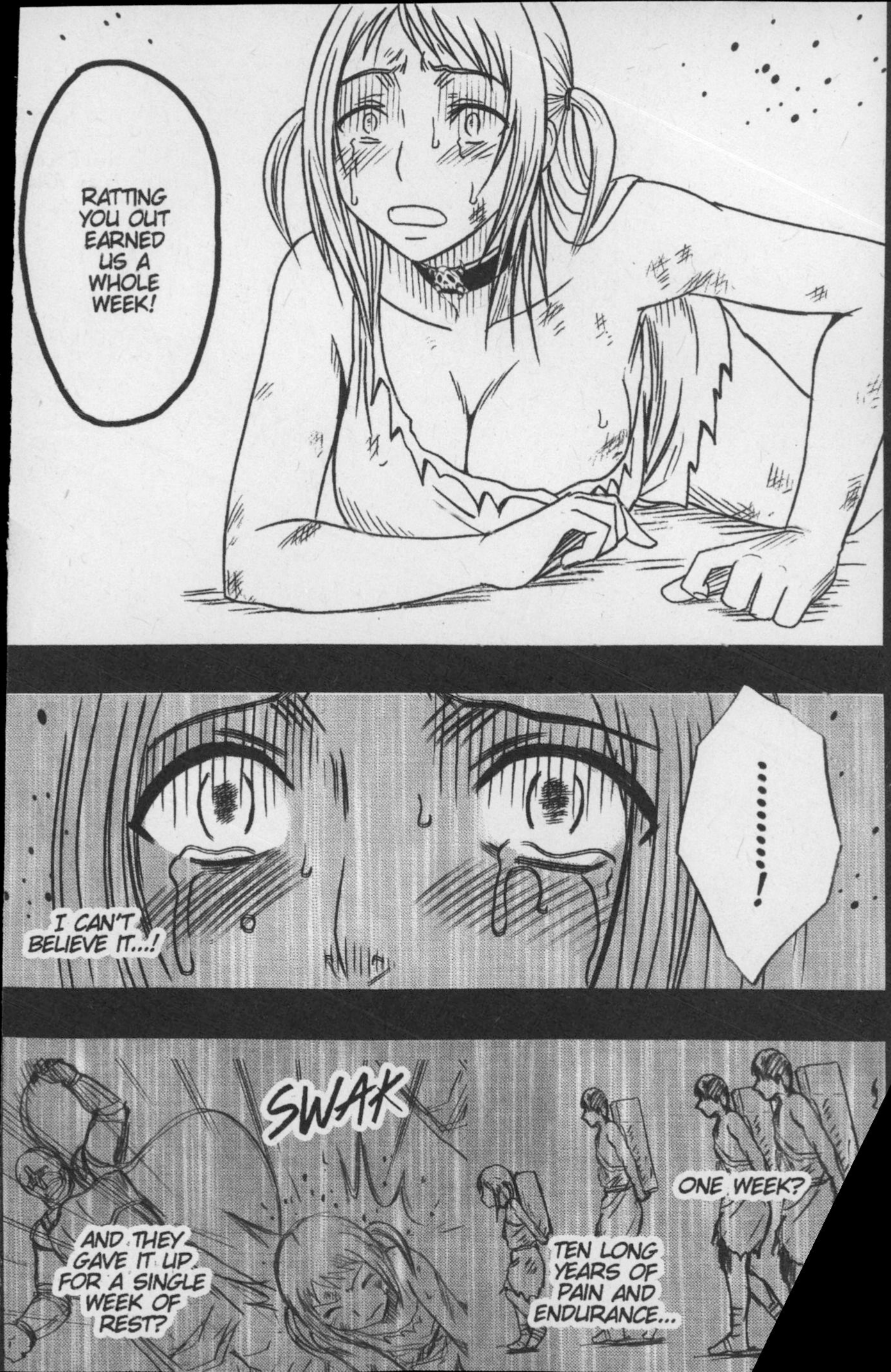
RATTING YOU OUT EARNED US A WHOLE WEEK!
......!
I CAN'T BELIEVE IT...!
ONE WEEK?
TEN LONG YEARS OF PAIN AND ENDURANCE...
SWAK
AND THEY GAVE IT UP FOR A SINGLE WEEK OF REST?

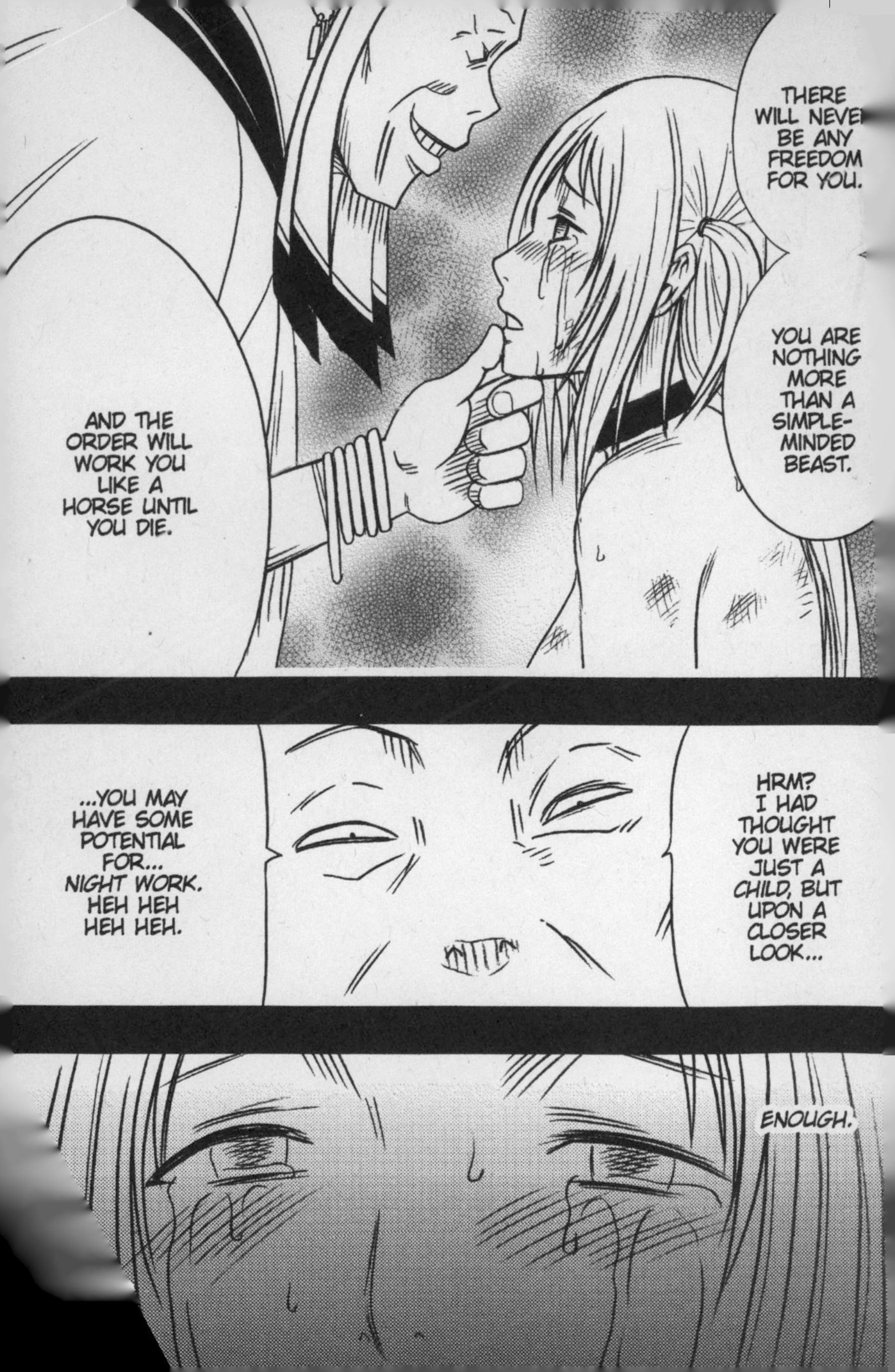
THERE WILL NEVER BE ANY FREEDOM FOR YOU.
YOU ARE NOTHING MORE THAN A SIMPLE-MINDED BEAST.
AND THE ORDER WILL WORK YOU LIKE A HORSE UNTIL YOU DIE.
HRM? I HAD THOUGHT YOU WERE JUST A CHILD, BUT UPON A CLOSER LOOK...
...YOU MAY HAVE SOME POTENTIAL FOR... NIGHT WORK. HEH HEH HEH HEH.
ENOUGH.

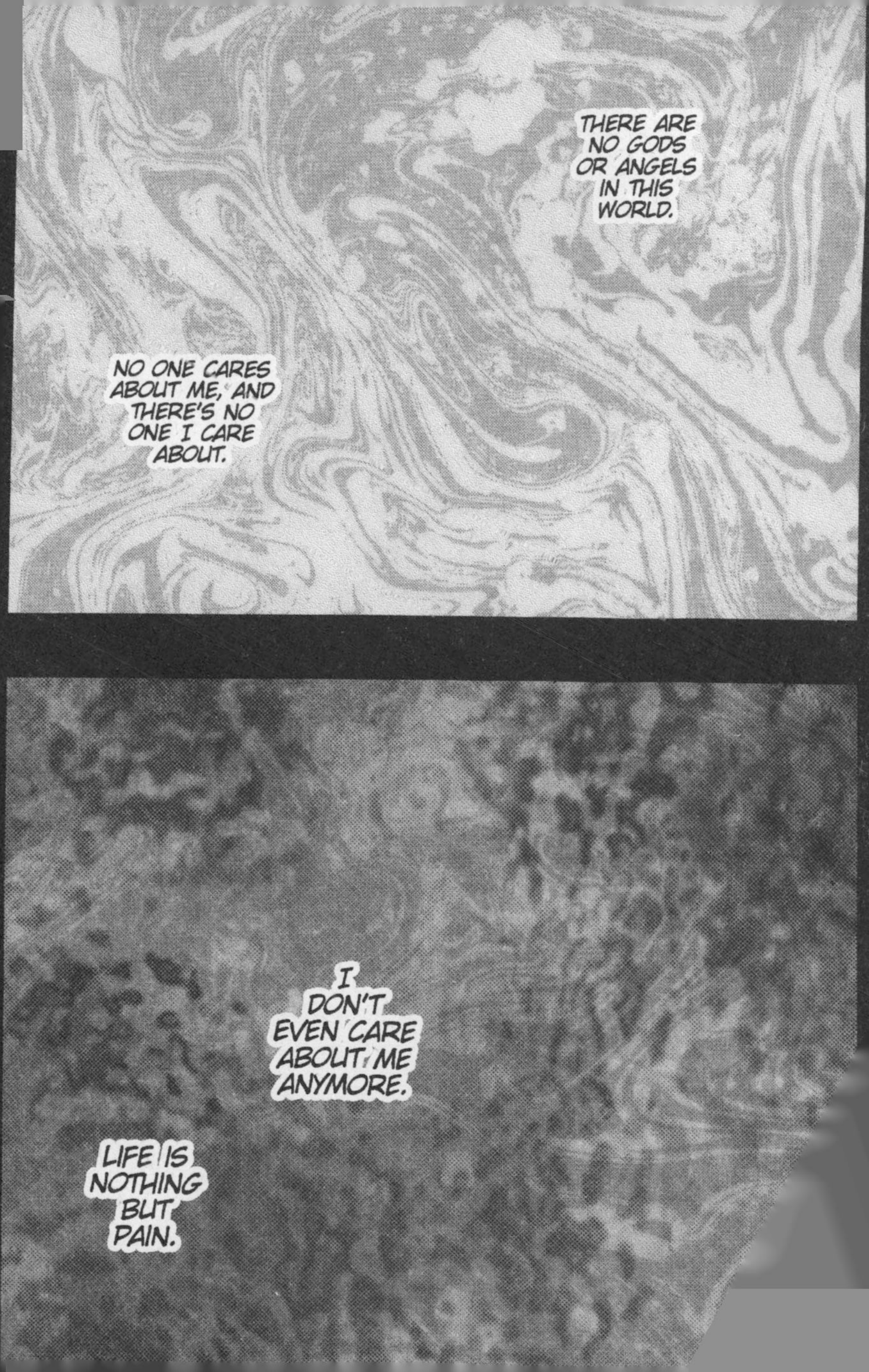
THERE ARE NO GODS OR ANGELS IN THIS WORLD.
NO ONE CARES ABOUT ME, AND THERE'S NO ONE I CARE ABOUT.
I DON'T EVEN CARE ABOUT ME ANYMORE.
LIFE IS NOTHING BUT PAIN.

ALL I
WANT
NOW...

...IS TO
DIE.

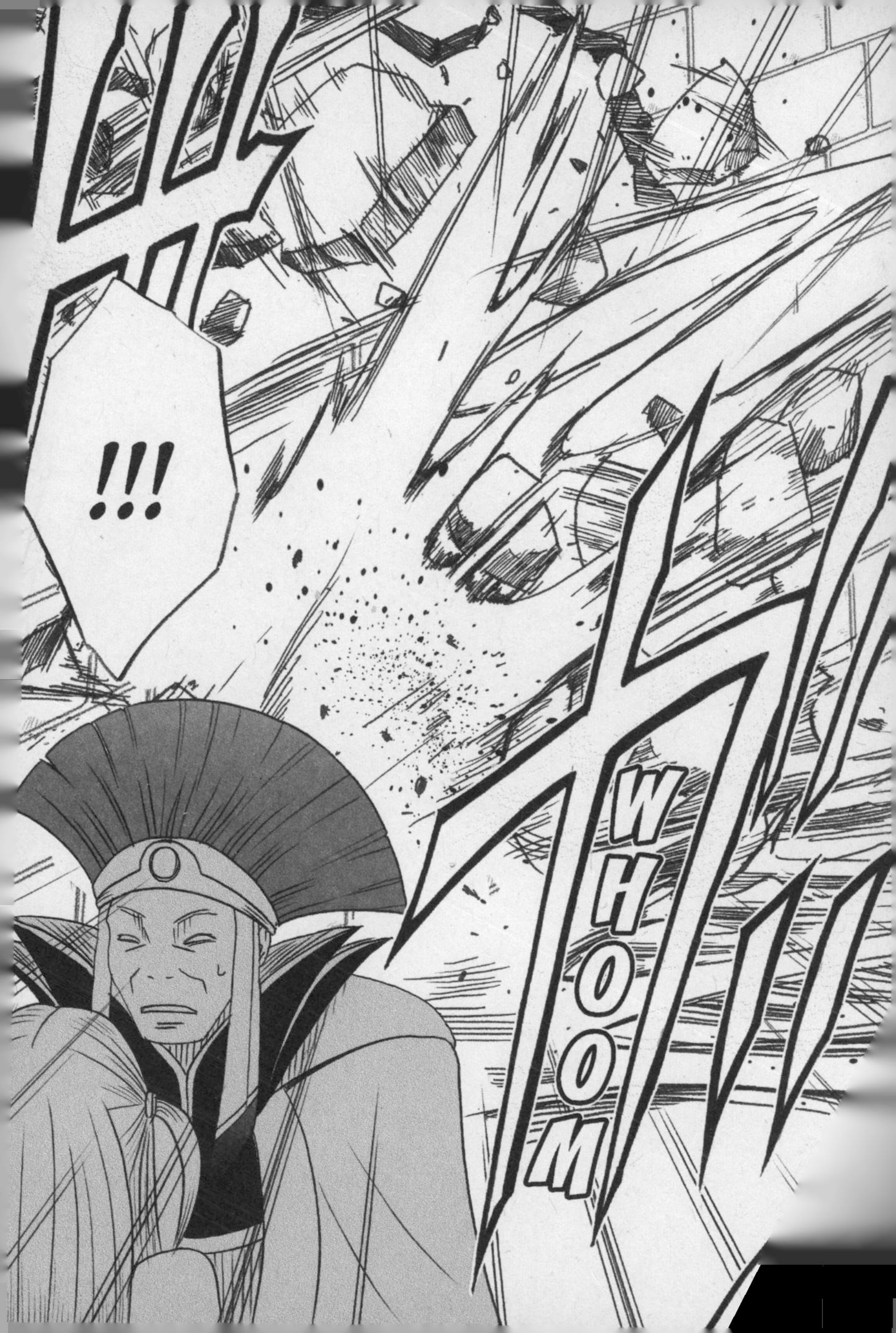
!!!
WHOOM

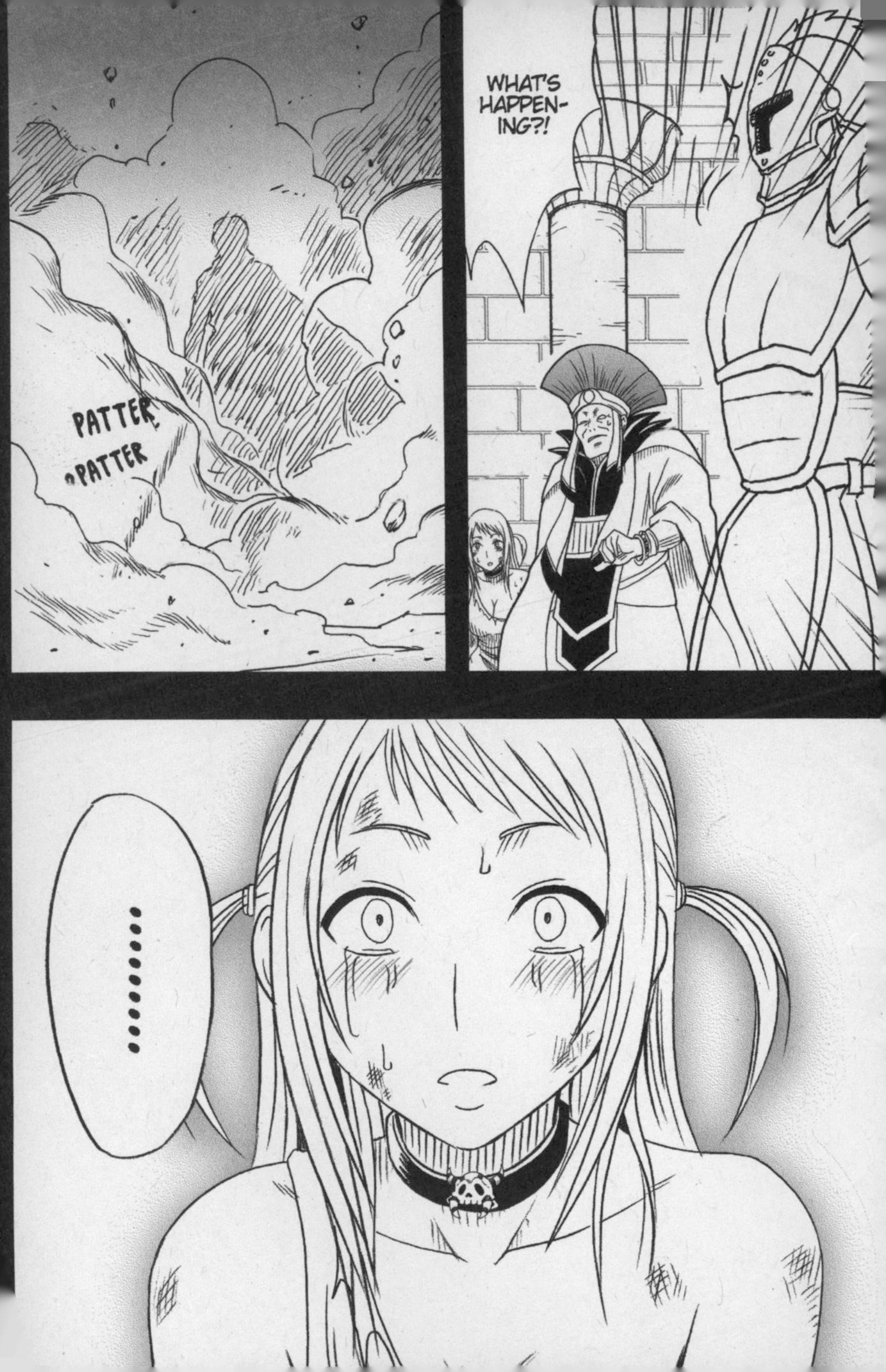
WHAT'S HAPPEN-ING?!
PATTER PATTER
....

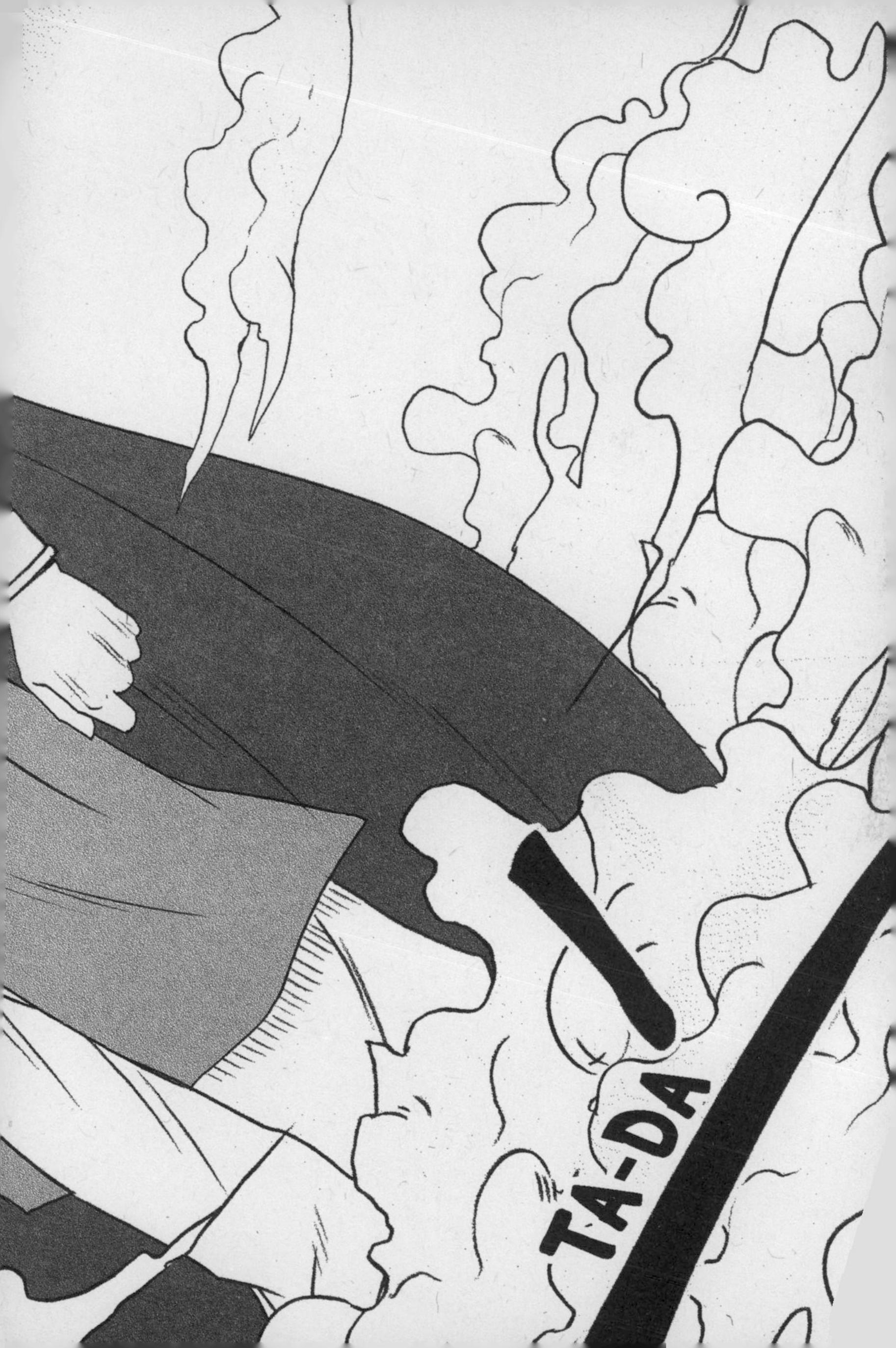
TA-DA

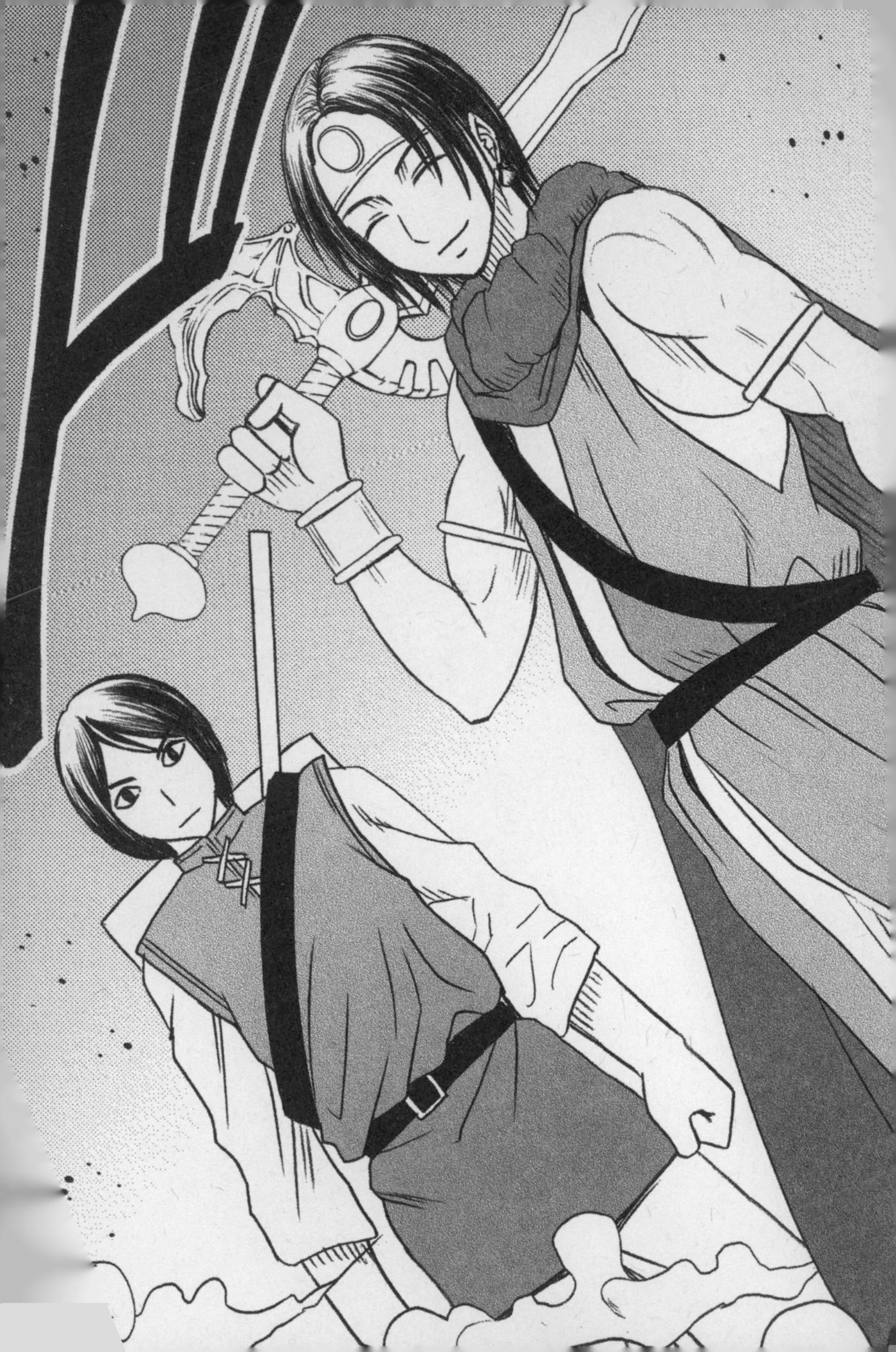

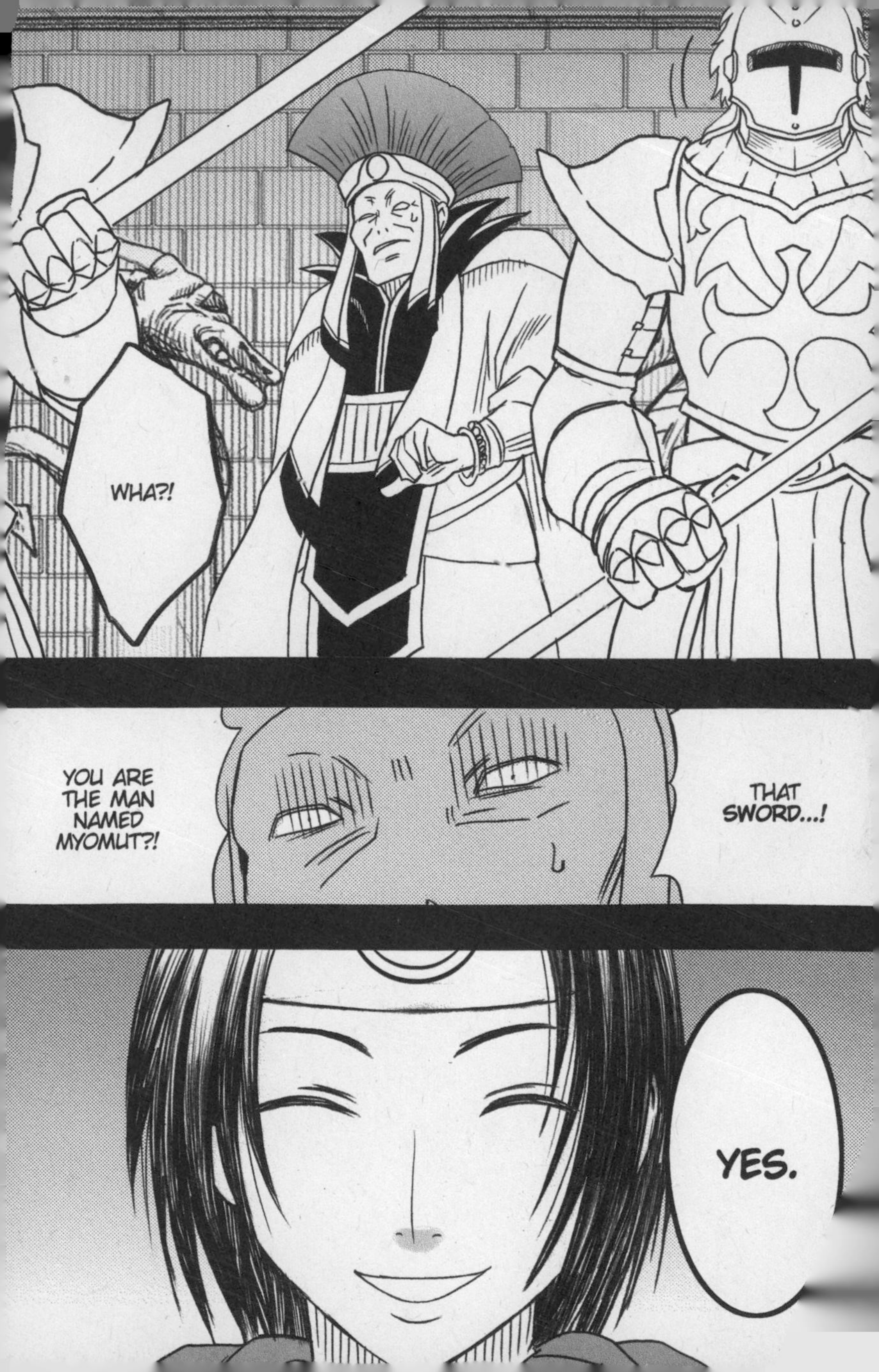
WHA?!
THAT SWORD...!
YOU ARE THE MAN NAMED MYOMUT?!
YES.

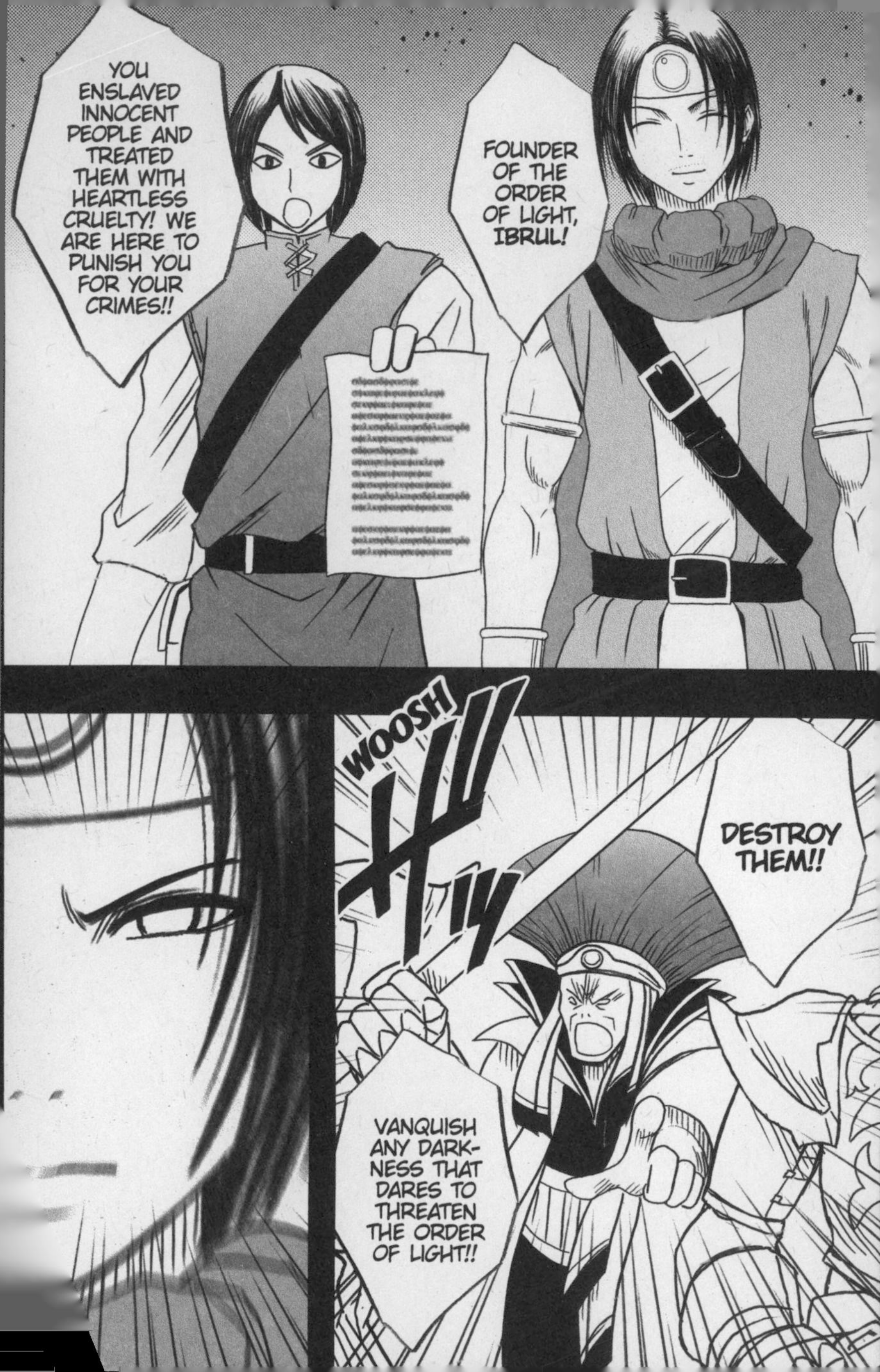
FOUNDER OF THE ORDER OF LIGHT, IBRUL!
YOU ENSLAVED INNOCENT PEOPLE AND TREATED THEM WITH HEARTLESS CRUELTY! WE ARE HERE TO PUNISH YOU FOR YOUR CRIMES!!
DESTROY THEM!!
WOOSH
VANQUISH ANY DARKNESS THAT DARES TO THREATEN THE ORDER OF LIGHT!!

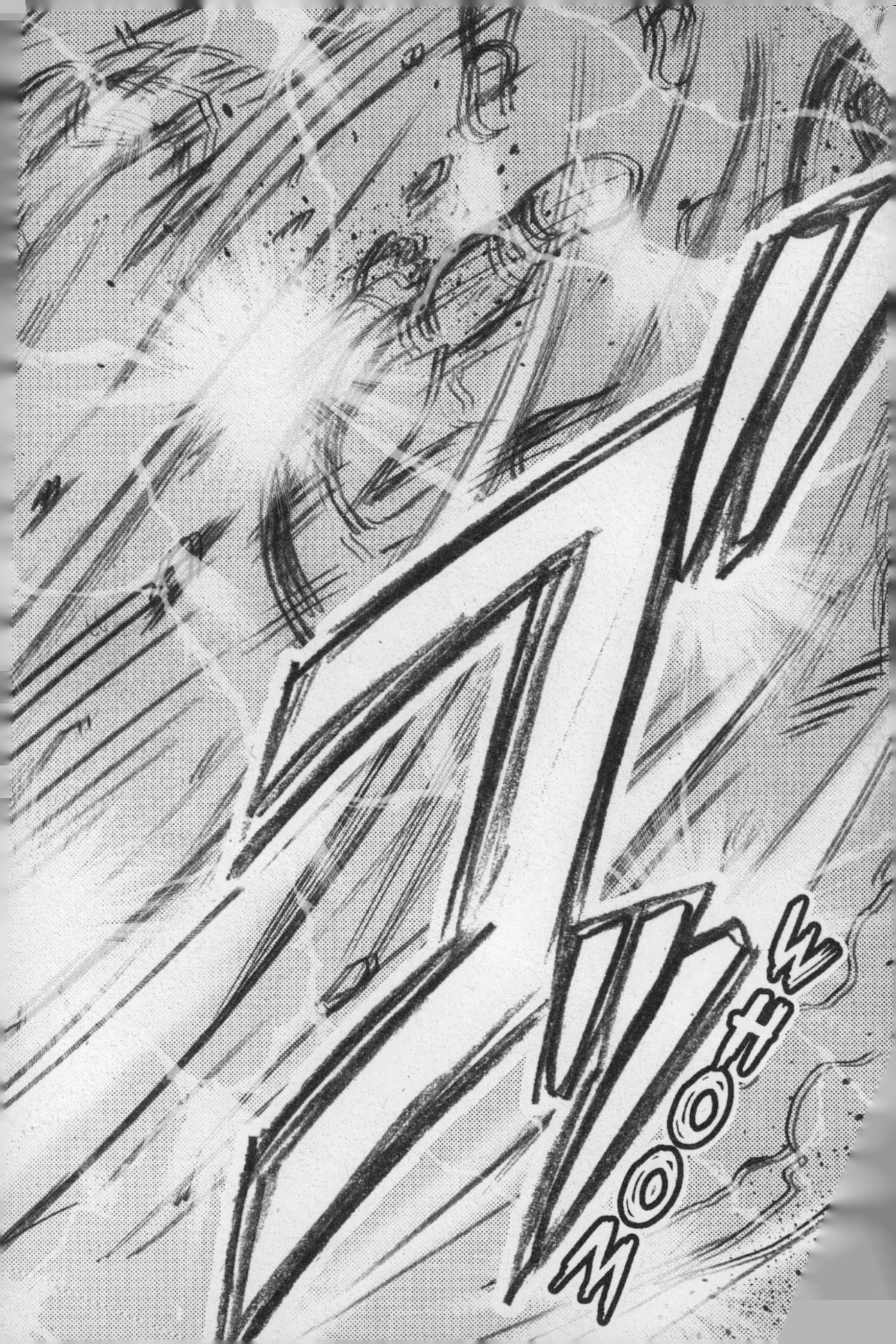
WHOOM

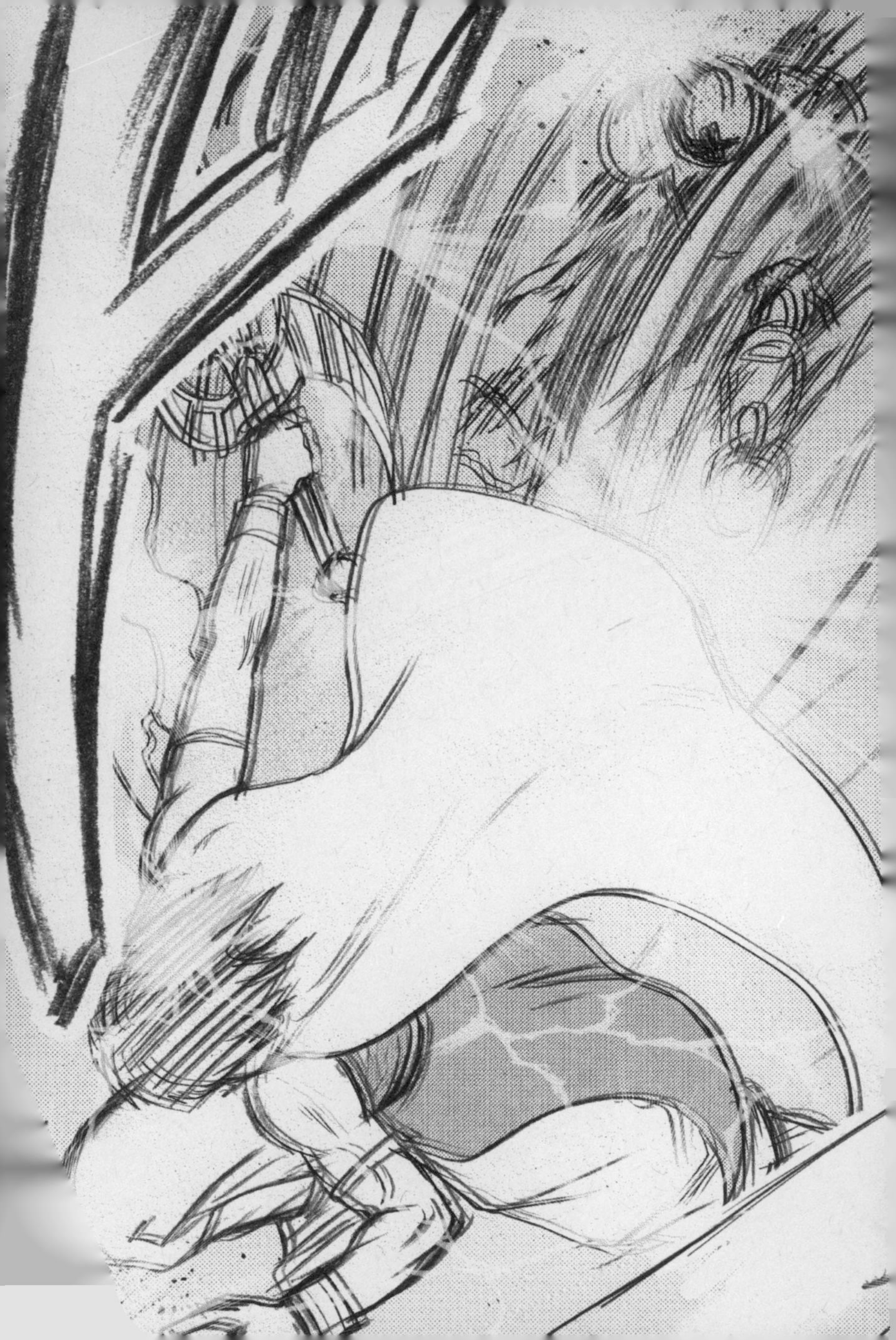

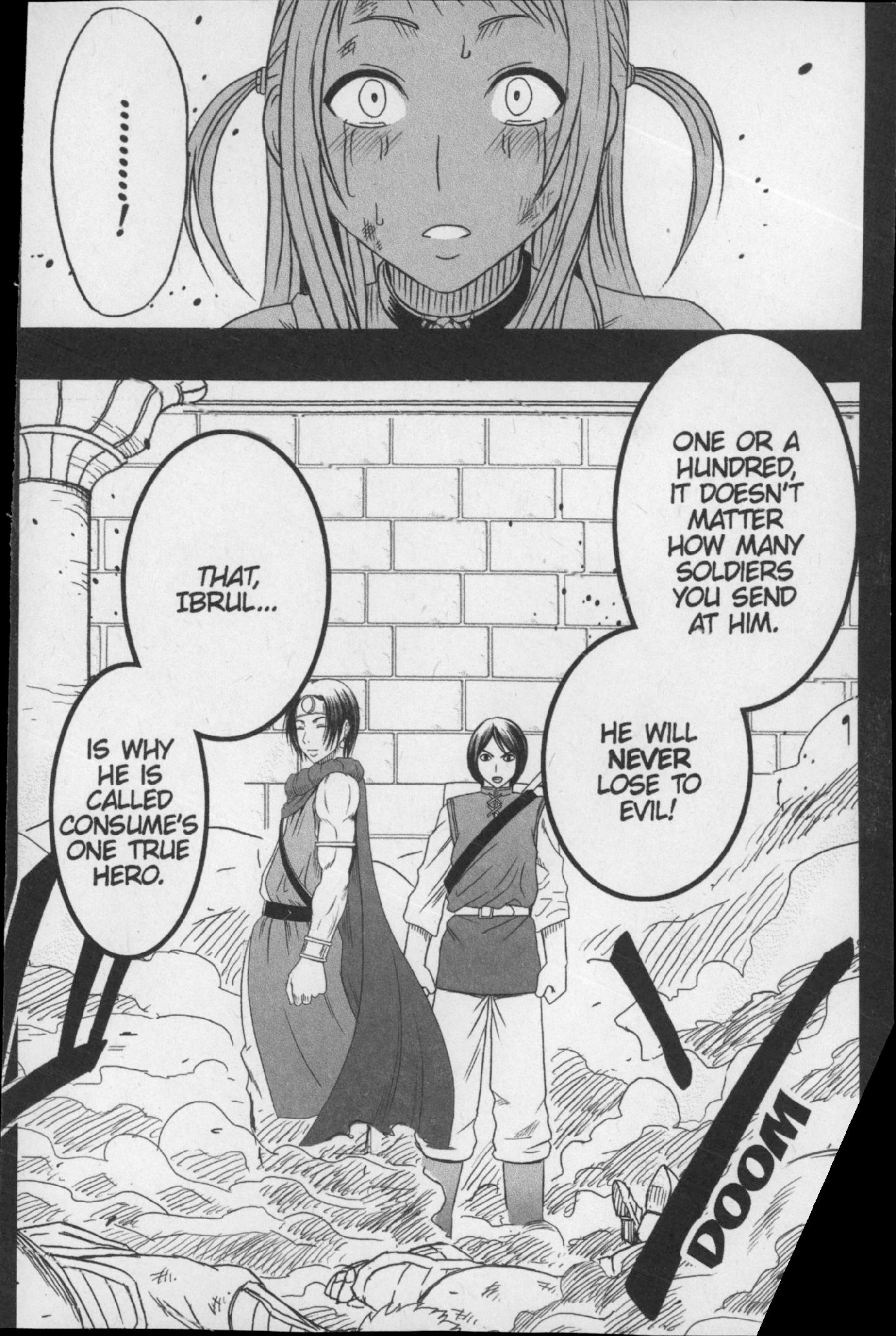
......!
ONE OR A HUNDRED, IT DOESN'T MATTER HOW MANY SOLDIERS YOU SEND AT HIM.
HE WILL NEVER LOSE TO EVIL!
THAT, IBRUL...
IS WHY HE IS CALLED CONSUME'S ONE TRUE HERO.
DOOM

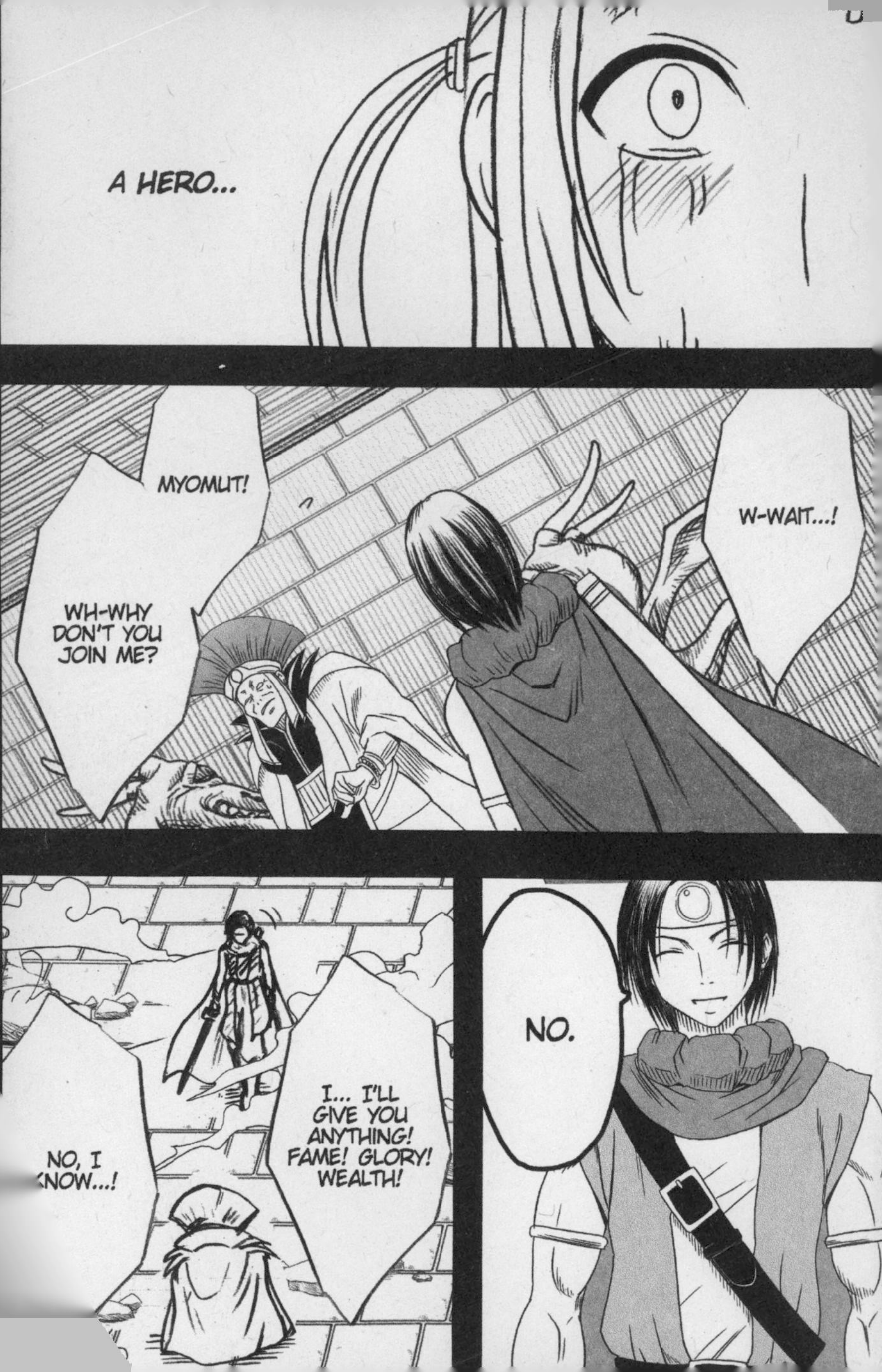
A HERO...
W-WAIT...!
MYOMUT!
WH-WHY DON'T YOU JOIN ME?
NO.
I... I'LL GIVE YOU ANYTHING! FAME! GLORY! WEALTH!
NO, I KNOW...!

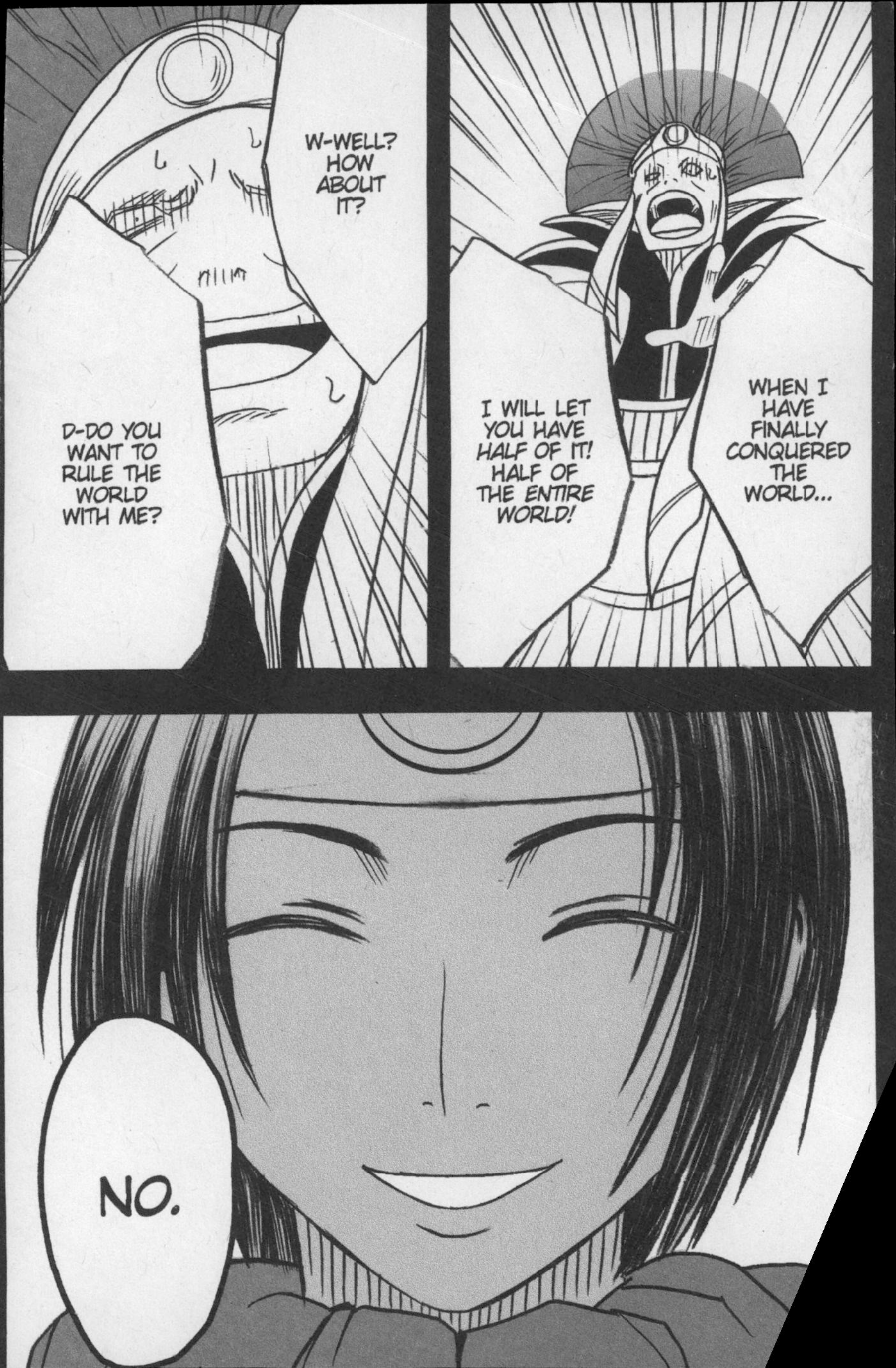
WHEN I HAVE FINALLY CONQUERED THE WORLD...
I WILL LET YOU HAVE HALF OF IT! HALF OF THE ENTIRE WORLD!
W-WELL? HOW ABOUT IT?
D-DO YOU WANT TO RULE THE WORLD WITH ME?
NO.

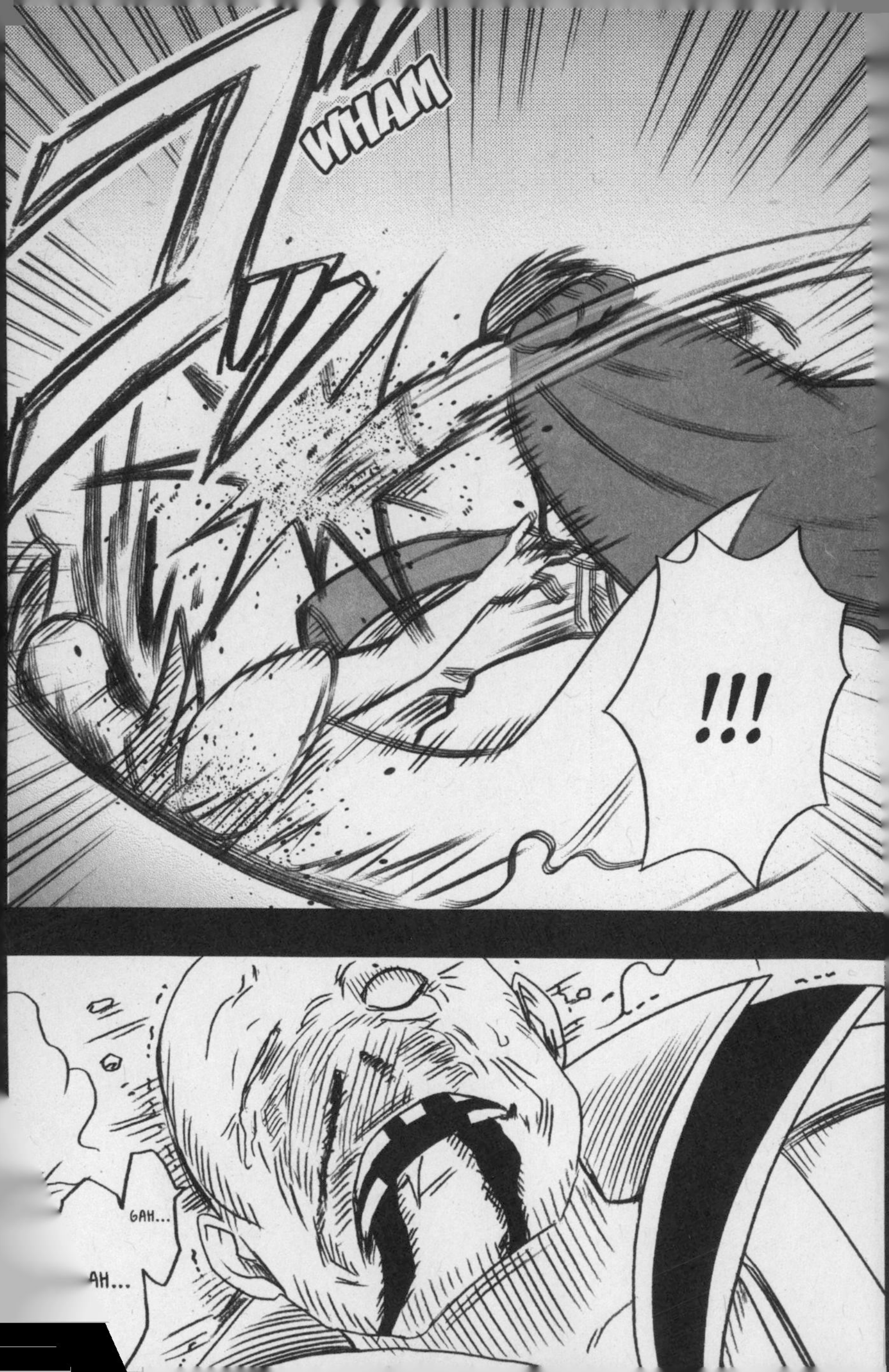
WHAM
!!!
GAH...
AH...

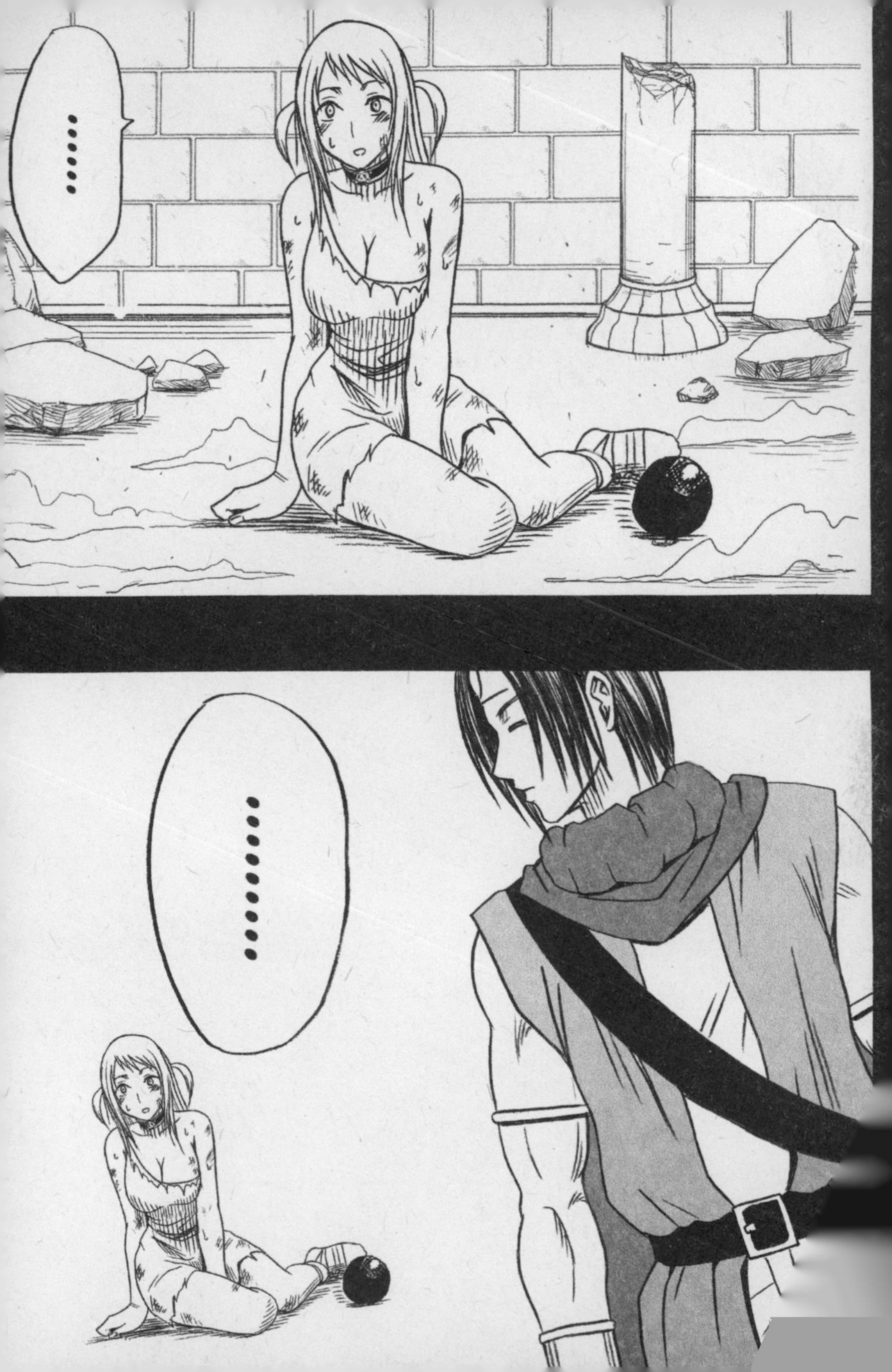
……
………

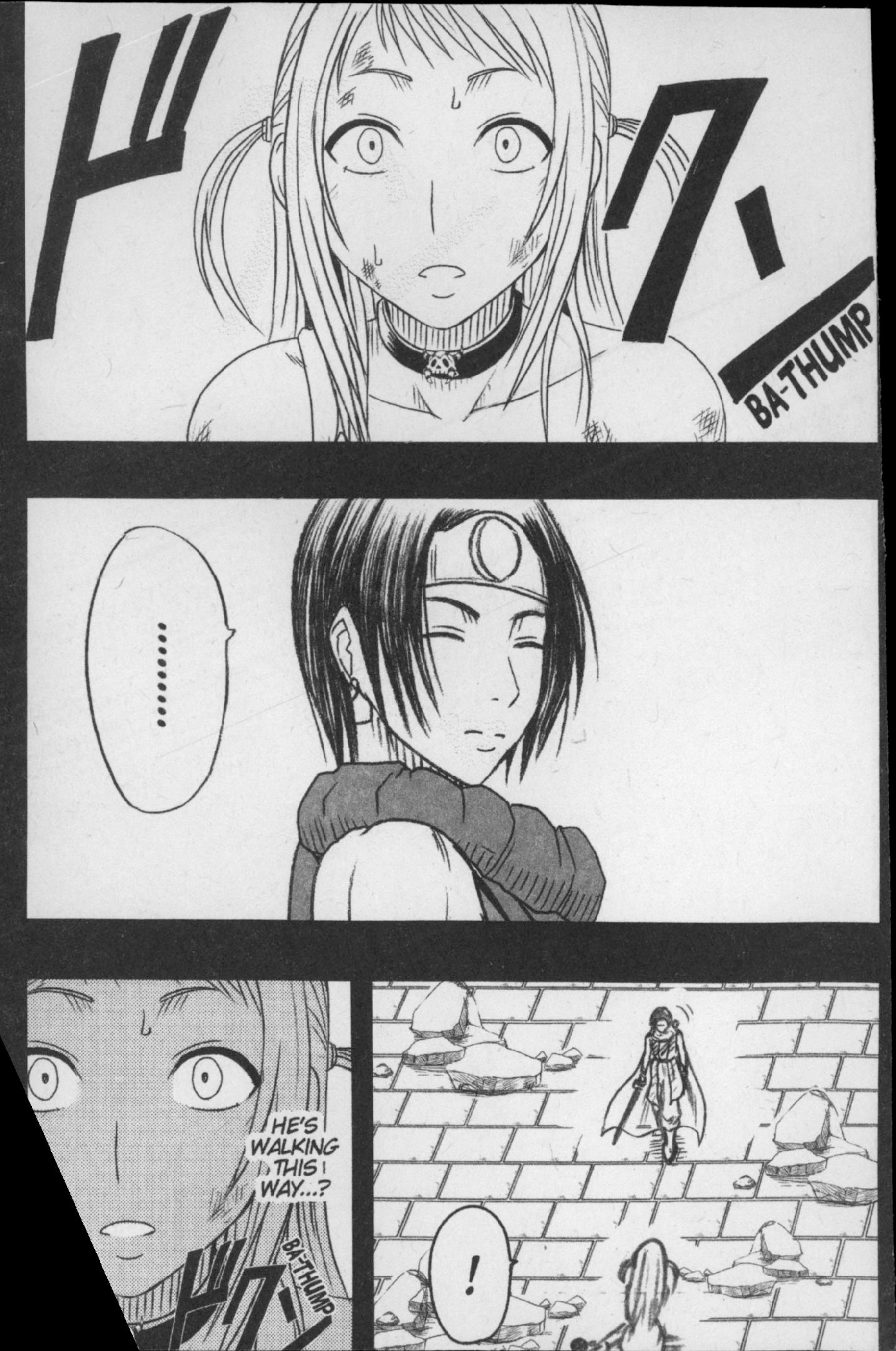
ドクン
BA-THUMP
……
!
HE'S WALKING THIS WAY...?
ドクン
BA-THUMP

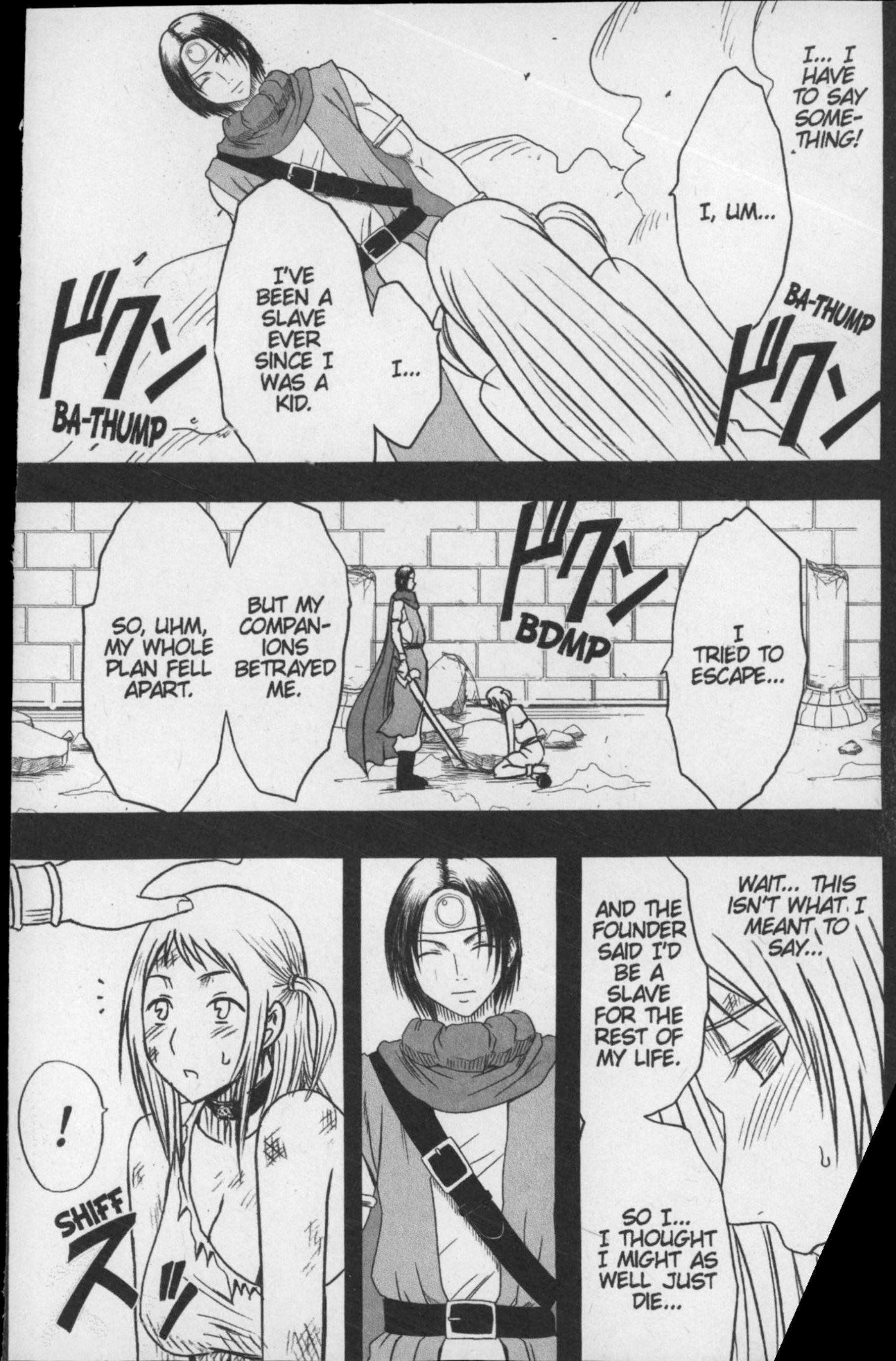
I... I HAVE TO SAY SOME-THING!
I, UM...
BA-THUMP
ドクン
I...
I'VE BEEN A SLAVE EVER SINCE I WAS A KID.
ドクン
BA-THUMP
I TRIED TO ESCAPE...
ドクン
BDMP
BUT MY COMPANIONS BETRAYED ME.
SO, UHM, MY WHOLE PLAN FELL APART.
WAIT... THIS ISN'T WHAT I MEANT TO SAY...
AND THE FOUNDER SAID I'D BE A SLAVE FOR THE REST OF MY LIFE.
SO I... I THOUGHT I MIGHT AS WELL JUST DIE...
!
SHIFF
スッ

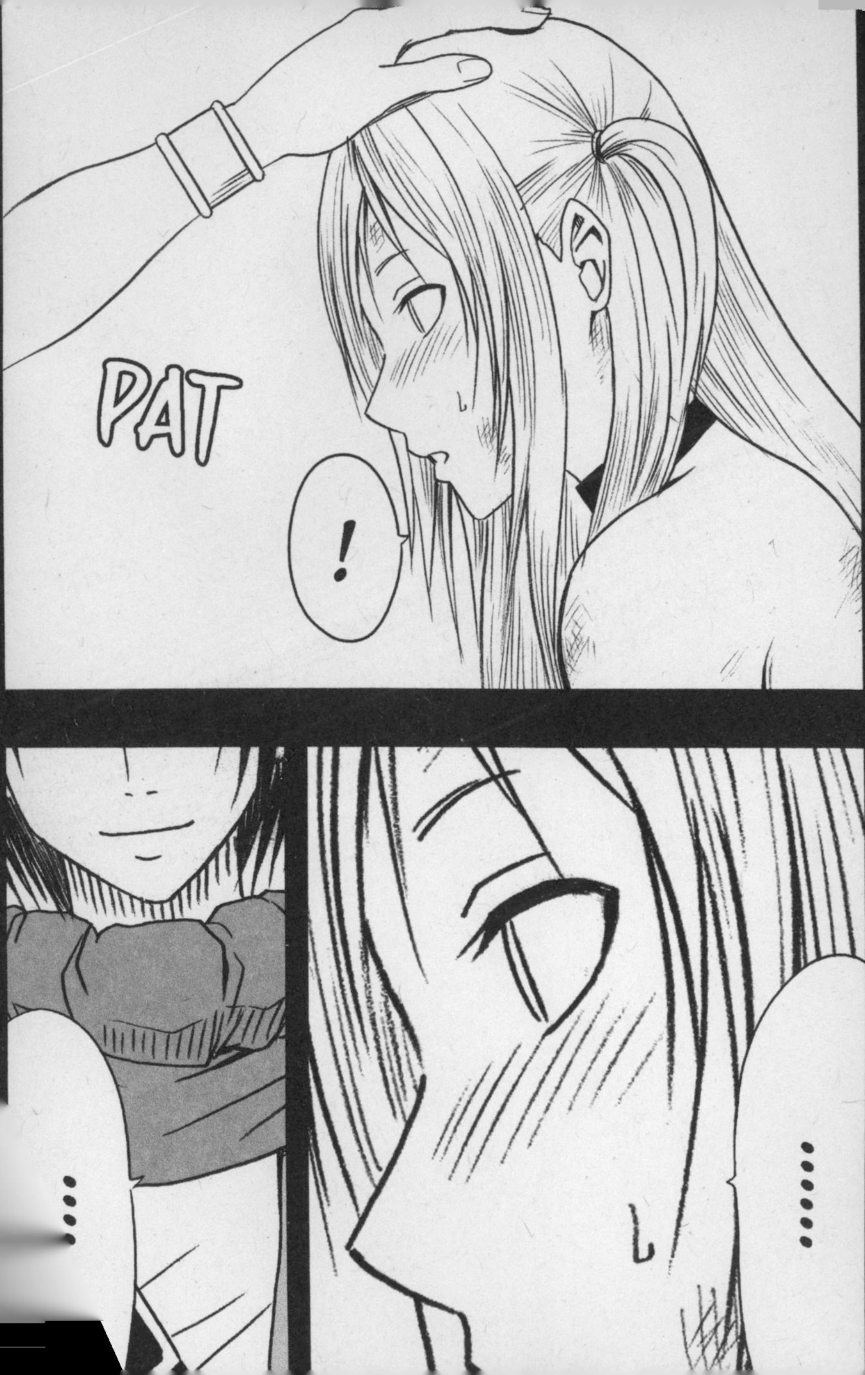
PAT
!
......
....

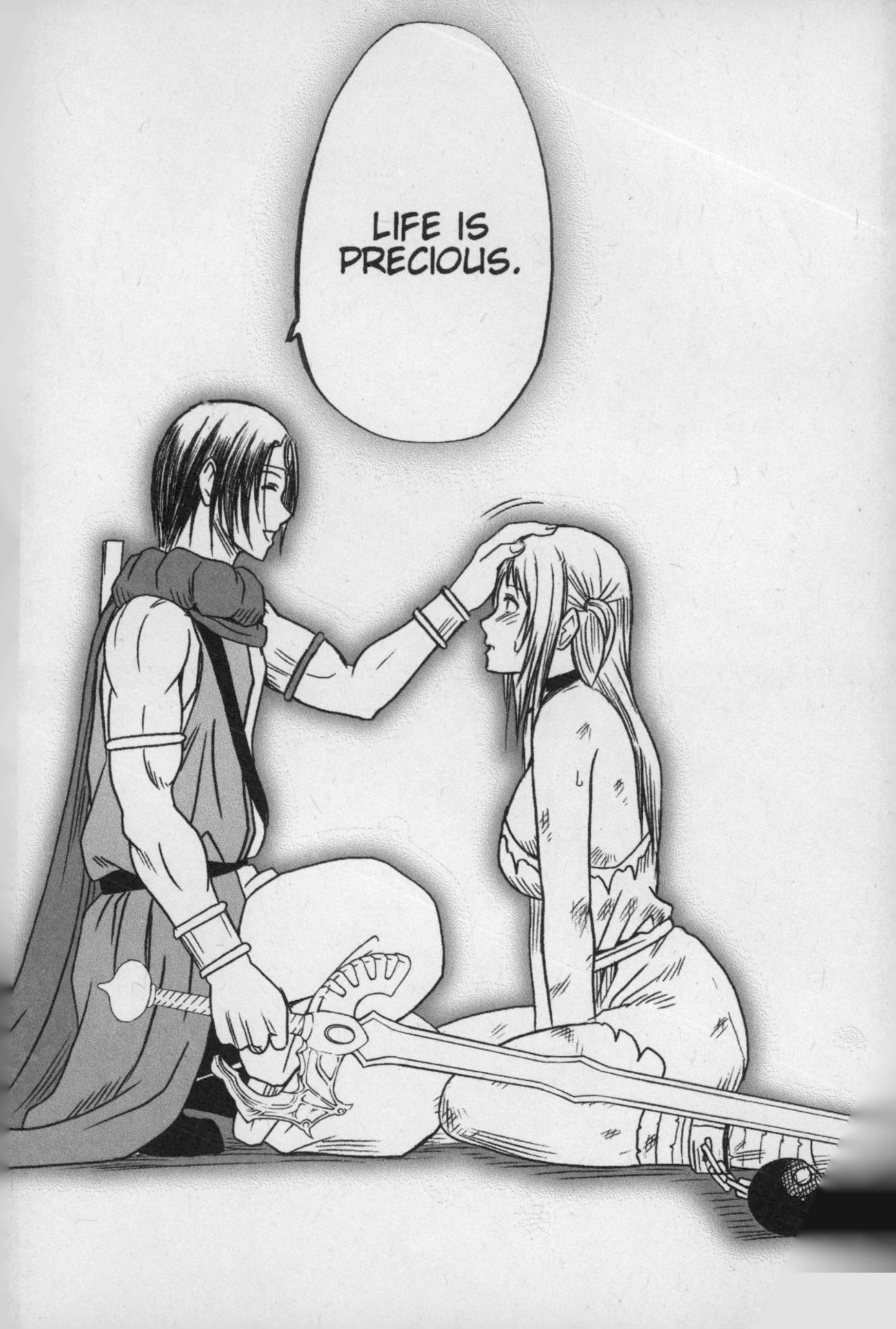
LIFE IS PRECIOUS.

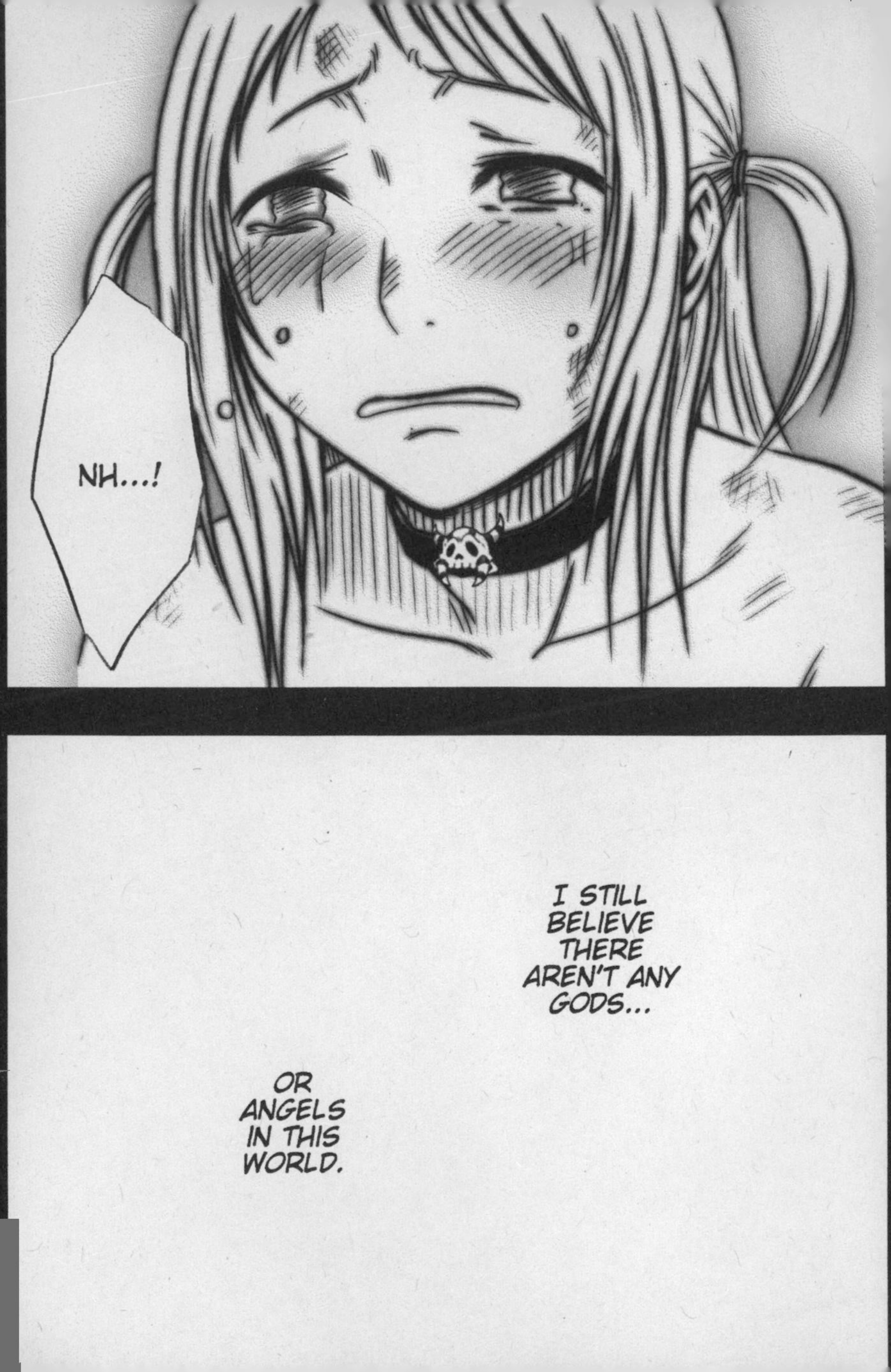
NH...!
I STILL BELIEVE THERE AREN'T ANY GODS...
OR ANGELS IN THIS WORLD.

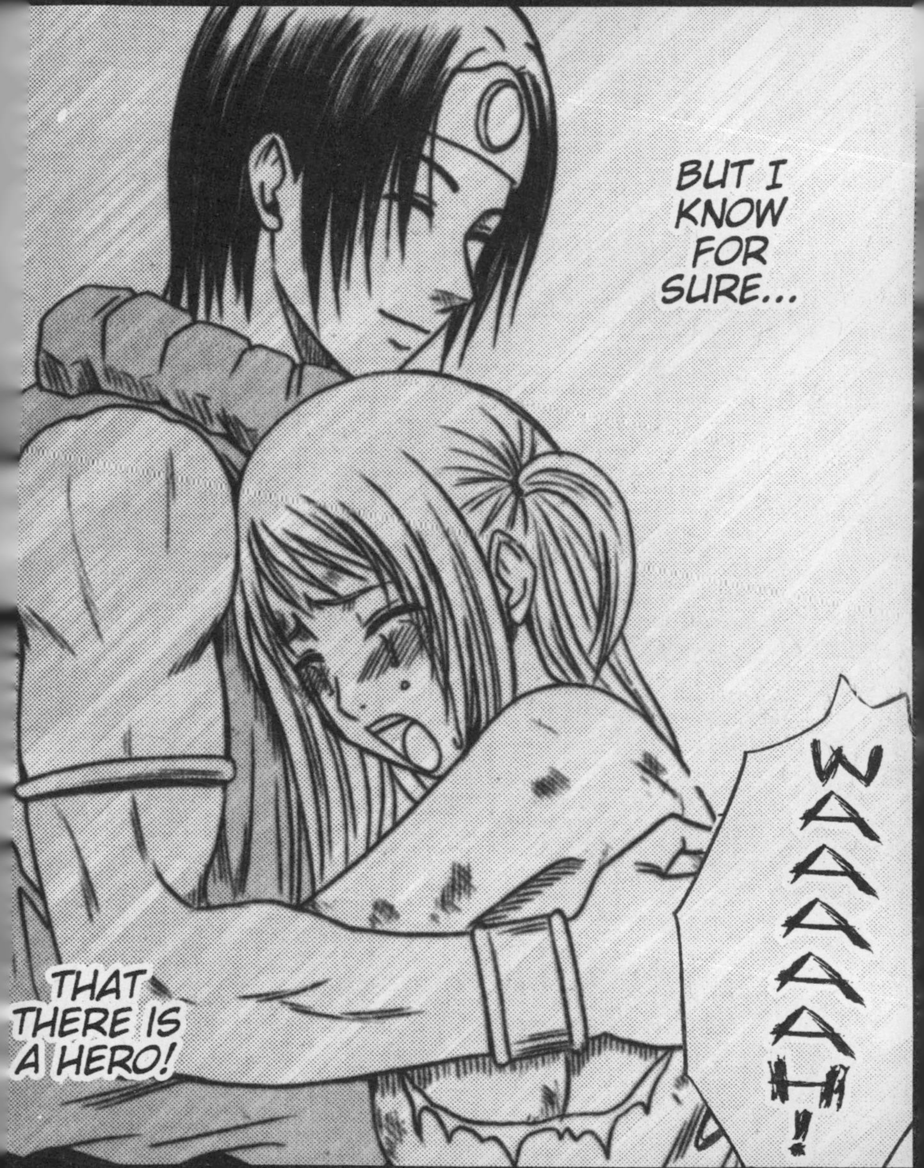
BUT I KNOW FOR SURE...
WAAAAAAH!!
THAT THERE IS A HERO!

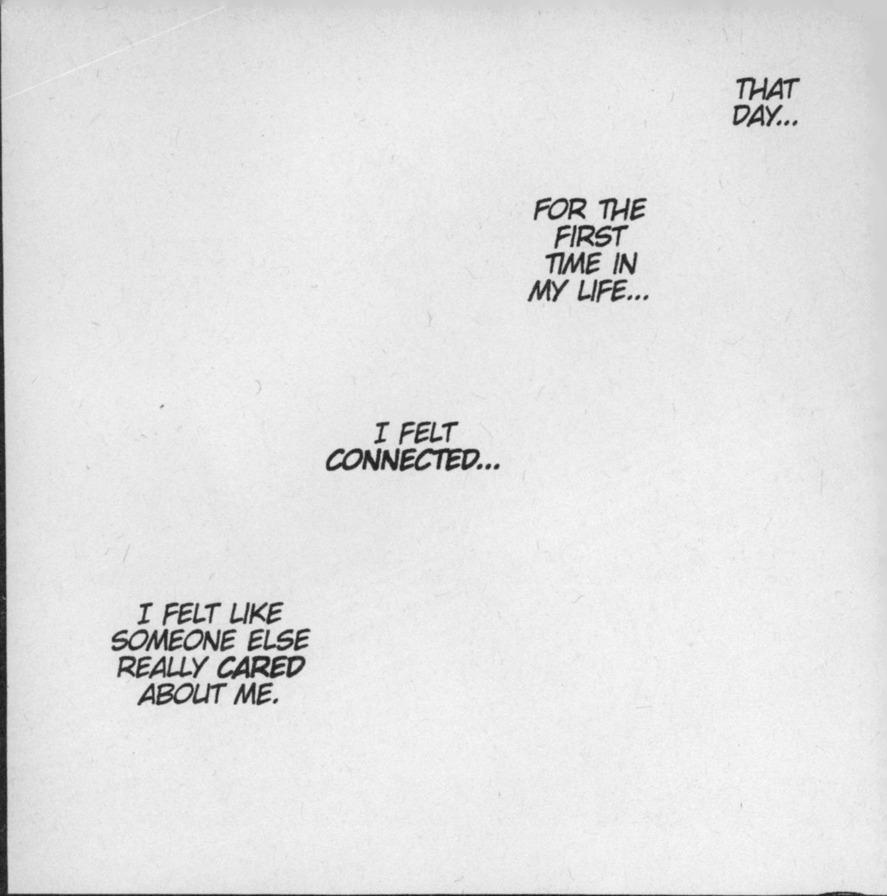
THAT DAY...
FOR THE FIRST TIME IN MY LIFE...
I FELT CONNECTED...
I FELT LIKE SOMEONE ELSE REALLY CARED ABOUT ME.

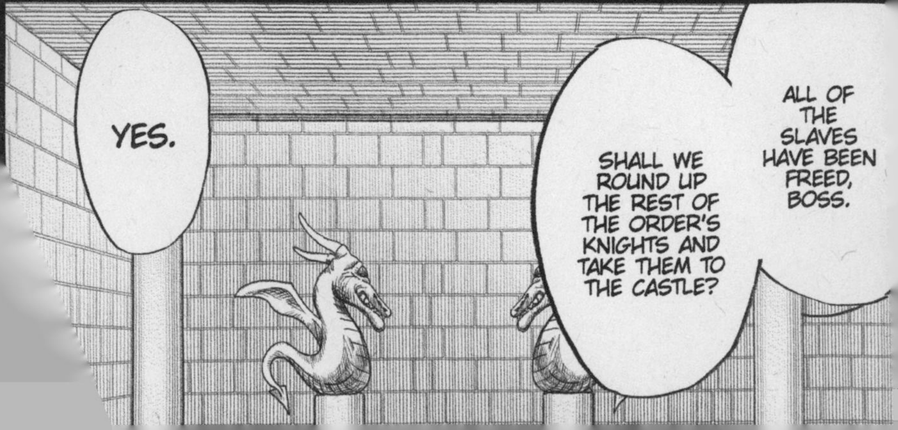
ALL OF THE SLAVES HAVE BEEN FREED, BOSS.
SHALL WE ROUND UP THE REST OF THE ORDER'S KNIGHTS AND TAKE THEM TO THE CASTLE?
YES.

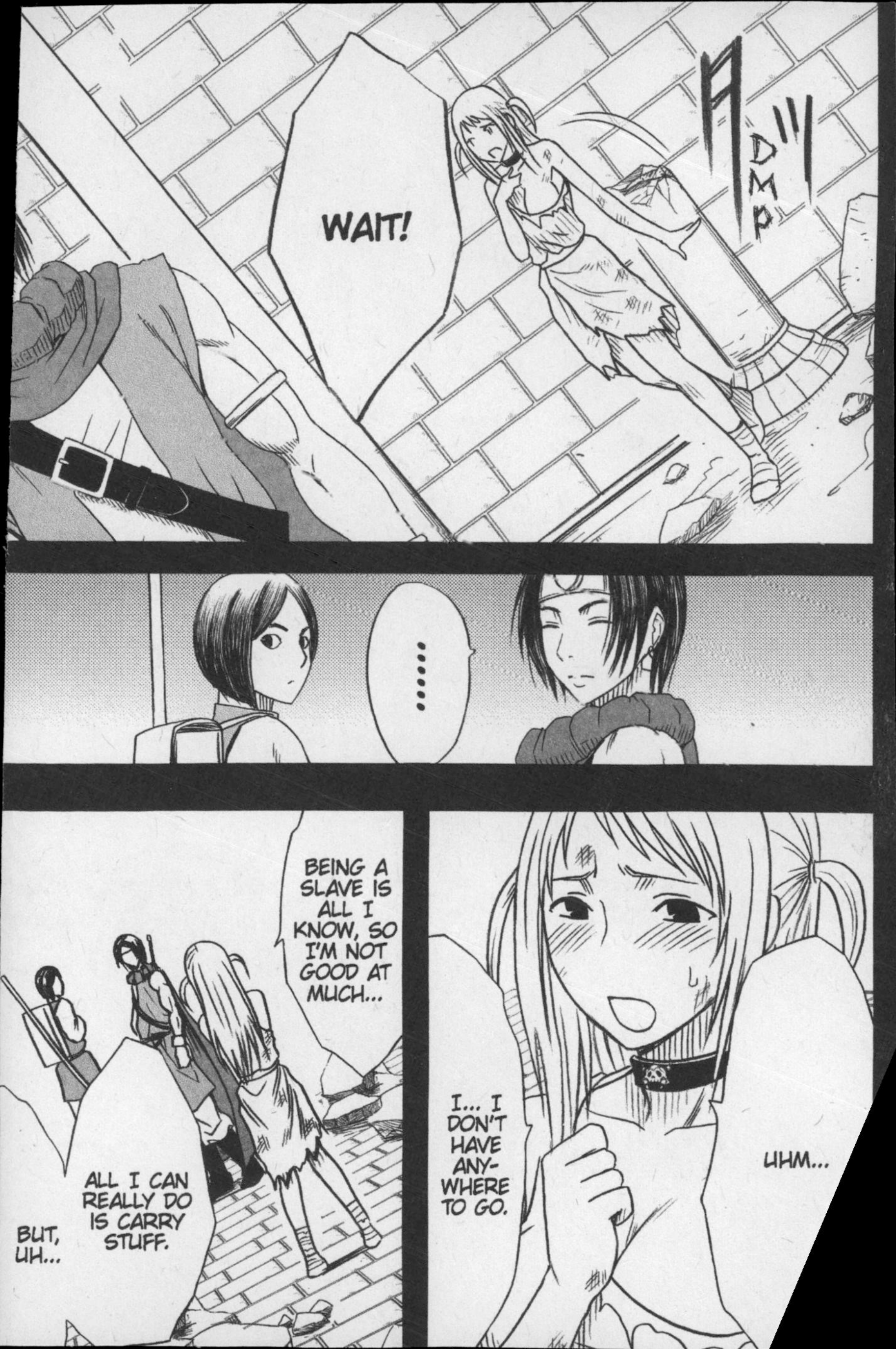
DMP
WAIT!
......
UHM...
I... I DON'T HAVE ANYWHERE TO GO.
BEING A SLAVE IS ALL I KNOW, SO I'M NOT GOOD AT MUCH...
BUT, UH...
ALL I CAN REALLY DO IS CARRY STUFF.

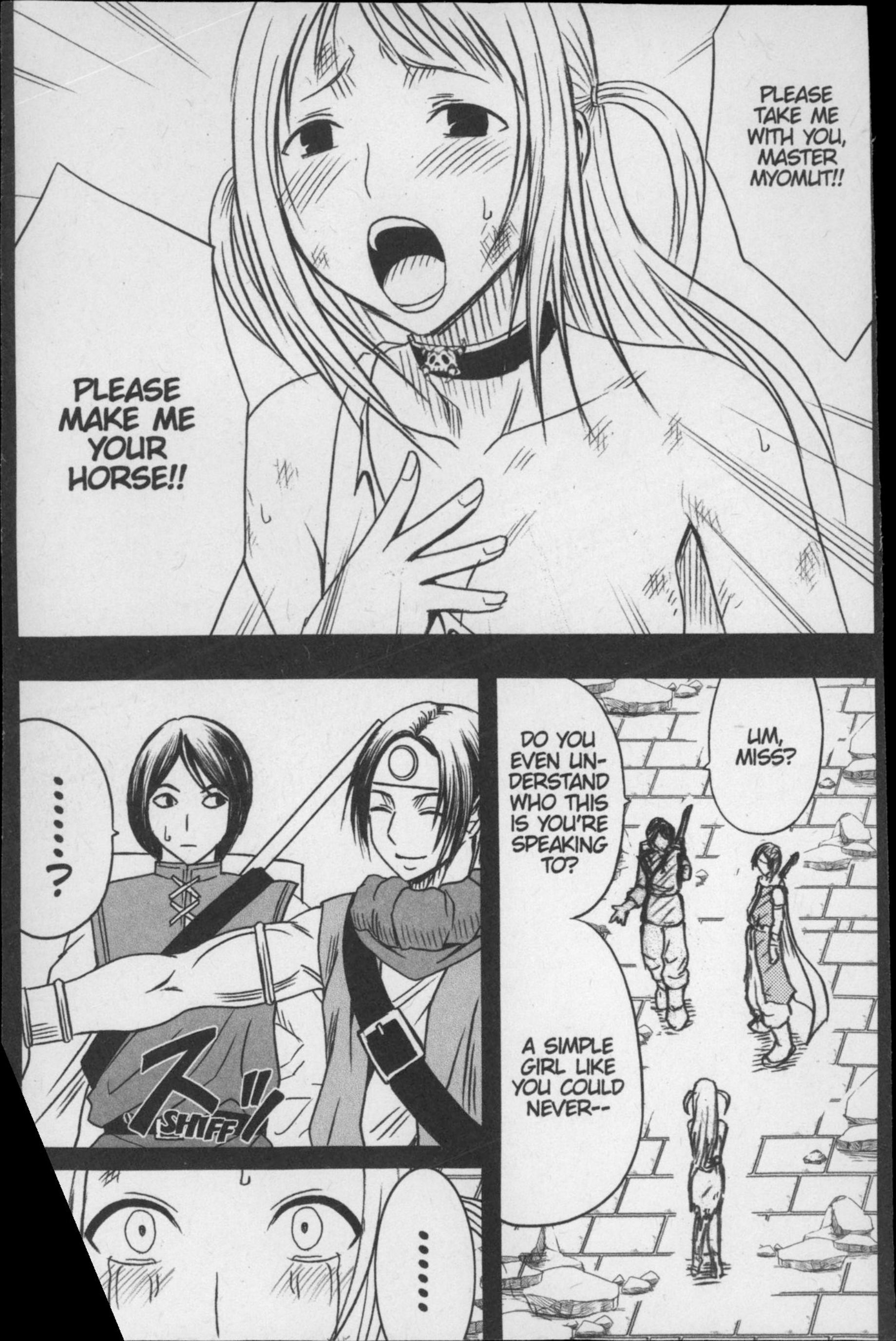
PLEASE TAKE ME WITH YOU, MASTER MYOMUT!!
PLEASE MAKE ME YOUR HORSE!!
UM, MISS?
DO YOU EVEN UN-DERSTAND WHO THIS IS YOU'RE SPEAKING TO?
A SIMPLE GIRL LIKE YOU COULD NEVER--
?......
SHIFF
......

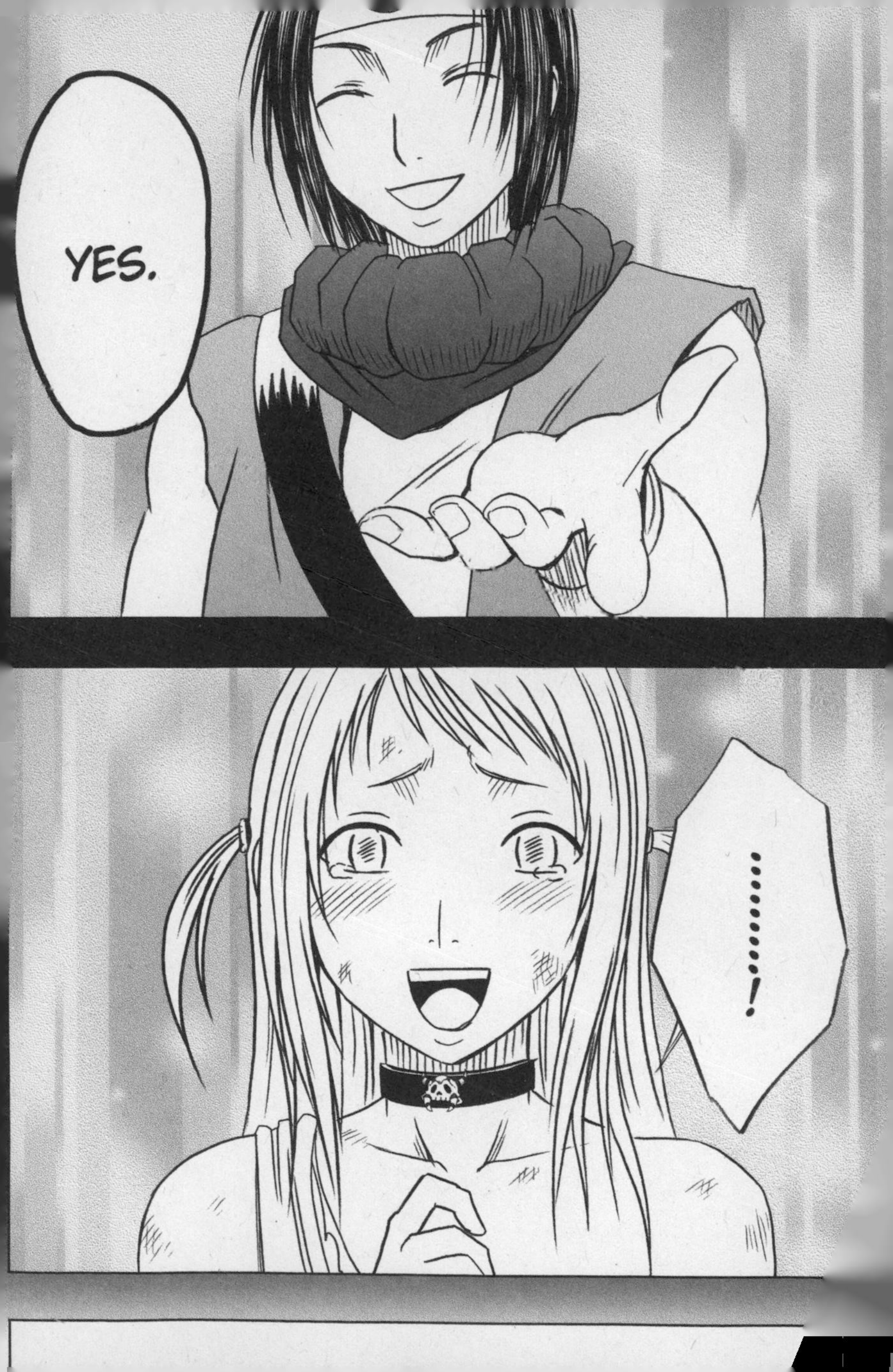
YES.
……!

AND
SO...

THAT'S HOW
I JOINED
MASTER
MYOMUT'S
PARTY.

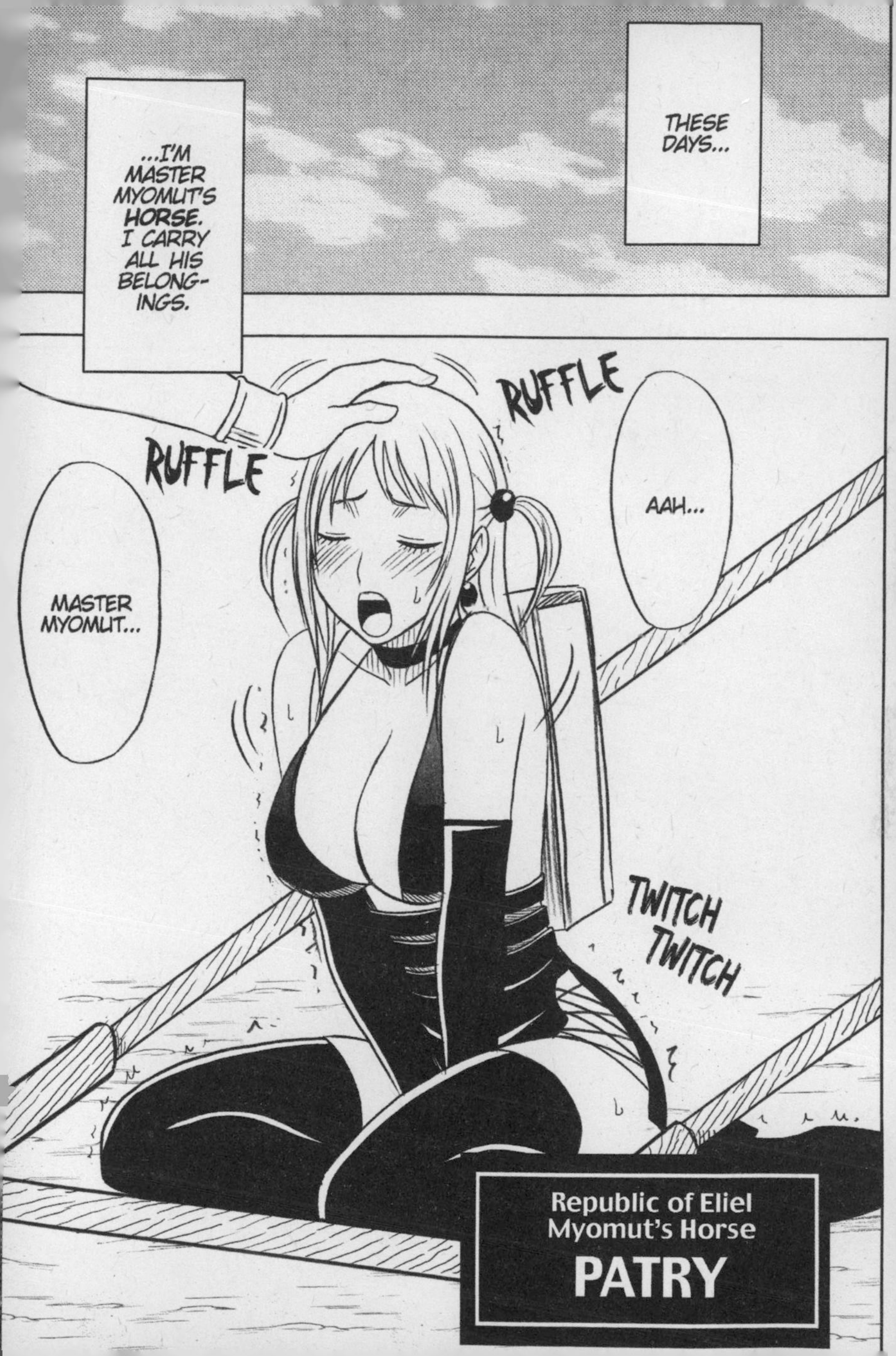
THESE DAYS...
...I'M MASTER MYOMUT'S HORSE. I CARRY ALL HIS BELONG-INGS.
RUFFLE
AAH...
RUFFLE
MASTER MYOMUT...
TWITCH TWITCH
Republic of Eliel Myomut's Horse
PATRY

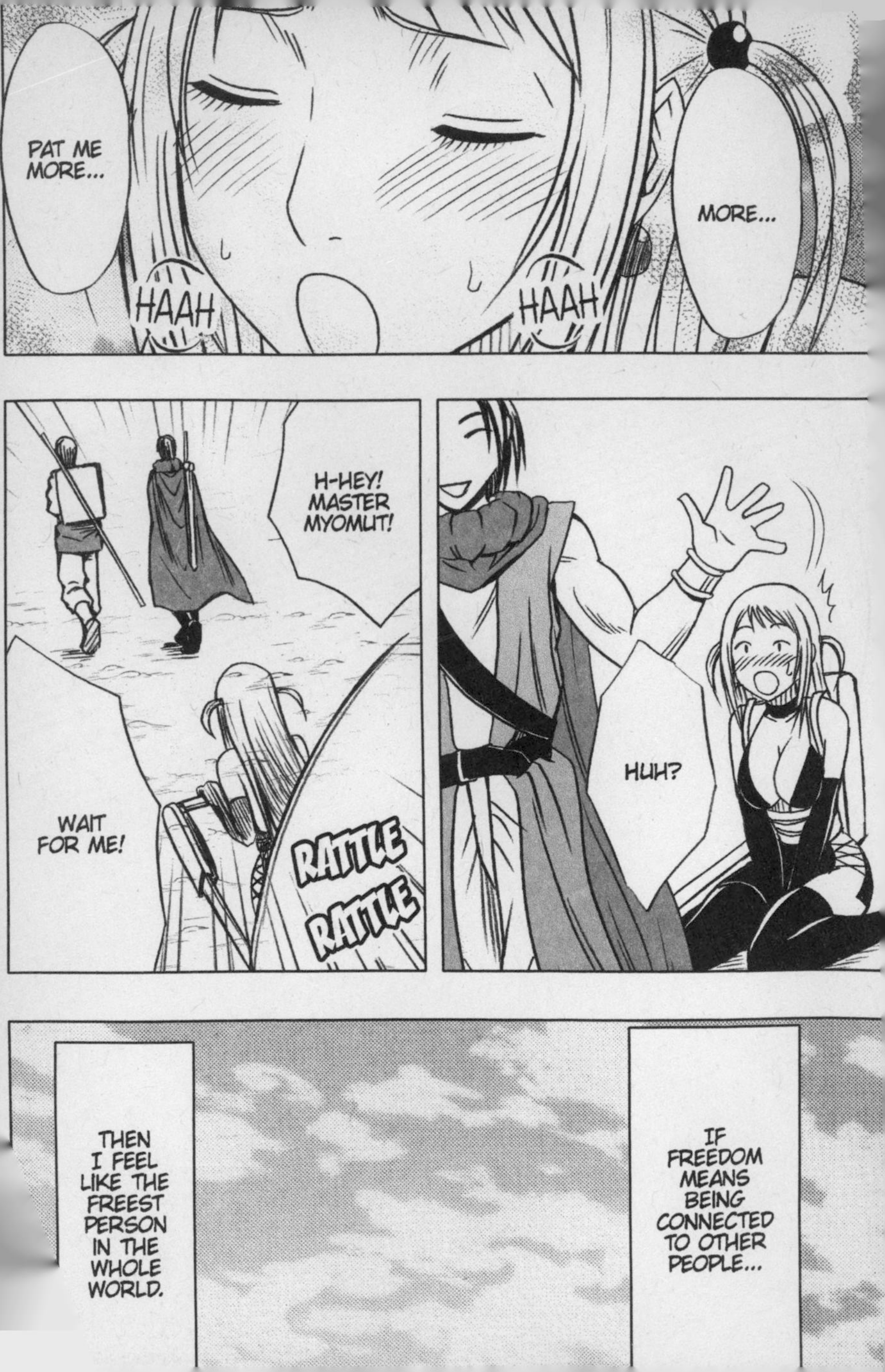
MORE...
HAAH
PAT ME MORE...
HAAH
HUH?
H-HEY! MASTER MYOMUT!
WAIT FOR ME!
RATTLE RATTLE
IF FREEDOM MEANS BEING CONNECTED TO OTHER PEOPLE...
THEN I FEEL LIKE THE FREEST PERSON IN THE WHOLE WORLD.

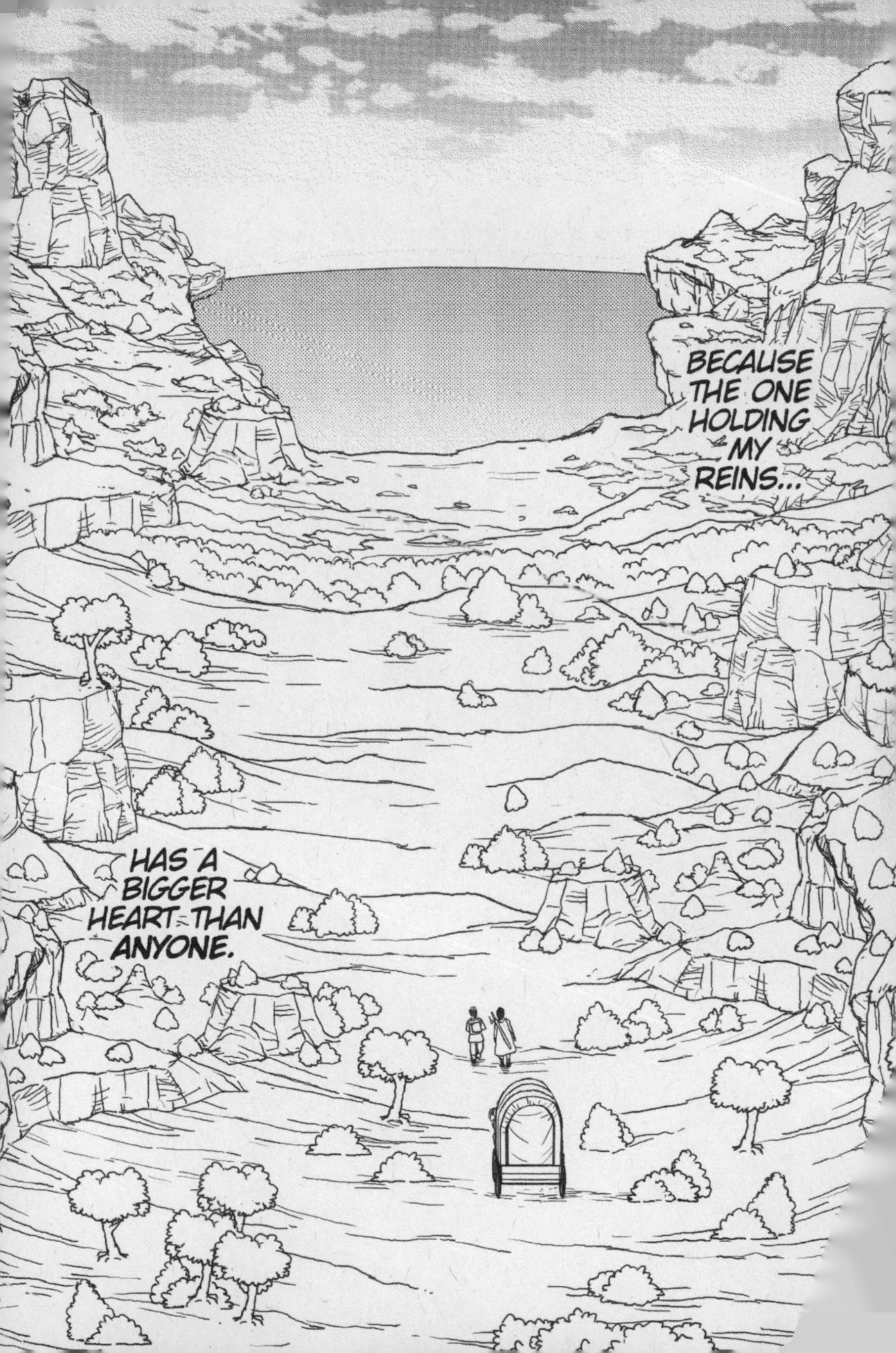
BECAUSE THE ONE HOLDING MY REINS...
HAS A BIGGER HEART THAN ANYONE.

ON THE SIDE STORY

I personally thought Myomut had a lot of promise as an awesome character, so I wrote a one-shot story about him. Everybody liked it. In fact, I received a lot of fan mail saying the one-shot was better than the main story, and they wanted to know what happened next.

Patry's line, "Please make me your horse," has garnered mixed opinions from readers. Patry always had a low opinion of herself and her abilities. She wasn't a good fighter, and wasn't very pretty. Living most of her life as a slave meant she had no education and no manners. She was convinced she was utterly unqualified to be part of a "hero's" party. Still, she wanted to go with Myomut so much, she came up with that line out of sheer desperation. I know it may still be a little hard for some, but if you could look at it in that light, I think it may make it a little clearer.

Also, Myomut may have Patry pulling his wagon, but he does not force her to do it. Patry enjoys doing things to help Myomut, and he understands this. The interplay between them at the beginning of the story wasn't Myomut being mean to Patry, it was just playful banter. (Having Patry to slow them down so Myomut has an excuse to save his strength is another reason.)

By the way, while Myomut usually only says "yes" and "no," he is capable of talking normally.

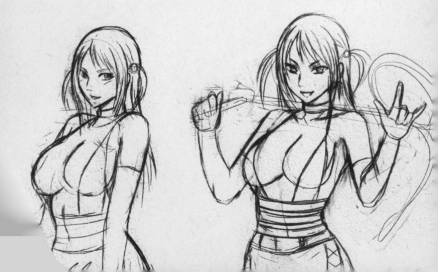

WORLD WAR BLUE

CHARACTER INTRODUCTION

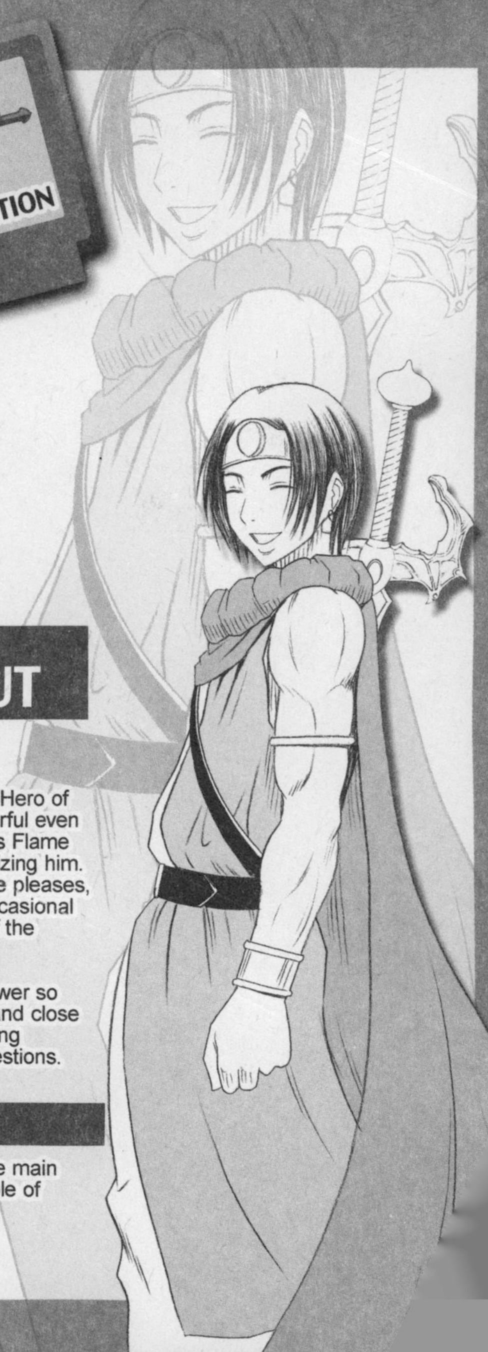

The Hero

MYOMUT

Eliel native.

He is called the one true Hero of Consume. He is so powerful even Marcus himself, Ninteldo's Flame Emperor, avoids antagonizing him. He generally travels as he pleases, but he will take on the occasional odd quest for the good of the country.

He exudes an aura of power so great that people who stand close to him are awed into asking nothing but yes or no questions.

Author Comment

He hardly talks during the main storyline, but he is capable of speaking normally.

WORLD WAR BLUE
CHARACTER INTRODUCTION

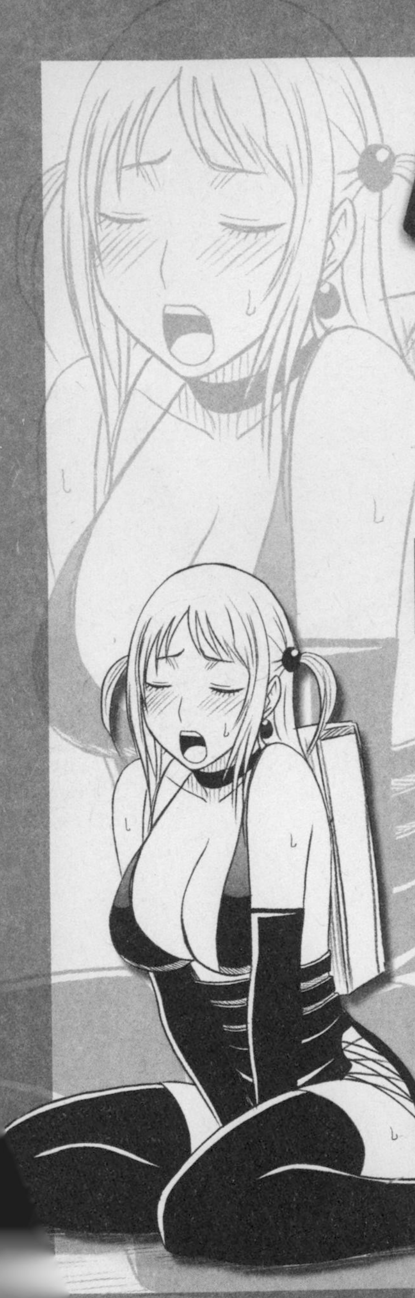

The Hero's Horse
PATRY

Eliel native.

Patry pulls Myomut's baggage cart. She has a huge crush on him.

She may have the genes of a killer, but besides her superhuman strength, everything else about her is normal. Myomut picked out her outfit for her.

Author Comment

I wanted to make her more of a secretary-slash-dominatrix type, but as I was writing the story, she kinda wound up as she is now.

PATRY

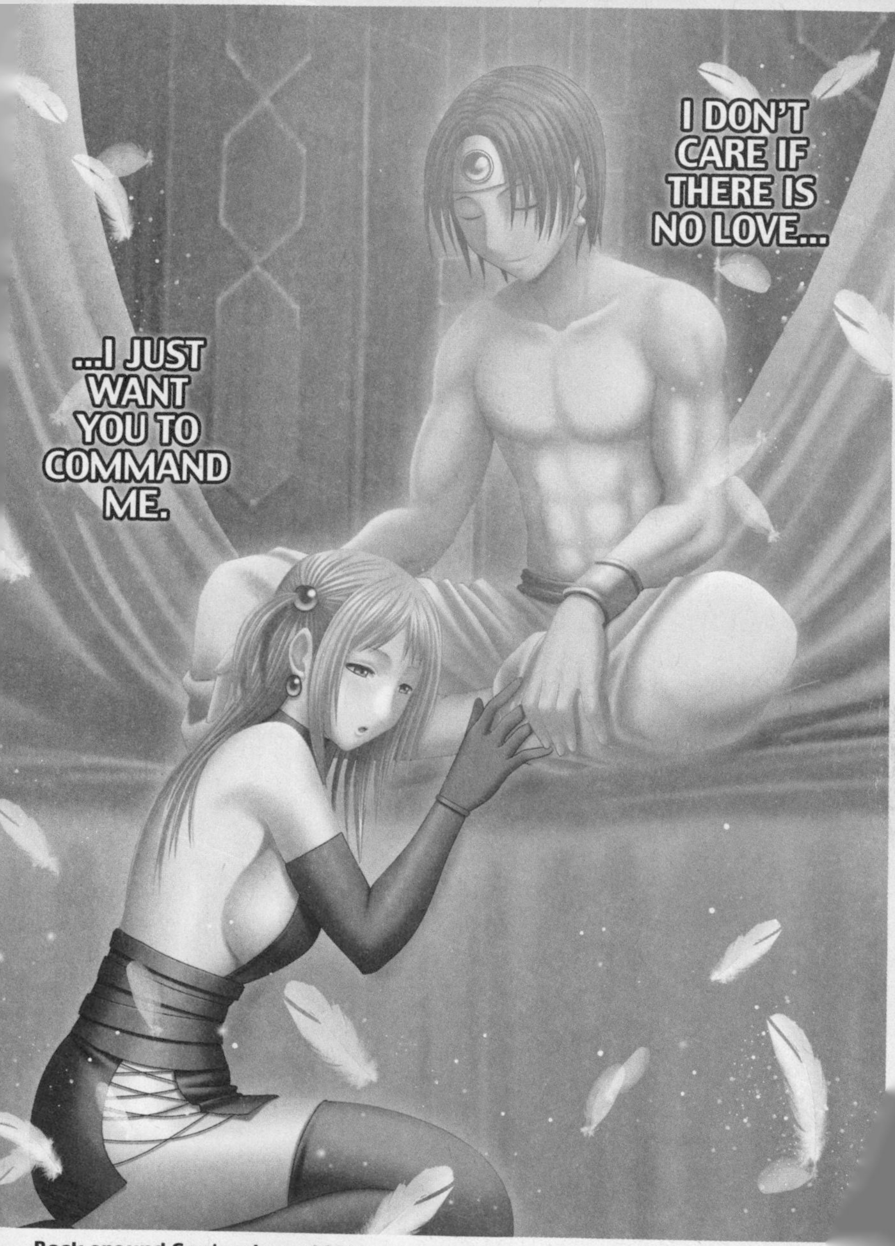
I DON'T CARE IF THERE IS NO LOVE...
...I JUST WANT YOU TO COMMAND ME.

Back around September of 2008, I ran a questionnaire on the website I wa
publishing this on at the time. It asked fans which character they wanted t
see more of. Myomut came in at #1, so I drew this pin-up. This is one of
Patry's mental pictures of her relationship with Myomut.

Perusing Video Game History

ON THE EDGE OF THE BLUE WORLD

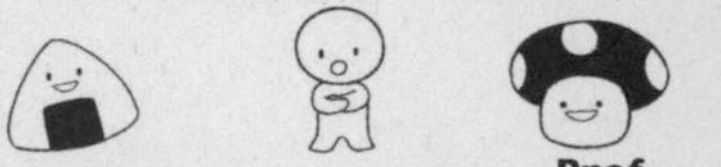

Dr. Onigiri Mr. Why Prof. Mushroom

Today's Topic

DRAGON QUEST

Mr. Why: Okay. Today we're going to take a look at the game that's so ridiculously popular it needs no introduction: *Dragon Quest* (originally known as *Dragon Warrior* in North America).

Dr. Onigiri: Oh, that one? Since it's so popular, everyone undoubtedly knows all about it already. Can't we just skip over it? I mean, it's not even a Sega game.

Prof. Mushroom: Whoa, whoa! We can't say we truly talked all about video game history if we left out one of the most popular series in the history of the medium. Ever since Enix put out the first one in 1986, it's been one mega-hit after the other.

Mr. Why: Yeah. Even I've heard of it.

Prof. Mushroom: So which was the first one you played?

Mr. Why: Ummm...I think it was *Dragon Quest V.*

Prof. Mushroom: Awesome, you picked the perfect one for this point in the story. Now, *DQV* was released for the Super Famicom in 1992. The Hero, his dad Pankraz having been killed, is made a slave of the Order of Light for 10 years. Then he has to contend with Ibul, the founder of the Order and a memorable villain.

Mr. Why: Yeah, I remember him! Oh, and you could make monsters part of your party, too! Which *DQ* did you like best, Prof.?

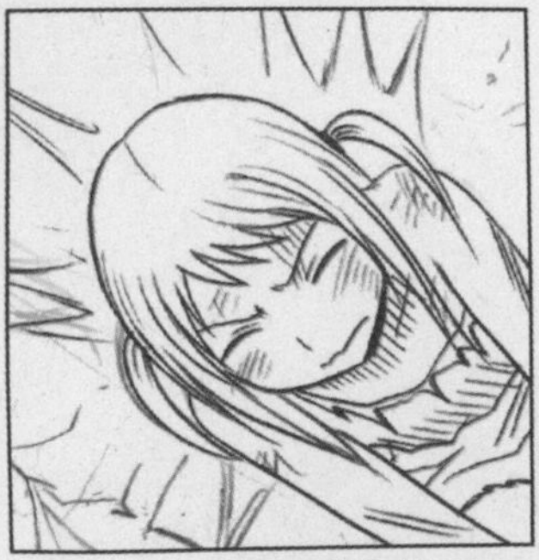

Patry spent 10 painful years as a slave in the Order of Light.

Prof. Mushroom: Hmmm... I think it was *DQIV*, for the Famicom. Released in 1990, it was a five chapter story that followed the Hero and his companions' battle against Necrosaro. It was a really intense drama. I loved watching how, by Chapter 5, all the characters I'd worked hard to raise and got so attached to come together. It was just like Meena, the fortune teller, said: "They started as little sparks, but in the end they became a bright beacon to lead the way." Also, this was the first game in the series to include the wagon, since you gathered so many followers.

Prof. Mushroom: The horse that pulls it is a mare named Patricia. By the last battle, you could blow a special horn and she would run right to you from anywhere. Another first in *DQIV* was battle commands. Back then, the idea that your characters would move on their own via AI (artificial intelligence) was new and exciting. But the AI turned out to be so dumb that most players hated it. Enix learned from that, and in *DQV*, they let you control party members more directly or give them individualized orders.

NO.

True Heroes never give in to evil, no matter what form it takes.

The Cursed Necklace (a.k.a. Death Necklace in the North American version) is an item only a certain person can remove for you. You can't take it off yourself.

Dr. Onigiri: YAAWN...maybe I should head home...

Mr. Why: Didn't *DQVI* have a horse and wagon too?

Prof. Mushroom: Yep. The horse was named "Peggy Sue," and she was really, really strong.

Mr. Why: Yeah, that's it!

Prof. Mushroom: Going all the way back to the original *Dragon Quest*, the Dragon King had some pretty amazing lines for the time. The most famous one was when he said if you joined him, he'd give you half of the world. I admit, I almost chose "Yes."

Dr. Onigiri: I remember equipping the Cursed Necklace out of curiosity. Boy, did I regret that.

Prof. Mushroom: Yeah, you almost can't help yourself.

To Be Continued... in Volume 4.

Enjoying the bonds of companionship, Patry is willing to follow the Hero to the ends of the earth.

WORLD WAR BLUE
CHARACTER INTRODUCTION

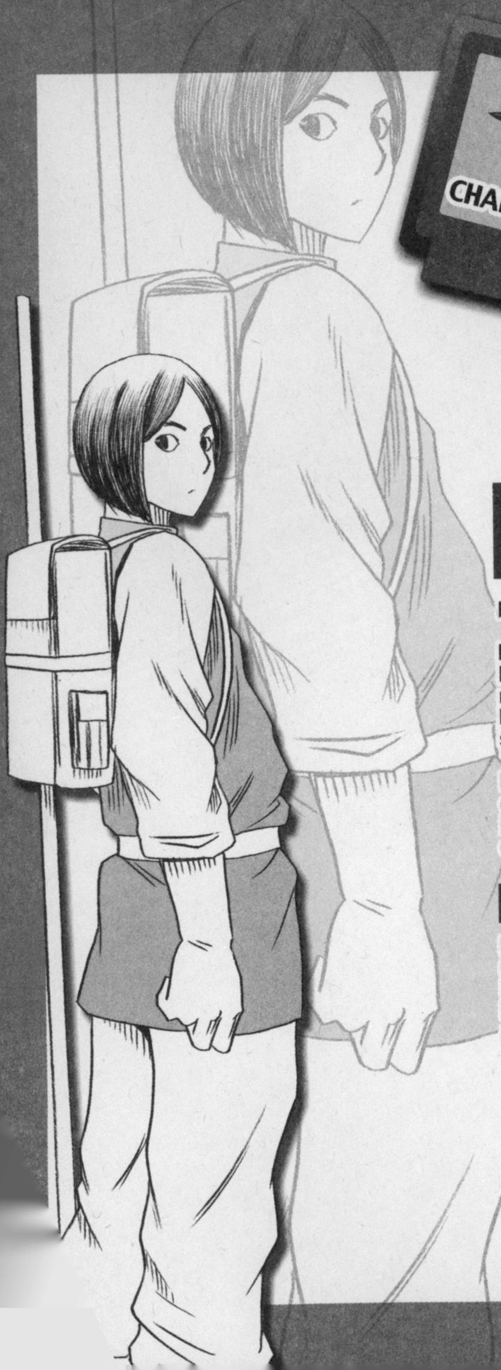

The Hero's Aide
MANOS

Eliel native.

Myomut's aide and manager, he was once part of Eliel's national police force. He calls Myomut "boss." He also has a scar on his shoulder.

He has no particularly outstanding skill in battle, but he's generally capable of doing anything fairly well.

Author Comment

Both Myomut and Patry are really distinct characters, so I've been trying to keep Manos as a more standard, normal type of guy.

MANOS

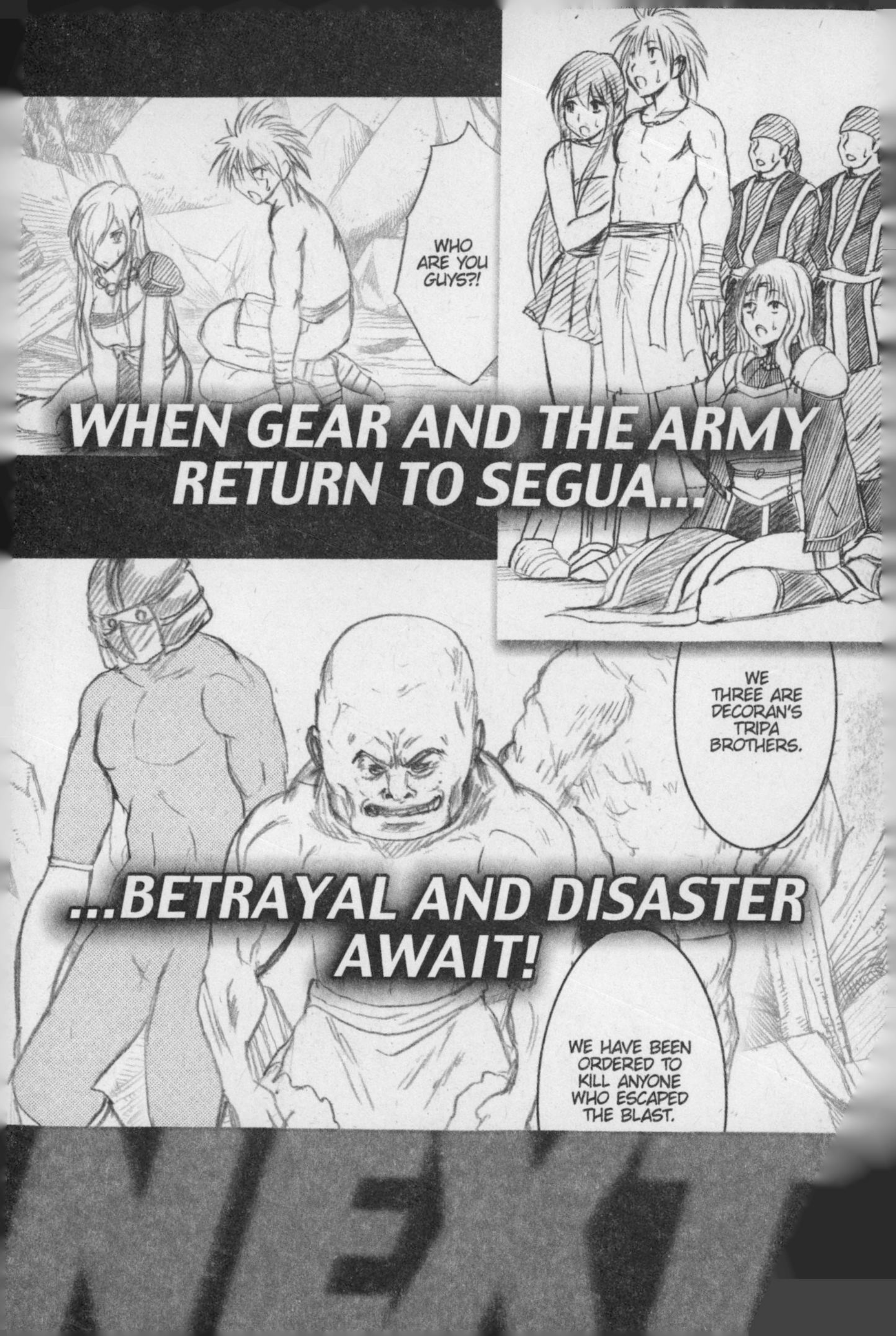
WHO ARE YOU GUYS?!
WHEN GEAR AND THE ARMY RETURN TO SEGUA...
WE THREE ARE DECORAN'S TRIPA BROTHERS.
...BETRAYAL AND DISASTER AWAIT!
WE HAVE BEEN ORDERED TO KILL ANYONE WHO ESCAPED THE BLAST.

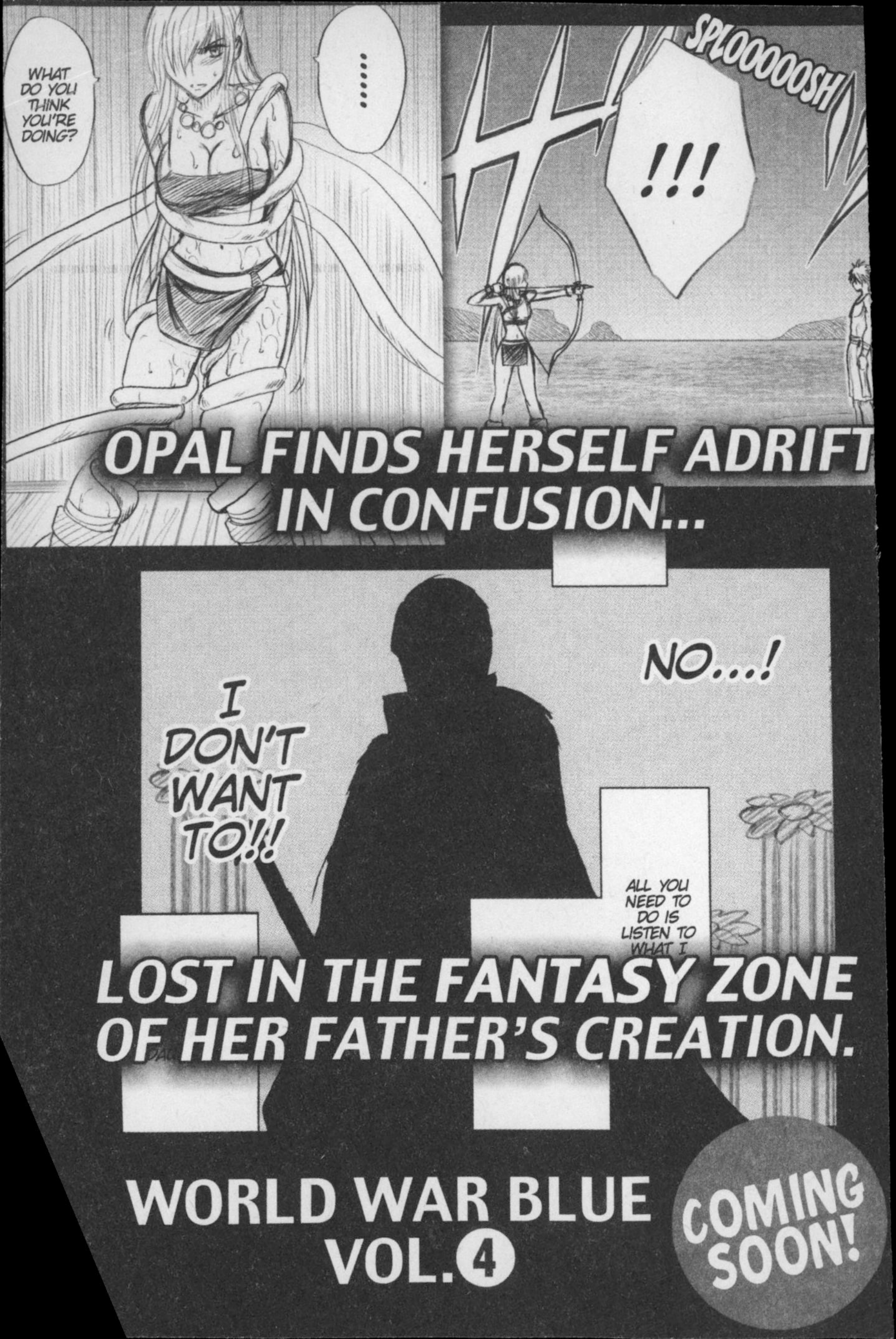
SPLOOOOOOSH
!!!
WHAT DO YOU THINK YOU'RE DOING?
......
OPAL FINDS HERSELF ADRIFT IN CONFUSION...
NO...!
I DON'T WANT TO!!
ALL YOU NEED TO DO IS LISTEN TO WHAT I
LOST IN THE FANTASY ZONE OF HER FATHER'S CREATION.
WORLD WAR BLUE VOL. 4
COMING SOON!

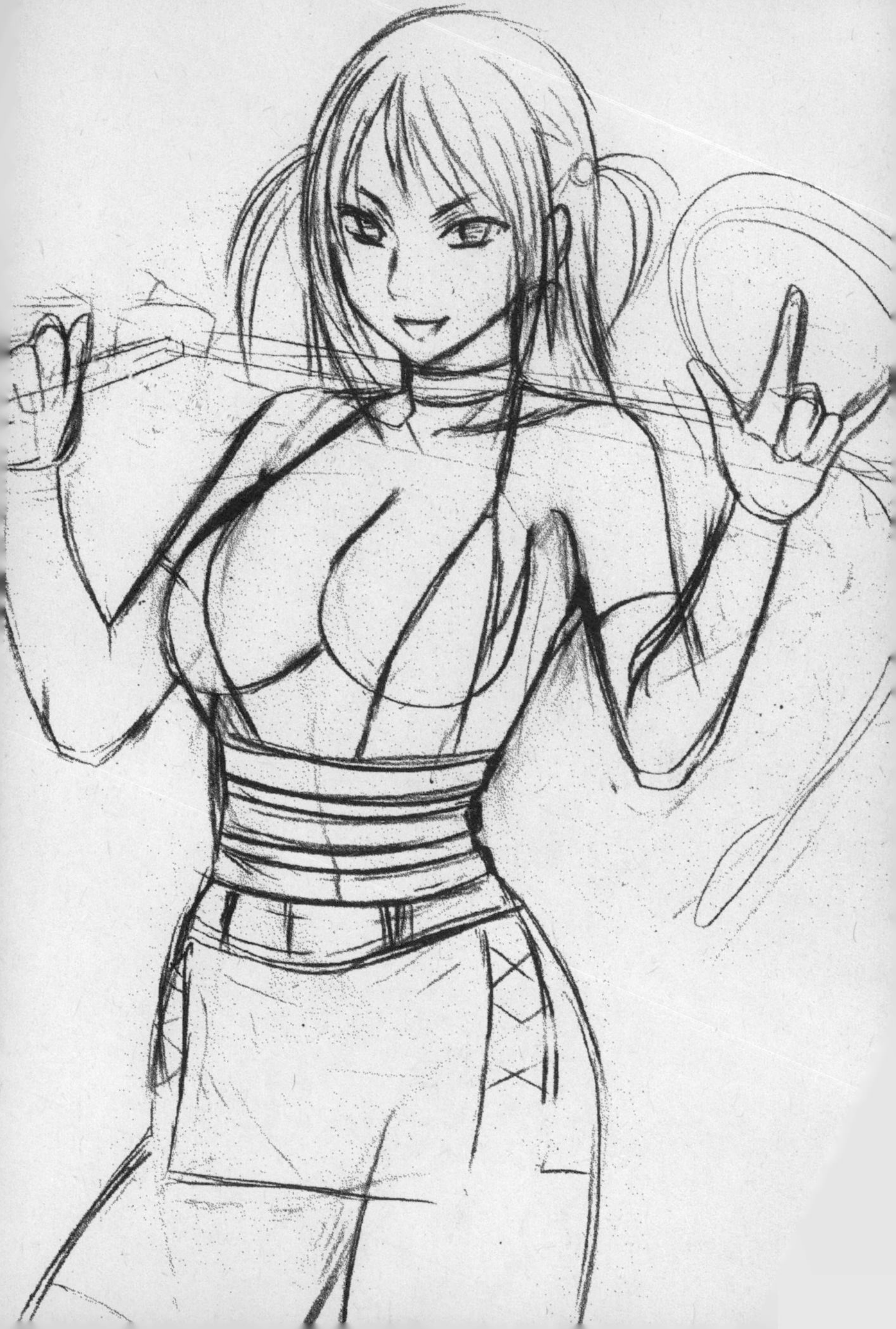

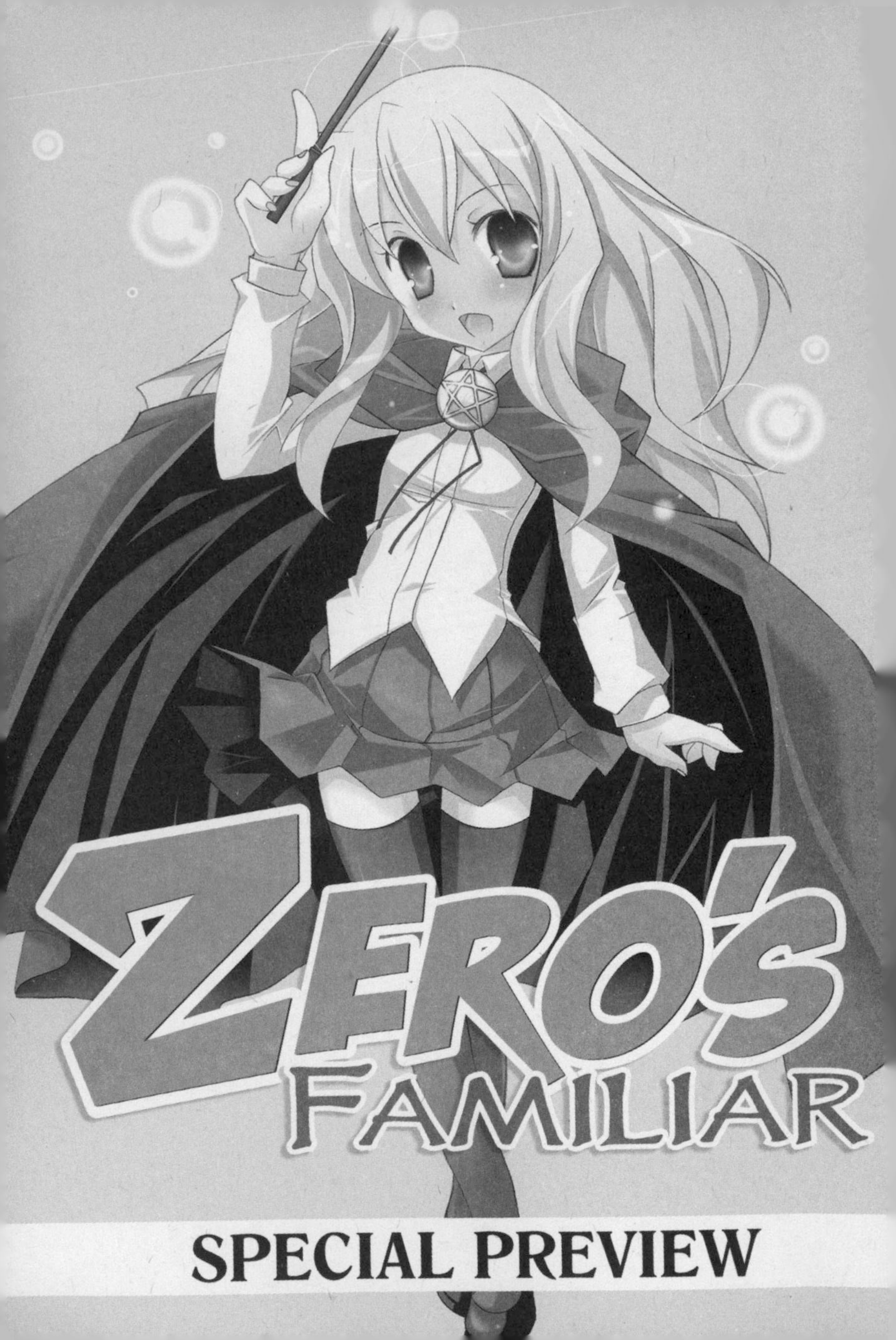
ZERO'S
FAMILIAR
SPECIAL PREVIEW

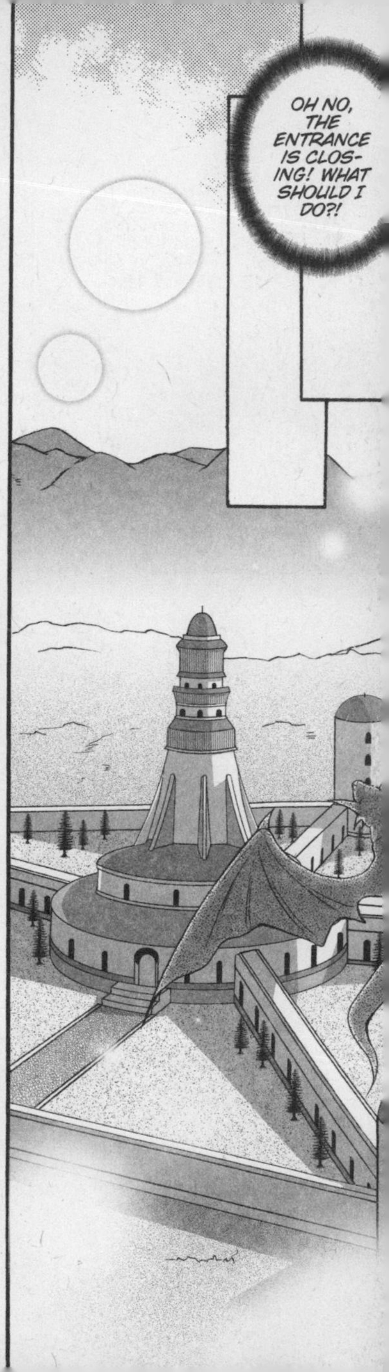
OH NO, THE ENTRANCE IS CLOSING! WHAT SHOULD I DO?!

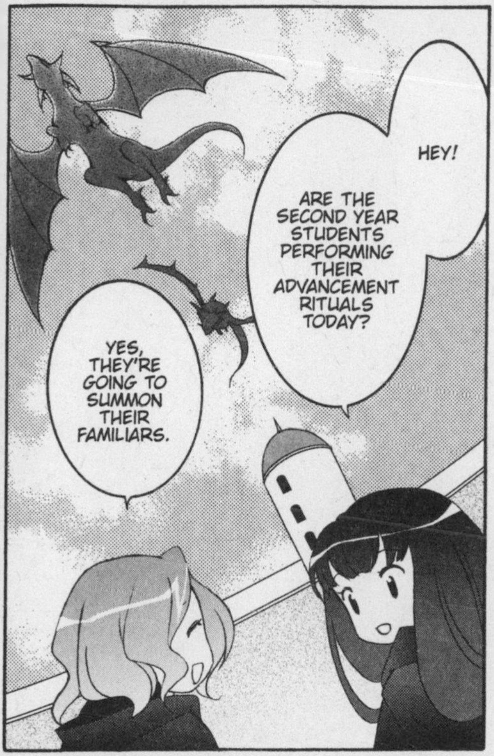
HEY!
ARE THE SECOND YEAR STUDENTS PERFORMING THEIR ADVANCEMENT RITUALS TODAY?
YES, THEY'RE GOING TO SUMMON THEIR FAMILIARS.

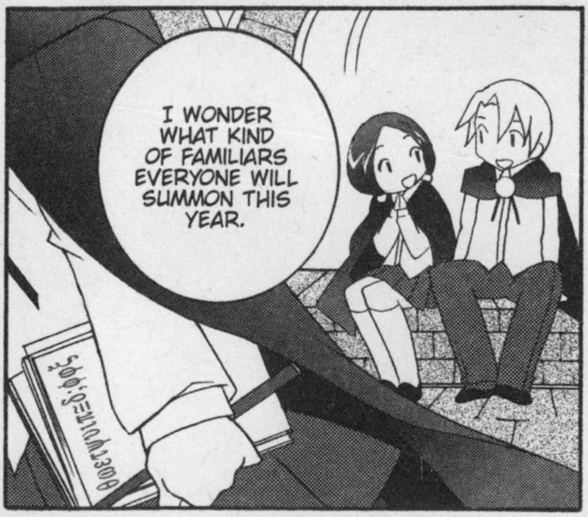
I WONDER WHAT KIND OF FAMILIARS EVERYONE WILL SUMMON THIS YEAR.

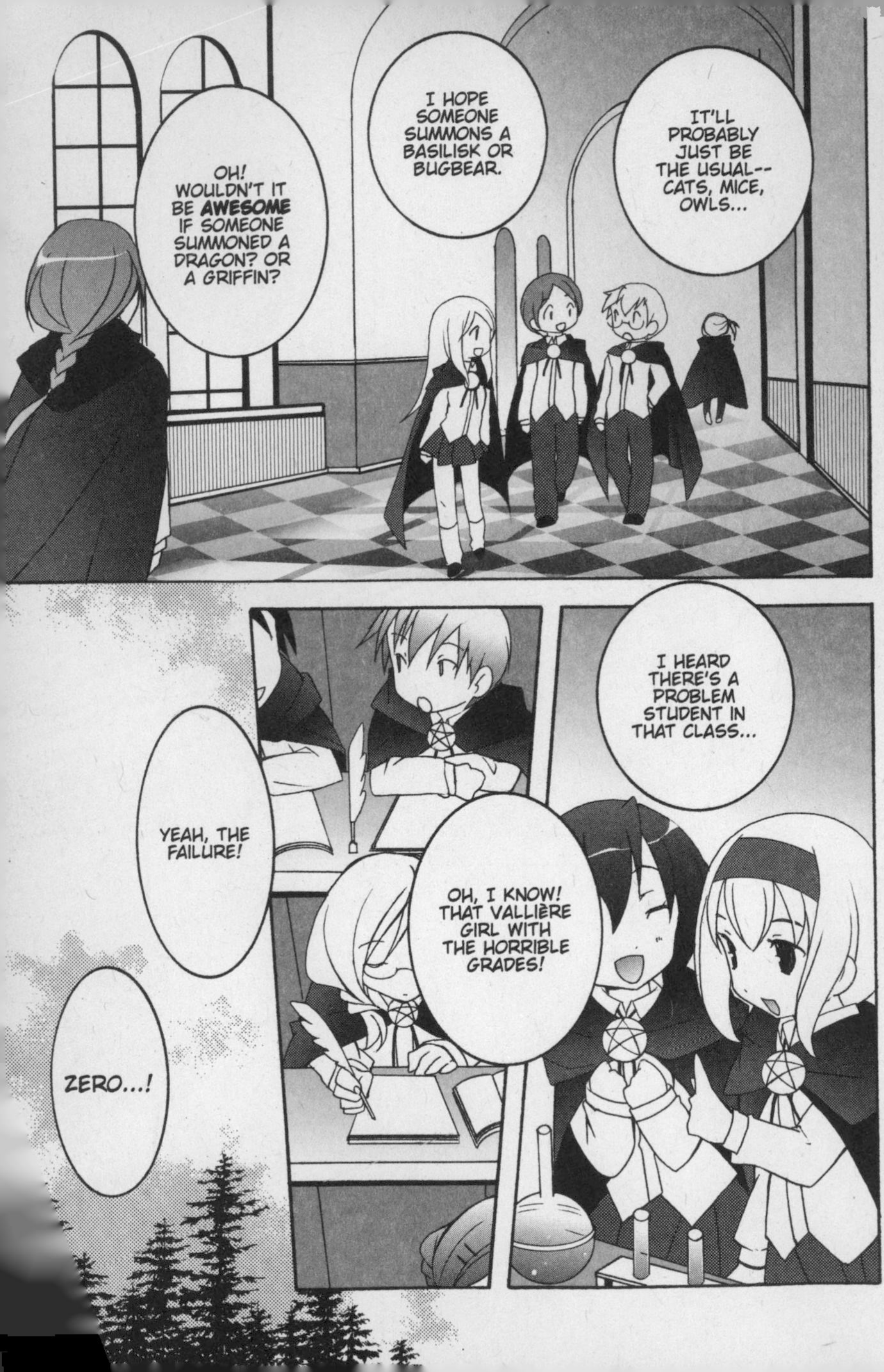
IT'LL PROBABLY JUST BE THE USUAL-- CATS, MICE, OWLS...
I HOPE SOMEONE SUMMONS A BASILISK OR BUGBEAR.
OH! WOULDN'T IT BE **AWESOME** IF SOMEONE SUMMONED A DRAGON? OR A GRIFFIN?
I HEARD THERE'S A PROBLEM STUDENT IN THAT CLASS...
OH, I KNOW! THAT VALLIÈRE GIRL WITH THE HORRIBLE GRADES!
YEAH, THE FAILURE!
ZERO...!

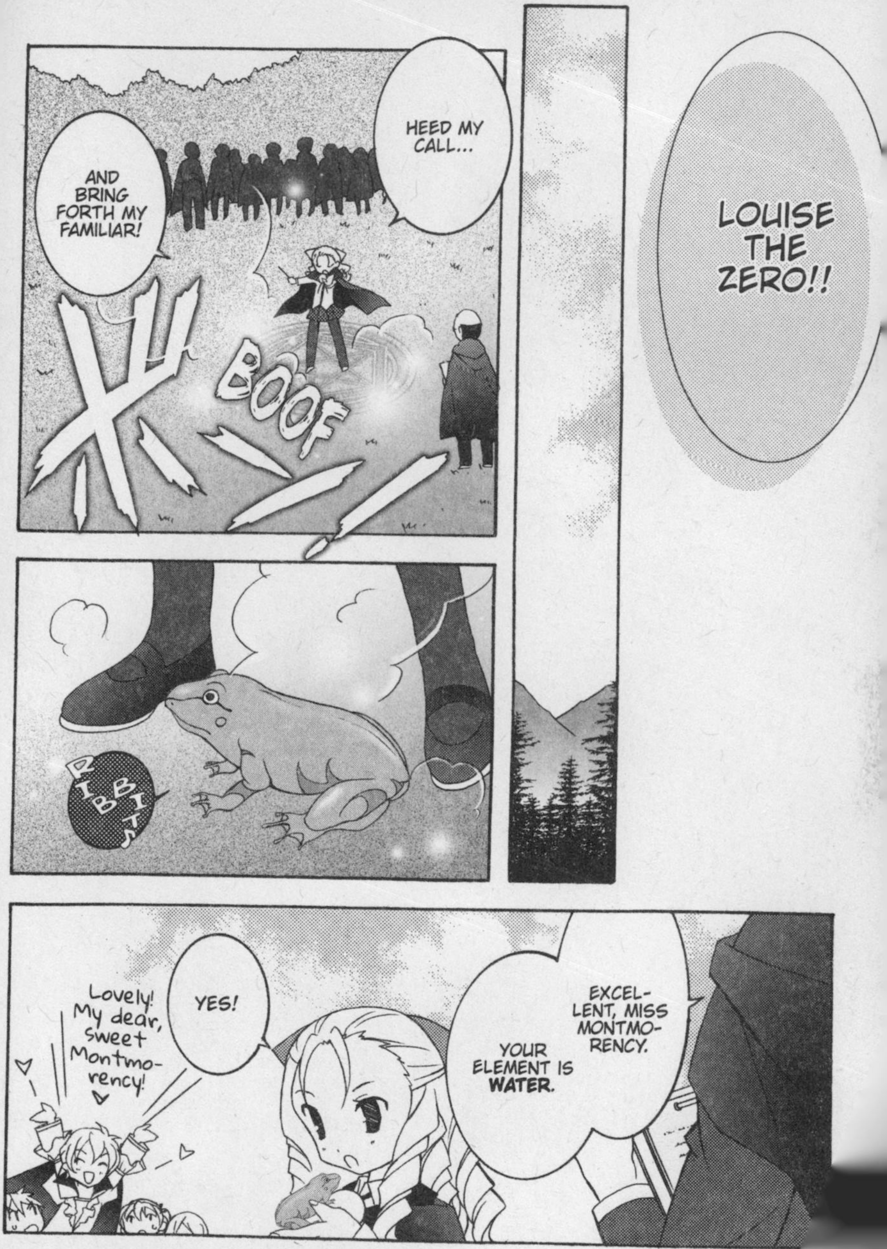
LOUISE THE ZERO!!
HEED MY CALL...
AND BRING FORTH MY FAMILIAR!
BOOF
RIBBIT
EXCEL-LENT, MISS MONTMO-RENCY.
YOUR ELEMENT IS **WATER**.
YES!
Lovely! My dear, sweet Montmo-rency!

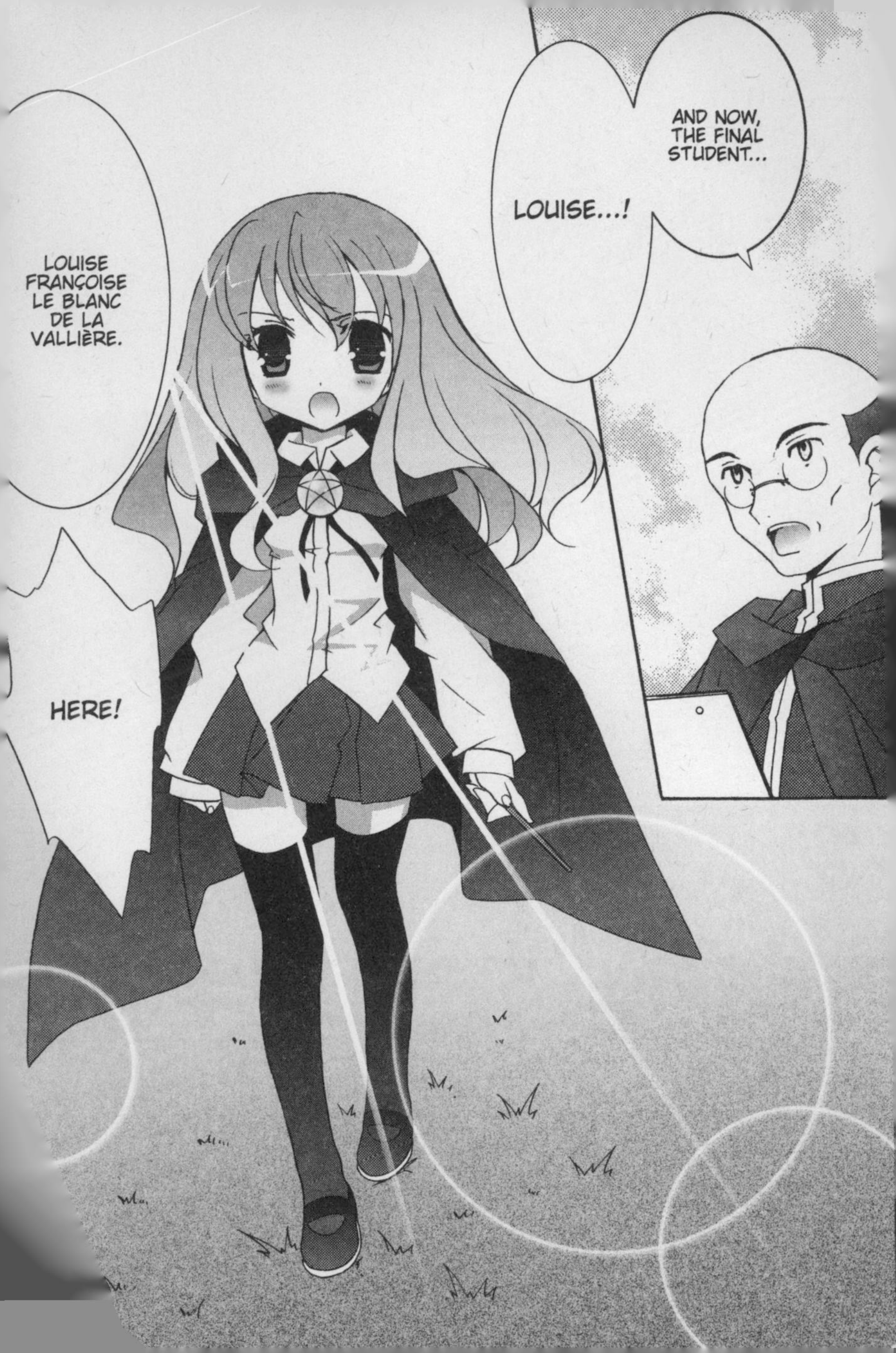
AND NOW, THE FINAL STUDENT...
LOUISE...!
LOUISE FRANÇOISE LE BLANC DE LA VALLIÈRE.
HERE!

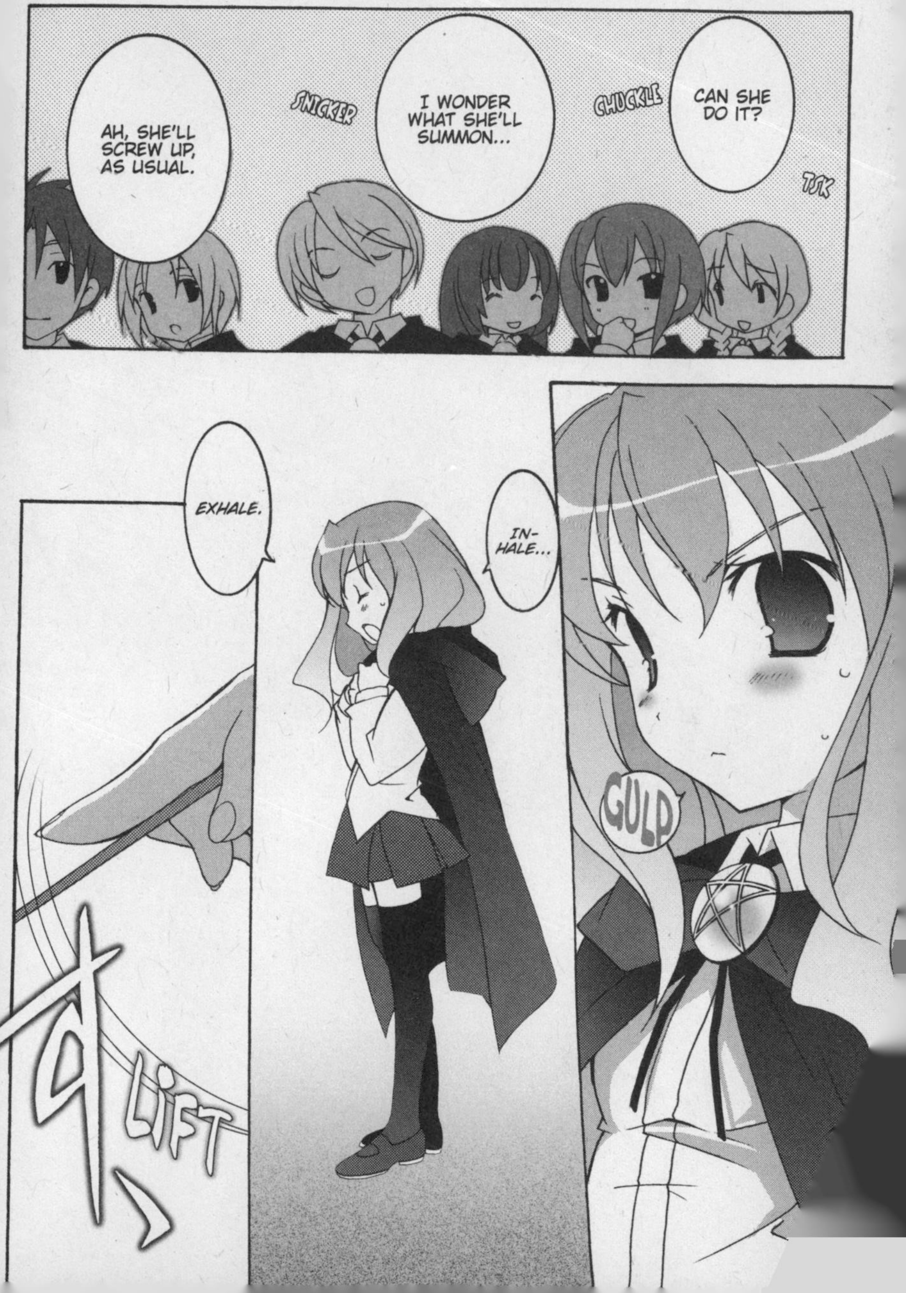
TSK
CAN SHE DO IT?
CHUCKLE
I WONDER WHAT SHE'LL SUMMON...
SNICKER
AH, SHE'LL SCREW UP, AS USUAL.
GULP
IN-HALE...
EXHALE.
LIFT

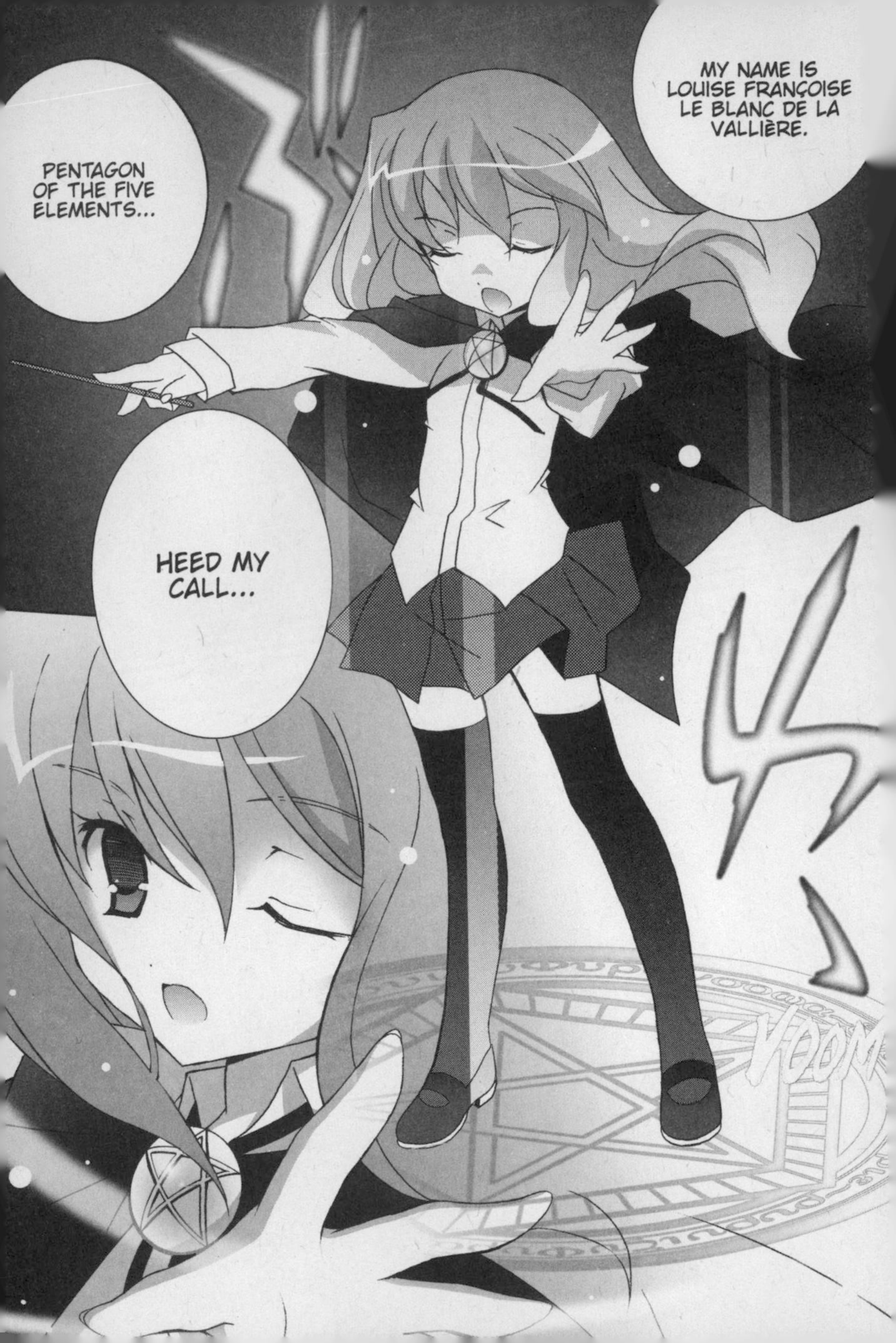
MY NAME IS LOUISE FRANÇOISE LE BLANC DE LA VALLIÈRE.
PENTAGON OF THE FIVE ELEMENTS...
HEED MY CALL...
VOOM

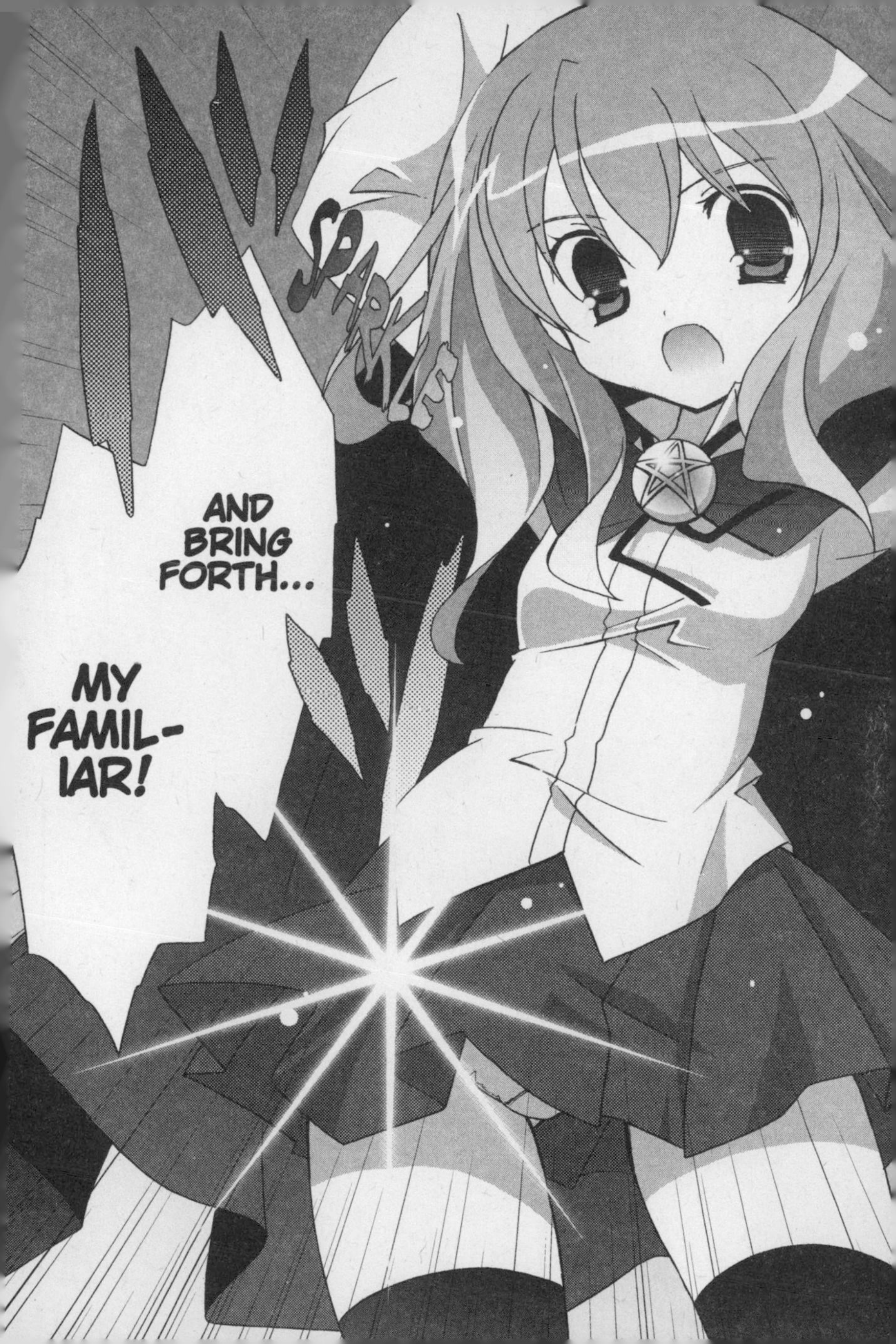
SPARKLE
AND BRING FORTH...
MY FAMIL-IAR!

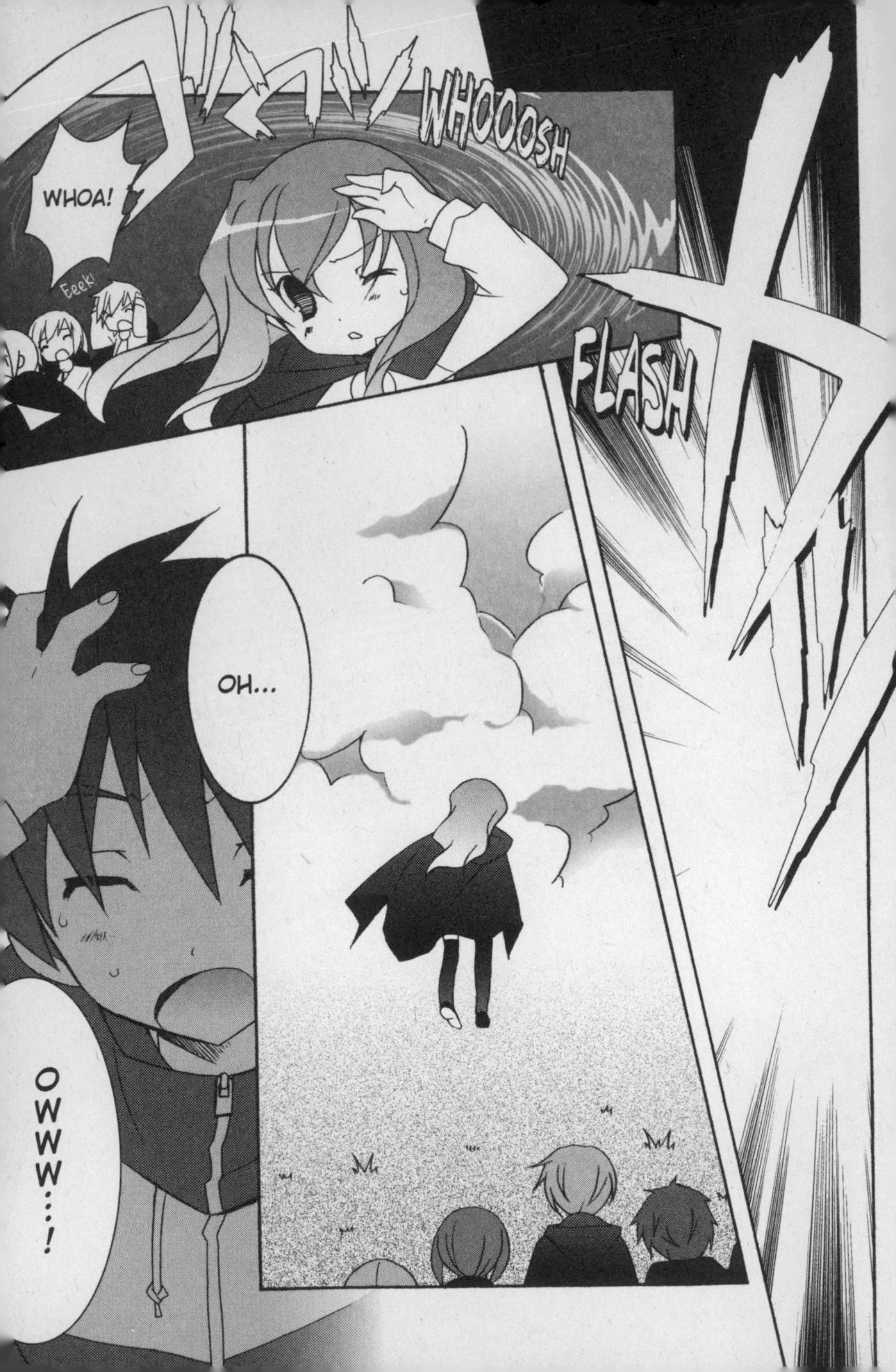
FLASH
WHOOOSH
WHOA!
Eeek!
OH...
OWWW...!

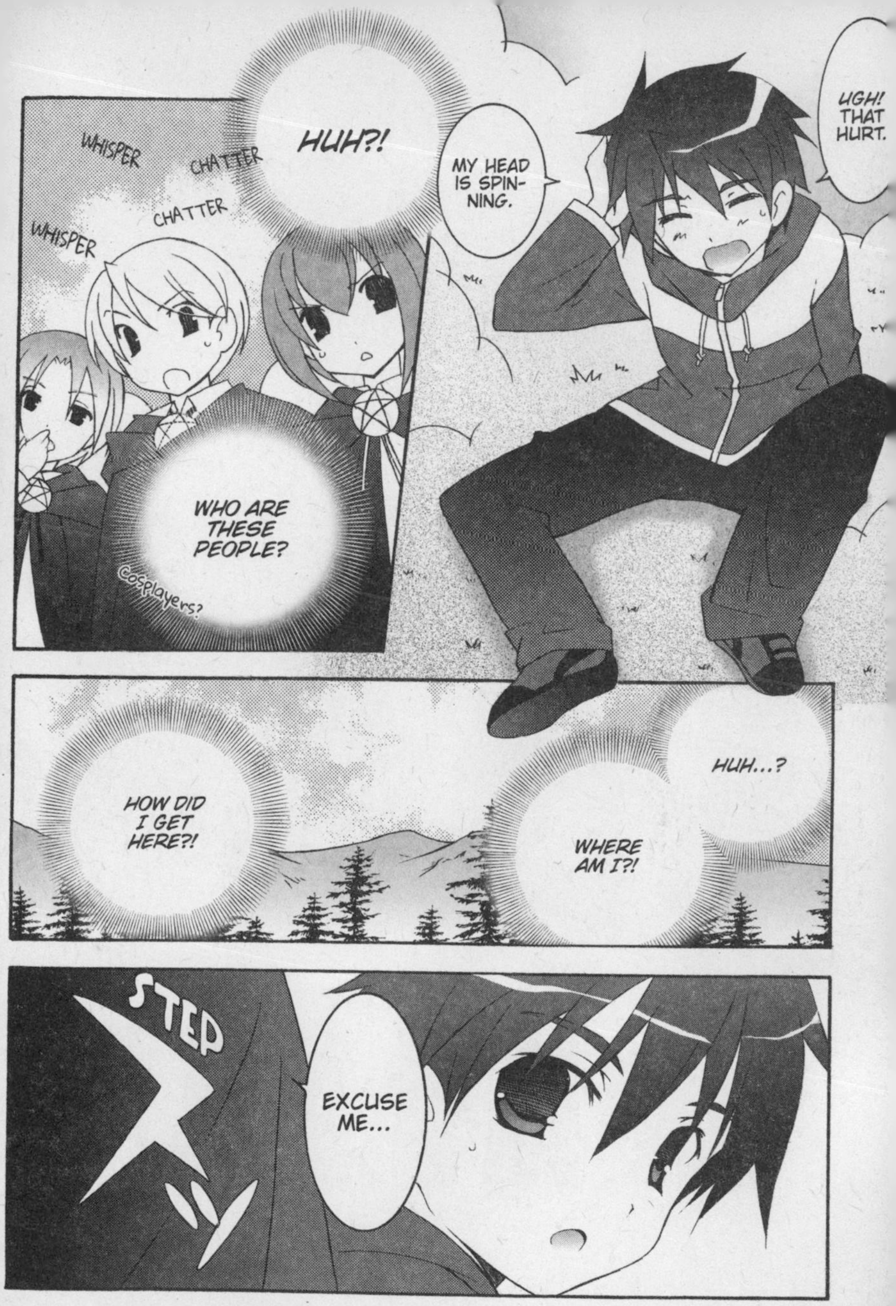
UGH! THAT HURT.
MY HEAD IS SPIN-NING.
HUH?!
CHATTER
WHISPER
CHATTER
WHISPER
WHO ARE THESE PEOPLE?
Cosplayers?
HUH...?
WHERE AM I?!
HOW DID I GET HERE?!
EXCUSE ME...
STEP

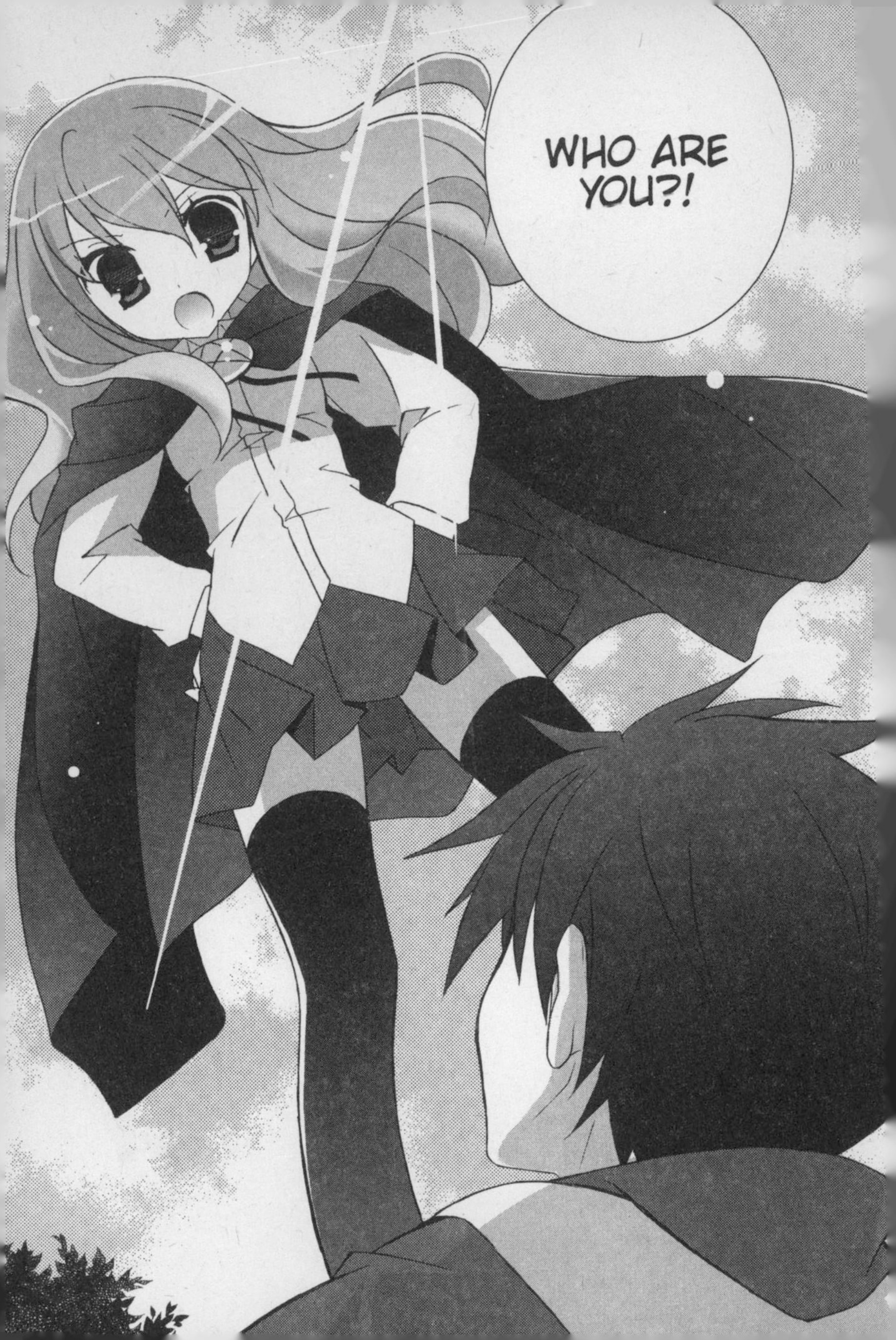
WHO ARE YOU?!

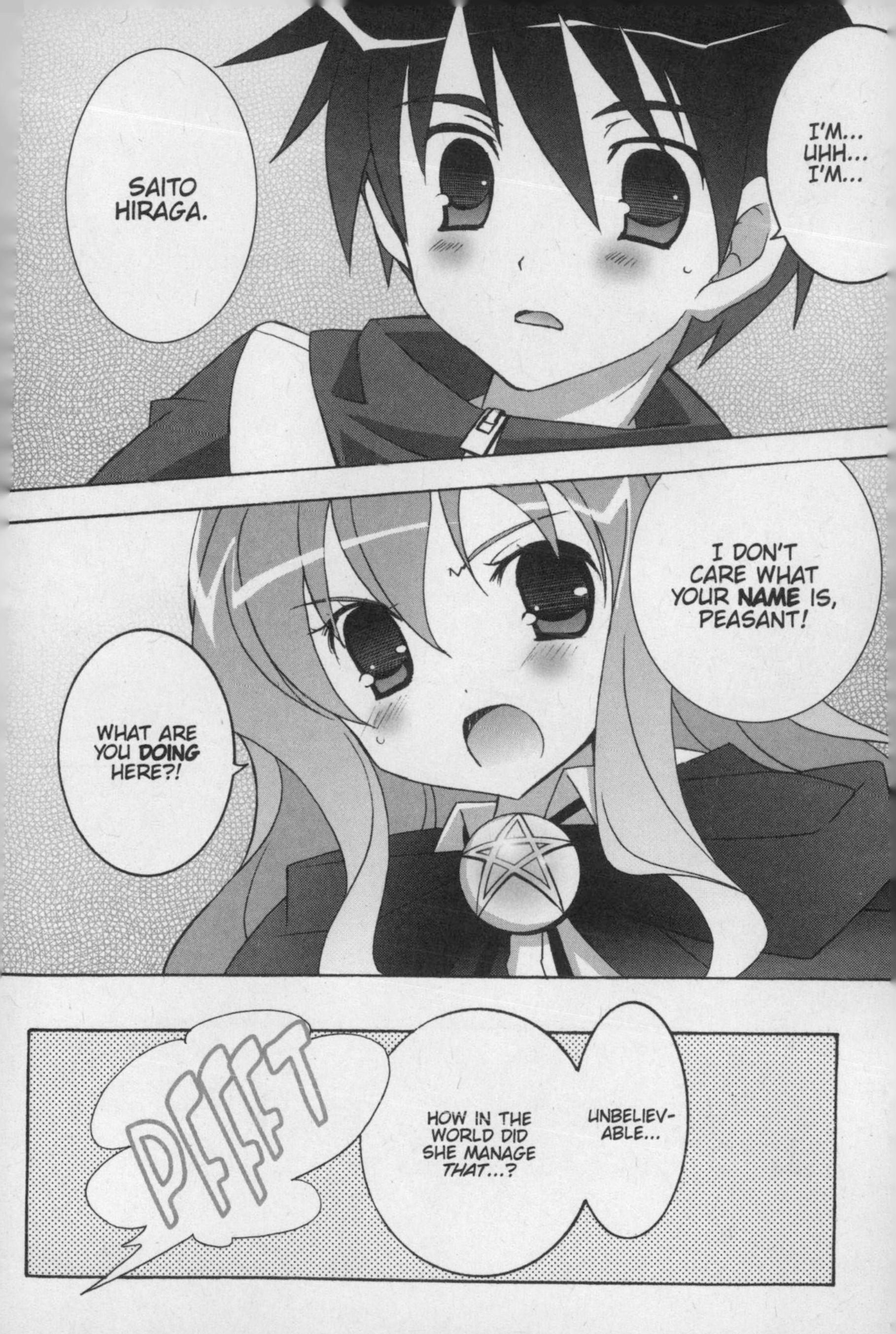
I'M... UHH... I'M...
SAITO HIRAGA.
I DON'T CARE WHAT YOUR **NAME** IS, PEASANT!
WHAT ARE YOU **DOING** HERE?!
UNBELIEV-ABLE...
HOW IN THE WORLD DID SHE MANAGE *THAT*...?
PFFFT

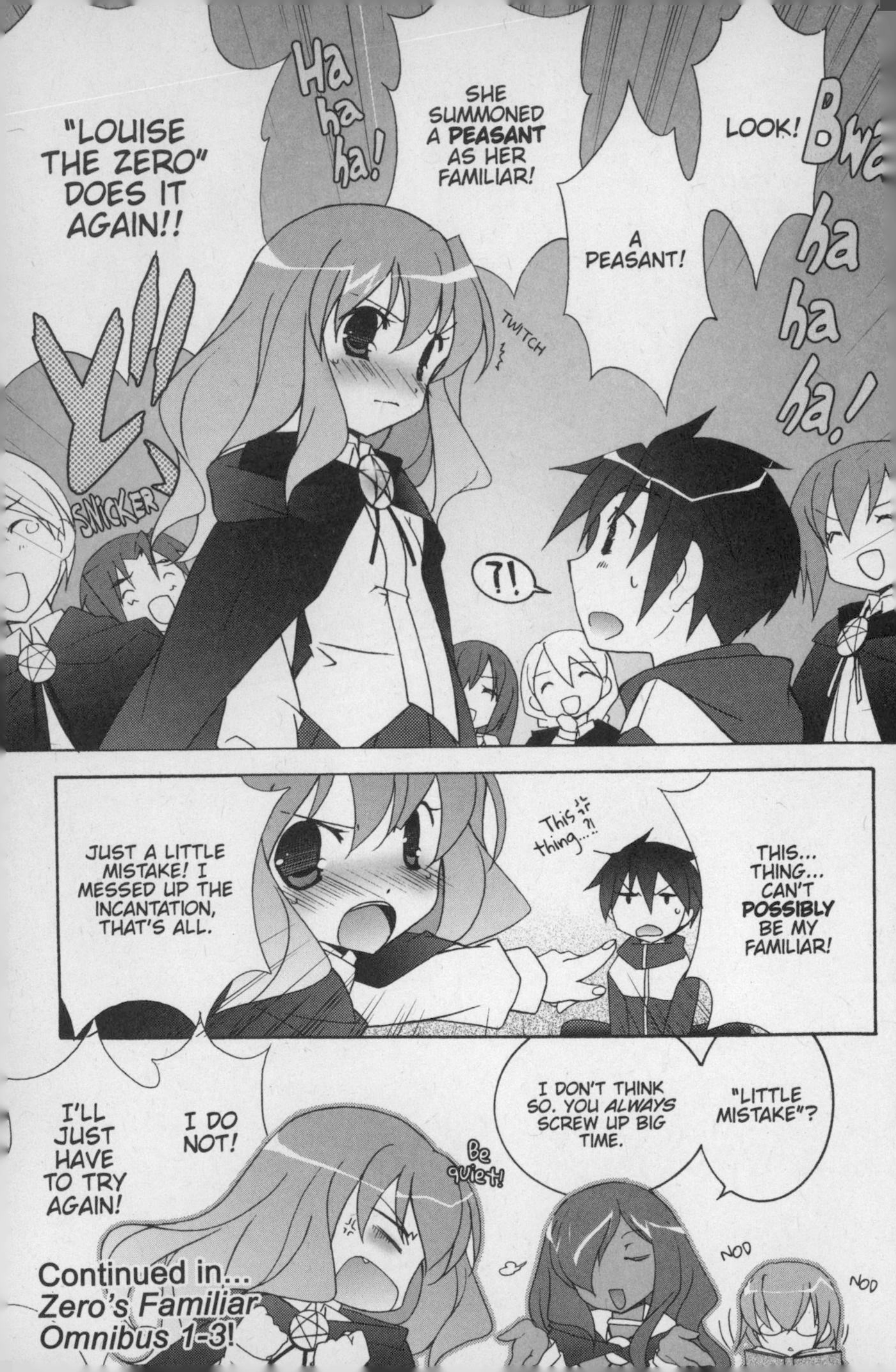
LOOK!
Bwa ha ha ha ha!
A PEASANT!
SHE SUMMONED A **PEASANT** AS HER FAMILIAR!
Ha ha ha!
"LOUISE THE ZERO" DOES IT AGAIN!!
TWITCH
?!
SNICKER
THIS... THING... CAN'T **POSSIBLY** BE MY FAMILIAR!
This thing...?!
JUST A LITTLE MISTAKE! I MESSED UP THE INCANTATION, THAT'S ALL.
"LITTLE MISTAKE"?
I DON'T THINK SO. YOU *ALWAYS* SCREW UP BIG TIME.
Be quiet!
I DO NOT!
I'LL JUST HAVE TO TRY AGAIN!
NOD
NOD
Continued in... Zero's Familiar Omnibus 1-3!

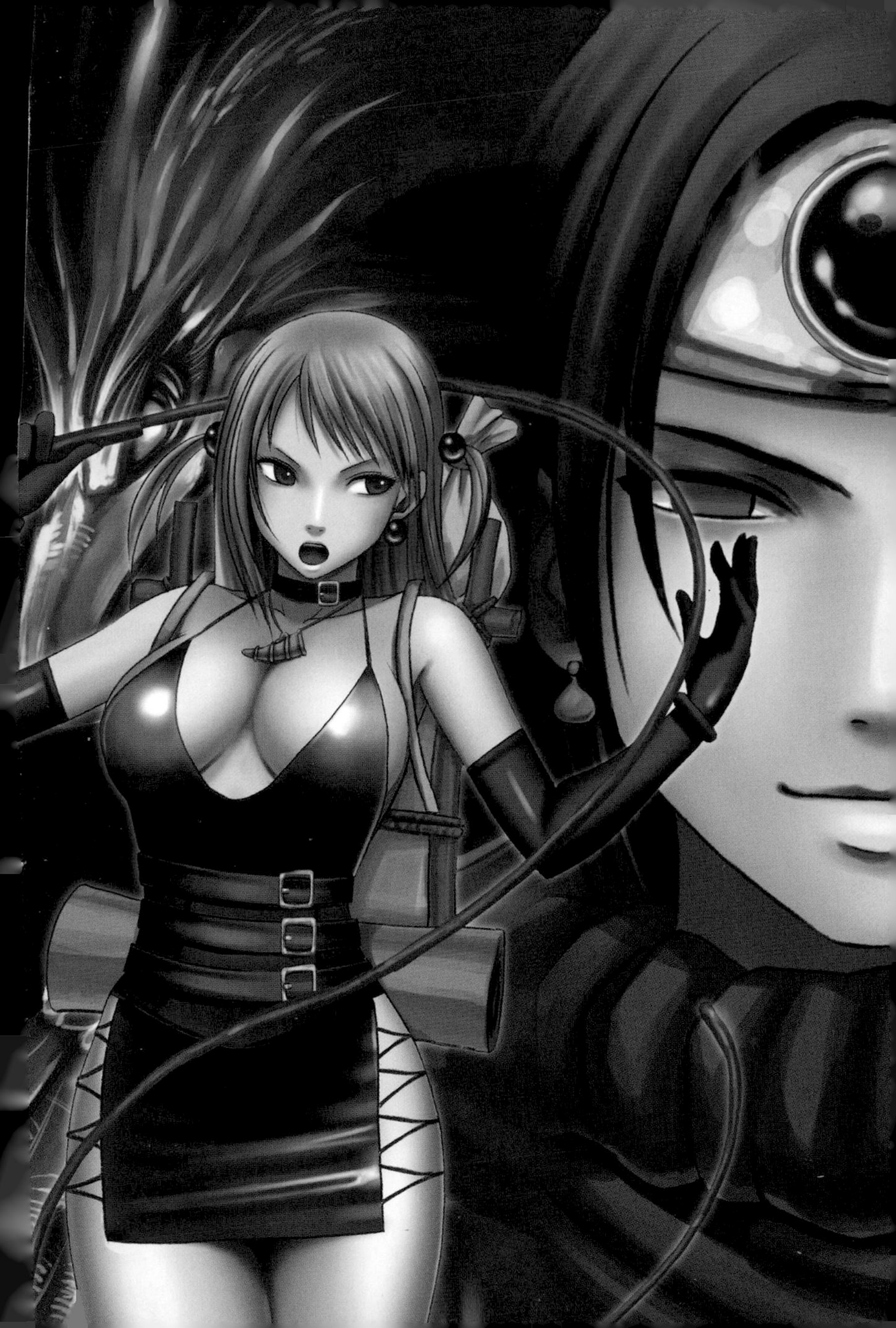

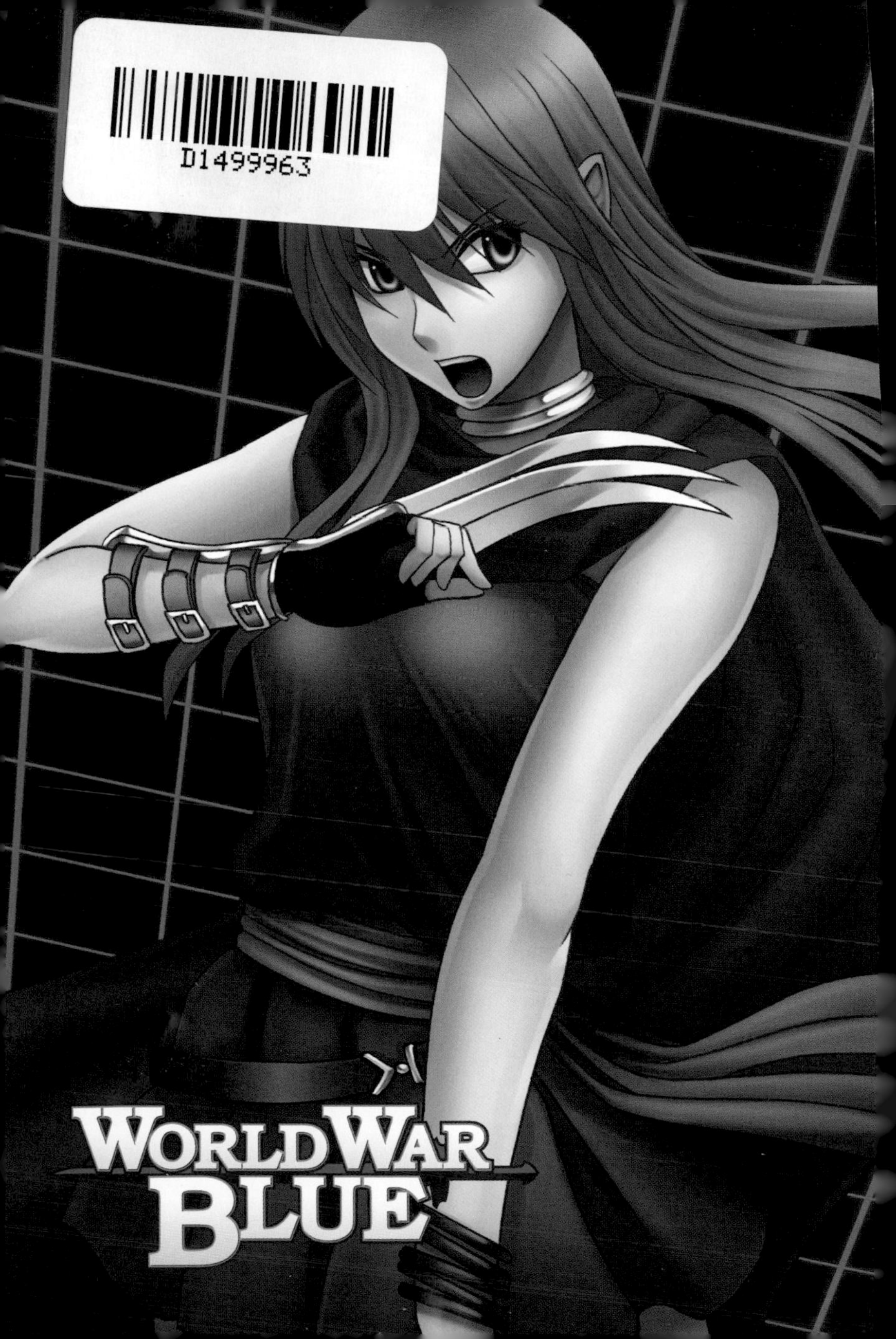
WORLD WAR
BLUE